AF361412

MARGHERITA COSTA, DIVA OF THE BAROQUE COURT

JESSICA GOETHALS

Margherita Costa, Diva of the Baroque Court

UNIVERSITY OF TORONTO PRESS
Toronto Buffalo London

© University of Toronto Press 2023
Toronto Buffalo London
utorontopress.com

ISBN 978-1-4875-4730-1 (cloth)   ISBN 978-1-4875-4731-8 (EPUB)
                                  ISBN 978-1-4875-4732-5 (PDF)

Library and Archives Canada Cataloguing in Publication

Title: Margherita Costa, diva of the baroque court / Jessica Goethals.
Names: Goethals, Jessica, author.
Series: Toronto Italian studies.
Description: Series statement: Toronto Italian studies | Includes bibliographical
   references and index.
Identifiers: Canadiana (print) 20230224385 | Canadiana (ebook) 20230224423 |
   ISBN 9781487547301 (hardcover) | ISBN 9781487547325 (PDF) |
   ISBN 9781487547318 (EPUB)
Subjects: LCSH: Costa, Margherita, active 17th century. | LCSH: Authors, Italian – Italy –
   Rome – 17th century – Biography. | LCSH: Sopranos (Singers) – Italy – Rome – Biography. |
   LCSH: Courtesans – Italy – Rome – Biography. | LCSH: Rome (Italy) – Court and courtiers –
   Biography. | LCSH: Rome (Italy) – Court and courtiers – History – 17th century. |
   LCSH: Rome (Italy) – Intellectual life – 17th century. | LCGFT: Biographies.
Classification: LCC PQ4621.C74 Z85 2023 | DDC 852/.5–dc23

Cover design: Alexa Love
Cover image: Woman Playing a Guitar. Simon Vouet, ca. 1618.
Metropolitan Museum of Art, New York, USA. Album/Alamy Stock Photo

We wish to acknowledge the land on which the University of Toronto Press operates. This land is
the traditional territory of the Wendat, the Anishnaabeg, the Haudenosaunee, the Métis, and the
Mississaugas of the Credit First Nation.

This book has been published with the help of the Lila Wallace – Reader's Digest Publications Subsidy at
Villa I Tatti, the Harvard University Center for Italian Renaissance Studies.

University of Toronto Press acknowledges the financial support of the Government of Canada,
the Canada Council for the Arts, and the Ontario Arts Council, an agency of the Government of
Ontario, for its publishing activities.

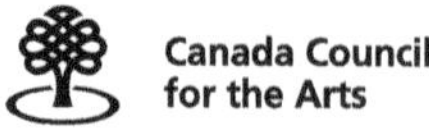

Canada

To Larry and Lauren Goethals

Contents

Illustrations

Acknowledgments

Writing a book is a long and humbling journey, one nearly impossible to complete alone. As I near harbour, I find myself in the debt of many. I have been fortunate to count Jane Tylus as a mentor and friend; her generosity in offering advice, lending a supportive ear, reading drafts, and lifting me up in myriad ways has been unflagging. Virginia Cox first encouraged me to see where my curiosity about Costa might lead; she has been a reliable touchstone as my research takes shape. My interest in Margherita Costa originates in a chance conversation with Sara Díaz at a conference reception a decade ago about whether any early modern Italian women wrote comedies. The question led us to translate and edit Costa's *Buffoons* together. The ideas in this book and my sense of Costa as a writer and performer are born of that collaboration; Sara's sharp and thoughtful approach to Costa's works permeates this study.

This book has benefited from a team of readers. Anna Wainwright and Shannon McHugh have read the book nearly in its entirety, offering astute feedback and comradery along the way. I also benefited from the early feedback of Danielle Callegari and Melissa Swain. Other colleagues graciously agreed to read drafts of individual chapters, and for this I warmly thank Bryan Brazeau, Kate Driscoll, Eugenio Refini, and Paola Ugolini. I also thank my departmental works-in-progress group colleagues at the University of Alabama: Matt Feminella, Micah McKay, Gina Stamm, and William Worden, as well as former colleagues Kelly Shannon-Henderson and Alexandra Perkins. At UA thanks are also due to Fabio Battista, who kindly helped check my translations, as well as to Michelle Dowd, Kelsey Guy, Douglas Lightfoot, Tricia McElroy, Russel Peterson, Daniel Riches, Claudia Romanelli, Kirk Summers, and Cheryl Toman.

For suggestions, conversations, feedback, and answers to my queries (even when they were sent out of the blue), I am indebted to many colleagues and friends, including Chris Barrett, Dario Brancato, Brian Brege, Alexandra Coller, Elizabeth Cohen, Suzanne Cusick, Maria di Maro, Derek Dunne, Beth Glixon, Valeria Finucci, Julia Hairston, Megan Heffernan, Robert Henke, Amanda Herbert,

Stephanie Leone, Marco Faini, Francesca Fantappiè, Margaret King, Marianna Liguori, Lia Markey, Alessandro Metlica, Gerry Milligan, Eric Nicholson, Kirsten Noreen, Carmen Nocentelli, Laurie Nussdorfer, Joe Ortiz, Katharina Piechocki, Courtney Quaintance, Meredith Ray, Julia Robarts, Diana Robins, Sarah G. Ross, Debapriya Sarkar, Janet Smarr, Maria Galli Stampino, Mihoko Suzuki, Mary Vaccaro, Kate van Orden, Emily Wilbourne, Owen Williams, and Enrico Zucchi. Francesco Tagliapietra offered helpful assistance with Latin paleography.

I had the good fortune to present this work in its more nascent stages at New York University, the University College London, the University of Miami's Center for the Humanities, the Università degli Studi di Padova, and at the annual meetings of the Theater Without Borders group. I am grateful to the organizers of these events and to participants for their helpful observations and questions.

Research for this project received financial support from the American Philosophical Society, the Folger Shakespeare Library, the Renaissance Society of America, the University of Alabama College of Arts and Sciences, and the University of Alabama Office of Research and Economic Development. While my fellowship at Harvard's Villa I Tatti was for a separate project, my time there permitted me to add many missing pieces to Costa's biography. For assistance in defraying the costs of publishing, I am grateful for the support of the Lila Wallace – Reader's Digest Publications Subsidy at Villa I Tatti and a grant from the University of Alabama College Academy of Research, Scholarship, and Creative Activity.

I am grateful to the patient librarians and archivists at the Archivio di Stato di Firenze, Archivio di Stato di Roma, Archivio di Stato di Torino, Archivio di Stato di Venezia, Archivio Doria Pamphilj, Beinecke Library, Biblioteca Civica di Padova, Biblioteca Giovardiana, Biblioteca Marciana, Biblioteca Nazionale Centrale di Firenze, Biblioteca Nazionale Centrale di Roma, Biblioteca Statale di Lucca, Biblioteca del Seminario Vescovile di Padova, Biblioteca Universitaria di Torino, Bibliothèque Mazarine, Bibliothèque Nationale de France, Folger Shakespeare Library, Newberry Library, Library of Congress, and Vatican Library. An especially hearty thanks goes to the UA Interlibrary Loan Department, who heroically processed scores of my requests.

I acknowledge the permission to reproduce portions of this book that have previously appeared in print. Select sections of chapter 2 appear in "The Bizarre Muse: The Poetics and Persona of Margherita Costa," *Early Modern Women: An Interdisciplinary Journal* 12, no. 1 (2017): 48–72; an earlier version of chapter 4 and the final section of chapter 5 appear in "The Patronage Politics of Equestrian Ballet: Allegory, Allusion, and Satire in the Courts of Seventeenth-Century Italy and France," *Renaissance Quarterly* 70, no. 4 (2017): 1397–448; and a portion of chapter 5 appeared in "The Singing Saint: The Martyrdom of St. Cecilia in Seventeenth-Century Literature and Theater," *Women Language Literature in Italy / Donne Lingua Letteratura in Italia* 2 (2020): 43–61.

I thank Suzanne Rancourt and her team at the University of Toronto Press for their expertise and advice in seeing this book into print, and to Anne Laughlin for her expert editing. The external readers shared useful feedback that have helped me to clarify the arguments and organization.

Behind this book stands my family. My in-laws, Simonetta Camuffo and Giorgio Bisotto, have graciously provided countless trips to and from Italian airports and train stations. My brother Jake and his family (Naaz, Liam, and Ian) have given me support with a dose of levity. My wife Alessandra Montalbano has been my bedrock since our graduate school days. I could have thanked her at any number of points in these pages as a departmental colleague, and I need not excuse the many evenings and weekends spent at my desk because she was doing just the same. But beyond the confines of work, she is my truest companion and the most brilliant person I know, and this book has benefited greatly from her influence. My parents, Larry and Lauren Goethals, made countless sacrifices for my education and then did not flinch when I told them I was dropping my plans for a career in law to study Italian Renaissance literature. Indeed, my father's first words were "Maybe you'll write a book one day!" I dedicate to my parents these first real fruits of everything they have given me.

MARGHERITA COSTA, DIVA OF THE BAROQUE COURT

Introduction

Sometime around 1618, the French artist Simon Vouet painted a female musician strumming a Spanish guitar, her lips slightly parted as if in song. The portrait, selected for this book's cover, dates to Vouet's years in Rome during the first decades of the century.[1] Sumptuously dressed in a full red skirt and green satin sleeves that fall suggestively from her shoulder, and framed in dramatic Caravaggesque lighting, the seated figure glances to the side as though lost in thought. Pictorial images of female musicians, including singers, were in ever increasing demand in the early seventeenth century. In roughly the same years, the Roman artist Ottavio Leoni drew a similarly positioned female singer playing the guitar, perhaps either modelled on or a model for Vouet's painting.[2] Leoni's image – one of his many portraits of *cantanti* – differs from Vouet's in the inclusion of a lightly sketched male figure whose hands grasp the woman's thigh and circle her waist, hinting at an erotic availability often associated with professional female performers.[3]

The identity of Vouet's and Leoni's sitters remain uncertain.[4] Yet we might well imagine these figures of female musicianship to represent contemporaries such as Margherita Costa (1600?– after 1657), a Roman singer, courtesan, and prolific writer who entitled her first poetry collection *La chitarra* (The Guitar).[5] This title, as Costa explained to her patron and dedicatee, Grand Duke Ferdinando II de' Medici of Tuscany, reflects the ambiguous nature of both the volume and its author. "The guitar," she wrote, "though it be a lowly instrument, is played by nearly everyone."[6] The declaration alludes to the tension between criticisms of the instrument as humble and unrefined and the evident enthusiasm for its versatile sound. Much like Costa herself, the Baroque guitar's repertoire ranged from "boisterous street music to the elegance of courtly performance."[7] Yet, Costa pointedly adds, despite its contested status the grand duke often deigns to include it among the more urbane instruments found at his court. So too, she implies, should she belong there.

Her argument proved persuasive. Margherita Costa won prominence and acclaim across the courts of Italy and France during the mid-seventeenth century.

She was, in the words of one of her celebrants, "la Signora Margherita Costa di poesia e di musica" – a woman of both poetry and music.[8] In addition to her performances in the chambers and on the opera stages of Baroque Europe, Costa published a remarkable fourteen full-length texts across an array of genres: historical writing, burlesque comedy, drama, equestrian ballet, pastoral opera, amorous letters, elegiac poetry, and laments. She deftly secured a steady stream of elite patronage – with benefactors including the Medici in Florence, the Barberini in Rome, and Cardinal Jules Mazarin and Queen Anne in Paris – while male academicians, poets, and librettists wrote poetry on her behalf. Italy offered earlier examples of itinerant performer-authors, most notably the actress Isabella Andreini (1562–1604), and of literary courtesans such as Tullia d'Aragona (c. 1501/5–1556) and Veronica Franco (1546–1591), but Costa was *sui generis* in both content and context. Unafraid to leap over the boundaries of decorum that delimited what women could and should write about, she blended the laudatory and the satirical, the stately and the risqué. A versatile and self-styled "bizarre" figure active in the very decades when Italian women writers encountered fewer opportunities and more hostility than in previous generations, Costa defies categorization as an early modern author.

Despite her successes as a performer, her enviable publication record, and her fascinatingly crafted persona – all of which led her to become "most venerated in Italy and abroad," in the word of one of her near contemporaries – Costa has remained a figure virtually unknown today until quite recently.[9] Several factors have contributed to her near absence in early modern scholarship. First, like so many of her female peers, Costa fell into the shadows cast by long-prevailing but erroneous assessments of women's place in the literary landscape of the Italian Counter-Reformation and its wake. Women had not ceased to write after the Council of Trent, as accepted wisdom had insisted, but instead wrote more and in a wider range of genres than ever before until the early years of the seventeenth century.[10] Second, the scant attention paid to her has often fixated on her activity as a courtesan. This, coupled with the salty nature of some of her writing, made it easy for many to moralizingly discount her. Finally, as a writer who, more than any other woman of the age, embraced the theatrical and exuberant aesthetic of the Italian Baroque, Costa has suffered from a general critical aversion to the period. Indeed, the Baroque's reputation as an era of "bad taste" has endured until of late.[11] As the literary Baroque finally receives the sort of re-evaluation that art, music, and theatre from the period have already enjoyed, figures such as Costa increasingly share the limelight with better-known writers like Giambattista Marino.[12]

After a long lull, the scholarly tide on Costa is quickly turning. In her watershed *Women's Writing in Italy, 1400–1650*, Virginia Cox highlights Costa's originality and argues that her works are "deserving of a far closer critical scrutiny than they have hitherto received."[13] Efforts to answer that call have included translations, dissertations, and a small but rapidly growing number of article-length studies, as well as a re-evaluation of the position of women like Costa in the field itself.[14] In a recent survey of innovations in the study of early modern women, Meredith K. Ray points to Costa as an important example of the kind of previously underexplored female writers that can rise to the surface when scholars "[deal] in flexible and innovative ways with questions of genre and interdisciplinary categories."[15] Similarly, Sarah Gwyneth Ross spotlights Costa as emblematic of a new, intentionally provocative scholarly category of "weird humanists" – that is, early modern writers who "by tugging on loosely classical threads, and sometimes even ripping holes in that venerable garment … ended up weaving for themselves something like distinct identities, separate from these other many ties that bind [religion, status, gender, geography, etc.]."[16]

This book marks the first full-length treatment of Costa's life, works, and relationship to the European courts and literary-theatrical circles in which she moved. Her biography has long been plagued by shadows and question marks. Although the first modern treatment of Costa dates to the mid-1920s, its author, Dante Bianchi, was largely dismissive of her on moral and aesthetic grounds and insisted – incorrectly – that there was no information to be found on her in Italy's archives.[17] Shorter encyclopedia entries and studies in more recent years have slowly begun to piece together her activities, and those very archives Bianchi set aside still have a great deal to tell us about this extraordinary woman.[18] The present book, however, offers the most complete and accurate picture of Costa's life to date.

Not merely a literary biography, this book is also a portrait of seventeenth-century courts, their concerns, and their entertainments. While some of the figures in Costa's orbit are familiar to scholars of early modernity, such as Cardinal Mazarin and Urban VIII, others, like Ferdinando II de' Medici and Turin's regent duchess Marie Christine of France, often have gone underdiscussed, particularly in anglophone scholarship. Similarly, it brings to light genres underrepresented in the scholarly record, such as equestrian ballet and "ridiculous" comedy, that – like Costa herself – combined the literary and performative arts to the delight of their audiences. Like the guitar to which she equated herself, this was a *virtuosa* able to harmonize her unique poetic voice with the rhetoric and tastes of the Seicento court.

Restoring Costa to her place in the constellation of early modern writers and performers, this book argues that she fused musical and literary roles by assiduously courting those noble and ecclesiastic benefactors able to shield her, through support of her publications, from the instabilities of a singing career. Central to Costa's continued success was her ability to become an astute monitor of tastes, from the burlesque to the sacred, and to adapt her authorial persona and the content of her writing accordingly. This study therefore asks what it meant to be "professional" in early modern Europe by looking at a woman who made a name for herself by adopting the literary-theatrical fashions of the cities she visited and by often making her patrons not merely her audience but the very objects of her writing. Uniting close textual readings of her publications with archival materials detailing her performance itinerary and social-cultural networks, it progresses chronologically through her life, geographically along the routes she travelled, and thematically via the genres in which she experimented.

Women Writers and Performers, Decorum, and the Patronage Structure

Costa was positioned between two overlapping eras of transition: the decline of the published female writer and the rise of the *virtuosa* soprano.[19] While an outpouring of publications such as Costa's would be enviable in any age, it is particularly remarkable at this moment in Italy – not because women's writing had not yet arrived there but rather because its heyday had largely come and gone. While sixteenth-century Italian presses printed the works of over 200 women, these numbers plummeted by the middle of the seventeenth century.[20] Shifting political landscapes had diminished the influence of the smaller Italian courts, where women had previously enjoyed visibility as the patronesses, subjects, and authors of literature. While men of the sixteenth century could demonstrate their urbanity through courteous attitudes towards women, the seventeenth century saw a sharp uptick in the circulation of misogynistic literature, leading even the prolific Lucrezia Marinella (known best for *La nobiltà et eccellenza delle donne*) to later caution her female peers away from study, stating "men do not want women as their partners in knowledge."[21] And while fashionable writing of the Cinquecento centred upon Petrarchan lyric and pastoral (safe terrain for even aristocratic women), the sensual and suggestive nature of the Baroque aesthetic made publication ill-advised for ladies with reputations to protect. Costa was by no means the only woman publishing in the mid-Seicento, even with these dwindling numbers – other prominent examples include the aforementioned Marinella and the nun Arcangela Tarabotti (both Venetian), while actresses and performers continued to write – but she was "the most distinctly 'seventeenth-century' of seventeenth-century female poets."[22]

While the women of the mid-Seicento faced obstacles to literary engagement that their predecessors of even the previous generation largely did not, singers and actresses were being increasingly stylized as "divas": celebrity performers of divine-like stature.[23] These included women such as Isabella Andreini, Vittoria Piissimi, and Virginia Ramponi in theatre, and Adriana Basile, Leonora Baroni, Barbara Strozzi, and Anna Renzi in music.[24] This enhanced visibility and status did not always translate into acceptance and approval, of course. Most notably, singers and actresses had to fend off accusations of indecency. Public performances by female singers were banned in papal Rome on the grounds of impropriety, though women could often be heard in the city's more intimate chambers. As Susan McClary has noted, many "skilled female musicians practiced their arts as courtesans, in which case the selling of the voice attached directly to the prostitution of the body and vocal prowess operated quite literally as siren song."[25] Virtuosity came with or at a price. Even if a singer (or actress) did not herself engage in such practices, her performance on stage could suggest sexual availability. Figures such as Andreini and Basile, symbols of cultural capital for the courts and patrons able to secure their services, took pains to shield their reputations from accusation and attack.[26] Female performers might take on husbands, or attentively negotiate the terms of their contracts, to avoid censure. Women writers similarly managed their images with care. Attention to reputation was not restricted to aristocrats like Vittoria Colonna. Even an "honest" courtesan like Veronica Franco felt the need to balance her poetic "frank eroticism" with professions of moral rectitude.[27]

At first glance, one might assume that Costa also cultivated the public persona of respectability and prestige so often required of early modern women. She enjoyed ties to the distinguished patrons of her age: Ferdinando II de' Medici, his wife Vittoria della Rovere, and other members of his family such as Cardinal Giovan Carlo; Charles of Lorraine, Duke of Guise, then exiled in Florence; Cardinals Francesco and Antonio Barberini, nephews of Urban VIII; Camillo Pamphili, nephew of Innocent X; Marie Christine of France, duchess and regent of Savoy; Cardinal Jules Mazarin and Anne of Austria, queen mother and regent of France; and, collectively, the Brunswick-Lüneburg dukes Georg Wilhelm, Ernst Augustus, and Johann Friedrich. She forged relationships with members of the literary establishment, who supplied celebratory verse for her earliest volumes of poetry and letters. She commissioned author portraits, and several of her volumes contain skilfully executed etchings. Her works frequently engaged her patrons' dynastic, political, and cultural interests, ranging from a history of Ferdinando II's journey to the Holy Roman Empire to verse applauding the dazzling success of the opera *Orfeo* organized in Paris by Mazarin and Queen Anne (in which Costa and her sister Anna Francesca starred). Framed in this light, Costa would seem to have followed the sixteenth- and early seventeenth-century model of self-legitimation strategies by which women obtained the authority needed to write, publish, and move within elite cultural circles. And to a certain extent, she did just that.

It would be inaccurate, however, to pigeonhole Costa within pre-existing categories by portraying her as simply having taken a familiar route to female literary achievement. Perhaps because her role as a professional itinerant performer already pushed her to the margins of social acceptance, Costa was exceptionally adept at navigating the increasingly rocky terrain of female authorship – and was not shy in doing so. A survey of her works, particularly those dating to her Florentine period, quickly reveals that Costa was in fact often remarkably uninterested in projecting the conventional persona of female decorum. Central to her strategy was the cultivation of a literary and theatrical persona as a "bizarre" – that is, capricious and unconventional – writer. Repeatedly underscoring her *bizzarria*, Costa emphatically declares in one poem that "with my Muse [whom she portrays as a wild banshee] I'll do as I wish," and cautions her reader in another, "don't raise your eyebrows at me."[28] Her poetry is filled with women who are sexually experienced and experimental; her comedy features dwarfs and hunchbacks cracking crude jokes. A volume that begins with poetry dedicated to the members of the Medici clan ends with verse describing, for example, a procuress who lost her nose "in the service of love."[29] Her collection of love letters expresses female desire and features a spectrum of "grotesque" lovers: the syphilitic, the lame, the deaf, the bald, the stuttering, and so forth. Particularly during the first half of her career, she in no way shrank from the kinds of language and subjects that were typically off-limits for women. Hers was often a burlesque world.

If we should take care not to categorize Costa as self-legitimating within the same mould as her female literary and theatrical predecessors, so too should we temper the urge to label her a "feminist."[30] While Costa claimed the liberty to write how she chose, and while she largely affirmed female sexuality at the same time that she acknowledged the challenges women faced (as exemplified by a poem about a mother's joy when her baby girl magically transforms into a boy, sparing the child future hardship), with regard to women, as in so many other facets of her work, it is hard to pin her down.[31] If in one poem she encourages women to take revenge on philandering lovers by pursuing some fun of their own, in another she urges them to abandon erotic adventures for the spindle and the hearth. Moreover, the libertine slant in Costa's poetics dates primarily from her early Florentine period and does not characterize her literary career writ large.

While Costa delved into the burlesque, then in vogue within male circles, and often embraced a lyric eroticism, her brand was by no means limited to it. She showcased her ability to engage diverse registers with disparate rhetorical aims, and alongside her libertine ladies are saintly heroines, grieving widows, and female regents. This versatility – the hallmark of her corpus – reflects the various cultural environments in which she was active. Although Costa forged a career as an accomplished singer in the chamber halls and on the stages of the day, she perhaps did not quite reach the celebrity of the period's most renowned singers, women like Baroni, Renzi, or Strozzi. The card up her sleeve was her literary engagement, nearly unmatched for her gender in its generic breadth, thematic and stylistic variability, and sheer quantity. Yet we can also make sense of her oeuvre by considering what is often its *fil rouge*: the courtship of her patrons and other benefactors.

When we look at how Costa responds to her patrons in print, it is clear that her focus on them went well beyond title-page dedications and fawning letters of gratitude.[32] This was a woman with her finger on the cultural pulse of each of the courts and cities she visited and who readily adapted to their tastes and political-rhetorical exigencies. Costa was not above complaining about the court, however. Her laments about competition among singers and the challenges posed by negligent or nefarious benefactors illustrate the hardships of being a professional performer and a female writer. However, Costa often recasts her itinerary into a narrative of neglect (in her old court) and nurture (in her new one – wherever it may be), putting each of her patrons in turn in the "unique" position of being able to recognize and appreciate her talents. This emphasis on her misfortune thus becomes another part of Costa's constructed persona of singularity and eccentricity.

Life and Works

Previous biographies of Costa's life have been short on detail, and information about her has been derived primarily from her publications. The trajectory of her career – previously hazy and unfamiliar to the modern reader – is fundamental to understanding how she crafted literary relationships to her patrons. It is therefore important to next consider Costa's movements and connections in detail. The following biographical profile, which significantly advances our knowledge about Costa, is not merely an introduction to this book but also to the woman herself.

Early Years in Rome

While Costa's date of birth is yet unknown, most estimates place it in the first decade or so of the 1600s. A will dated 1635 describes her as the daughter of "Cristoforo Costa *romano*."[33] Cristoforo makes an appearance in Janus Nicius Erythraeus's satirical novel *Eudemia* (1637) as an unnamed father who describes his beautiful daughter's "most sweet voice" and skill on the lyre, gifts that attracted droves of listeners. These spectators' interest was not simply a matter of musical appreciation: Costa is identified as "*Pleura*, the well-known prostitute," a pun on *pleurum,* the Greek word for "rib" that translates to *costa* in Italian. This occupation was necessitated in part by the need to cover the many expenses of the father, whose lack of virtue the novel's speakers condemn.[34] Erythraeus (pen name of Gian Vittorio Rossi) does not offer any clues about her age, save the fact that she is married to a young man (*adolosce*[*ns*]) and her brother is not yet twenty.

Costa's will contains the "tell-tale sign" that she was indeed a courtesan, at least at this stage of her career: following Roman regulations, she leaves one-fifth of her estate to the Convertite, a monastery for reformed prostitutes.[35] At the same time, the document also demonstrates her relative success: among her bequests are a house on Via della Lungara in Trastevere and a vineyard outside Porta Portese, as well as a collection of pearls, diamond necklaces and rings, and a coral crown.[36] It is unclear whether these material goods prove Costa's success as a courtesan or as a singer, or both. In addition to a necklace to be given to the church of San Francesco a Ripa, where she hoped to be buried, she left sizeable funds to her brother Paolo (a Barberini bravo whom Erythraeus calls both a talented singer and the murderer of a rival),[37] to her sisters Anna (whom the Barberini would later help join a convent) and Anna Francesca, and to her "little sisters" Barbara, Vittoria, and Olimpia.[38] Like Margherita, Anna Francesca was also a professional singer – one who enjoyed the steady patronage of Giovan Carlo de' Medici, became an opera impresario (*Ergirodo*, 1653), and is believed to have been the mistress of Charles II of England.[39] Margherita's husband was Giovanni Galbiatti, with whom she had a contentious and likely estranged relationship ("ho con lui di qualsivoglia sorte"); she leaves him 260 *corami* (decorative leather panels) in turquoise and gold on the condition that her widowed mother, Dorotea, named her universal heir, have no further interaction with him.[40] The will further states that her heirs could secure a portion of the money needed for the remaining payments for the vineyard from Papirio Capizucchi, a member of Rome's patrician class and, according to subsequent baptismal records, the future father of her child.[41] Capizucchi evidently was her principal early patron, the kind of *amico* that high-ranking courtesans – and singers – enjoyed.

In addition to opening a rare window onto Costa's familial context, Erythraeus is also the source for the episode for which Costa has been most known: a musical rivalry that inspired composer Domenico Mazzocchi's *La catena d'Adone*.[42] In 1626, Giovan Giorgio Aldobrandini commissioned the opera (an adaptation of cantos 12 and 13 of Marino's epic *L'Adone*), which features a confrontation between the characters Venus and Falsirena. It was initially intended to stage a historical rivalry between two female singers: a certain "Cecca of the Swamp" and Margherita Costa. The two women had the backing of Giandomenico Lupini and Aldobrandini, respectively.[43] Such competitions were common, but this one alarmed Aldobrandini's wife enough that she put a stop to it. When the opera debuted in February, the women had been replaced by castrati.[44]

While the *Catena d'Adone* did not go according to plan, Costa did sing before other elite audiences in Rome. Evidence to this effect is provided by Ludovico d'Agliè (a Turinese ambassador who oversaw the Roman palace of Cardinal Maurizio of Savoy), who hired Costa and other musicians for a 1627 dinner for the Count of Soissons.[45] Costa surely also participated in *veglie* or *conversazioni*, formal or intimate discursive gatherings (at times in connection to an academy) at which female singers were known to perform.[46] Evidence of Costa's familiarity with prominent men in Rome is also seen in poems from her first verse collection; adopting the poetic persona of a *bella donna* (beautiful woman), these are addressed to the Venetian ambassador Angelo Contarini, the patrician Federico Colonna, and the visiting future king of Poland, Wladyslaw IV, among others.

Florence

Costa would soon depart for Florence. It has generally been assumed that she arrived in Tuscany after the *Catena d'Adone* incident or, more likely, on the heels of Ferdinando's 1628 journey to the imperial court, a trip which initially brought him to Rome and that was the subject of Costa's first (undated) publication. There is also some reason to believe that she performed in Ferdinando's first major cultural event, the festivities for the 1628 wedding of Margherita de' Medici and Odoardo Farnese of Parma, which included the opera *La Flora*.[47] While the archival documents are cursory regarding the hiring of musicians for that event, support is found in Erythraeus's *Eudemia*, where Pleura's father asserts that his family has only recently returned to Rome after "King Anthimus … invited us to his sister's wedding with the greatest enticements and hosted us for eight whole months," a version of events that the satire's protagonists dispute as mere cover for her having been summoned to that city by a john but expelled soon after due to the various scandals she caused.[48] Two contemporary manuscript keys to the work identify Anthimus with Ferdinando.[49]

If Erythraeus's chronology can be trusted, Costa may have travelled to Tuscany first in 1628 and returned once again in the mid-1630s. While her will places her in Rome in 1635, in September 1636 she sold her Trastevere vineyard (first purchased in 1633) and her daughter Giovanna Vittoria was baptized in Florence earlier that March. A second daughter, Vittoria Maria, was baptized there in May 1637.[50] The baptismal records list the girls' fathers: Giovanna's the aforementioned Papirio Capizucchi, Vittoria's the bravo and bandit Tiberio Squilletti (1595–1678).[51] Capizucchi soon faded from the picture, but Costa's relationship to Squilletti would endure, proving a defining (if disruptive) lodestone for her movements and her legacy over time, including as a reoccurring figure within her publications. In addition to shedding light on matters of paternity, these records demonstrate Costa's integration into Florentine socio-cultural life. Her eldest daughter's godfather was Giovan Carlo de' Medici, while the youngest's was the grand duke himself (represented at the ceremony by Ferdinando Saracinelli, court librettist and soon one of Costa's poetic celebrants).[52]

Florence would become singularly important for Costa. There she cultivated enduring bonds to the Medici and forged connections with the city's literary elite. Florence was where Costa launched her publishing career and proved to be most prolific – producing nine printed volumes, a handful of pamphlets, and at least one manuscript– as well as where she could afford to experiment widely in genre and register, moving between Marinist poetry to dynastic epic to equestrian ballet to burlesque comedy.

While Costa likely had already begun composing verse in Rome, she first entered the world of print with the aforementioned history of Ferdinando's voyage to the court of the Holy Roman Emperor (*Istoria del viaggio d'Alemagna del serenissimo gran duca di Toscana Ferdinando Secondo*).[53] The work, published sometime after 1632, meticulously traces the young grand duke's movements and diplomatic receptions in the various cities he visited. As chapter 1 will demonstrate, Costa was the editor, not the author, of the work – as she herself acknowledges. This raises the fascinating questions of why such an important history came to be entrusted to a then-unpublished Roman courtesan and singer, and what role, if any, its publication played in securing her status in Florence in the 1630s.

Costa's literary career began in full force in 1638, when she dedicated two poetry collections with musically themed titles to Ferdinando, *La chitarra* (The Guitar) and *Il violino* (The Violin). These volumes were clearly designed to make a splash. Like all of Costa's publications save her last, they are in quarto rather than the more pedestrian and ubiquitous duodecimo format. Prominent Roman and Florentine writers contributed celebratory verse applauding Costa's musical and lyric skills, and the leading Florentine draftsman of the day, Stefano della Bella, supplied an author portrait for *La chitarra*. Within this elegant packaging, however, the reader encounters amorous and often burlesque lyric. Her first (and heftiest) verse collection is a malformed dwarf, she claims, and her muse is ugly and uncontrollable. The two volumes pivot between an often audacious *bella donna* in the *Chitarra*, who addresses first Costa's patrons and elite acquaintances and then an assortment of desired or disdained lovers, to a largely ventriloquized male voice in *Il violino*. Alongside ambassadors, aristocrats, and even the future king of Poland, the cast of characters includes jealous lovers, pining ladies, *virtuosi*, pretty boys, nymphs, and shepherds.

Costa published two additional volumes the following year. An innovative adaptation of the popular letterbook genre, her *Lettere amorose* (Love Letters), dedicated to Giovan Carlo, featured epistles and poems exchanged between a host of imagined characters: more traditional pairs of lovers and beloveds, followed by unexpected couples that include, for example, a witch and her bald lover, a courtesan and her greedy client, and a hunchback and a one-eyed woman. The collection, which introduced a new portrait of the author by an unknown artist, proved Costa's most popular during her lifetime: subsequent editions were published in 1643, 1651, and 1674, and the work was partially anthologized in the *Scelta di lettere amorose* (1656), which itself saw several reprints. Her second publication of the year, dedicated to Lorenzo de' Medici, is entitled *Lo stipo* (The Cabinet).[54] It consists of seven highly versatile "drawers" associated hierarchically with gems, from precious to fake, and presents verse ranging from encomia to burlesques.

These two works, as well as the earlier *Istoria*, bear false imprints. Venice is identified as the publication city of the *Istoria*, with no publisher named, and *La chitarra* and *Il violino* are both described as having been printed in Frankfurt by one "Daniel Watsch."[55] However, Julie Robarts has demonstrated that the decorative devices found in *Lo stipo*, *La chitarra*, and *Il violino* are those of Massi and Landi, the Florentine publishers who would officially print all of Costa's works in the city beginning in 1640, and that there is every reason to assume that the *Lettere amorose* are also under their imprint.[56] These publications date to a period of time in which Florence sought to evade Roman censorial control over the book market.[57]

The next year, 1640, was the most prolific of Costa's career. It also marked a clear, albeit somewhat temporary, shift in her register, as a new quartet of texts allowed her to more fully showcase her literary versatility – to demonstrate the "variety of my songs," as she put it to Ferdinando.[58] Setting aside her earlier interest in bawdy topics, she took up the dynastic concerns of her patrons, themes that had guided the *Istoria* and informed her occasional verse. This comparatively sober stylistic turn also saw her works' first accurate imprints. This series began with *Flora feconda* (Fertile Flora), a short epic about the grand duke and duchess's first pregnancy, framed as the Mediterranean journey of Zephyrus and Flora to Jove's oracle to request permission to procreate.[59] When the Medici child died after only a few days, however, Costa had to quickly revise the poem. She further proved her range by rewriting it again later that year, transforming the epic into a drama (possibly a *dramma in musica*) under the lightly tweaked title *La Flora feconda*.[60] Costa had delivered the original *Flora* poem to Ferdinando alongside another work: a gift manuscript of an equestrian ballet libretto, the *Festa reale per balletto a cavallo* (Royal Fete Horse Ballet).[61] Equestrian ballet was a spectacular form of early modern musical theatre that blended horsemanship and the military arts, vocal and instrumental music, and *ballet de cour* in a manner that promoted the political messages of the courts staging them. The first if not the only female-authored libretto of its kind, Costa's manuscript was an innovative take on the genre that blazoned her patrons' names across the very heavens. However, the work proved impossible to stage due to the recent sad circumstances at court. Costa revisited these same themes –the political interests of her benefactors as intertwined with troubled hereditary politics – in a collection of historical and pastoral laments, *La selva di cipressi* (The Cypress Forest), dedicated to Charles of Lorraine, Duke of Guise, a French exile in Florence who had recently suffered the deaths of his two sons, in a volume combining elegiac verse for them, members of the Della Rovere and Medici families, and a variety of cultural, political, and military figures with pastoral laments.[62]

In 1641 Costa returned to the unconventional components of her earlier compositions with the ribald *Li buffoni* (The Buffoons), the first comedy published by a woman in Italy.[63] Although no evidence has yet come to light regarding the performance history of *Li buffoni*, its dedication implies a staging during Carnival. Dedicated not to a Medici family member but instead to one of their buffoons, Bernardino Ricci, known professionally as "il Tedeschino" (who doubles as the comedy's protagonist), this is the prurient tale of a princess unable to entice her prince into their marriage bed because he is so consumed by baser pleasures. Though set in Morocco, the "ridiculous" comedy's ragtag cast of dwarfs, hunchbacks, and madmen satirizes the Medici court. The prologue insists, however, that not only are the play's buffoonish antics acceptable to the Medici but in fact they represent the family's preferred form of entertainment.

It has been suggested that Costa's subsequent departure from Florence was prompted by outrage over this comedy.[64] However, she left several years later, in 1644, and her companion Squilletti in fact thanked Leopoldo de' Medici for helping her publish it.[65] The family continued to support and follow Costa throughout her career. Some months after *Li buffoni* went to press, for example, Costa was due to perform in Venice, presumably on loan by the Medici per common practice. After being mistreated in that city, she ultimately avoided the commitment by professing to be unavailable. As Pier Francesco Rinuccini (son of librettist Ottavio Rinuccini) wrote to Mattias de' Medici in November 1641, "these men [presumably the organizers] will learn with no little distaste about the absence of Signora Margherita Costa from these theatres," adding, however, that "they should blame themselves and the poor way they treated her [....] I cannot but praise her resolution."[66] If Costa suffered slights in other corners, she still enjoyed the backing of the Medici and their agents.

Costa's departure from Florence was instead connected to Squilletti. Born in Catanzaro, Squilletti had been a bandit operating under the guise of a hermit (alias "Fra Paolo") before making his way from Rome to Florence and the employ of Ferdinando.[67] Costa was intimately connected to his scrapes and adventures. Her thinly fictionalized poem *Tirsi trafitto* (Tirsi Stabbed) details a thrilling episode in 1639, when a would-be assassin stabbed him in the neck, and she herself received a letter of warning from an old acquaintance in Rome, Camilla Perugina, about new plots to murder him (by arson or poison) in 1641.[68] The stabbing, and Squilletti's remarkable survival, thrilled Florentine chroniclers, who inaccurately claimed that during his convalescence – a period in which he sought amorous distractions from low women – he first met Costa and published poetry under her name.[69] The pair, whose relationship in reality dated to at least 1636, decided to leave for Rome together. Despite having assisted the Medici against the Barberini during the War of Castro (1642–4), Squilletti requested and secured a papal bull of absolution from Urban VIII, after which the couple set out in early 1644.[70]

Return to Rome

Costa and Squilletti arrived in Rome in mid-February, professing to the Barberini that they wished to become penitents. The chronicler Giacinto Gigli attributed Squilletti's successful rapprochement with the papacy not only to this claim, which was sure to please Cardinal Francesco, but also to the direct influence of Costa, "a famous prostitute, who was friendly with a man who had an in with the Barberini."[71] Gigli recorded with dismay the warm welcome Squilletti received: "The famous thief and violent killer Fra Paolo was greeted with carriages and baggage wagons, and went to stay [temporarily] in the house of Don Taddeo Barberini … where he was honoured, and he travelled in Don Taddeo's carriage to everyone's amazement." Rumour had it that he was to receive a canonship at St. Peter's and a salary from the Barberini. "But," Gigli concludes, "the whole populace was curious to see how things would turn out, since no one could believe that he – accustomed to betrayal, blackmail, and murder – could become a good man."[72] Fellow chronicler Theodoro Ameyden agreed, stating that Romans found this reception "monstrous."[73]

Costa would allude to this return in a later poem addressed to Francesco Barberini, in which she thanks him for his clemency.[74] First, however, she veered hastily from the rowdy *Buffoni* to a new project guaranteed to interest this ecclesiastic benefactor: *Cecilia martire* (Martyr Cecilia).[75] The four-canto hagiographic epic invites comparisons between its author and St. Cecilia, the Roman patron saint of music, and between her dedicatee's uncle (Urban VIII) and Cecilia's confessor (Urban I), while also furnishing a flattering portrait of the family's spiritual and architectural endeavours. Costa worked quickly, completing the work by the summer. However, in July the pope died. The day before the conclave, the Austrian cardinal Ernst Adalbert von Harrach noted receiving a copy, describing its author not as a new penitent but instead as "a woman of little repute, the mistress kept by Fra Paolo," whom, he suggestively adds, his nephew the imperial diplomat Count Ferdinand Ernst von Waldstein also likely knew quite well.[76]

Urban's death imperilled the status of the Barberini and their circle. The increasingly hostile environment in Rome after the election of Innocent X (Giovanni Battista Pamphili) and the resentments built up over the long twenty years of Urban's papacy soon resulted in their flight to France. Deprived of her previously powerful backers, Costa turned to the new papal family. She delivered to Camillo Pamphili, Innocent's nephew, the undated manuscript of a long poem entitled *Le sette giornate, o vero Il viaggio di Loreto* (Seven Days, or The Voyage to Loreto). A recent addition to the list of Costa's known works, it presents as a conversion poem that explores a wealth of courtly divertissements, from banquets to games, in a rather libertine manner before taking a spiritual turn.[77]

Costa's textual relationship to the Pamphili remained limited, with no other known dedications. A figure such as Olimpia Maidalchini, Innocent's formidably influential sister-in-law (and Camillo's mother), might ordinarily attract Costa's pen for individual poems. However, her next publications would not appear until a few years later, in France. Even so, according to an August 1645 *avviso*, the Costas – "quite defamed and public women in this court" – had obtained Olimpia's protection thanks to renumerations offered her, which "let them put the arms of Her Excellency above their door and ... permitted them to travel by carriage without any regard [for the rules that usually forbid this luxury to courtesans]."[78]

Shortly before obtaining these privileges in Rome, Costa faced another turn of fate. In November 1644, Squilletti was arrested in Florence with compromising documents in his possession while requesting an audience with Ferdinando II. He would spend the rest of his days imprisoned in the Bargello. When an appeal failed and an escape plan resulted in his being held in shackles, he responded with a hunger strike that prompted a flurry of letters between the warden and Giovan Carlo. The former reported that "that woman of his" had arrived in December but was not permitted to see him lest scandal erupt.[79] By February Squilletti once again used her spiritual salvation as a bargaining chip, requesting permission to see her under the pretence of convincing her to join the Convertite or return to her mother's home.[80] His request was granted, although it is unclear whether the meeting took place; by May Squilletti was again asking for her, promising that he merely wanted her to collect his belongings since he was no longer prey to "amorous passion" and complaining that she had refused.[81] As will be seen below, Squilletti would continue to create headaches for Costa over the years to come, even if their relationship had cooled. The singer would be economically, if no longer emotionally, on the hook for the bandit.

On the Road

During these tumultuous months, Costa received an invitation to the court of Marie Christine of France, regent duchess of Turin. Costa's January 1645 contract reveals that she received a salary more than twice that of the other chamber singers already there employed; it also makes the first reference to Costa as a widow.[82] Costa's visit coincided with a series of lavish spectacles held in the wake of the Siege of Turin, in which Christine had successfully defended her regency against her brothers-in-law Tommaso and Cardinal Maurizio. Costa was likely hired to perform at these events celebrating the legitimacy of Christine's rule; she would echo many of their political-military themes in a poetry collection dedicated to the duchess two years later, *La selva di Diana* (Diana's Forest).[83] Presenting the duchess as the titular goddess, this verse collection foregrounds historical and fictional women, including Christine's sister-in-law and fellow regent, Anne of Austria, at whose French court Costa would soon sing.

In the mid-1640s, a window for Italian music and theatre had opened in Paris, driven by the tastes of Cardinal Mazarin, the powerful Italian-born chief minister who virtually ruled alongside Queen Anne during the minority of Louis XIV.[84] Mazarin's agents in Italy recruited artists, composers, singers, and scenographers to Paris, including Anna Francesca Costa for Francesco Sacrati's *La finta pazza* (1645) and Francesco Cavalli's *Egisto* (1646).[85] Two years later Luigi Rossi's *Orfeo* — the first Italian opera written for a French audience — starred Anna Francesca as Eurydice and Margherita as Juno, alongside famed castrati Atto Melani and Marc'Antonio Pasqualini.[86]

Costa would portray her voyage to France as a flight from an inhospitable Rome, omitting any mention of her royal invitation or the difficulty Mazarin's agents had in securing her acceptance.[87] Mazarin tasked his representatives (Cornelio and Giovanni Bentivoglio in Florence and Paris, and Elpidio Benedetti in Rome) with selecting and transporting the musicians, as Giovanni explained in a letter: "Since her Majesty the Queen has decided to have a good number of singers in Paris this winter for both her chambers and the theatre, [we are to] write to Signora Francesca Costa and her sister Signora Margherita, who is now in Venice, to come to France with other musicians that might be found [in Florence] and Venice."[88] This reference to Margherita's presence in Venice in 1646 has led

Ellen Rosand to speculate that she may have been performing in one of the city's operas, perhaps Monteverdi's *L'incoronazione di Poppea*.[89] While Anna Francesca was already a familiar face in Paris, the men expressed growing exasperation with her sister's delayed response. Benedetti wrote to Cornelio in October and November to promote "Signora Felice," a budding soprano in the service of Mattias de' Medici who would make a fine alternative if Costa declined since, he added in a barb, "[Felice's] advantage is as great as the age difference between 17 and 47."[90] All was settled by December, when Benedetti reported that Margherita had alerted him to the cast's need for a contralto.[91] The *Orfeo* musicians arrived in January – without Felice.

The French court explored sponsoring an additional event that season. Under consideration were Giovan Battista Andreini's 1622 musical comedy *La Ferinda* and Costa's *Festa reale* horse ballet, the manuscript (which she had apparently carried with her) now dedicated to Mazarin.[92] A staging of the ballet was not to be, however, in part because Anne's enthusiasm for *l'Orfeo* led to encore performances through May. Mazarin instead helped Costa print a trio of works with Sébastien Cramoisy, the powerful publisher nicknamed "the king of rue Saint-Jacques" (the hub of the book industry) and director of the Imprimerie royale.[93] Her *Festa reale* was realized now in print, if not in performance, seven years after she had first delivered the original manuscript to Ferdinando II.[94] She included poems of thanks for the cardinal's assistance in *La tromba di Parnaso* (The Trumpet of Parnassus), a verse collection dedicated to Anne that honours a variety of figures connected to the French court, including key collaborators in *Orfeo*.[95] The third volume was the aforementioned *Selva di Diana*, which concludes with a poem professing gratitude for the "honours received in Paris by Her Majesty the Queen of France."[96]

Most of the Italian singers returned home in May.[97] They received 200 *doppie* from the crown, and Mazarin presented the women with diamonds "of great value."[98] The Costas' paths diverged: Anna Francesca departed for Rome, with a letter of recommendation addressed from Mazarin to the French ambassador François du Val, while Margherita returned to Florence bearing one for Ferdinando II.[99] Margherita appears to have moved regularly between cities. She may have been in Rome in early 1648, when the Florentine ambassador to Rome reported speaking to Anna Francesca's sisters and mother when Giovan Carlo was unsuccessfully attempting to locate her,[100] and in April 1649 she returned to the Eternal City once more from Turin, where she had been employed again at Christine's court.[101] A Roman *avviso* of February 1650 alleged that the "famous courtesan named Margherita Costa" had been arrested when the investigation into a *pizzicheria* (grocer) heist led to her home, where the culprits (whom she named as an illegitimate Colonna son and members of the Savelli and Tovaglia families) had divvied up the haul.[102] While *avvisi* should be read with caution – they are hardly infallible documents – this one assists us in tracking Costa's movements, if not observing the sorts of predicaments in which she may have found herself.

The Venice Question

A poem by fellow writer Isabetta Coreglia offers us promising clues to Costa's next movements. An admirer of Costa's music and literary style who dedicated several poems to her, the Lucchese poet praised in one sonnet "Margherita 'Comica' in the role of Isifile in *Giasone*."[103] A companion sonnet on the facing page for "Anna 'Comica' in the role of Medea" points us to Francesca Cavalli's famed *Giasone*; it went on the road after its 1649 premiere in Venice, and its cast featured singer Anna Renzi when it arrived in Tuscany in the mid-1650s.[104] It is tempting to imagine that Coreglia saw Costa take the stage when the opera arrived in her native Lucca that September; however, it is more plausible that the production took place in Florence sometime between May and July, since by mid-August Costa had moved on to Venice.

Costa arrived in the Serenissima bearing a 26 June 1650 recommendation from Desiderio Montemagni, Giovan Carlo's secretary, to which the Florentine ambassador Francesco Maria Zati responded on 13 August. The cardinal instructed Zati to facilitate "a full introduction … [of] this *virtuosa* to the Academy of [Venetian] merchants," a task to which the ambassador promised to dedicate himself.[105] Costa's confirmed presence in Venice in this period is a new and important addition to her biography, which has long been particularly hazy in the years after the 1647 *Orfeo*. Despite Zati's vows of assistance, Costa's time in the city appears to have been fraught with difficulties. In March 1652, her daughter Giovanna penned a letter to Giovan Carlo, her godfather, stating that Margherita wished to leave Venice but that the same obstacle which had driven mother and daughters northward impeded their return south: the creditors "of that devil Captain Tiberio [Squilletti]." They had hounded poor Margherita before, forcing her to escape to the stormy "swamps" of Venice. To her letter Giovanna appended a list of the "debts of Captain Tiberio incurred while we were held [*tenute*] at home by force" and "while we were hostages [*schiave*]." Giovanna entreated Giovan Carlo to secure a one-month moratorium from these debts. "Save me," her letter pleads with mounting fervour, "from the precipice that readies my funeral bed."[106]

Giovanna's entreaty is yet another testament to Squilletti's enduring impact on Costa, one that by then negatively dictated her movements and saddled her with financial obligations and, it appears, even captivity by an unspecified party. The cardinal answered the call, earning Giovanna's profuse thanks a month later.[107] Later that year the Costas were still in Venice, however. In December 1652, Giovanna entreated Montemagni to have the cardinal intervene in another conflict, this one between the Costas and a rival Medici singer, Anna Maria Sardelli, who was tarnishing their names within Venetian theatre and music circles, thereby jeopardizing their future.[108]

In spite of (or perhaps because of) these hardships, Costa brought her final full-length work to press in Venice: the 1654 *Gl'amori della luna* (The Moon's Loves), a pastoral drama about Diana and Endymion that may in fact be a libretto. Its dedication to the three ducal brothers of Brunswick-Lüneburg (Georg Wilhelm, Ernst Augustus, and Johann Friedrich), and a paratextual reference to four years spent under "foreign skies," have led to speculation that Costa journeyed north to Germany. Those skies were surely Venetian, however, and the dedication recognizes the German brothers' growing role in the city's opera scene. Their enthusiastic visits to its stages earned them thirty libretto dedications between 1654 and 1688, making Costa one of the first to recognize and appeal to their mounting influence.

Costa's overtures to the Brunswick-Lüneburg dukes as well as the correspondence between Florence and Venice all indicate that Costa was likely performing on the Serenissima's stages. Supporting this assumption is a sonnet by Vicentine poet Paolo Abriani that praises "Signora Margarita Costa, the sorceress Nerea at the Teatro Sant'Apollinare" – that is, a role in Cavalli's 1651 *Rosinda*.[109] Abriani notes the singer's Roman origins, making an identification with our same Margherita Costa likely if not assured. Yet Costa's other engagements in Venice present something of a historical puzzle. The account books of Marco Faustini, brother of the librettist and impresario Giovanni Faustini, record the hiring of a "Margarita da Costa" for two other Cavalli operas performed in that same theatre, *La Calisto* (1651) and *L'Eritrea* (1652).[110] It happens, however, that there was indeed a Margarita da Costa (of as-of-yet uncertain origins) in Venice, but her death in 1653 precludes speculation that she is the same woman under study here.[111] Faustini's records note that the soprano who sang in these two operas was hired in agreement with Marc'Antonio Correr, to whom both librettos are dedicated and in whose papers this other Margarita's name appears.[112] The fact that Costa's own drama of two years later revisits the mythological subplot of *Calisto* – the story of Diana and Endymion – in a volume published by the same printer (Andrea Giuliani) is suggestive but hardly definitive.[113] The timing of the final *Eritrea* performance on 23 February 1652 also happens to coincide with a letter from Giovanna to Giovan Carlo three weeks later stating that her mother was ready to leave Venice. Is this a case of a slight confusion of names in the account books, or were there indeed two Margherita [da] Costas singing in Venice in the very same years? A decisive answer is not yet possible, and it is even conceivable that one woman performed in *Rosinda* and the other in *Calisto* and *Eritrea*. While Costa's precise activities in the Serenissima remain somewhat veiled, her presence there in the 1650s nevertheless marks an important addition to our knowledge of her movements.

Later Life

Costa's last known publication is a broadside commemorating a carousel that Maffeo Barberini (the younger) staged for the newly converted Queen Christina of Sweden, whose 1656 arrival in Rome was greeted with a variety of spectacles, from processions to fireworks.[114] Recently returned to Rome themselves, the Barberini had everything to prove as they sought to re-establish their cultural might through three operas, as well as through the hotly anticipated tournament. Costa's sonnet memorializes this elaborate affair.

We last see Costa in letters sent the following years. The first was sent to Mario Chigi in Rome on 4 May 1657.[115] This plaintive epistle presents Costa as a "widow and poor *virtuosa*" in need of assistance due to the upkeep of her two daughters (one the wife of a Flemish captain stationed in Crete, the other unmarried). To better catch Chigi's attentions, Costa included a sample of her poetry. She chose her recipient strategically: the brother of Alexander VII, Mario had recently been named commander of the papal army. Her connection to the Chigi family was likely facilitated by Mattias de' Medici, governor of their native Siena, a hypothesis supported by the fact that she was also sending letters to Mattias himself from Rome in this same period.[116] These letters thanked Mattias for various favours and acts of generosity (including the provision of a litter) before broaching the subject of her straitened circumstances. Wishing to return with her daughters "to our nest" – presumably meaning Florence – but stuck in Rome facing "the oppression of malicious men," Costa's requests centre on trying to maintain access to the services of a man (one Fortunato Berto) who assisted with her affairs.[117] In a message sent a month after her entreaty to Chigi she lamented that, with Berto no longer able to help her without Mattias's blessing, she and her daughters were left at the financial mercy of their enemies in Rome.[118] In what may be her final known letter, one without a date but possibly composed in early 1658 at the end of a long and circuitous career, she describes herself as a "foreigner" stranded in an unspecified city with her daughters and in need of assistance from the Medici patrons to whom she had so long pledged her service.[119]

The date and circumstances of Costa's death remain unknown, as are those of her sister Anna Francesca, though the latter had died by at least early 1677.[120] Margherita's younger daughter Vittoria also joined the ranks of professional performers. In 1664, one Francesco Cardinali recommended her to Ippolito Bentivoglio as "niece of the departed Checca Costa, who sings quite well and is very attractive," adding that "she sang for three years in Florence in the productions staged at the theatre on Florence's Via del Cocomero in Ottonaina's company and was very well received."[121] Constructed in 1650 with the assistance of Giovan Carlo, the Teatro del Cocomero offered a particularly robust calendar of comedies and operas in these years, including Giacinto Andrea Cicognini's 1661 *L'Orontea*; its cast list contained both a Maddalena Ottonaina and a "signora Vettoria" and is therefore likely one of the productions alluded to by Cardinali.[122] Margherita's musical career – but not her literary one – had passed on to the next generation.

Poetic Celebrants, Literary Relationships, and Readership

The congratulatory poems that introduce Costa's earliest volumes with praise for her literary and musical skills are among our best indicators of the circles in which she moved. While there is no indication that she gained academy membership, as had select predecessors like Isabella Andreini and Margherita Sarrocchi, most of her male celebrants were members of prominent groups: the Umoristi in Rome, the Crusca in Florence, and the Incogniti in Venice, among others.[123] Costa's relationship to the infamously libertine Incogniti is especially curious. Not only did her Florentine works treat many of the same subjects on which they published, with comparably Marinist arguments and registers, but portions of her *Lettere* would later be anthologized alongside examples from academy members. Several of Costa's celebrants were also librettists with whom she likely had performative, as well as poetic, ties: Tronsarelli (librettist of the aforementioned *La catena d'Adone*) and Ferdinando Saracinelli. Costa's most pivotal relationship within this male coterie was with Alessandro Adimari of Florence, whose academy membership spanned the peninsula (Fiorentino, Alterato, Linceo, Incognito) and whose own publications provided clear models for her own.[124] We can hazard that Adimari was her primary literary ally at the Medici court and attribute her ability to publish there to his influence, rather than to Squilletti's pen as the chroniclers had claimed.

Although Costa was never the recipient of a full volume of encomiastic verse as were celebrity singers like Adriana Basile, Leonora Baroni, or Anna Renzi, she garnered high praise in individual poems.[125] The Neapolitan Marinist poet Giovanni Fontanella (a contributor to the Basile volume who celebrated numerous women, including Lucrezia Marinella and Artemesia Gentileschi), for example, included a sonnet to Costa in his 1640 *Novi cieli*, dedicated to Ferdinando II. Here he professed that no conventional appellation sufficed – woman, siren, muse, Pallas, Venus – since her many virtues placed her in a class by herself.[126] In his 1641 *Rime* dedicated to Benedetto Guerrini, another Marinist poet, Lorenzo Morassini, included a sonnet lauding "Margherita Costa, spirited miracle of poetry" within a section of verse celebrating Florentine and Aretine figures, calling her "the tenth and most famous" of the Muses.[127]

Of particular interest are the aforementioned poems by Paolo Abriani and Isabetta Coreglia, who applauded Costa's roles in *Rosinda* and *Giasone*, respectively. Abriani commends Costa's performance as the sorceress Nerea, pairing thematically appropriate praise for her "sweet incantations" and "magical notes" with recognition of her virtuosic ability to stir feelings of "contempt, love, cruelty, pity, and fervour" in her listeners.[128] Virginia Cox has suggested that Coreglia's manuscript verse collection reveals "the influence of Costa's more vivacious model" on the writer, a "poetic discipleship" somewhat toned down in the Lucchese poet's case due to her higher social station.[129] This *Raccolta di varie composizioni* contains several poems about Costa. The first, whose title transforms "Margherita Costa *romana*" into the anagram "Grat', hormai, sirena canta," praises the singer-poet born on the Tiber and made famous on the Arno who, now that she has also come to Lucca's own Serchio, can be confirmed first-hand as a modern-day Pindar.[130]

In addition to the poems applauding Costa's performance as Isifile, several others may reference her: a sequence of three male-voiced amorous poems about "Margherita" that directly follow one of Coreglia's most Costian compositions, *La musa libera* (The Free Muse), as well as correspondence verse on women's virtue (or lack thereof) conducted between "Elisa of the Tiber" ("Elisa" being Costa's pastoral name in her autobiographical verse) and Nerina (Coreglia's own poetic alias).[131]

Several contemporaries placed Costa alongside other notable women. Giovan Francesco Loredan, founder of the Incogniti, gave her illustrious female company in his *Bizzarrie academiche*, praising those "admirable women … the infinite Teanos, Sosipastras, Zenobias, Aspasias, Corinnas, Sapphos, Costas, Marinellas, Tarabottis, and a thousand others" who were exceptions to his broader discourse on female inferiority.[132] The Neapolitan poet Giambattista "Titta" Valentino similarly included her in his "gallery" of exceptional women alongside Lucrezia Marinella, Laura Terracina, Veronica Gambara, and Vittoria Colonna; the octave dedicated to Costa generously likens her to Tasso and Ariosto, since "she wrote just as well and just as much."[133] The following century, Francesco Pentolini's 1777 *Le donne illustre* measured her against the likes of Thalia (muse of comedy and pastoral poetry), Homer, Ariosto, and Tasso before settling on an ultimate comparison with Ovid ("al Sulmonese").[134]

Pentolini's identification is rooted in Costa's own corpus, which explores a variety of classical exemplars but none so much as Ovid, whom Costa – true to her age – innovatively adapted, particularly regarding questions of gender.[135] Her works also reveal deep literary ties to more contemporary models, in addition to the aforementioned Adimari. Foremost among these was Marino, whose theatrical and rule-bending approach to authorship (characteristics even more heavily emphasized by his followers) made imitation of him unthinkable for most women. Costa's identity as a performer keen to test literary and social boundaries made her particularly well-suited to Marinist poetry and thus able to buck the downward trend in publications by women in the Seicento. This was especially true during her time in Florence, which she astutely identified as being amenable to such style, including from a woman's pen. But Costa – like Marino himself – adapted her register as necessary and could also draw upon his more sober, sacred verse. She further displayed a creative familiarity with predecessors such as Petrarch, Boccaccio, Ariosto, Tasso, and Andreini.

Costa's volumes filled the selves of her patrons. Caution is advisable when considering the holdings of individual libraries – a volume's presence is no guarantee that it was read. Nevertheless, an overview of Costa's representation in libraries helps us appreciate the degree to which her work was being collected, and by whom. The case of Vittoria della Rovere is particularly notable because it also allows us to reassess the grand duchess's modern reputation, which until recently was largely defined by Eric Cochrane's dismissal of her as "that stuff-necked religious bigot."[136] Just as recent studies of her patronage activities, particularly of women, have revised this blunt assessment, the inventory of her library similarly shines new light on her tastes; in addition to numerous festival books, opera librettos, and especially comedies, Vittoria's shelves contained seven of Costa's publications, making her the best-represented female writer in the grand duchess's library.[137] The Barberini were also major holders of Costa's volumes.[138] Alongside the *Cecilia martire* dedicated to him, Cardinal Francesco possessed eight of her Florentine publications.[139] Camillo Pamphili acquired the highly disparate *Cecilia martire* and *Lettere amorose*, in addition to the *Sette giornate* manuscript.[140] Costa's works pop up in other collections beyond those of her patrons. Most notable is the presence of her *Buffoni* and one of the *Flora* works in the library of Galileo; the former is particularly striking because the telescope of the scientist (whose period of house arrest overlaps with Costa's years in Florence) features prominently but satirically in both the frontispiece and the script.[141] Near-contemporary bibliophiles also possessed copies of her texts: Barberini librarian Cassiano dal Pozzo; the literato Prospero Mandosio; Giovanni Giacomo Amadei, canon of Bologna's Santa Maria Maggiore; the Venetian librettist Apostolo Zeno; the Belgian biblio- and Italophile Albert François Floncel, and the French jurist Pierre de Maridat. At the end of the nineteenth century the poet Giosuè Carducci would acquire several of her volumes for his immense library.

Costa's *Lettere* saw several Seicento editions and were anthologized at the end of her lifetime in the 1656 *Scelta di lettere amorose*, where she appeared alongside authors (Ferrante Pallavicino, Luca Asserino) associated with the Incogniti, among others. After being published in several editions, the *Scelta* was placed on the Index of Prohibited Books in 1683.[142] The poet and playwright Luisa Bergalli next included Costa in her important 1726 survey of women writers, with selections – *La mia musa è svegliata e già ripiglia* on Costa's wild muse and two other poems also drawn from *La chitarra* – that were later replicated in other collections, creating an enduring but limited micro-canon.[143] More varied selections came with Jolanda de Blasi's 1930 anthology of women writers, which presented the *Buffoni* prologue alongside a newly varied set of verse and letters.[144]

Li buffoni has drawn the most interest in our own day. It was Costa's first modern edition (to date the only one in Italy) through its inclusion in Siro Ferrone's 1986 *Commedia dell'arte* anthology; the comedy was also translated into English in 2018. Most curiously, it was rewritten and performed as a dialect comedy on the Mediterranean immigration crisis by a company of psychiatric patient-actors as part of Bologna's Arte e Salute association.[145] Interest in Costa's other works is also expanding, evidenced by translations of her *Lettere* and a selection of her poetry.[146]

As a performer, Costa was intimately familiar with the musical forms of her day, and while she does not appear to have tried her hand at any formal musical compositions, one imagines that her virtuosity as a singer included improvisations. At least one poem "by Signora Costa" (*Oh Dio, voi che mi dite*) was set to music by the Roman composer Marco Marazzoli.[147] This verse would later be extracted and reset by the musician-composer Cesare Morelli in manuscripts written out for his pupil, the English diarist and parliamentarian Samuel Pepys. It was subsequently reproduced by the copyist and composer Daniel Henstridge and French music printer Christophe Ballard's *Recueil des meilleurs airs italiens*.[148]

Reception and Legacy

As has been the case for many women writers, especially courtesans, scholarly responses to Costa have often been steeped in questions of personal reputation, and the actual content of her works has slid to the backburner. With some exceptions, like the satirist Erythraeus, Costa's contemporaries had written favourably about her. In his seventeenth-century *Bibliotheca romana*, for example, Prospero Mandosio praised her skill, erudition, supposed knowledge of Latin, and esteem by refined men.[149] But for her first modern biographer, Dante Bianchi, the arguments of Costa's defenders such as Mandosio "fall apart" when compared to negative assessments like that of the nineteenth-century Costantino Arlia.[150] Upon encountering a laudatory entry on Costa published in the 1880 *Bibliografia romana*, a passage modelled on Mandosio's that cited his correspondence with the famed Medici librarian Antonio Magliabechi regarding Costa's reputation, Arlia had objected heartily.[151] Arlia transcribed another of Magliabechi's letters as "proof" of his true assessment, a missive whose repudiation of Costa is hardly as damning as Arlia evidently held it to be:

> Those who knew Costa unanimously affirm to me that she was blessed with most singular talents and incomparable modesty and courtesy. It's true that for a period she practised the prostitute's arts, but it seems to me that this can be skipped over, since it's not necessary for someone composing a catalogue of literary figures to include their defects … Certainly all those who knew her presented her to me as most modest, courteous, a *virtuosa* in a hundred different things, and quite devoted … The word is that she was kept by [Squilletti] because he provided protection, but according to what someone who knew her well told me, there was a prominent figure who loved her.[152]

Disregarding Magliabechi's argument that such details ought not sway assessments of a writer's value, Arlia points to Costa's courtesanship and relationship to Squilletti as disqualifying. Magliabechi's true opinion, he insists, surely was that reported by his disciple Anton Francesco Marmi, who, in addition to noting Costa's low birth and prostitution, stated that "the assorted poems published under her name were not hers, but in Magliabechi's assessment, those … of Fra Paolo [Squilletti]."[153] However, Marmi's notes elsewhere also incorrectly describe the buffoon Bernardino Ricci as Costa's husband (Arlia overlooks marginalia in another hand disputing this) and declares that the *Istoria* "is known to have been set forth by Benedetto Guerrini," not mentioning (as Magliabechi had) that Costa herself highlighted Guerrini's role.[154] Costa's sexual impropriety and the authenticity of her works were inextricable matters for these commentators.

Inevitably chilling would be the assessment of Benedetto Croce, famously no friend to either Baroque poetics or women's writing and who correctly identified the convergence of the two in Margherita Costa. He dismissed her as having "scribbled" poor quality works that served only to demonstrate her ignorance.[155] Such assessments, particularly as coloured by continued devaluation of Seicento literary culture, have also bled into the view of some of Costa's recent biographers, who have suggested that she be considered primarily in "sociological terms" and that her publications have "only historical value as a documentation of seventeenth-century taste and as a source of information about her contemporaries."[156] Yet the more we learn about Costa, even previously sceptical scholars are beginning to look at her in a fresh new light as a versatile and unique figure who opens up new windows onto seventeenth-century Italy.[157]

Indeed, others had shared Mandasio and Magliabechi's positive assessments. Reflecting on her *Festa reale*, the seventeenth-century French music and dance theorist Claude-François Ménestrier praised her "genius and talent for poetry," an appraisal with which the Florentine bibliophile Giovanni Cinelli Calvoli (who possessed several of her works) explicitly concurred.[158] The following century the literary historian Girolamo Tiraboschi, although echoing the by-then prevailing view that the Baroque was characterized by works of inferior quality, nevertheless listed Costa among its notable poetesses.[159] Francesco Saverio Quadrio did the same, placing Costa alongside her male contemporaries and conceding that, while he personally found sparse wisdom in her works, she had been "acclaimed by the literary men and princes of her day."[160] Even the occasional Ottocento reader would observe that "she had an exquisitely poetic brilliance in epic, in lyric, in drama, and in satire."[161]

Curiously, the nineteenth century saw waves of interest in the story of Costa and Squilletti, due in part to a publication of his *Vita*.[162] Many Italian literary scholars shared Arlia's distaste for the couple, with one noting that Costa's *Lettere* were so scandalous that it hardly mattered which of the two was their true author.[163] In contrast, the journalist and writer Enrico Montazio needlingly asked Alessandro Ademollo – no fan of Costa's – "You do know that there's a fabulous story or even a novel to be written about Fra Paolo and the poetess Margherita?"[164] English-speaking audiences were ahead of him; in 1833 a translated version of the biography circulated in magazines from the *Monthly Traveller* (later part of the *Boston Herald*) to the immensely popular *The Lady's Book* under the title "Squilletti, The Celebrated Bandit."[165] These accounts no longer claimed that Squilletti published a volume under the name of a loose woman but instead "dedicated

[it] to the charming Margherita Costa, his favorite, and a most accomplished woman." The pair even appeared in a late nineteenth-century Florence guidebook in the entry about the Bargello, where Squilletti had been long imprisoned; in this revisitation, "the celebrated singer and favorite at court, Marguerite Costa, loved him and protected him as far as lay in her power" – a further romanticization that nevertheless reflects the continued intertwining of their stories and restores to her the favourable reputation that Magliabechi described Costa as having enjoyed.[166]

Book Synopsis

While the current volume is not Montazio's imagined novel, it is perhaps a guide-book to the remarkable life and career of Margherita Costa. This study reveals a woman who navigated the hardships of being an itinerant professional performer and a female writer in an increasingly inhospitable literary climate by savvily evaluating the tastes and needs of her patrons and shaping her works accordingly. From the burlesque to the sacred, the elegiac to the satirical, her texts attest to her virtuosic ability to forge a publishing career by attending to the literary and performative currents in the courts, cities, and intellectual circles in which she moved and by placing her benefactors at the core of her publications.

Chapter 1 begins with Costa's first publication, the *Istoria* on Ferdinando II's journey to the court of the Holy Roman Emperor. Presenting for the first time the documents to which Ferdinando's secretary Guerrini gave Costa access, this chapter identifies her as the history's editor, rather than its author, while arguing that the work's principal themes – diplomacy and spectacle – shaped her approach to the literary brokering of patronage.

Chapter 2 examines the burlesque literature and theatre of Costa's early career. While she crafted a literary persona as a "bizarre" new Sappho guided by an unfettered muse, I argue that this move reflected her evaluation of the Florentine literary climate – both the city's tradition of comedic writing and the tastes of her male Medici patrons. This chapter examines the theatrical and grotesque elements of her Florentine works (*La chitarra, Il violino, Lo stipo, Lettere amorose,* and *Li buffoni,* as well as the later *Sette giornate* manuscript), paying particular attention to how she wed encomiums to her patrons and their associates with satire, bawdy humour, and libertine poetics.

Chapter 3 pivots to works composed in support of the dynastic ambitions of Costa's patrons in Florence. It traces how Costa's *Flora* epic and drama intertwine favoured political-genealogical iconography associated with the Medici and the Della Rovere with revisitations of familiar mythological episodes. It ties these concerns to the funereal *La selva di cipressi,* which similarly blends verse about these historical personages with idylls featuring pastoral women – including several modelled on Costa herself – who decry their misfortunes in a rewriting of literary tradition, from Ovid to Tasso.

Chapter 4 expounds upon these dynastic themes by considering Costa's equestrian ballet libretto and her efforts to have it staged in both Florence and Paris. Costa identified such equestrian spectacles as being especially dear to her patrons, insofar as they displayed both technological innovation and military-political rhetoric. Tracing the progression of her *Festa reale* libretto from a sumptuous gift manuscript to a printed volume, this chapter examines the manner in which Costa collaborated with artists and engaged in contemporary debates on astronomy. At the same time, the chapter also showcases her willingness to satirize these same lofty court pursuits in her *Buffoni*.

Chapter 5 examines Costa's relationship to ecclesiastical patrons, the Barberini in Rome and, when the family went into exile following the death of Urban VIII, in Paris. Alongside elegiac and occasional poetry, the chapter especially considers Costa's sacred epic *Cecilia martire*, written for Cardinal Barberini. The poem's rhetorical deftness is highlighted by positioning it amid the many texts that circulated after the discovery of St. Cecilia's body in 1599 and by examining the adaptations Costa made to conventional narratives that served to foreground the protective relationship between the woman and her pope.

Chapter 6 centres on Costa's attention to female regents as patronesses in *La selva di Diana*. In this work Costa lauds three women who invited her to sing before them: Marie Christine in Turin; Queen Anne in Paris; and a Roman noblewoman, Lavinia Lopez Buratti. Dense with allusions to performance and applause, this volume celebrates the military and cultural authority of powerful women. This chapter investigates the performance histories of Costa's appearances before these women and her assiduous presentation of their individual cultural-political campaigns within her verse.

Chapter 7 concludes the book by turning from Costa's literary overtures to her benefactors to the criticisms of court and patronage culture found throughout her works. It first examines *Gl'amori della luna* as a portrayal of the danger and violence that lurk behind courtly competition and rivalries such as those she encountered in Venice – thanks to the nefarious character of Envy, a favourite topos in her oeuvre. It next traces Costa's self-portrait as a beleaguered *virtuosa* and exile across her autobiographical verse, and her criticisms of both courtiers and the inattentive princes for whom they perform.

Costa's is an extensive and largely unplumbed corpus, one that encompasses her wide musical, performative, and literary interests. Her career as a soprano took her from city to city, but above all it was her boldness and savvy as an author that secured her fame. While seeking to offer a comprehensive view of Costa's career and her relationship to her patrons as well as her poetic interlocutors and predecessors, this book places a remarkable woman back on the stage as a diva of the early modern court.

Chapter One

Editing History

A look at Costa's literary career needs to begin with her presumed earliest – and her historically thorniest – publication. As its title suggests, the *Istoria del viaggio d'Alemagna del serenissimo gran duca di Toscana Ferdinando Secondo* details Ferdinando's 1628 journey to the court of the Holy Roman Emperor just before he reached his majority and assumed political power from his two regents, Maria Maddalena and Christine of Lorraine, who had ruled on his behalf since Cosimo II's death in 1621. Costa's thick volume is a detailed diplomatic history of this six-month voyage. It meticulously records not only the grand duke's movements but also the multitude of honours he received along the way, concluding with his triumphant return to Florence, neatly timed to his eighteenth birthday. Of acute personal, political, and symbolic significance, the trip marked Ferdinando's debut on an international stage.

At least four years later, Costa similarly enjoyed a milestone of her own: her entry into the world of publishing. Likely the singer had already begun composing verse while back in her native Rome, but with her edition of the *Istoria* she initiated what would become a lifelong literary career. The *Istoria* was also the first of her many works – full-length published texts, individual poems, pamphlet poems, a manuscript – connected to the Medici family. Dedicated to the Spanish ambassador to Tuscany, the quarto volume runs to nearly 400 pages and includes a virtually day-by-day account and over a dozen diagrams and tables, as well as several participant lists. It bears what is surely a false Venetian imprint, with no listed publisher or date. Nevertheless, this is clearly a work intended to be taken seriously, its weighty subject matter mirrored by its precise organization and format.

In addition to being the first volume printed under Costa's name, the *Istoria* has raised the most questions about her literary activity. Some of these doubts about Costa's legitimacy arise from her own acknowledgment in the preface that, not having been an eyewitness to the events she recounts, she relied on the papers of Benedetto Guerrini, Ferdinando's secretary at the time of publication. This disclosure made it easier for some contemporaries and scholars to discount the authenticity of her works altogether. However, in recent years, scholars largely have accepted Costa's authorship of the text at face value.[1] In fact, the *Istoria* replicates contemporary diplomatic records almost verbatim. Drawing on archival evidence, this chapter argues that Costa was not the history's author but rather its editor. This new assessment of her role in its composition ought not diminish her literary stature. Indeed, reclassifying the project in this way aligns with what Costa herself tells the reader when she explicitly draws attention to her reliance on official documents.

The identification of Costa as the editor of this single publication within her fourteen-volume printed corpus elicits two important questions. First, why were these documents – which, as we shall see, detail an event of paramount importance to the Medici – entrusted to an as-of-yet unpublished female singer (and, at least previously, a courtesan) from Rome at all? Second, what can this publication tell us about Costa's movements and relationships and how it might have influenced her later poetic and theatrical works? Answers to the first question may prove elusive, barring the discovery of documentary evidence outlining channels that for now lie beyond the historical curtain, although Henk Th. Van Veen has argued that the Medici grand dukes looked to foreign panegyrists, rather than native Florentines, to delicately tip the balance between praising the principate and honouring the city's republican roots towards the former.[2] While the curious circumstances surrounding the volume's production may remain obscure, we can assess its early fruits: Costa's decades-long relationship to the Medici and the avenues by which she courted these and other patrons. We turn first to an evaluation of Ferdinando's journey, its political significance, and the *Istoria*'s relationship to ambassadorial records, before then examining the lessons on how to cultivate powerful benefactors – particularly through the medium of spectacle – that Costa gleaned from her experience working with these historical-diplomatic materials.

The Voyage and Its *Istoria*

Ferdinando's journey was of the utmost importance for Tuscany. While all of the family's travels of this scope were carefully monitored, with preparations painstakingly organized and belongings and participants thoroughly inventoried, this case was especially so. Ferdinando's expedition to the court of the Holy Roman Emperor (his uncle, also named Ferdinand II) marked the end of his minority. The two so-called *tutrici*, his mother and grandmother, had governed for the previous seven years.[3] An imposing Sustermans canvas commissioned to celebrate the beginning of Ferdinando's reign captures this dynamic. The work, *The Florentine Senate Swears Allegiance to Ferdinando II de' Medici* (1625), memorializes the ceremony, which was attended by the Florentine senate and the Council of Two Hundred in the great *salone* of Palazzo Vecchio. Before the gathered men sits the ten-year-old Ferdinando, sandwiched between the more visually imposing female regents.[4] Now Ferdinando was nearly an adult and prepared to take the reins of power. He set out in February, the anniversary of his father's death, and therefore of his own role as grand duke. His travels took him first to Rome and then to major cities on the way to Prague and back. Upon his return home on his birthday in July, he would formally assume the power that went with his title.

It has generally been assumed that the volume dates to the immediate aftermath of Ferdinando's trip. However, Costa's preface states that the account is "gathered from the writings of Benedetto Guerrini, currently His Highness's chamber secretary."[5] This acknowledgment is important for what it tells the reader about the history's creation, but it also provides clues to chronology. Guerrini's promotion to secretary occurred in 1632, four years after the trip, which is therefore the *terminus post quem* for publication.[6] While the imprint lists the publication city as Venice, it was almost certainly Florence (as would also be the case for Costa's next four works).[7]

The later dating is also confirmed by the other elements of the *Istoria*'s preface. Costa opens what she calls her "little history" – a text that, as noted, runs to nearly 400 pages – by underscoring the honour that the publication brings her, and by establishing the grandeur of her subject matter.[8] How could a simple figure such as she – with her "weak pen" and "meagre intellect" – even tackle such a topic?[9] The question allows her to launch into hyperbolic praise for the grand duke and the early successes of his governance. He is, she states, "a prince of noblest birth, endowed with great magnanimity, gifted with great worth, a true example of praiseworthy behaviour, a reflection of goodness, the seat of every virtue, and a most abundant fount of truth and sincere piety."[10] While the rest of Europe has been ravaged by warfare, his state has enjoyed greater tranquillity and prosperity than any other.[11] His family needs no introduction, united as it is through marriage to every other crown, no matter how modest or great. This final statement was likely intended to satisfy the need to at least cursorily recognize Ferdinando's regents, women whose efforts contributed to the soundness of the Florentine state Costa here champions but whom she is careful to avoid commending directly, focusing instead on the current male ruler. Costa then directs her tribute to Ferdinando's response specifically to the 1630 plague (and, depending on dating, its brief return in 1633). What prince has ever so embraced his subjects, as a father does his children, when disease struck his city with fear? He gave his own riches to assist his people, visited the downtrodden, and tearfully prayed to the Almighty on their behalf. Under his rule the skies calmed and the air cleared, the poor were succoured and the rich heartened (all epistemologically important details, putrid air and the wretched living conditions of the poor being associated with the spread of disease).[12] In short, he restored his city to a state of health. Amid this avalanche of praise, the adjective to which Costa repeatedly returns is *pietoso*: Ferdinando is merciful. With clement words and deeds, he – "almost a new David" – reanimated the souls of a people who had seemed lost.[13] Costa's references to Ferdinando's efforts to combat the plague, like Guerrini's secretarial post, date the *Istoria* to the 1630s rather than to 1628.

Costa's comparison between Ferdinando's diplomatic journey and his control of the pandemic – moments in which he cut his teeth internationally and domestically – sheds light on the delayed timing of the publication. As Giulia Calvi notes, since the plague struck just after Ferdinando assumed power, "the great epidemic was the first test of political responsibility which the young grand duke underwent."[14] Costa was not alone in highlighting his relative success. After the second wave of illness passed in 1633, Ferdinando commissioned a history of the plague (and his handling of it) from his librarian, Francesco Rondinelli. The proem to Rondinelli's *Relazione del contagio stato in Firenze l'anno 1630 e 1633* (Discourse on the Contagion in Florence, 1630–1633) applauds in the strongest of terms the "heroic virtue" of the grand duke for the wise and skilled leadership that allowed the city to suffer far fewer deaths and less social upheaval than its northern peers.[15] The *Relazione* also includes a *canzone* by the poet Francesco Rovai "praising the *pietà* of the most serene grand duke of Tuscany in the calamitous period of 1630," as well as a celestially themed panegyric by the astronomer Mario Guiducci lauding Ferdinando's "heroic beneficence" in saving Tuscany from war and disease.[16] Costa's preface echoes Guiducci's favourable portrayal of the literal and political-military state of health in which Ferdinando kept the city, indicating a textual influence or, just as likely, a common vocabulary with which the Medici's supporters touted the achievements of the young grand duke. Costa's introductory remarks tie Ferdinando's successful navigation of this recent moment of crisis to his earlier and first triumph, that of the diplomatic journey to Germany. This commentary on the origins of his authority might help explain why a history of that 1628 trip came to be published at least four years after the fact, in the wake of the plague.

Also potentially telling is the dedicatee. In a volume of this nature, one might expect a dedication to one of the Medici or to another prominent Florentine. Instead, the volume is dedicated to "Giovanni de Erasso," that is, Juan de Eraso, the Spanish ambassador to Florence. The reasons underlying this selection are not spelled out, but Costa would address a poem to Eraso in *Lo stipo* (1638), in a section reserved for important personages and cultural entities in Florence.[17] In the 1630s, before he was later dispatched to Genoa, Eraso helped arrange Giovan Carlo's appointment as generalissimo of the Spanish navy and communicated Spain's demands that Ferdinando fulfil Tuscany's long-standing obligation to provide support for their military needs (requests that the grand duke was keen to evade as much as possible).[18] One wonders whether the genesis of the project and Costa's involvement in it perhaps had something to do with the identity of this dedicatee who, depending on the timing, might have been softened by backchannel flattery and who, Costa's dedication suggests, will appreciate the gift more than anyone else due to his affectionate reverence for Ferdinando.[19]

Ferdinando's journey occasioned a number of other compositions. In several instances these were printed editions of the various works performed for him. These ranged from a slim collection of sonnets by Giulio Strozzi that were set to music by Claudio Monteverdi and sung in Venice, to an elaborate festival book commemorating a tournament held by the Accademia dei Torbidi in Bologna.[20] A manuscript account of the grand duke's movements in Rome circulated in multiple copies.[21] Also coming out of Rome was an anonymous encomiastic *canzone* celebrating Ferdinando, a work whose author describes himself as a singer who breaks out into song when he recognizes the heroic grand duke despite the latter's efforts to travel "incognito" (that is, without the standard fanfare typical of major state entries).[22]

The *Istoria* fits within a constellation of writing tied to Ferdinando's 1628 voyage, but its comprehensive approach stands out. The text offers a daily window onto the activities of Ferdinando and his brother Giovan Carlo, who accompanied him. Although Ferdinando wished to travel without the usual pomp, his arrival in Rome was thoroughly documented and debated (the Savoyard ambassador Ludovico d'Agliè, for example, reported extensively about Ferdinando's movements and motivations, concerned that he perhaps sought the title of king).[23] After several weeks in Rome, the brothers began their voyage north, stopping at important cities and courts along the Italian peninsula: Loreto, Bologna, Ferrara, Venice, and Verona, among others. Beyond the Alps they spent an enjoyable period at Innsbruck, hosted by their aunt, Claudia de' Medici. Following stays in cities such as Munich, they were received by their uncle in Prague. At the completion of their trip, they looped back south, returning to Innsbruck and paying visits to Piacenza, Parma, and Modena. These cities became stages for the rites of diplomacy, the choreography of royal etiquette, and theatrical display. The *Istoria* follows the Medici's reception, exhaustively recording the details of precedence, protocol, honours paid, and gifts exchanged. These are apparent in diagrams that visually represent the seating arrangements of the grand duke, his brother, and their hosts at dinners, spectacles, and the like. These images are designed to measure the treatment of Ferdinando through physical proximity to the emperor and other powerholders.

Given that the imperial court in Prague was Ferdinando's final destination, his arrival and stay there may seem rather anticlimactic to the reader, since the emperor's entertainments do not live up to those of other courts and the Italians themselves seem rather disappointed with Bohemia. Arguably, however, Prague is not the real terminus of either the journey or its printed history. Both reach their apex when Ferdinando returns to his own court. On 12 July, he reached the family villa of Pratolino where, to the regents' approval, all of Florence's noblemen and courtiers greeted him before he travelled on to the city, whose streets were filled with cheering crowds.[24] The *Istoria* describes the final stage of his journey as such:

> On Friday the 14th of July, the day he reached his eighteenth birthday and the period
> of his minority ended, he took control over the absolute governance of his state.

His deputies and advisers, together with the rest of the senators, gathered in the new apartments in Palazzo Pitti to pay their respects and signal their obedience to His Highness, and rejoice with him his assumption of absolute power. His deputy Niccolò dell'Antella recited the words on behalf of the public while His Highness sat on an elevated throne under a baldachin to receive these acts of obedience.[25]

Il seguente venerdì a quattordici di luglio, giorno del suo natale, e nel quale l'Altezza sua finì li diciotto anni della sua età, ed in conseguenza spirò il tempo della sua età pupillare, prese il possesso dell'assoluto governo de suoi stati; essendo però venuti li signori luogotenente [*sic*], e consiglieri con tutto il resto de senatori nel Palazzo de Pitti nella sala terrena dell'appartamento nuovo a rendere osseguio, ed obbedienza a Sua Altezza, ed a rallegrarsi con lei, che havesse preso il sudetto governo assoluto, e il signor Niccolò dell'Antella come luogotenente fece in nome publico le parole mentre l'Altezza sua stava a sedere in un rilevato solio sotto il baldacchino a ricevere questi atti di obbedienza.

The volume no longer needs visual diagrams to illustrate the proximal relationships of power. Ferdinando now sits alone, fully vested in his authority. While Costa's preface praised the sovereign's *pietade*, the history of his journey ends on the word *obbedienza*, obedience. This concluding image recalls – and supersedes – the 1625 Sustermans canvas. The new ceremony in 1628 not only granted Ferdinando sole occupancy of the throne and baldachin (excising Maria Maddalena and Christine, at least on paper) but also moved from the storied *salone* in Palazzo Vecchio to Ferdinando's own apartments in Palazzo Pitti, the politically themed redecoration of which would occupy the coming years.[26]

The political significance – practical as well as symbolic – of Ferdinando's trip is evidenced by the several thousand pages of pertinent letters and reports held at the Archivio di Stato of Florence from those six months.[27] They document every aspect of the trip, from the laborious preparations and negotiations that took place behind the scenes to the minutiae of diplomatic honours and recognitions paid to the brothers. While brokering an audience for the grand duke with a resistant Urban VIII, for example, the frazzled secretary Andrea Cioli lamented that he was "dog-tired."[28] While some of these materials are letters between the Medici, the vast majority are *relazioni* (reports) from members of the Tuscan diplomatic entourage. That news from Ferdinando's travels was followed with rapt attention back in Florence is also evident in eighteenth-century chronicler Francesco Settimanni's historical compilation from these months, where entries about the trip eclipse nearly all other Florentine news.[29]

As Costa herself foregrounded, the *Istoria* relies on such documents. Quoting her preface in his papers, Medici librarian Antonio Magliabechi later noted that Benedetto Guerrini "played a big part" in its production.[30] In point of fact, the *Istoria* replicates nearly verbatim the reports and letters sent back to Florence, with alterations primarily of an occasional and very minor nature. Specifically, the text duplicates the many reports sent by Geri Bocchineri, Ferdinando's private secretary.[31] Not only does the *Istoria* reproduce more or less entirely (with occasional emendations or additions) the body of these letters, but it also incorporates the diagrams contained in them. As but one example of the nearly complete overlap between Bocchineri's records and the *Istoria*, we might consider a description of a hunt and subsequent meal in Prague on 20 May. Bocchineri's letters and the history give an identical account:

> They went up to a loggia to watch [the] bear and bull hunt. The loggia had three arches: their Majesties occupied the middle one, the grand duke and the prince [Giovan Carlo] the one on the right, and the archduchesses that on the left. When the hunt ended, the empress, the grand duke, and the prince went on horseback to a nearby park to shoot at deer. They then returned to the lodge, where they supped, sitting at the table in the following manner [...].[32]

> Salirno sopra una loggia a vedere la detta caccia, che fu d'orsi et d'un toro, la quale loggia faceva tre archi; in quel di mezzo stavano loro Maestà, in quella man dritta il gran duca con signor principe, nell'altro a man manca le serenissime archiduchesse; finita la caccia l'imperatrice, il gran duca, ed il signor principe andorno a cavallo al barco quivi vicino a tirare a cervi; poi tornorno al casino, dove cenorno, sedendo a tavola in questa forma [...].

Following the passage in both works appears the same sketch of the seating arrangement around the table (figs. 1.1 and 1.2). Rather than an isolated occurrence, this kind of replication is characteristic of the *Istoria* and is found throughout.

Unsigned *relazioni* offer many of the very same descriptions and diagrams communicated in Bocchineri's missives, including this one, making it difficult to determine which came first and who, if anyone else, was involved in their production. Guerrini's signature does not appear on any document regarding the journey contained in the archival files.[33] Yet Costa is clear in stating that she relied on his papers, suggesting either that he had assembled the *relazioni* or that he had a copy of these documents, to which he had provided the singer full access.

Given this pattern of verbatim replication, it would be inaccurate to describe Costa as the history's author. She crafted a dedication and preface, supplied periodic transitions between the daily accounts, made assorted minor tweaks, and inserted the occasional extra detail. An attentive eye might also note that the title page states the volume has been dedicated to Eraso by her ("dalla Margherita Costa"), rather than being explicitly a work of her authorship ("della signora Margherita Costa"), as all her other publications would read. It is as of yet unclear whether the concluding entry, on Ferdinando's triumphant return to Florence and formal assumption of power, also derives from some other documentary source (the episode would not have been described in the advisers' missives sent back to Florence, of course, though it conceivably could be tucked

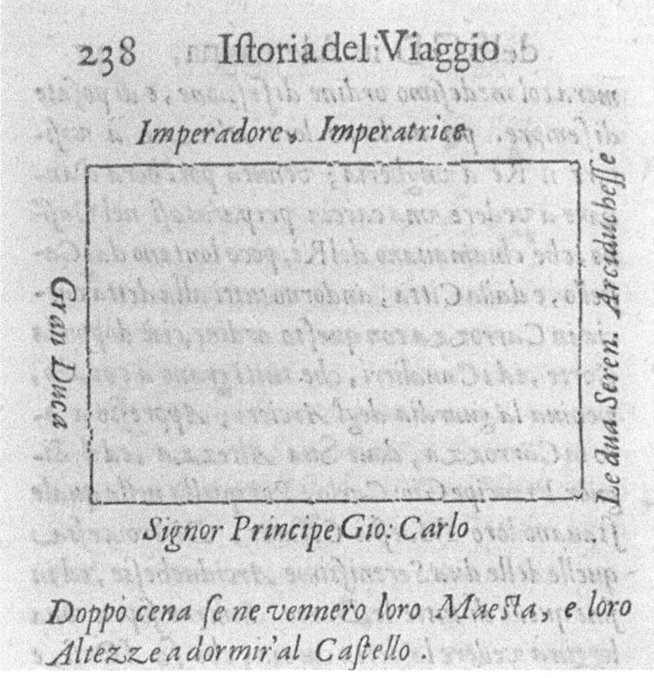

Figure 1.1. Margherita Costa, detail from *Istoria del viaggio d'Alemagna del serenissimo gran duca di Toscana Ferdinando Secondo* (after 1628), entry for 20 May, showing the seating arrangements of (clockwise) the emperor, empress, the archduchesses, Giovan Carlo, and Grand Duke Ferdinando II (p. 238). Courtesy of the Newberry Library.

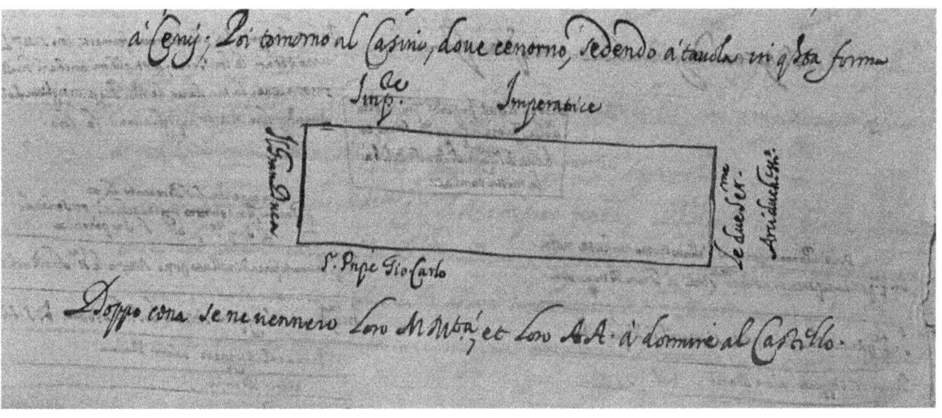

Figure 1.2. Geri Bocchineri, detail from a 28 May 1626 *relazione*, recording the events of 20 May, showing the seating arrangements of (clockwise) the emperor, empress, the archduchesses, Giovan Carlo, and Grand Duke Ferdinando II (ASF MdP 6270 f. 174r). Printed with the permission of the Ministero della Cultura / Archivio di Stato di Firenze.

away elsewhere in the archive) or if Costa may have played an expanded role in the composition of that particular episode. It is also plausible that Costa originally had a somewhat different project in mind: in her preface she states that she had initially planned to augment this history with a biography of the grand duke. Advised that writing a *vita* on a still-living subject was inauspicious, however, she consented to limit her scope to the journey itself, thereby changing her own role. Briefly stated, Costa is best described as the *Istoria*'s editor.[34]

A claim of this kind must be made carefully. As already discussed in this book's introduction, Costa would counter attacks on her authenticity as a writer repeatedly throughout her career, a situation to which her explicit acknowledgment of Guerrini's role surely contributed at least in part. The problem was one that Costa's peers frequently confronted in the seventeenth century – a period that Virginia Cox has termed "a golden age for denials of female authorship" – as attitudes towards women writers shifted away from the comparative openness of the previous century.[35] While the Cinquecento was generally welcoming, the authors and commentators of the intervening centuries often have proven less so, and scholars of gender in the early modern period have been compelled to dismantle attacks (both old and new) on women's legitimacy that seek to strip away their attributions. Part of this process has involved broadening our conceptualization of authorship and recognizing the manifold ways in which women participated in literary and intellectual life.[36] Precision in describing the *Istoria*'s composition is thus crucial, for Costa's biography as well as for scholarship in the field. Establishing the author/editor distinction for this first publication of hers helps set up a contrast with her later poetic and dramaturgical works, for which there is no persuasive reason to question the authenticity.[37]

Rather than take this categorization of Costa's (self-acknowledged) editorial role as a rationale for casting a shadow across her other works – or, inversely, for seeing it as yet another example of censorial or restrictive criticism of an early modern woman writer – it may be fruitful to consider the issue from another perspective. We might reframe the question not as "Why did Costa print this account under her name?" as if she sought to suit her own purposes (as her detractors imply) but rather "Why was it entrusted to her when every other part of Ferdinando's journey was so meticulously organized and evaluated?" The question of this being an illicit, "pirated" work is off the table. Costa's long-standing relationship to Ferdinando, who would become the godfather of her second daughter, and the continued Medici protection she enjoyed indicate that the *Istoria* was authorized, even if it circulated under a partially false imprint. Her involvement seems especially curious when we consider that the Guerrini were newcomers to Florence, after Benedetto's father, a notary, arrived from nearby Marradi and obtained Florentine citizenship in the early 1620s. The family's social position was on an upward climb, one bolstered especially by Benedetto's promotion at court from chamberlain to secretary, and one, we might imagine, that could have been even furthered by the publication of such a history under his own name, were decorum to allow it from someone in his position.[38]

In the absence of documentary evidence, it is difficult to answer with any certainty the question of why the history landed in Costa's hands. It is evident, however, that she would have been either selected or approved for the project. What is also clear is that the volume would launch what was to become one of the most prolific literary careers of early modern women, particularly in the Seicento, and textually cement the relationship between Costa and the Medici.

Literary Lessons from the *Istoria*

The reassessment of Costa's role in the *Istoria* from authorial to editorial, as well as the more precise dating of its production to 1632 or thereafter, help make better sense of her subsequent career. The chronological clarifications narrow what once seemed like an improbably long gap of ten years between Costa's first and second publications, the *Istoria* supposedly in 1628 and then *La chitarra* in 1638. This is especially the case given her remarkable and rapid burst of activity between 1638 and 1641, with eight full-length publications. Moreover, while versatility characterizes Costa's corpus, which boasts an impressive breadth of genres, it is nevertheless true that the *Istoria* stands apart from her other publications, which gravitate more towards poetry and theatre than to the particulars of diplomatic history. A precise and measured account, the text exhibits none of Costa's characteristically baroque flourishes. The exception is its adulatory preface, which is far more of a piece with the tone and style of her other works. The body of the *Istoria* is for her oeuvre an anomaly, and a role as editor improves – rather than detracts from – the logical coherence of her subsequent literary endeavours.

Although we cannot identify Costa as the author of the *Istoria*, the contents of that history were by no means extraneous to her career and literary style. To the contrary, her work on it was likely foundational for a writer who became particularly attentive to patrons, their tastes, and their messaging across the decades and cities in which she published. This heedfulness to political rhetoric and deference might well have been a lesson ingrained while bringing a history to print which follows minutely the performance of diplomatic protocols.[39] We might take as an opening example the continuity between the memorable final scene in the *Istoria*, in which Florence's elites and citizens perform "acts of obedience" to their grand duke, and that found in the first poem of the 1638 *Violino*, in which that same citizenry honours him at the feast of St. John the Baptist (patron saint of Florence): "Today, all bow at your feet, Sire, and to you render their due gift of obedience."[40] The line alludes to the annual practice of the Tuscan territories performing their subjugation to Florence.[41] Concern for patrons' image campaigns and cultural enterprises would not be limited to Costa's works for the Medici but also guide her publications for subsequent benefactors, as the chapters of the present book will demonstrate.

The final scene in the *Istoria* removes the two *tutrici* from their previously visible role, and they are similarly absent from Costa's preface panegyric on the early successes of Ferdinando's reign. Likewise, mention of them is missing from her later works, save oblique references to Medici marital unions with the French and Austrian crowns. This includes the 1640 *La selva di cipressi*, for instance, a volume of funeral verse in which several Medici men are honoured, including the two regents' husbands, Ferdinando I and Cosimo II, but from which Maria Maddalena and Christine themselves remain conspicuously absent, their recent deaths notwithstanding. The choice to repeatedly sidestep them was unusual for any writer at the Florentine court, let alone a woman, particularly given how active they proved as patrons.[42] Others took care to cultivate them. Predecessors such as Isabella Cervoni and Maddalena Salvetti, for example, composed encomiastic verse for Christine of Lorraine upon her marriage to Ferdinando I, and Cristoforo Bronzini dedicated his multi-volume dialogue *Della dignità e nobiltà delle donne* to the then-widowed Maria Maddalena.[43] While Costa would later focus on (other) female regents in her 1647 *Selva di Diana*, she omitted Christine and Maria Maddalena, maintaining throughout her Florentine works a singular focus on Ferdinando II's journey to power, without acknowledgment of the authority and influence of his *tutrici*.

While the minutiae of protocol are positioned front and centre in the *Istoria,* dry diplomacy is not the only material the text offers its readers. State- and stagecraft were complementary practices in early modernity, and Ferdinando's journey not only facilitated political-diplomatic relations across numerous borders, it also presented the Medici brothers with a wealth of artistic, architectural, and performative treasures to behold. The latter occupy an especially prominent role in Costa's *Istoria* and the records from which it derives. These celebrations are a veritable catalogue of courtly entertainments: innumerable comedies, concerts, *intermedi*, ballets, jousts, parades, regattas, orations, masquerade balls, and spiritual plays, in addition to religious rituals and official state audiences. As Paola Barocchi has suggested, the panorama of artistic, performative, and (I would add) recreational encounters that the journey afforded both Medici brothers allowed them to "concretely measure the value of the figurative [arts] in contemporary civil life and to develop [their own] projects for the future" – an education in the rhetorical power of performance and festival that built upon the interest in theatre that their mother Maria Maddalena had instilled in them.[44] The lesson for an up-and-coming Costa assembling the volume was therefore not only that of paying homage to powerful benefactors but also of courting them through spectacle. She would do the same through a burlesque comedy, a mythological epic and drama, and an equestrian ballet, as well as through her highly theatrical verse and letters.

We can detect traces of the *Istoria*'s influence in the first canto of the *Flora feconda*, for instance, a spectacle-rich epic in which the couple Zephyrus and Flora (figures for the grand duke and duchess) undertake a dynastic journey not dissimilar to that of Ferdinando. One of the *Istoria*'s lengthiest descriptions of a performance is of a sacred opera, Stefano Bernardi's *Maddalena peccatrice*, which received much acclaim when staged in Salzburg on 8 June 1628 at the Hellbrunn Palace's stone theatre, an outdoor stage built into a former quarry. One entered the theatre "through a hole like a cave's," the *Istoria* states, and there Magdalene first "appeared … in fully ornate dress, surrounded by cupids (*amoretti*) and revelling in her own beauty."[45] She later removes her finery and replaces the putti with angels. When Zephyrus similarly approaches Venus's cove in *Flora feconda*, he encounters a scene reminiscent of the pre-conversion, carnal woman of the Salzburg production. Zephyrus arrives "where the leafy cavern arches" and finds a festive scene: Joy, Song, Sound, Dance, Play, and Peace fill the space with harmony and movement as a chorus of a thousand *amoretti* flit above, all in celebration of the goddess's beauty.[46] The continuities between the two cave settings indicate that Costa likely recollected and adapted specific performative episodes from the *Istoria* when crafting this tale of Zephyrus's/Ferdinando's epic voyage and the myriad spectacles that dot it.

Also notable in the *Istoria* is the range of entertainments, from formal affairs to improvised or farcical amusements. Indeed, while Ferdinando often tired of the former – understandably the umpteenth masquerade or banquet might bore an eighteen-year-old – he reliably delighted in the latter. While passing through the snowy mountains of Umbria, for instance, the grand duke himself improvised a *palio* run by village peasants wearing large snowshoes, "a ridiculous thing."[47] On his return trip through Innsbruck, he was treated to a "most ridiculous fete" – a joust fought without swords by riders on bareback, with the combatants continually slipping and falling from their horses.[48] Costa likely would have witnessed first-hand Ferdinando and his brothers' taste for such divertissements, but the inclusion of these "lower" pleasures in the history might well have paved the way for the prologue of Costa's burlesque comedy *Li buffoni* in which Buffoonery insists that it is she, not the more dignified Ancient Comedy, that the Medici actually prefer. And perhaps one may see mirrored in that work's buffoon Tedeschino, who falls from a hobbyhorse that he humiliatingly rides for the entertainment of the princess, those tumbling Austrian horsemen whose antics had pleased the young grand duke.

In short, the descriptions of performances attended by Ferdinando and Giovan Carlo, and the act of curating them for her *Istoria*, likely informed Costa's political imagery and approach to drama, while the work's emphasis on diplomacy and protocols underscored for her the avenues by which powerful men could be approached and represented. Theatricality (including in its more ridiculous forms) and patronage courtship would be pillars of her subsequent literary career. While Costa's acknowledgment of her reliance on the pages furnished by Guerrini in assembling the volume made it easier for some, in both her own day and over time, to question the legitimacy of her subsequent publications – accusations she would swat away in several later poems – it instead offers an intriguing case of how the early editorial project established Costa's textual ties to the Medici and provided key models for how she might continue to develop that relationship through her own writing. The result would be a torrent of publications to follow shortly thereafter, and Medici protection in some form or another, into the 1650s. In other words, identifying Costa as the the editor rather than author of the *Istoria* is not only unambiguously accurate in this instance but also results in a shift in thinking that allows us to reframe her other literary activities. In the next chapter, we turn to how Costa captured the "ridiculous" amusements and appetites of the Florentine court in publications that fused the lessons about courtly rhetorical messaging and entertainments driven home by her work on the *Istoria*.

Chapter Two

Bizzarria, Burlesque, and Buffoonery

Buffoonery is the life and soul of the court.

Pietro Aretino[1]

In 1638 Costa began a publishing blitz that defined her Florentine period and crystallized her role as poet and playwright. Over just four years, she published eight full-length texts and a number of poems in pamphlet form, and penned an additional manuscript libretto. In the first two years alone, she published nearly 500 poems (150 of which accompanied fictitious love letters). While some of these clearly date to, or at least speak to, her Roman period, they were edited, finalized, and printed during her time at the Medici court. This output is impressive in its quantity as well as in its range of genre and register. Chapters 3 and 4 will examine her more pointedly dynastic works (the epic *Flora Feconda* and its dramatic rewrite, *La Flora feconda*, the elegiac *Selva di cipressi*, and her horse ballet libretto, *Festa reale*). In this chapter we begin with the publications that most set Costa apart as a unique and, in her words, "bizarre," writer. These works embrace an eroticism, irreverence, and burlesque flair rarely associated with early modern women's writing.

Costa's first verse collections, *La chitarra* and *Il violino* (1638), wed her musical and literary identities while staking bold new territory for women's writing. She followed these up the next year with a book of *Lettere amorose* and a volume of panegyric verse, *Lo stipo* (1639). These publications contain encomiastic and amorous poems, idylls, and letters replete with myriad lovers and beloveds in various states of yearning, disgust, heartbreak, jealousy, lament, and amusement. They also place elite historical figures alongside more dubious or nefarious characters. Costa populated her works with an array of Baroque subjects unafraid of unconventional passions and capricious behaviours.

These were by no means underground or surreptitious publications. They bore dedications to the Medici men: Grand Duke Ferdinando, his uncle Lorenzo, and his brother Giovan Carlo. Costa presents her unorthodox works as rough, unattractive, even monstrous, yet fully in keeping with their tastes. *Lo stipo* offers an illuminating example. Costa organized the volume according to the metaphor of a *stipo*, an elaborate and sumptuously decorated cabinet popular in sixteenth- and seventeenth-century Florence whose many compartments conceal precious objects.[2] This clever structure allowed Costa to showcase her poetic versatility in a single volume that progresses down a hierarchy of "drawers," from priceless jewels to worthless counterfeits, pivoting from encomiastic verse for the ruling family and members of the city's elite to more daring offerings, as seen, for example, in "The Syphilitic Astrologer." Palazzo Pitti had just recently acquired a particularly lavish ebony *stipo* from Claudia de' Medici when Ferdinando passed through her Innsbruck court during his 1628 voyage. Costa warns her dedicatee, Claudia's brother Lorenzo, that her own cabinet is coarse and poorly built, yet it too hides precious gems inside: that is, the Medici themselves honoured in verse form.

In short, Costa courted her Medici benefactors through unexpected literary routes. She intertwined her appeals to her patrons' self-promotional interests and their fascination with grotesque bodies and entertainments, on the one hand, with her *sui generis* perspective on love and gender on the other. The results were new, unusual *canzonieri*. In *La chitarra* she reappropriates the voice of the *bella donna* (beautiful woman) typically employed by male Marinist poets, in *Il violino* and *Lo stipo* she also ventriloquizes male perspectives, an approach which also informs her *Lettere* and its poems, where men and women engage in risqué epistolary and verse dialogue. These two threads – her cultivation of the Medici through unconventional texts and her unusual exploration of amorous themes – culminate in her most "burlesque composition" of all, the 1641 *Li buffoni*.[3] The first comedy published by a woman in Italy, the play recounts the marital woes of Princess Marmotta of Fessa, who suffers because her husband, Prince Meo of Morocco, prefers the company of dwarfs, hunchbacks, and prostitutes to their marital bed. In this work, which is a clear parody of Medici Florence, Costa professes "to invent nonsense, represent hooey, and imitate poppycock" in an absurd world of courtly shenanigans.[4] Costa dedicated the comedy not to a Medici but to one of their court buffoons, Bernardino "il Tedeschino" Ricci, who doubled as one of its protagonists.

Medici court culture of the Seicento has often been viewed negatively by historians as an entrenchment of absolutism and, especially after the death of Cosimo II, a moment of stagnation ushered in by Ferdinando's two "sanctimonious" regents.[5] Ferdinando and his brothers have thus tended to be overshadowed by previous (or, in the case of Cosimo III, subsequent) generations.[6] Yet they commissioned and collected art, supported academies, invested in the new sciences, and became important opera impresarios.[7] Costa's peculiar but prolific literary-theatrical activity in Florence, and the relationships she forged to members of the grand ducal family, help animate our picture of Ferdinando's court.

This chapter looks at the unique ways in which Costa constructed her literary persona, revealing a tension between depictions of her as, on the one hand, a Sapphic tenth Muse, and on the other, as a poet beholden to a wild, unfettered literary power capable of producing only ignoble or monstrous works. Centring on her own *bizzarria* – that is, capriciousness – Costa casts her burlesque touch and buffoonish pursuits as not only sanctioned by the Medici but actually representative of their tastes. After establishing Costa as a Marinist writer, the chapter looks at how she employs her literary persona as an unconstrained, burlesque author to innovatively reframe questions of gender, focusing especially on women's sexual appetites and agency (or lack thereof). Concluding the chapter is a look at two instances in which Costa subsequently re-evokes but also reframes her previous burlesque engagements, the *Sette giornate* conversion poem and her last, late-life pamphlet poem for Ferdinando II.

Front Matter: Imagining Costa's Literary Persona

Two images visually bookend Costa's literary career in Florence. Both are from the hand of renowned Florentine draftsman Stefano della Bella, a versatile artist known especially for his representations of Seicento theatre, spectacle, and other facets of courtly life.[8] The two works introduce Costa's first and last full-length texts written at the Medici court, *La chitarra* and *Li buffoni*. Together they provide a nuanced view of how Costa framed her literary endeavour.

The first is Costa's portrait (fig. 2.1).[9] The image invites a consideration of her complex musical and authorial identities. Della Bella has dramatically encircled the poet with symbols of performance: rich curtains suggestive of court spectacle, open part-books, and musical instruments. Spanish guitars are most conspicuous, but a horn and a pipe also peek out. A Latin couplet by Alfonso de Oviedo Spinosa (who also contributed two celebratory poems) names Costa the tenth Muse. Both the couplet and the inscription on the cartouche declare that she has been depicted without her rightful crown of laurel, symbol of poetic greatness. In a version of the portrait used the following year in her *Lettere amorose*, the couplet is removed and the inscription is replaced with the previously missing laurel, by then more clearly earned.[10] Laurel similarly graces a second portrait by an unknown artist first printed in *Lo stipo* (fig. 2.2).

The *Chitarra* portrait presents Costa in a dramatic and ennobling way that visually likens her to two of her important poetic influences. Costa's most reliable celebrant and local literary model, Alessandro Adimari, published his 1631 translation of Pindar's verse with similarly theatrical imagery. Musical instruments – a lyre, a violin, pipes – line a page draped with sumptuous curtains (fig. 2.3). A comparable arrangement, with the incorporation of laurel and palm leaves, is found in the frontispiece to early editions of Giambattista Marino's *La sampogna* (fig. 2.4). Among the decorative elements are assorted instruments – the titular

Figure 2.1. Stefano della Bella, portrait of Margherita Costa, in *La chitarra* (1638). Courtesy of the Biblioteca del Seminario Vescovile di Padova.

Figure 2.2. Portrait of Margherita Costa, in *Lo stipo*, *Flora feconda* and *La selva di cipressi*. Image courtesy of the Charles Deering McCormick Library of Special Collections and University Archives, Northwestern University Libraries.

panpipe, as well as a trumpet and drum – and an open book. A preparatory drawing for Della Bella's portrait reveals that the artist had experimented with an identically placed book atop the cartouche, an even more pointed echo between Costa's image and Marino's volume (fig. 2.5).[11] The book in Marino's image is clearly a volume of poetry. The book in Della Bella's preparatory drawing might be a musical part book, like the one the artist subsequently placed at the bottom of the page next to the titular guitar. The volume at the top of the portrait shown in figure 2.1 has been turned inward such that the reader sees only its spine as its pages flutter, purposefully obscuring its identification as either a musical or literary collection.

As Amy Brosius notes, Costa's author portraits feature a "sartorially modest" but still fashionable woman whose appearance situates her within a tradition of printed depictions of female performers, from actress Isabella Andreini in her

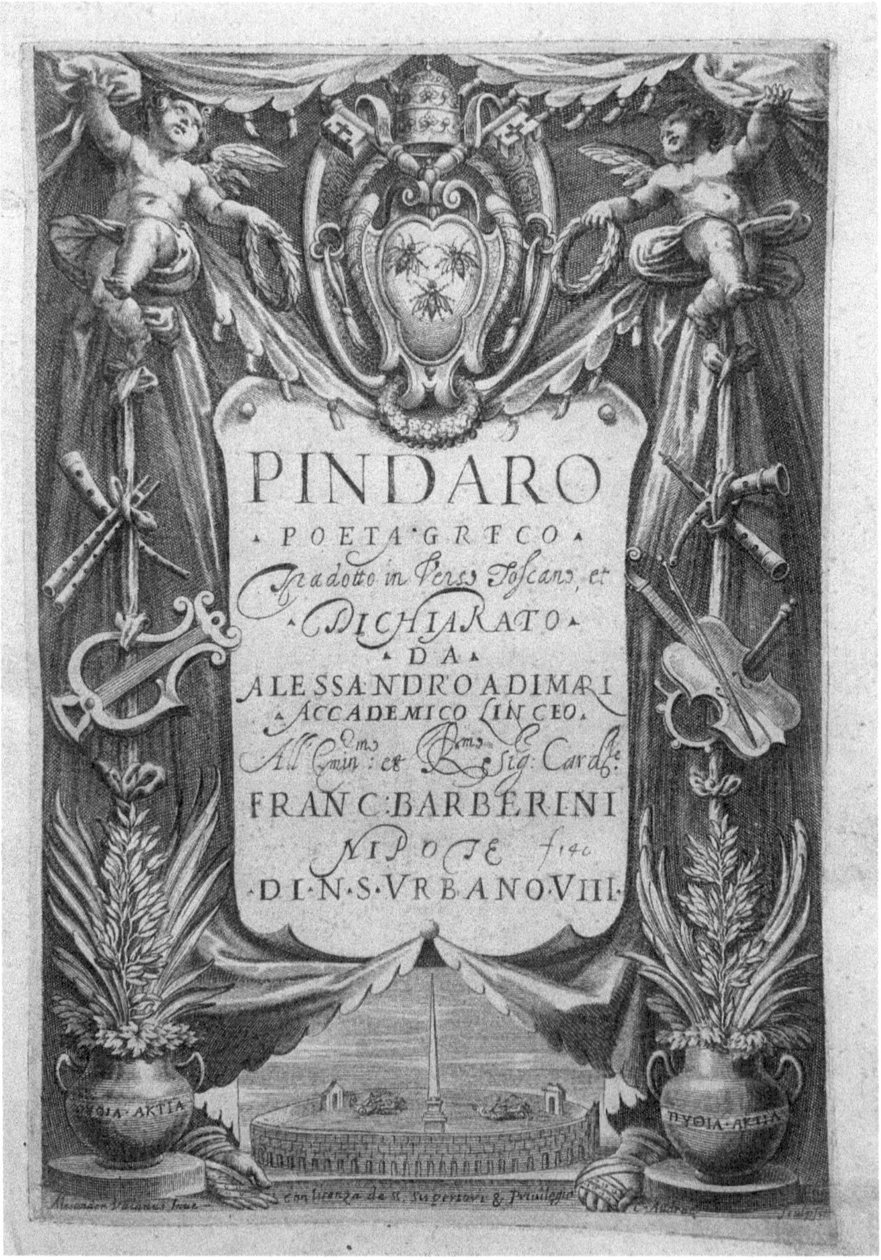

Figure 2.3. Carlo Audran, after Alessandro Vaiani, engraved title page to Alessandro Adimari, *Ode di Pindaro* (1631). Newberry Library, Chicago (Y 642.P4196).

Figure 2.4. Engraved title page to Giambattista Marino, *La sampogna* (1621). Newberry Library, Chicago (Case Y 712.M3617).

Figure 2.5. Stefano della Bella, preparatory sketch for portrait of Margherita Costa. Gallerie degli Uffizi, Gabinetto Disegni e Stampe degli Uffizi, n.623 O.

1601 *Rime* to singer Adriana Basile in the 1628 verse collection dedicated to her (fig. 2.6).[12] Details such as lace and starched collars, strings of pearls, pendant earrings, medallions, and flowers woven into the sitter's hair frame Costa within the conventions of female portraiture and communicate economic status and social acceptability.[13]

The pricier format, male-authored prefatory verse, and portraits might suggest that Costa, like so many early modern women, sought to give herself a veneer of sophistication, accomplishment, and acceptability. However, the very theatricality of Della Bella's image, and the visual connections it makes to a figure like Marino are the first indications that Costa might not engage in quite the same processes of self-legitimation as her peers and predecessors. Once the pages of her book are flipped open, Costa does not insist at all that she is decorous and "honest" but

Figure 2.6. Nicolas Perrey, portrait of Adriana Basile, in *Il teatro delle glorie della signora Adriana Basile* (1628). 252–401q, image 9920, used by permission of the Folger Shakespeare Library.

rather that she is *bizzarra* – capricious, unconventional, and subject to an indomitable muse.

This ambiguity is highlighted by Costa's title itself: *La chitarra*. Costa stresses in her dedication to Ferdinando that the guitar was widely considered a "lowly instrument."[14] Often used to accompany soloists, it appeared in both popular and courtly contexts, yet was rarely shown in the hands of the socially elite.[15] Playing the guitar had sexual connotations that underlie the alluring appearance of the female guitarists seen in Simon Vouet's and Ottavio Leoni's portraits discussed in the Introduction. Guitars also often appear in the hands of *commedia dell'arte* performers, who incorporated them into their performances. The actor Francesco Gabrielli, known for the *zanni* role of Scapino, holds both a guitar and a mask in his 1633 portrait by Carlo Biffi. Comedian Carlo Cantù ("Buffetto") strums a guitar in a 1646 portrait by Della Bella. While in Florence, under the patronage of Cosimo II, the French artist Jacques Callot (one of Della Bella's primary artistic models) executed a series of *commedia*-inspired *Varie figure gobbi*, caricatured dwarfs and hunchbacks who duel and play musical instruments; in figure 2.7 we see one such character pressing a guitar against his protruding belly.

Costa herself insisted in *Li buffoni* that among the court buffoon's tricks of the trade was "grabbing a guitar and hacking away at it."[16] While she acknowledges the guitar's lowly reputation in her *Chitarra* dedication, she reminds Ferdinando that the instrument is nevertheless "played by nearly everyone." She concludes by stating that surely the grand duke "will not refuse to occasionally include even [the guitar] within the harmony of the various instruments" found at his court.[17] Like the versatile instrument, Costa too hoped with this publication to solidify her place among the writers and performers in Medici circles. *La chitarra* sets the tone for Costa's Florentine literary career, alerting her readers to both her virtuosity and her peculiarity.

The second Della Bella image that illuminates Costa's approach to publishing and patrons is the frontispiece to her comedy *Li buffoni* (fig. 2.8). At first glance, the reader might be impressed by the Tuscan architecture and environs, with cypress trees peeking out on the horizon, and the layout of the stage scenery, which evoke the many examples memorialized in festival books for Florentine operas. This impression is quickly belied by the characters depicted in the streets of the city, which, as we shall explore in greater depth below, is a parody of Medici Florence set in the rambunctious kingdom of Morocco. As its title suggests, this "ridiculous comedy" (*comedia ridicola*) presents a cast of characters dominated by buffoons, dwarfs, hunchbacks, and madmen. In Della Bella's foreground a cluster of these figures dance and sing tauntingly around two birdcages in which are imprisoned a court buffoon and a prostitute. Costa's characters recall the kinds of "grotesque" figures that Callot depicted while at the Medici court, as seen in figure 2.7. Indeed, Della Bella's circle of burlesque dancers echoes Callot's etching *La ronde* (fig. 2.9), part of his provocative series *Capricci di varie figure* (1617) for Cosimo II's brother, Lorenzo de' Medici.[18]

Figure 2.7. Jacques Callot, *Masked Comedian Playing the Guitar*, from *Varie figure gobbi*, 1616–22. Courtesy of The Metropolitan Museum of Art (www.metmuseum.org), bequest of Edwin De T. Bechtel, 1957.

Like the various male performers – whose formation, movements, and buffoon-ish attire find close parallels in the *Buffoni*'s frontispiece – Callot's central female figure also has an equivalent in Della Bella's etching, the woman who appears on the lower right. While the position of her hands and feet and, to a lesser extent, her dress mirror Callot's, she is distinguished by the lute she grasps. Visually tied to the *Ronde* and reminiscent of the *commedia* actors represented with musical instruments in hand, she is identifiable with one of Costa's two prologue speakers: Buffoonery (*Buffoneria*). The play's prologue makes the case for Costa's brand of irreverent writing. It takes the form of a *contrasto* between Buffoonery and Ancient Comedy (*Comedia Antica*) over the genre of comedic performance.[19]

Della Bella's etching emphasizes the theoretical centrality of this exchange. Across from young Buffoonery stands Ancient Comedy, whose feeble, lonely steps

Figure 2.8. Stefano della Bella, frontispiece to Margherita Costa, *Li buffoni* (Florence, 1641). Courtesy of The Metropolitan Museum of Art (www.metmuseum.org), bequest of Phyllis Massar, 2011.

Figure 2.9. Jacques Callot, *La ronde*, from *Les caprices*, Series A, 1617. Courtesy of The Metropolitan Museum of Art (www.metmuseum.org), Harris Brisbane Dick Fund.

separate her from the sprightly dancers before her.[20] While Ancient Comedy opens the play, initially appearing to be the authorial voice, her influence is quickly undermined by the arrival of her rival, Buffoonery. Ancient Comedy levels at her the attacks circulated against her particular comedic genre by theatre's detractors (who disparaged performance writ large) and proponents (who wished to distinguish skilled artistry from tomfoolery) alike: she is drunken and debauched, feeds on the fruits of cheap appreciation, and is the laughingstock of the wise. But Costa's Buffoonery voices a counterattack, accusing Ancient Comedy of being outdated, hypocritical, pedantic, and envious of her superior success: "It pains you that I've taken away your part. / Let's at least split the difference, my friend, take heart, / let mine be the practice, and yours be the art."[21]

In this battle of the "classic" versus the "bizarre," Buffoonery bests her adversary by arguing that conventional forms of literature and theatre no longer appeal to the masters of the Florentine court, who prefer the "witty words / of sharper, merrier intellects" – that is, the burlesque, bizarre, and buffoonish.[22] "Here the only Greek that's any good," she insists in a doubled reference to comedic history and to wine, "is the one that's drunk in the morning."[23] After Buffoonery asserts that to her "the Heavens have entrusted … the care of the Medici," Ancient Comedy acquiesces: "To this great name, and not to your words, / I am forced to yield."[24] Bowing before the august hero of the Arno, whose kingdom she deems the glory of Italy, she takes her leave of the "Medicean Stars," the name given by Galileo Galilei to Jupiter's moons.[25]

This *contrasto* cleverly pre-establishes Medici approval for Costa's satirical endeavour. It closes with Buffoonery, now commanding a stage from which she banishes "unwelcome, solemn voices."[26] Florence is a city nourished by laughter – where mirth should be embraced, bitter words silenced, and audiences delighted by "buffoonish loves."[27] Even the ancient Romans preferred mimes to earnest intellectuals, she adds, and "if the buffoon is the salt of the meal, / without buffoonery the scene has no appeal [*sciocca è la scena*]."[28] The prologue's genre contest between Ancient Comedy and Buffoonery thus ends with the assertion that without buffoonery, theatre (and the Tuscan court) would be *sciocca* – that is, both foolish (an oxymoron) and, in Tuscan idiom, flavourless.

Like the humble guitar, both snubbed and desired, Costa fought for her place at court. Her own versatility – in genre, register, and content – made her adept at literary and theatrical play as a way of crafting her multifaceted authorial persona and approaching the literary trends of her day. This ability to be many things at once was evident during her extended residency in Florence, where she launched her publishing career and composed ten of her fifteen total works. By adopting a burlesque approach to a number of these texts – one that combined professions of humility with an attention to Florentine courtly pastimes – Costa participated in the city's long-standing comedic literary climate, stressing that in so doing she satisfied the express tastes of her Medici benefactors. Her pen could dare to be baroque and buffoonish because, quite simply, it pleased the court. Della Bella's etching implicitly confirms their approval: below the actors sits a well-dressed audience whose members attentively watch and comment on the spectacle before them.

Prizing Pleasure

As we saw in the last chapter, Costa learned an important lesson from the official reports she used to assemble her first publication, the *Istoria*. These *relazioni* sent back to Florence from each of the many cities Ferdinando visited on his trip to the Holy Roman Empire revealed that the grand duke's enthusiasm for lofty entertainments, from orations to *sacre rappresentazioni*, could prove limited when he found them tiresome. Burlesque spectacles, however, were sure to please him. On at least one occasion Ferdinando had himself organized an absurd *palio* of mountain peasants running clumsily while wearing snowshoes. As Buffoonery declares in the comedy's prologue, Ferdinando and his court gravitated towards pleasure and amusement. Costa's publications indulged in the kinds of courtly entertainments, amorous passions, and "monstrous" bodily displays that appealed to her patrons, as well as providing the forms of encomiastic verse they expected.

Jest and audacity long had a place in Florence's visual arts. As Helen Langdon has stated, "juxtaposition of the solemn and the grandiose with the burlesque and the eccentric runs through the city's culture."[29] We have already seen examples such as Callot's *Varie figure gobbi* and *Capricci*, executed under the auspices of the French artist's Medici patrons, and works by Della Bella, but the Florentine tradition also encompasses images ranging from the "visi mostruosi" (monstrous faces) invented by Leonardo da Vinci to the drawings of seventeenth-century artists like Antonio Francesco Lucini, who assembled an album of duelling *caramogi* (hunchbacked dwarfs), and Baccio del Bianco, known especially for the caricatures he executed under the Medici.[30] Baccio's images included *caramogi* shown, in the words of contemporary Filippo Baldinucci, "in acts and movements so new and so bizarre that no one had ever seen anything quite like it."[31] Baccio also enlivened court events by dashing off humorous portraits of attendees, cavaliers, and ladies, rendered "ridiculous beyond words"[32] Through drawings of this sort, members of the court could themselves temporarily join the world of the burlesque. Costa's verse invited them to do the same.

The early modern period exhibited a fascination for "human exotica." Dwarfs, hunchbacks, and fools were fashionable additions to rulers' collections of physical "marvels" and were charged with providing carnivalesque divertissements for the court in the form of wrestling, mock jousts, races, and so forth: "They were curiosities, monstrosities, deemed both repellent and attractive, and were often used to satirize the chivalric, the noble, and the beautiful at court."[33] As the dwarf in Ben Jonson's Italian-set *Volpone* declares, he and his companions held up a mirror to that courtly community because they were tasked with offering "pleasing imitation / Of greater men's actions, in a ridiculous fashion."[34] The display of "grotesque" bodies was common, but the Medici were particularly fond of such spectacles. As Barry Wind puts it, "the Florentine penchant for images of deformity is widely manifest."[35] The family historically employed a number of dwarfs, from Cosimo I's favourite, "il Morgante" (Braccio di Bartolo, famously captured in a nude portrait by Bronzino), to all of the little people in the employ of Ferdinando and his kin who appear as characters in Costa's *Buffoni* (Pedina, Gobbo, Catorchia, Scatapocchio). These figures were not merely on the Medici payroll, they often were members of the household and, like court buffoons, had access to the most intimate of the family's chambers.[36]

The Medici desired the display, antics, and performances of these "collectibles" as well as their commemoration in literary as well as visual formats. Costa not only fills her burlesque works for the Medici with portrayals of *caramogi* and physical others – as in her comedy *Li buffoni* for which Della Bella provide the spirited frontispiece depicting such players – but she also casts her very literary enterprise as yet another grotesquerie that should attract the Medici's curiosity. These works sent an unmistakable signal that she belonged within Medici court culture in a manner that targeted the varied interests of Ferdinando, his brothers, and his uncle.

The climate of the "grotesque" fostered by the Medici in divertissements and the arts dovetailed with Florence's burlesque literary tradition, of which the family was supportive.[37] With important fourteenth- and fifteenth-century roots, including works by figures like Lorenzo de' Medici, this embrace of the sexual, sardonic, and irreverent elements in carnivalesque poetry and song rose to greater prominence over the course of the sixteenth century. The genre championed by Francesco Berni and his followers, who ranged from scholars to artists, found its practical and etymological origins in the *burla*, the joke or jest.[38] Chafing at the perceived artificiality and stuffiness of predominant tastes, these writers argued that – in the words of Anton Francesco Grazzini (called "Il Lasca") in his 1548 anthology of *poesia giocosa* – "Petrarchisms, refinements, and Bembisms have nearly half-glutted and annoyed the world," necessitating a "burlesque, light, merry, loving, and, so to speak, companionate style" to counterbalance them.[39] A decade later, Grazzini would again highlight the Florentine appetite for comedic and unorthodox verse through a collection of irreverent, comedic *canti carnascialeschi* (carnival songs), from Lorenzo the Magnificent to his own day.[40]

The Florentine tradition of *poesia giocosa* intersected in the seventeenth century with the new Baroque aesthetic, as seen in the works of figures like Alessandro Adimari, Michelangelo Buonarroti the Younger, and Jacopo Soldani.[41] While Gabriello Chiabrera held special sway in the city, where he had enjoyed close patronage ties to Ferdinando I and Cosimo II for thirty years, Marino's legacy also had its place there, albeit it a more limited fashion.[42] Indeed, Florentine writers like Adimari bridged the style and arguments of the two.[43] Articulating an unconventional perspective, Marino – who, like Grazzini, displaced the Petrarchism that had been the hallmark of fashionable writing for previous generations – famously declared that the true rule of literature was knowing how and when to break the rules according to the tastes of the age.[44] The high theatricality, innovative irregularity, wit, and "marvellousness" of the Baroque period (for which Marino was the towering, though not uncontested, figure) cracked open the lyric repertoire, shifting away from the lofty poetics that had so tired Grazzini a few generations prior, to embrace new quotidian, imperfect, or unexpected subjects. Franco Croce has observed that "the emphatic representations of the most deformed aspects of reality can, by interweaving with wit, be presented as delightful demonstrations of capricious inventiveness."[45] This democratization of poetic subject was matched by a reimagined structure for the *canzoniere* (a process already initiated by Guarini and Tasso in the previous century), with an expansion of represented forms (madrigals, *canzonette*), new organizational frameworks by which poems were classified by theme or mode, and the assignment of descriptive titles to individual components.[46] The impact on Costa's poetics is evident in, for instance, the arrangement of her *Stipo* into "drawers" associated with different qualities of jewels, from gems to junk, or the poems of *La chitarra* describing, for instance, a woman speaking "jokingly to a cavalier who during Carnival showed up with a mask in the shape of a pyramid that made him look like Daphne."[47]

Among the changes that the Marinists introduced was a new vision of women and of bodily integrity. In part this involved a shift away from the comparatively open attitudes shown towards women in the previous century. As Cox observes, "the 'rule' of deference to women was particularly tempting as a transgression opportunity: the more so since an attitude of profeminist gallantry had been the default polite gender pose for so long" that its displacement offered "a greater scope for scurrility and the display of satirical wit."[48] On the one hand, this shift made joining the literary arena increasingly challenging for women writers, unless they were willing to engage with these same tropes – as Costa undoubtedly was. On the other, attitudes towards women as literary objects moved away from upholding the singularly chaste beauty embodied by the Petrarchan ideal. In her place arrived a multitude of women.[49] This included the poetic figure of the *bella donna*, a woman in and of the world who addresses her own personal relationships, amorous entanglements, and quotidian encounters in prosopopoeial verse. Costa would reclaim the *bella donna* as her lyric persona of choice throughout her hefty *Chitarra* collection.[50] This new repertoire also included "beauties" previously unthinkable: darker-skinned, ugly, or disfigured women.[51] Yet it was not only women who underwent this new poetic examination: the Marinists were also keen to explore other forms of physical alterity, with a particularly attentive eye on dwarfs, hunchbacks, and other disabled figures.

These transformations in the female poetic object, and the language with which she could be addressed, reflected the influence of the libertine circles to be found especially in the Venetian Accademia degli Incogniti.[52] Prizing boundary-shifting debate accomplished through virtuosic expression indebted to Marino's influence, writing prolifically, cultivating relationships to singers and the city's opera scene, and exhibiting an erotic sensibility (one that often privileged a male perspective while denigrating the female), the Incogniti have come to represent a certain cultural freedom in word and act that echoes in Costa's persona and publications.[53] Julie Robarts has argued that not only are there thematic continuities between Costa's works and the conversations and publications of the academy, but that she used her compositions to confront and contest their appropriation of the female voice.[54] As noted in the Introduction, a selection of her *Lettere* would be posthumously anthologized alongside those of Incogniti members, and the academy's infamous founder Giovan Francesco Loredan (who also wrote a biography of Marino) listed her among exceptional ancient and modern women. The Incogniti's influence was felt in Florence. Costa could find a model for the intersection of Florentine literary tradition and a libertine, Marinist aesthetic in figures like

Adimari, her primary poetic interlocutor and the only celebrant to put his congratulatory stamp on each of her first four collections. Besides being a member of the esteemed academies of the Lincei in Rome and the Fiorentini and Alterati in Florence, Adimari was an Incognito and therefore served as a conduit between Venetian and Florentine cultural circles.

Indeed, Costa could look to Adimari as an example of how to pivot from more scholarly endeavours, such as translation of Pindar, to the burlesque and bizarre. Adimari sponsored court events such as a 1615 "monster race" ("corso de' mostri") and composed a volume of love poems devoted to unattractive women, from the bald to the slovenly, which would influence her *Lettere*.[55] Through a series of manoeuvres – testing the boundaries between genres, finding her own Marinist voice, and identifying her comedy as a "burlesque composition" – Costa highlighted her participation in these "untraditional traditions," just as she did by creating her own literary cast of unconventional characters. Engaging in these literary forms meant stepping away from the style and subjects typically permitted to women, but it allowed her to insinuate herself into key literary currents of the moment and of her court.

Central to this effort was her appropriation of *bizzarria*, a term whose meaning was evolving in the early modern period, from the medieval definition of "irascible" to "capricious" and "spirited," and only much later to "out of the ordinary."[56] *Bizzarria* was the product of "sharp and lively conceits and inventions" and therefore epitomized the hyperbolic wit and ornamentation characteristic of seventeenth-century literary, artistic, and theatrical style. Marino himself wrote of the "novità e bizzarria dell'invenzione" (novel and bizarre invention) of his works.[57] The concept crept into titles of the mid-Seicento as a banner of originality and even fashionability. This is seen in works such as Callot's *Capricci*, composer Marco Marazzoli's opera *Il capriccio* (whose first lines declare the work a "strana bizzarria"), and Loredan's *Delle bizzarrie accademiche* (1638, 1646), as well as two volumes of *Bizzarrie poetiche* (1635, 1636), written by Giulio Strozzi and set to music by Nicolò Fontei for Barbara Strozzi. Observing that *bizzarria* was a "defining quality" of the Baroque, Robert Holzer finds that the term became a "virtual advertisement for fine musical poetry."[58]

While some contemporaries pushed back against the "bizarre age" as the trendy pursuit of short-lived astonishment as a remedy for boredom, the pejorative use of *bizarre* by art and cultural historians as a synonym for "Baroque" itself traces back to the eighteenth-century disparagement of this period as an era exemplifying "bad taste."[59] The architectural theorist Antoine-Chrysostome Quatremère de Quincy, for example, offered one of the most extensive analyses of the concept. Couching his discussion in ethical terms, he described bizarreness as a moral departure from the gravitas of the Renaissance masters, a movement prompted by artistic envy and competition – "an affected search for extraordinary forms, whose only merit consists in novelty itself." He nevertheless distinguished bizarreness from what he saw as the slightly more permissible category of capriciousness. While acknowledging that something of the capricious is implicitly contained in the bizarre, he suggested that "the first seems to be the child of imagination, the second the result of character." Caprice was for him the playful – but juvenile – bending of rules, but *bizzarria* was the anarchic obliteration of them: "caprice produces a childish game whose consequences can ... be dangerous, the bizarre engenders a system that is destructive of order and of the forms dictated by nature."[60]

Quatremère de Quincy's criticism was aimed at architects like Borromini, but one assumes he also objected to the likes of Marino and the *marinisti*. What Quatremère de Quincy and other later critics called slavery to fashion, the Marinists saw as stylistic liberation.[61] Costa herself echoes the Marinist perspective in the dedication to *Li buffoni*. "The usual is always the same," she states in the opening line, "but the unusual is far more novel."[62] While such an emphasis on novelty as an end in itself is precisely what disturbed critics of Baroque aesthetics, Costa argues that delight comes from an experience of the new rather than the tried and true. Novelty – in her case through a blending of the grotesque, burlesque, and Marinist – was a means by which she could please her Medici benefactors while honing her own unique literary persona.

The Bizarre Muse

Abandoning the decorum typically embraced by women writers, Costa embraced capriciousness as a central facet of her early authorial and public persona in Florence. The final autobiographical poem of *Lo stipo*, a volume dedicated to Lorenzo de' Medici (recipient of Callot's *Capricci*), provides a telling example. Despairing that Benedetto Guerrini, Ferdinando's secretary, urged her to burn some of her works, the poet vows to abandon her craft. This pledge is, of course, utterly contradicted by the publication of the volume itself. Cursing all aspects of love and literary enterprise, Costa first assails her own manner of writing:

> Damn the Muses,
> and damn he who invented poetry.
> Damn my indirect style,
> which now renews my misfortune.
> Damn my speaking with my own words,
> damn my bizarreness,
> and damn the moment and hour
> in which I discerned my fair dawn in Apollo.

> Maladette le muse, e maledetto
> Fia colui che trovò la poesia.
> Maledetto il mio stil poco diretto,

> Ch'oggi rinova la sventura mia;
> Maladetto il mio dir con il mio detto;
> Maladetta di me la bizarria
> E maladetto sia quel punto, ed hora,
> Ch' in Apollo scorgei mia vaga aurora. [63]

Like many of her day (especially but by no means exclusively women), Costa often feigns humility about her "rough and lowly style." Such protestations are well-suited to this context – a poet witnesses the destruction of her verse – but something more than conformity to a rhetorical norm is at play here. With a truly Baroque flourish, Costa lists no fewer than 105 different things to curse, including the fact that her style has been so well received.[64] In the lines cited, which inaugurate the poem's litany of maledictions, Costa introduces her literary efforts as *sui generis*. Employing a style and a language all her own, she presents herself as a poet of the bizarre.

It is not just this persona that Costa curses – and thus highlights – in the *Stipo* poem, but also her faith in the Muses who had led her down the thorny path of "bizarre" literary engagement. The evocation of these inspirational goddesses is a poetic commonplace, yet on this too Costa puts her own unique stamp. As noted above, the couplet on Costa's portrait (fig. 2.1) proclaims her a tenth Muse. The epithet "Tenth Muse" originated in acclamatory descriptions of Sappho, first in an epigram attributed to Plato and later revisited by figures such as Boccaccio and Poliziano during what has been termed the "Sapphic Renaissance."[65] Sappho, considered a paragon of classical verse, became "*the* recovered female voice of the mid-sixteenth century," her epithet frequently conferred on early modern female poets and patrons.[66] Through Spinosa's allusion to the Greek poet, Costa adopts in her first poetic publication an image of female literary excellence that places her within a class of predecessors that included Vittoria Colonna, Gaspara Stampa, and Isabella d'Este.

In many respects, the choice is apt. Known for her love poetry and (despite fifteenth- and sixteenth-century attempts to downplay the fact) indecorous sexuality, Sappho makes a natural model for Costa's *canzoniere amoroso*. As its title suggests, *La chitarra* shares Sappho's association with music – Sappho having, in the words of Boccaccio, "t[aken] up Phoebus' plectrum," a tool she is credited with having invented.[67] She is traditionally portrayed with a flower garland or laurel crown of the sort that Costa, Spinosa insists, deserves but does not yet wear. The *Chitarra*'s celebratory poems reinforce this association of Costa with her classical forebear. They call for the laurel or a "crown of daisies" (*margherite*) to adorn her brow, while praising her "golden plectrum," "serene and melodious plectrum," "richly virtuous plectrum," and "plectrum transformed into [Love's] bow and quiver." Alongside portrayals of Costa as a Siren, they compare her to that "legendary diva on the Greek lyre," declaring her a "new Sappho made a Muse."[68]

Yet if the frontispiece and prefatory verse set up Costa as a Sapphic tenth Muse, her first poem quickly reinterprets that image. Inaugurating both the publication itself and Costa's first real literary activity in Florence, this *capitolo scherzoso* acts as her literary manifesto of sorts. Here she attributes her audacity – and her peculiarity – to her equally bizarre muse. This is no Clio, Erato, Calliope, or other classical Muse of Parnassus, she emphasizes. Recalling Spinosa's couplet, Costa instead invents a new Tenth Muse: Simona of Elicona, the untamed groundskeeper of Helicon. In place of Sappho's elegant musical pick, she grips a "rusted plectrum" and *zampogna*, a bagpipe associated with lyric poetry (and with Marino's volume that her frontispiece recalls).[69] A scrawny, malnourished firebrand with a bearded and bestial face, she does not share in the refined beauty of the traditional Muses. Nor does she sail on wings like her sisters; her clipped ones keep her earthbound, her homeliness matched only by her fury. In short, she is the aberrant inverse of the traditional inspirational divas, a figure far more likely to be found among courtly "grotesques" than in the company of the gods. With this portrait, Costa draws the Baroque fascination with the tainted "dark lady" (over the unblemished Lauras of yesteryear) into the seemingly impenetrable world of poetic illumination. Literary enterprise is the product of a contentious relationship between the poet and this wild Muse:

> She shouts, she thrashes, she screeches, she curses,
> begs me to let her speak the truth,
> and puts assorted things in my head.
> Since I don't want to get off track,
> I tighten the reins and beat her down,
> and give no thought to her rampages.
> Yet if you look closely at my verses,
> you won't see dactyls and spondees,
> but scraps for cooking fritters.

> Grida, s'abbachia, stride, e maledice,
> e priega ch'io li lasci dire il vero,
> e varie cose in testa mi predice;
> Ed io, ch'uscir non vuoglio dal sentiero,
> tiro la briglia, e li do bastonate,
> e stimo la sua furia quanto un zero.
> Però se i versi miei ben riguardate,
> non vi parranno dattili, o spondei,
> Ma scartacci da cuocer le frittate.[70]

More harpy than Muse, this alter ego says and does what it wishes. If Costa's verses do not follow the typical patterns – if her style is defined by bizarreness – it is because her Muse instigates more than she inspires.

In the figure of this volatile Muse, who embodies the rhetoric of authorial un-worthiness, Costa fuses the two early definitions of *bizzarria*: capriciousness and irascibility. The poet, who avers to be more interested in passion than Parnassus, presents herself as the unwilling instrument of a most unlikely goddess, her literary engagement as "imposed by the Muses," and her pages as nothing but fritter paper.[71] Rhetorically, this manoeuvre absolves Costa from the responsibility of having written about amorous subjects in an often indecorous and potentially reproachable manner. Such declarations also conveniently freed her from the conventions that constrained register, content, and metre (in contrast with that original Tenth Muse, renowned for her metrical forms). Anything goes, she asserts, provided that her style is never forced (*stirachiato*) – an echo of Grazzini's suggestion a century earlier that burlesque writing depended on the avoidance of "rime … stiracchiate."[72]

Yet just as she would later do in *Li buffoni*, whose prologue insists that the Medici actually prefer the burlesque and bizarre to the tested and timeworn, in the opening poem Costa suggestively leaves open the possibility that her style might just please readers – so much so that some may doubt her authorship (as indeed proved to be the case). "I know that there will be more than six people, even dozens," she states, "who will say that if the verses are good, they can't be mine."[73] But, she continues, "I've kept my Muse sharp the whole year long, and I don't bother to versify by counting on my fingers" – that is, counting both her detractors and her metre.[74] As the two identities fuse, Costa's desires align with those of her inspirer: "With my Muse I'll do as I wish … and I'll sing without fear that Heaven, Hell, earth, or evil fates conspire against me."[75]

Costa concludes *La chitarra* with another *capitolo scherzoso* that returns to many of these same themes. Here Costa fully embraces her Muse, who brings her victory and – in a sexual pun – sings out each time she is strummed.[76] Readers must indulge Costa's bizarreness (*la mia bizzarria*), product as it is of this mad (*pazza*) and irrepressible divinity.[77] Costa spurns the grave matters of state and antiquity as worthy subjects for such a Muse. Women are not meant, she declares, to write "in serio modo," in a serious way. Veering from the lessons of female authorship passed down from the aristocratic, widowed Petrarchists Vittoria Colonna and Veronica Gambara, Costa claims erotic and burlesque topics to be within women's purview.[78] So if she selects amorous themes and presents them in an unconventional manner, she warns, "don't raise your eyebrows at me or disdain me" and "don't disturb my serene song for '*è bello ogni mal detto in una dama*,'" meaning that every poorly executed phrase – or every curse – is beautiful when it comes from a woman.[79]

Literary and Corporeal Grotesques

While the *Chitarra*'s concluding *capitolo scherzoso* might assert that every coarse word from a woman has its beauty, this is not how Costa generally framed her own writing. As noted, like most early modern authors, she apologized for her rough style. Within this convention, Costa stands out for being particularly insistent, and inventive, in portraying her literary humility, as seen in her bestial Muse.

In describing *Il violino* as a gift to Ferdinando on the feast day of John the Baptist, patron saint of Florence, for instance, Costa insists that it falls short of the glimmering, golden offerings she envisions being presented by others (symbols, as noted in chapter 1, of the Tuscan people's subjugation to the grand duke). Rich only in misfortunes, Costa has naught to offer but her paper ("pure" and "nude") and her ink ("dark," "dim, poorly applied, and black").[80] This gift, she repeats, is *nudo* and *ignudo* – poor, naked, unembellished. Her volume is itself a supplicant, its only redemption that the grand duke might show mercy to Costa as a foreigner (*straniera*).[81] In thanks, she promises, "my fragile pen will be / the nuncio of your joys."[82] Here, more explicitly than anywhere else, Costa sets the glorification of her benefactors as the core objective, the humble gift, of her literary enterprise.

More telling still is a sonnet that introduces *La chitarra* as another gift for Ferdinando. If the volume's title refers to a musical instrument with complicated associations, as seen above, and if its opening *capitolo* describes a Muse who is the capricious inverse of her classical sisters, this sonnet presents the project itself as another courtly grotesque of precisely the sort that pleased her Medici patrons. "I gift to you," she writes, "a dwarf, hunchback, cripple, [a work] poorly composed." Like the wild Muse, her volume rides through Parnassus with neither bridle nor spurs, and only Ferdinando's own whip (*sferza tua*) can tame it. She urges the grand duke to accept this small deposit (*caparra*) of her devotion, though it be "a dwarf, or a guitar."[83] Going far beyond the description of her literary efforts as *rozzi*, Costa declares that "I birthed (*partorito*) an obscene and unseemly monster." Composed entirely of imperfections, it is a "crippled and malformed dwarf."[84] Description of a volume nearly 600 pages long as "dwarfish" drips with irony. Strikingly, she applies the Baroque fascination with deformity and irregularity not merely to her literary characters but to her very act of writing. She dares present such a "monstrous *parto*" (offspring/work) before Ferdinando's feet because "in the courts of great princes such things are still allowed as humorous and facetious."[85] Ferdinando's was indeed a court par excellence for grotesque entertainments, as we have seen, and Costa situates her *Chitarra* as the literary equivalent of the "human exotica" with whom the family so famously loved to surround itself.

Costa elsewhere would frame her literary choices as having the court's implicit or explicit blessing. In *Lo stipo,* verse lauding the Medici family members, political and military figures of importance in Florence, and the city's literary academies – many of them dependent on the Medici – is coupled with satirical and risqué poems. These latter include poems voiced by reformed courtly figures (the gambler, the dandy, and the courtier himself) as well as verse depicting, for instance, a randy older woman in search of a young lover.[86] Costa's structure cleverly allows for such unusual juxtapositions, since the hierarchy of jewel "drawers" lets her place valuable gems and metals (garnet, diamonds, emeralds, rubies, gold, pearls, etc.) alongside a collection of everyday "fakes" (alabaster, bohemian diamonds, false gems). Henk Th. Van Veen has argued persuasively that the aggrandizement of the Medici necessitated the aggrandizement of Florence itself, due in no small part to its unique political transition from republic to grand duchy.[87] Through the contents of her *Stipo*, Costa fashioned a courtly *Wunderkammer* that placed in close proximity the glories of Medici family, elements of Florence itself, and civic or social oddities.

If the supplicatory aspect of her style is presented organizationally in *Lo stipo*, in the *Lettere amorose*'s dedicatory poem to Giovan Carlo it is introduced narratively. Costa declares that the Arno itself expressly encouraged her to write an erotically themed volume. One day upon overhearing her lament her adverse fortune while she stood along its shores, the anthropomorphized river presented her with a vision of Amore "writing love letters on the green laurel."[88] The Arno urged her to do the same. Costa thus fills her pages with amorous exploits at the request of Medici Florence itself. If Love is her inspiration, and the Arno her advocate, Giovan Carlo is her shield (*scudo*) and safe harbour – images that wed his appointment the year prior as the generalissimo of the Spanish navy with his patronage duties.[89] As she completes her letters, a temple arises in his honour; its walls are decorated with his heroic deeds, and upon its altar she reverently hangs her book. Just as he fends off the Ottomans, so too can he hold misfortune and criticism of her at bay.[90] The reader of the *Lettere* soon discovers that the Arno's, and therefore the Medici's, sanctioned love letters extend far beyond the sorts of paramours found in previous examples of the genre. While the first half of her volume presents stock images of lovers (at least at first glance), the second half presents unexpected couplings of lovers with physical or social "deformities," from dwarfs to the deaf.

Nowhere is Costa's attribution of her bizarre, burlesque style to Medici appetites more evident than in *Li buffoni*. Given this context, the work merits extended consideration. We have already seen above Buffoonery's victory in the prologue as the symbol of grand ducal tastes. Costa labels the three-act work a *commedia ridicolosa*, a subgenre of *commedia dell'arte* of Roman origin typically performed by nonprofessional actors, often at courtly palaces or in the homes of academicians, that incorporated linguistic pluralism and was often published in duodecimos designed for quick consumption.[91] Costa's version deviates from this model in its more elegant quarto format. It is a theatrical work about the court, for the court.

The play takes place in the kingdom of Morocco, likely a nod to Ferdinando's commercial and imaginative interests in the Mediterranean, seen in Medici portraitist Justus Sustermans's depiction of him wearing an elegant kaftan and turban.[92] Although ostensibly set in northern Africa, Costa's script parodies the Medici court itself. In addition to the Tuscan-inspired environs depicted in Della Bella's frontispiece (fig. 2.8), other symbols of grand ducal Florence abound. The Uffizi (begun under Cosimo I and completed under Francesco I) are mentioned repeatedly, characters imagine urinating drunkenly into the telescope (an instrument associated with Galileo that fascinated Ferdinando), and, as Teresa Megale has demonstrated, nearly all the characters – from dwarfs to cooks – are based on historical personages in the employ of the Medici.[93] In Costa's fictionalized principality, these assorted caricatured figures become the advisers and administrators of the state, creating a court of pleasure-seeking fools and eccentrics. Effective administration falls to the wayside.

Costa alerts the reader to the unusual make-up of the players through an additional character list included alongside the traditional *dramatis personae*. Most of the characters are mental, physical, and linguistic others: "loons, buffoons, and dwarfs," many of them foreigners (a Turk, German, Croatian, and Spaniard) who have been "Italianized" and who add a macaronic flair to melees, blundering hunting expeditions, verbal sparring, and acrobatics. These individuals range from the chief huntsman (Gobbo, "a freak of nature who looks like a dwarf but is hunchbacked") to the valet (Michelino, "a crazy Italianized German" who speaks, often nonsensically, in a thick singsong accent). Even Prince Meo himself is a "born fool."[94] Acts 1 and 2 both culminate in a whirlwind of fisticuffs and verbal mayhem featuring these eccentric characters.

Among the few characters who do not appear on this unflattering list is Tedeschino, one of the court's two buffoons and the historical figure to whom the comedy is dedicated. Tedeschino's counterpart, Baldassare, is an "Italianized Spaniard" who ultimately is revealed to be Princess Marmotta's long-lost brother. Meo's joy at the surprise discovery of this in-law (his tenure as a buffoon notwithstanding) prompts him to abandon his shenanigans and to return to his marital bed. Costa prefaces her list of misfits with a letter to the reader in which she warns that, alongside *Li buffoni*'s "variety of languages," one will encounter "an array of styles."[95] Her readers should not fault her for these irregularities, she states, because they are necessary to depict faithfully this motley crew. Publishing a work of buffoonery demands an unconventional approach.

Costa's presumed model for her tale is Flaminio Scala's *commedia dell'arte* scenario *La forsennata principessa*, in which the prince of Morocco abandons his betrothed (Alvira, princess of Portugal) for the princess of Fessa.[96] The lone tragedy among Scala's scenarios, it likely featured Andreini as the titular jilted and maddened Portuguese princess Alvira, a role that recalled her performance of the similarly abandoned heroine in *La pazzia di Isabella*. While Isabella always regains her wits after virtuosic displays of madness in the comedy, the tragic Alvira drowns herself. While Scala's *Forsennata principessa* in fact ends with the death of all its noble characters, abandoning the stage to buffoons, servants, and commoners – a survival of the *parti ridicole* of *commedia dell'arte* within the tragedy – Costa's script undoes the tragedic in favour of the ridiculous, populating her realm from the start almost exclusively with buffoonish figures. The eccentricities of the buffoon (seen as simultaneously virtuosic and transgressive) and the dwarf highlight the comparative cohesiveness and constancy of a court. By shifting the balance between regular and irregular inhabitants in her fictionalized principality, Costa displaces the regular, which, deprived of its dominion, is no longer able to define itself vis-à-vis these counterparts.

The *Buffoni* also took inspiration from the Medici court itself. In around 1640, just before the comedy's publication, Sustermans included among his portraits of the family one "Mad Meo," a local madman and possible buffoon financially supported by the grand duke. The historical counterpart of Prince Meo – Costa's "born fool" – Mad Meo's fine courtly attire clashes with his mottled, sluggish appearance.[97] Several years earlier, in 1637, Della Bella produced an etching for Vittoria della Rovere depicting one of the family's preferred buffoons: Costa's dedicatee and protagonist Bernardino Ricci, known as "il Tedeschino, the Cavalier of Pleasure." Like Susterman's portrait, the work parodies courtly pretence: in a pastiche of equestrian portraiture, a handsomely dressed Ricci straddles a fine horse, the city of Florence visible behind him and the caption below heralding him as "the most esteemed statesman of his age."[98] This ironic appellation points us to a mid-1630s dialogue published by Ricci entitled *Il Tedeschino, overo Difesa dell'arte del Cavalier del piacere* (Tedeschino, or the Defence of the Art of the Cavalier of Pleasure), explicitly echoed in *Li buffoni*.[99] This satirical work challenges the efforts of contemporary comedian-authors like Pier Mattia Cecchini and Nicolò Barbieri to shield their craft from accusations of indecorousness by distinguishing it from base buffoonery.[100] Ricci's interlocutor Tedeschino draws on classical and modern authorities, from Plato to Castiglione, to laud buffoonery as one of the liberal arts. Since it is uniquely able to bring delight, all other arts (grammar, rhetoric, poetry) work in its service. Those who condemn it have simply failed to achieve it. Bringing laughter to all, and especially to the prince for whom divertissement is not gratuitous but imperative, the true buffoon is an indispensable fixture of court.

While Costa's comedy similarly dispenses with the posturing of a Cecchini or Barbieri, it also toys with Ricci's defence of buffoonery. While her Tedeschino is not a physical or linguistic "other" in a principality otherwise dominated by misfits, he is universally despised. Although he is the sole character who aspires to actually help govern the rudderless principality (a nod to Della Bella's portrait), and while he flaunts his superior performance skills, other characters mock him as a "dimwit of diplomacy" and as an ass who repels rather than entertains audiences.[101] While one of the longest scenes in the comedy is dedicated to his comedic repertoire (improvised poetry and song, dance, guitar playing, acrobatics, and pantomimed horsemanship), these are antics that he performs both reluctantly and disastrously, to great comedic effect. Costa uses Tedeschino's ineffectiveness, both physical and social, as an apologia to remind her readers that this parody of Medici Florence should not be taken too seriously. As Pietro Aretino said, "buffoonery is the life and soul of the court."

While at moments the comedy dips into biting humour, the prologue's *contrasto* between Ancient Comedy and Buffoonery insisted that the Medici were in on the joke, so to speak, and that they approved of Costa's theatrical undertaking. This message is borne out by a 24 November 1640 letter in which Tiberio Squilletti, Costa's companion, thanks Leopoldo de' Medici for facilitating its publication.[102] Conceivably Costa may have intended originally to print the comedy under his name before choosing a buffoon as her dedicatee for the ribald play. If Pier Maria Cecchini had envisaged a comedy free of "dishonest material, obscene words, and gross acts," Costa instead offers one composed entirely of those elements.[103] Sexual puns, crude gestures, and scatological humour are the bedrock of her burlesque and grotesque players, who, with the Medici's endorsement, together satirize the Florentine court.

The Voice of a Female Marinist

Costa staged Medici support for her *bizzarria* by filling her poetry, letters, and comedy with the burlesque figures favoured at their court and by employing a *giocoso* style common in the Florentine literary and artistic tradition. Her works – which she presents as simultaneously grotesque and sanctioned – brim with the sorts of pleasurable entertainments dear to these benefactors, from hunts and tournaments to banquets and buffoonish carousing. However, if in these publications Costa embraces the literary themes and style of the Baroque in a manner few women could, with arguments she shapes to fit her Medici patrons' tastes and expectations, they are also vehicles by which she interjects her own unique take on one of the era's favourite literary-theatrical themes: aberrant, available, or unattractive women. In other words, within this frame Costa capably asserts her own voice as a rare female Marinist in a way that the Florentine literary climate allowed, pointedly answering, challenging, rewriting, and supplementing prevailing representations of women and gender by the era's male writers.[104] In the following section, we trace Costa's reconfigurations of gender, first in her use of the ventriloquized male voice before moving to her reappropriation of the female figures commonly found in Marinist and burlesque writing, and then considering finally the ways in which she complicates women's socio-political position.

Ventriloquized Male Voices

While the prevailing voice in *La chitarra*'s is female, as we shall see, these proportions are reversed in *Il violino*. Women do play an important part in enriching the volume's emotional repertoire: notable examples include a woman who, jealous over her lover's infidelities, takes her own life, and a mother whose baby daughter is suddenly transformed into a son – a "victory" that spares the child the tribulations of a woman's life.[105] The latter is particularly curious because this twice-born child ("parto due volte partorito al mondo") is first named Maria Vittoria – only a slight transformation of Vittoria Maria, Costa's second daughter, then just over a year old. However, much of the volume ventriloquizes male amatory anguish – not in the sorrowful yet measured tones of a Petrarchan lover but instead in emotional outbursts more characteristic of the "feminized" lament, which was becoming increasingly popular in vocal performance.[106] The connection to lament is especially palpable in the section of Chiabreran *canzonette*, whose musicality hints at a possible performance.[107]

The idylls are filled with cries and accusations. The first, for instance, presents the case of a distraught lover who has discovered a love letter written by his lady to another. Through his angry outburts and insults, Costa parrots the language of misogyny, lambasting, for instance, the "iniquitous, fraudulent, and wicked sex" – a sex, the man continues, that is "a horror to the world, / a perverse and impious sex, / the sex where deception roosts."[108] The lady's angelic visage disguises her infernal nature: she is a new Alecto (*novo Aletto*), wreaking havoc on earth.[109] These accusations carry over into the speakers' next idyll, a parodic rewrite of Marino's *Trastulli estivi* (itself an adaptation of Ovid's *Amores*), describing the rape of the *verginella* Lilla.[110] Here we see the pursuit of the identically named *giovanetta* who, like her predecessor, feigns resistance before she is caught.[111] But while Costa's narrator initially believes that he will follow in the footsteps of his Marinist forerunner – who had proven a "conquering warrior" – he instead finds himself faced with his just deserts: her physical desires now awakened by the attack, Lilla forsakes him for another's embrace. Distraught, he concludes the poem with a condemnation of *her* cruelty: "wicked monster / … / will your merciless and foul desire be sated / by my death?"[112] Costa has repositioned the poem from the section dedicated to "amori" in Marino's *Lira* to one of the idyll laments in *Il violino* (Costa's answer to *La sampogna*) simply through the erotic vendetta of the female victim.

Costa breaks up the *Violino*'s sequence of poetic laments with surprising and at times even joyous verse. Amid all the jealous lovers, for instance, we find one who instead delights in the attentions his lady receives from other men. For what merits could a woman possibly have, he asks, who is *not* surrounded by admirers?[113] And while others might seek out beautiful women, one lover professes to his homely paramour – a squinty, grey-haired, dark-skinned, black-toothed, wrinkled, bloodied, slovenly lady – that "every other beauty of your ugliness I adore."[114] Even the complaint-laden *canzonette* reveal exceptions to male misery, such as a lover who relishes in how his beloved toys with him.[115] These oscillations between plaint and pleasure are encapsulated by the volume's culminating dialogue between pastoral lovers, Filli and Tirsi, who speak the anguished language of Petrarchan antithesis – their final individual strophes playing with variations of *ardo* (I burn) and *ghiaccio* (I freeze) – but who ultimately depart from that model (as did their Marinist and Tassian predecessors) by declaring in unison, in the volume's final line, "let every heart burn with the ardour of love."[116]

The Bella Donna *Speaks for Herself*

While the *Violino* moves between female and male perspectives, ventriloquizing the latter in often remarkable ways, the *Chitarra* from earlier that year favours the female voice in the literary analysis of love. Of the more than 200 poems in the collection, only a few are dedicated to other topics and only a handful adopt a male viewpoint. Through this first verse collection, Costa stakes out space for a woman's perspective within a poetic terrain almost entirely occupied by male writers who were busily redefining womanhood within the evolving Baroque *canzoniere*.

Marino and his followers presented a newly accessible woman, the *bella donna*, a figure more adventurous, more imperfect, and often less conventionally attractive than the irreproachable, blond Beatrices and Lauras previously found in literary tradition. At times the male poetic persona spoke directly to this lady – as in Pier Francesco Paoli's "On a splinter in the *bella donna*'s finger," for instance – but often he ventriloquized her, as in "*Bella donna* to her lover held up in bed with gout."[117] In comparing the formerly idealized Renaissance beloved and the new Baroque woman, whose ugliness, deformity, or imperfection attracted Marinist writers, Patrizia Bettella has suggested that essentially "the woman's position in lyric poetry does not change" because "she continues to appear as the object at disposal of male poets' various agendas."[118]

Costa's *Chitarra* presents a key counter-example to Bettella's observation and to the emergence of the male-authored *bella donna*. Costa reappropriates this figure for her own agenda. Across hundreds of pages of verse, Costa gives new voice to the *bella donna* as a multifaceted woman who articulates her own passions, from desire to disgust. Costa highlights the flexibility of this persona in her final *capitolo scherzoso*, where she professes to have "feigned that a thousand chains / bound my heart, soul, and life in love / ... / I feigned to freeze in the cold, to burn in the fire / when I neither froze nor burned / but did so only to amuse myself a bit."[119] Robarts has astutely tied this passage depicting versification as theatrical acting (rather than any real moral threat) both to Andreini's similar admonition in the proemial sonnet of her *Rime* to "not believe / in their feigned ardors" since "as in theaters, in varied style, I have played now a woman, now a man" and to Ovid's late-life insistence in his *Tristia* that his erotic works were "unreal and fictitious."[120] The lines excuse the audacity of the effort and, at the same time, highlight the virtuosity of the accomplishment, here in adopting a literary persona to an impressive array of voices and attitudes.

Costa's fictitious *bella donna* intimately addresses notable historical personages, figures with whom Costa interacted in Rome and Florence, thereby uniquely fusing the new topos with more traditional encomiastic verse. Costa does not greet, thank, miss, desire, reject, or challenge her benefactors – the *bella donna* does. These range from Giovan Carlo on the occasion of his joust (in which he strikes others with his sword but slays her with his eyes) to Wladyslaw IV, the prince of

Poland (whose love for her she first declines in one poem and then resolves to reciprocate in another).[121] In the volume's other examples – far too numerous for a full accounting here – the *bella donna* alternatively invites, dismisses, pines for, suffers jealousy over, mocks, and accuses a host of lovers. This variety in content is matched by that of poetic form: octaves, sonnets, idylls, and *canzonette*. Notably, in several poems the *bella donna* advises her female peers, but that counsel ranges from the insistence that one should not just "love a single lover at a time" to a call for women to abandon love altogether and instead to have as their "sole thought and desire / spinning and darning."[122] If we can point to an underlying narrative thread in this *canzoniere*, it is the several dozen poems regarding the *bella donna*'s tumultuous relationship to her lover Tirsi in Rome and a move to a new paramour and life in Florence (with suggestive parallels to Costa's own movements and relationships to Capizucchi and Squilletti).[123]

Choosing a Lover from Medici Grotesques

Although *La chitarra* is almost single-mindedly devoted to developing the voice of the *bella donna*, one poetic sequence ties her brand of irreverently amorous verse directly to Florentine literary-performative court history in a manner that allows her to insert a new female voice, previously missing. This three-part *tenzone* caters to the city's enthusiasm for burlesque entertainments, reprising a past debate on erotic tastes and offering a definitive female perspective. The first of these is a reprint of an earlier poem originally published anonymously but attributed by Costa to librettist Andrea Salvadori (and included in his posthumous 1668 *Poesie*). The work, entitled *I caramogi palio e mascherata* (The Dwarf Race and Masquerade), circulated on the occasion of two comedic dwarf palios run along Via Maggio, in front of Palazzo Pitti on 26 and 28 August 1629, during Ferdinando's early reign. Addressed from *I caramogi, overo gl'amanti abbozzati* (The Dwarfs, or The Rough-Hewn Lovers) to "i signori begl'imbusti" (Ser Dandies), this is a ten-octave poem and accompanying letter in which the dwarfs declare themselves far better suited than their rivals to lovemaking.[124] "Whatever pleases is beautiful" ("bello è quel che piace"), they declare, and therefore their statures as "half men" make them preferable to the dandy – that "African monster" with a woman's head and a beast's body – since they adore all women, fair and ugly alike.[125] Proof of their superior desirability lies in the choice of the "wise queen of Lombardy": that is, Ariosto's episode in which the knight Iocondo glimpses the queen in the heated embrace of a dwarf, a "hunchbacked and disformed monster," despite having the handsomest of royal husbands.[126] The attentive reader recalls the encounter's concluding detail, which the dwarfs here conveniently omit: so repulsed is Iocondo that he re-evaluates his anger over his own wife's comparatively acceptable dalliances.

Salvadori's original pamphlet poem was answered by a second 1629 publication, the *Risposta de begl'imbusti a' caramogi*, an anonymously authored reply by the Dandies to the *Caramogi* (Angelo Solerti hazarded a possible attribution to Adimari, based on his involvement with similar events).[127] Rather than reprint the original response, as she had done with the first poem, Costa tables it and instead crafts her own *risposta* under the same title. Of her predecessor's text she maintains only its repetition of Salvadori's initial precept ("bello è quel che piace") and its summation of the dwarf as a "shortcoming of nature."[128] In many ways hers is the more successful of the two, as it challenges Salvadori's points one-by-one and replicates his rhyme scheme. Here the Dandies fancy themselves proud eagles, and their rivals mere monkeys.[129] While they concede that Ariosto's queen foolishly assented to a dwarf's lovemaking, they add that at least she did not chose the villain Mandricardo as her paramour – a humorous retort, given that only a few cantos prior (*Orlando furioso*, canto 24) he had mortally wounded Zerbino, the Scottish king whose name became synonymous with the dandy.

By rewriting the Dandies' *risposta*, Costa sets the stage for her addition of an entirely new component to the *tenzone*. Not only has she inserted herself into this earlier parodic debate – reproducing Salvadori's *proposta* and recrafting her own *risposta* – she steps in almost a decade after the original exchange in order to settle the question by supplying the missing perspective of the *donne* themselves (*Delle donne agli begli'imbusti e caramoggi* [*sic*]). The ladies revise the original precept put forth by Salvadori: delight determines beauty ("bello è quello che diletta"), and both the dwarf and the dandy bring them to laughter, not to loving.[130] Women desire neither "false, afflicted, and arched limbs" nor "curled locks."[131] Nor do they believe the tale of the Lombard queen, since "what we want are Tancredis and Mandricardis" – that is, svelte heroes.[132] The "rough-hewn lovers" should shelve their copies of Ariosto, the "Ser Dandies" can stash away their paintbrushes: women are looking for someone far more satisfyingly virile. In the *tenzone*, Costa picks up the thread of a Medici-connected performance, tying it off definitely through the addition of a poem in which women finally get to articulate their own desires.

New Letter Writers, from Divas to Dwarfs

In the *Lettere*'s dedicatory poem to Giovan Carlo, which vaunts his appointment as generalissimo of the Spanish navy, Costa insists that the concerns of love and war go hand in hand. She was likely aware of Giovan Carlo's interest in the epic amorous tradition, which a few years prior led him to commission decorative cycles for his villa depicting the stories of Ganymede, Psyche, Orlando, Erminia, and Armida.[133] After figuratively worshipping in his heroic temple, she reminds him of the bonds between Mars and Venus. Just as Spanish ships will permit Giovan Carlo, a new champion of arms, to more readily reach the sea-borne goddess, so too should he remember that the Greeks cast Venus herself as a warrior (*Vener guerriera*).[134] If Venus straddled those roles, so too does Costa. In the pages of her *Lettere*, where she explains the arts of love, she seems "here a Venus, there an Alcides [Hercules]."[135] Both lover and warrior herself, she gives voice to men and women who verbally spar more often than they caress.

With this dedicatory poem, Costa stakes her territory in the vibrant tradition of the letterbook, whose authors ranged from figures such as Pietro Aretino and Veronica Franco in the Cinquecento to Andreini and Marino in the Seicento.[136] Unlike Aretino, Franco, and Marino, whose epistolary collections addressed historical personages, Costa followed the model of Andreini and others in penning inventive amorous missives. This branch of the tradition begins with writers such as Girolamo Parabosco, whose *Lettere amorose* boasted more than a dozen editions over a century.[137] Volumes such as Parabosco's offer readers myriad takes on the subject of male passion and desire for a rarefied beloved. On occasion the lady responded. Andreini's posthumously published 1607 *Lettere* offered a departure from this model, both in form and in content. Her letters ruminate on human emotional experience through the use of both male and female personas, exchanges that Meredith Ray has persuasively described as hermaphroditic voices reflecting not merely Andreini's ability to ventriloquize and shape-shift as a renowned *commedia dell'arte* actress but also her strategic aim to showcase her rhetorical versatility as an author.[138]

Costa's volume takes Andreini's approach even further. As her dedication promises, her *Lettere* give voice to men and women. Gone, however, are the ruminations on loftier topics – Andreini's epistles on the nature of friendship, for instance, or on the death of a child. Instead, Costa's interlocutors are consumed entirely by their passions, and every missive receives a response. As Ray notes, in Costa "we can see the distillation of the hermaphroditic epistolary voice of Andreini's *Lettere* into an even sharper and ultimately comic guise, as the genteel *innamorata* origins of this device give way to the influence of the literary baroque."[139] The volume is evenly divided between seemingly stock images of lovers-beloveds and unexpected couplings. Echoing these comic themes are poems (primarily madrigals) for each of the 150 individual letters, *proposta* and *risposta* verse that complements the discursivity of two-, three-, four-, and even five-part exchanges through dialogically mirrored and adapted rhyme schemes.

The burlesque couples that make up the second half of Costa's *Lettere* have unsurprisingly drawn most of the sparse attention this volume has received to date, but it is worth underscoring how unconventional even the initial "stock" figures are.[140] In these lively explorations of longing, jealousy, distance, and disdain, women not only respond to but also initiate the discourses – a departure from early modern tradition, but one that evokes the classical *Heroides* model, particularly in the latter's use of so-called double letters (that is, letters that are paired with a response). Robarts has noted the echoes with Ovid's *Ars amatoria*, not only in Costa's repeated paratextual references to the "art of love" ("arte d'Amore") but also in the learned stratagems for writing letters in an eloquently simple and compelling fashion such that the recipient will want to respond.[141] Costa's letter writers dispute, insult, implore, and even persuade one another. These are not the demure and decorous ladies presented in other amorous letterbooks. Responding to a "Lover to his diva, yearning for even greater pleasure" (particularly from her lips), for instance, the lady retorts that the previous bestowal of her amorous favours "did not depend on your childish desire but rather on my absolute will" – an unusual statement of female erotic agency soon followed by her acquiescence to another rendezvous.[142] Another exchange calls the bluff of the supposedly pure courtly love tradition: when a cavalier writes to "his diva" that the sight of her transforms him, she responds haughtily that his lower station offends her, though she desires other paramours.[143] Such notable examples of female sexuality also appear in the second half of the volume, seen in the complaints of a male lover upset that his cloistered beloved is enamoured of another woman, and of a stingy scholar whose courtesan responds to his jealousy by wryly declaring that women like her relish variety: "In such misadventures the adventure is to prey upon ever more prey, to have a pair of lovers, to change one's garb … and, finally, to sell one's beauty at uncommon and varied prices!"[144]

The blandly conventional epithets of the women in the first half ("donna" and "diva") are belied by their unorthodox behaviour, which sets the stage for the transition to the volume's unconventional pairings. The burlesque characters of Costa's *Lettere* are inspired by works such as Adimari's *Tersicore*, published by Massi & Landi and dedicated to Giovan Carlo's uncle, Lorenzo, two years prior (1637).[145] This collection of "poetic *scherzi* and paradoxes on female beauty" presents fifty different ways in which ugly or unappealing women – fat, pocked, mad, fickle, blind, toothless, pregnant, even dead – are beautiful in the eyes of their lovers. Adimari's was a take on a popular Marinist theme; Giovanni Leone Sempronio, for example, famously included in his amorous verse lame, stuttering, and dwarfish beauties alongside female dancers, acrobats, servants, and the like.[146] As we saw above, Costa had already experimented with the male voice in verse on the subject of female homeliness in *Il violino*. These paradoxical protests of love and admiration for "women's imperfect perfections" highlighted Seicento poets' virtuosic wit.[147] As Bettella has observed, "attributes that in idealized female representations were considered undesirable are presented as attractive; this ploy allows the poets to display their deftness in exploring arduous and unthinkable combinations of beauty and deformity."[148]

Many of these "grotesque" attributes reappear in Costa's volume, but they are no longer the sole purview of women. Costa introduces the question of *men's* desirability into the Baroque repertoire on appearance and disfigurement. Alongside letters from a lover "to his ugly lady," "to his deceitful lady," and "to his lame lady," we find epistles addressed from a woman "to a stutterer," for example.[149] Just as frequent are exchanges between equally "Other" speakers: "a slovenly woman to her gasbag lover," for instance, "a mute lover to his deaf lady," and "a lover blind in one eye to his lady with a big hooked nose."[150]

Unsurprisingly, perhaps, the collection reprises the erotic *tenzone* from *La chitarra* seen above. Dandies and dwarfs populate Costa's epistolary cast. Here the lady still responds to the dandy with revulsion: in both of their sequences, the *zerbino* and the *bella donna* trade a volley of insults, and his effeminacy is the only consistently denounced quality in the *Lettere*. In the case of dwarfs, however, one receives only words of disdain from the *bella della*, while another succeeds in his amorous pursuit of her. The madrigals in the latter merry exchange adapt lines from the *Caramogi's* poem first written by Salvadori and later reproduced in the *Chitarra*, passages which measure Luigi Pulci's Morgante and the half-giant Margutte against each other, while in her epistle the lady congratulates herself on following the path of the "wise" queen of the Lombards in selecting a dwarf as a lover and chastises the man (that is, both Iocondo and Ariosto himself) who revealed her secret.[151]

Not all are happy matches in the *Lettere*: one lady, for instance, mockingly addresses her "excessively young lover" as "more a hummingbird than an owl" (two euphemisms for the male genitalia).[152] But in something of a nod to the *Tersicore's* "imperfect perfections," many delight in their shared passion and comically mirrored "defects." When a syphilitic lover declares to his lady with scabies that – in a humorously logical extension of the Petrarchan antithesis – just as every bitterness is sweet, so too is every blemish beautiful, she merrily replies that "we are happier than all others, having the good fortune to be so well coupled."[153] The *Lettere* become a bizarre catalogue of amorous matches and mismatches.

Getting around Fessa

The *Buffoni* is rife with the sexual humour and physical comedy we would expect from a ridiculous, burlesque work, particularly one centred around another sexual mismatch: that of Princess Marmotta, who wishes to have a physically satisfying marriage, and Prince Meo of Morocco, who wishes to avoid his wife's bed at all costs. An innovative take on the comedic topos of the *malmaritata* (unhappy wife), Marmotta suffers not from her husband's age or impotence but from his preference for dwarfs and prostitutes over her. The play's erotic context is broadcast to the audience from the start with Marmotta's own court of origin: the kingdom of Fessa. The name alludes to the historic Fez, but "fesseria" refers to nonsense, and as an adjective "fessa" describes a foolish woman while as a noun meaning "slit" it alludes crudely to the female genitalia.[154] Because her brother was abducted by corsairs as a child, Marmotta is the sole heir to Fessa. The plot focuses on the act – or absence – of copulation between Marmotta and her husband. Quarrelling over their conflicting sexual expectations, Meo abdicates his governing responsibilities to Marmotta in order to devote himself to shenanigans with court buffoons and rendezvous with prostitutes. "It falls on you to keep an eye / on matters pertaining to the kingdom," he declares, "and not to figure out if I'm on the hunt or want to love."[155] Marmotta finds no solace for her husband's amorous-authoritative demission in this opportunity to rule in his stead: "Oh lord, it's up to me to govern the state? / ... / ... Oh poor Marmotta!"[156] Aghast at the prospect of governing the kingdom of Morocco herself, she decides that her best course of action is to retreat back to the land of "Fessa."

Lest the erotic connotations of Marmotta's homeland escape readers, Costa supplies an extended comparison of the two courts in the comedy's longest scene, in which the princess describes her homeland to her maid Bertuccia. The defining element of Fessa is – fittingly – its women. Descriptions of the city are rife with barely veiled sexual innuendos. Its palaces "are superb, and since it's a rather humid spot, they have great big buttresses so they stay erect."[157] The streets are long and clean, free from any wayward puddles produced by earlier rains. The hospitable women will gladly welcome a stranger and "do what they can to make him feel at home."[158] Should the contrast between Fessa as a place of sexual fulfilment and Morocco as a site of unwelcome abstinence not yet be abundantly apparent, Marmotta clarifies: "In short, in my kingdom / the fertile plains are better tilled / than this country's hills."[159]

Fessa relies on male acquiescence to female desire. Erotic satiety is primarily a female prerogative, as "[the women] make love with everyone openly. / But, you know, modestly."[160] Men dare not impede the whims of their wives: "The men stay put and let them do as they wish. / If a woman dons a beautiful dress, / a beautiful necklace, a beautiful ring, / she need not account to her mate for a thing."[161] To capture the essence of her female compatriots, Marmotta describes them not as authoritative but rather as "bizarre" – that is, socially and erotically self-determined to the point of capriciousness.[162] In contrast, Morocco is characterized by the sorts of entertainments dear to men such as Ferdinando and his brothers: carousing and revelry, hunts, feasts, wines, and sport with dwarfs.

What might at first blush appear a proto-feminist position on gender roles shifts by the time we reach the final scenes. When Meo learns that he has male kin – Baldassare, the buffoon discovered to be Marmotta's long-lost brother and therefore the rightful heir to Fessa – he renounces his pastimes, resumes governance over his court, promises to satisfy his wife, and locks up the buffoon Tedeschino and his prostitute in bird cages. What was needed all along, Costa implies, was simply someone who knew his way around Fessa. Politically that kingdom will remain a patriarchy, passing from father to son, with no complaint from a Marmotta whose interest in its throne was merely consolatory. Now that her husband yields to her uxorial desires, she has no interest in returning, much less in ruling. If Costa gives voice to a female protagonist, that woman wishes merely to be the foremost among the prince's divertissements. Rather than the annihilation of order telegraphed by the theorist Quatremère de Quincy in his complaints about the dangers of the Baroque bizarre, the comedy concludes with the restoration of social structures as husband and wife are reunited. Bizarreness becomes not a new system unto itself but rather a reprieve from the ordinary.

A Bizarre Confession

Many of these themes – as well as passages taken directly from *La chitarra*'s opening and closing *capitoli* – would reappear in one of Costa's later works: *Le sette giornate, o vero Il viaggio di Loreto*.[163] The seven-canto manuscript poem is addressed to "Signore Conte" Camillo Pamphili, who had risen to a greater level of prominence upon the 1644 papal election of his uncle, Innocent X. By that time, Costa had returned to Rome from Florence. Together with Squilletti, she arrived in the Eternal City professing herself to be newly penitent.[164] As indicated by the manuscript's titular allusion to the biblical week and to Loreto, the pilgrimage site of a shrine believed to be the Virgin Mary's house, the work is a conversion narrative of sorts. The cantos are categorized first by types of entertainment before taking a spiritual turn. The narrative threads binding these sections together are loose, giving the poem a sketch-like feel, but Costa herself emerges as the protagonist – "I was, am, and will be Margherita" – in this journey through the Marche region.[165]

Courtly divertissement itself – in the form of feasts, hunts, comedies, stories, and card games – is the central subject of the first five cantos. Rather than retrospective professions of contrition, Costa offers a sampling of comedy, sexual suggestiveness, and unapologetic secularity. Even the opening pages demonstrate that this is no ordinary tale of newfound faith. The first canto describes an encounter with "a scoundrel in crimson" to whom her dedicatee had conspired to expose her.[166] When the cardinal tries to seduce her, she clobbers him with a wooden rod and, as he rolls under the bed, she beats him with a bed warmer.[167] The next four cantos follow suit. In the third, for example, Margherita sees two performers approach who, singing and playing the lute, lead members of a *commedia dell'arte* troupe. The company stops to stage "without discretion a comedy so ridiculous that everyone was cracking up laughing."[168] Positioning herself as a spectator, Costa outlines the antics of the Zanni, Pantalone, and other actors, essentially composing a scenario within her poem.[169] To Margherita's surprise, in the middle of one scene the Innamorato begins to recount her recent imbroglios at court. Taking this outing of her private affairs as a sign, she decides to join their wandering troupe: "I therefore resolved to travel the world with them, and in their company to laugh, and jest, and play the madman."[170] Curiously, Margherita presents herself not as one of the singers tasked with attracting spectators to the performance, or even as the Innamorata, but instead as one of its *parti ridicole* actors.

This choice reflects Costa's integration into the *Sette giornate* several passages drawn with only minimal alteration from the first and last *Chitarra* poems concerning her authorship seen above. The manuscript opens with nineteen lines taken from the final *capitolo*, a section that includes the passage about her Muse being "strummed."[171] Canto 3 similarly begins with twenty-three lines redeployed from the same poem, the verse on Costa's insuppressible Muse now used to excuse the preceding canto's criticism of the count's favourite pastime of hunting.[172] Similarly, the first seventy-two lines of "The Story" – nearly half the canto – replicate the full portrait of the bizarre Muse from *La chitarra*'s opening *capitolo scherzoso*.[173] The practical result is that it is Costa's unorthodox Muse, and not the Virgin of Loreto, who sanctions and guides most of her composition. The borrowed verses offer themes of poetic victory in place of piety, the mount of Helicon instead of Purgatory, *bizzarria* rather than grace. The narrative lack of control embodied by this frenetic figure who had given rhetorical cover to Costa's amorous poetry sits oddly in a work ostensibly about contrition and faith.

The tone shifts in the sixth canto ("Repentance"). Margherita falls asleep and has a spiritual vision of Penitence, who warns that if she does not repent, Atropos (one of the three Fates, often depicted with shears) will cut her life short. She cautions that "you will be left voiceless and immobile," a threat of death that also has a dire secondary meaning for an itinerant professional performer.[174] Awakening, Margherita goes to the Holy House of Loreto, where she experiences an infusion of celestial love. In the final canto, ("Conversion") she "renounce[s] the world," along with all the tools of both female beauty and courtiership.[175] In a manner that recalls Costa's burlesque catalogue of curses in the final *Stipo* poem, however, the canto offers not a blanket condemnation but rather an item-by-item list, resulting in a veritable inventory of devices. This enumeration includes the usual items condemned in religious literature, such as cosmetics and jewellery, but it also consists of somewhat more unexpected items, such as "Arabic scents on my breasts."[176] Costa imaginatively restores these various implements to their "rightful" owners: her foundation is rendered to bricklayers, for example, while myrrh (a common ingredient in facial creams and mouthwash) is left to those suffering from head lice. Turning to her own cultural activities, she abandons her "madness to musicians and poets, [her] plumed pen to pupils."[177] She concludes the work by vowing to withdraw from the spotlight:

> I want to live as a solitary handmaid,
> since this is key to a happy and carefree life,
> and in a narrow cloister, a narrow cell,
> far removed from opportunity,
> fall asleep to the sound of church bells.

> Io viver voglio solitaria ancella
> Che questo è il viver felice e giocondo
> Et in angusto claustro, angusta cella,

Col star lontano dall'occasione
Gir a dormire a suon di campanella.[178]

Despite this vow to enter the convent – and a pointed self-comparison to the Virgin Mary – Costa continued to sing, travel, and write, her broken vow of isolation and silence by now familiar tropes to her readers.

This new devotional posture does not prompt Costa to temper the tone or content of the preceding cantos. The first five cantos lack the retrospective self-condemnation one might expect in a conversion narrative. While it might be tempting to regard the text as evidence of Costa's newfound religious zeal, particularly when paired with her St. Cecilia poem from the same period, it seems just as likely that she appended the final two cantos to a text already in progress, one structurally and thematically consistent with her previous works. The unanticipated spiritual turn of Costa's poem parallels abrupt changes in Pamphili's trajectory as well; although he had been promised a choice secular post as commander of the papal military and governor of the Borgo after his uncle's election, Innocent reversed course and named him a cardinal. Like Costa in her pledges of silence and solitude, Pamphili would soon break his vows, shedding his cassock in order to marry. Costa may have amended a text originally about early modern entertainments – a subject well suited to a man whose mother (the formidable Olimpia Maidalchini) famously enjoyed such pursuits – to better fit her presumed addressee's new station.[179] Given the work's borrowings from *La chitarra*, conceivably Costa also may have composed the first five cantos while in Florence and added the final two upon her arrival in Rome. While the context of the composition is uncertain, what is apparent is that two "Margheritas" emerge from the *Sette giornate*: one a neophyte shunning the trappings of beauty and courtiership, the other an itinerant woman in and of the world and characterized by her *bizzarria*.

Conclusion

In 1655, at the end of her career, Costa would dedicate her final work to the Medici: a poem celebrating Ferdinando's forty-fifth birthday. Although she had come and gone over the intervening years, and though she had complained of her treatment in Florence in the dedication to her most recent publication (the 1654 Venetian libretto *Gl'amori della luna*, dedicated to the dukes of Brunswick-Lüneburg), this pamphlet poem strikes a very different tone. After six octaves of panegyric for the grand duke – a heavenly sun who sweeps away the storms of despair – in the second half Costa pivots to her own station. If shortly before she had lamented her misfortunes in Florence, now, a year later, she presents the years spent there as her best thanks to the patronage of this princely Apollo, by whose influence the laurel has graced her locks. Though she ought to have stayed on the Arno "where

I had been happy," she – like so many of her fictitious lovers and beloveds – had foolishly strayed away.[180]

Although she is lowly and unworthy of redemption ("son vile è vero, e non mert'io ristoro"), she writes, now that she nears death she throws herself at his mercy. In addition to asking the grand duke to again favour her work, she implores him to safeguard her "two unhappy *parti*," specifying that "if once I dedicated my *parti* to your highest image, / now I consecrate my *parti* at your feet."[181] The language cannot but recall her first dedication to the grand duke in the *Chitarra*, which she had described as a "monstruous *parto* [offspring/work]." Here Costa plays on the double meaning of *parto* – possibly referring to new compositions, but most likely referring to her two daughters (the youngest of whom was Ferdinando's goddaughter); two years later she would write to Mario Chigi soliciting his assistance for their support. Costa beseeches the grand duke to secure the future of her children, as he had once done for her burlesque compositions.[182]

In Costa's brand of burlesque writing, *bizzarria* is at least in part a means of bringing her readers and spectators to familiar destinations by way of unfamiliar routes – not unlike her own winding career path. Yet these respites from the ordinary and expected also engendered a powerful female voice that demanded autonomy and refused to stay silent, despite the author's feigned vows to the contrary. The rhetoric of an unfettered, ugly Muse and a "grotesque" corpus allowed Costa herself simultaneously to embed herself into Medici circles and to move freely – between the courts of Europe, between musical and literary engagement, between diverse genres and registers, and between tradition and innovation. By constructing a persona of bizarreness – that is, of capriciousness and novelty – she skirted the dictates of convention and the obstacles inhibiting women writers, thereby forging a path of literal and literary itinerancy.

Chapter Three

From the Golden Oak to the Weeping Cypress: Epic, Lament, and Dynastic Messaging

In 1640 Costa moved away from her "bizarre" compositions of the previous two years, works that fed the Medici's appetites for grotesque humour and embraced a Florentine tradition of burlesque literature. The change would prove somewhat temporary, since in 1641 she would publish her ridiculous comedy *Li buffoni*. During this particular year, however, she pivoted in subject and register from the amorous exchanges characteristic of her previous texts to more pointedly enco-miastic works in varied genres. Surely not coincidentally, these are Costa's first volumes issued with accurate imprints (in this case, with the Florentine publishers Massi & Landi) and the permission of the Florentine inquisitors. She also rede-ployed the laurelled author portrait that first appeared in *Lo stipo* (fig. 2.2).

These new compositions focus on the troubled dynastic aspirations of her pa-trons. The first, *Flora feconda*, was a short mythological epic dedicated to Ferdi-nando II and originally intended to celebrate Vittoria della Rovere's first pregnancy. It details the Mediterranean voyage undertaken by Zephyrus and Flora – figures representing the grand duke and duchess – to plead for progeny at Jove's oracle in Dodona, Greece. However, the Medici child died a mere two days after his birth in December 1639, rendering Costa's volume suddenly inappropriate.

Shortly thereafter, on 30 January, Costa sent a letter to Ferdinando, one later published in a collection of missives by "illustrious men."[1] At first news of Vit-toria's pregnancy, Costa states, she had set aside other ongoing projects in order to compose a suitable work for the occasion and thereby participate in Tuscany's collective joy. Framing the sad turn of events as yet another of Fortune's blows against her, the letter pleads for Ferdinando to allow publication of the poem to move forward. Even more notable than this entreaty is its justification. The child's death, Costa writes, deprived her of the opportunity to prove her devo-tion to the Medici through the diverse forms of poetic composition of which she was capable ("[la] diversità de' miei carmi"). With this new work Costa could demonstrate both her loyalty and her literary virtuosity within another, loftier genre.

Costa had hardly neglected to sing her patrons' praises before this. Her first publication minutely detailed Ferdinando's journey to the imperial court and lauds his response to the 1630 plague, *La chitarra* addressed an assortment of prominent men (and, less frequently, women) that Costa encountered in Rome and Florence, and four of the *Stipo's* seven "drawers" honoured members of the Medici family, Tuscan academies, and military, diplomatic, medical, and cultural figures in their orbit. But while her earlier poetic volumes are emblematic of Costa's curious fusion of the burlesque and the adulatory, *Flora feconda* sheds erotic and satirical elements in order to focus on a more unadulterated approach to patron appeal. The historied genre of epic offered Costa a more traditional means of glorifying her benefactors while expanding her literary repertoire.

Costa's plea was successful, and not only because she was permitted to publish after adapting the text to accommodate the new circumstances (accomplished by supplying an additional canto in which the infant is lifted to the heavens). The year 1640 would prove her most productive and versatile. In the fall she transformed the epic into a drama – possibly *in musica* – dedicated to Vittoria della Rovere under the nearly identical title of *La Flora feconda*. Between these two projects, she composed a volume of elegiac verse, *La selva di cipressi*, dedicated to Charles of Lorraine, Duke of Guise, a Medici kinsman who similarly suffered the premature deaths of two sons during his family's exile in Florence.

Costa's dynastic writing from this year was not limited to the sombre theme of losing one's children. In late January she presented Ferdinando the updated *Flora* poem together with an equestrian ballet libretto manuscript.[2] The work, the *Festa reale*, is the subject of chapter 4's analysis of this curious genre, one of the era's most spectacular means of celebrating a court and its sovereign. Composed contemporaneously and delivered together, the *Festa reale* and the *Flora feconda* poem were intended to exalt the Medici and herald the arrival of their next generation – that is, until Cosimino's premature death ruled out any fetes.

The year thus began with a set of dynastic projects designed to honour Costa's benefactors and prove her literary breadth. As her letter to Ferdinando articulates, the epic genre – with its focus on heroic enterprises, mythological encounters, and genealogical prophecies – could readily satisfy these entwined objectives. *Flora* is constructed around the promise of Medici imperial reach, an epic theme coursing across their adventures throughout the Mediterranean. The unanticipated introduction of mourning and hindered familial legacies did not, however, impede Costa's literary efforts. Rather, they became a unifying thread for her works of this year, one that opened varied avenues by which she could explore the issues of lineage and sovereignty so dear to her patrons. Flora, promised offspring by Jove himself, could rightly object to the cruelty of her loss. Needing to find a suitable means of negotiating that unfortunate twist of fate, Costa opted to represent the child's death as an apotheosis but included scenes of parental grief. These passages afforded her the chance to incorporate into her work a new side of complaint poetry, a mode in which she had already experimented throughout the original cantos in Homeric, Virgilian, and especially Ovidian episodes innovatively adapted to highlight the sort of versatility she assured Ferdinando was to be found in her poem.

As a singer and poet, Costa would have been familiar with the tradition of amorous laments found in classical and contemporary literature and transformed into famed stage performances in music. She likely sang them herself, conceivably even with her own lyrics. The lamenting abandoned woman par excellence was Ariadne. Her desperation upon being forsaken by Theseus, whom she had helped defeat her father's Minotaur, is heard in Catullus's *Poem 64* and subsequently in Ovid's *Heroides*. Ariosto modelled the lament of his heroine Olimpia (jilted by Bireno) upon these sources in the *Orlando furioso*, which in turn informed Giovanni Andrea dell'Anguillara's highly successful Cinquecento expanded translation of the *Metamorphoses*, where Ariadne's brief lament in the original is replaced with a full-throated complaint. Anguillara's account subsequently influenced the expression of grief in Ottavio Rinuccini's libretto for Monteverdi's renowned opera *Arianna* (1608), which established lament as a favoured medium to showcase singers' virtuosity in opera and chamber music.[3]

In *Flora*, Costa readapts these Catullan and Ovidian sources, offering her versions of female- and male-voiced complaint poetry. To this she now could add parental lament, especially an outpouring of maternal anguish, which adopted many of the non-verbal (beaten chests, pulled hair) and verbal expressions (cries of pain, professions of imminent death) of its amorous counterpart. Through the figures of Zephyrus and Flora, Costa memorialized the grief of the grand duke and duchess. As we shall see, however, Costa would soon begin to temper expressions of paternal sorrow.

Parental lament would become the point of departure for her other publication of that year, the collection of "funeral" ("funebri") poems. The "golden oaks" of Jove's Dodonian oracle become a "cypress forest," a conventional symbol of mourning. The volume's first poem dramatizes Charles of Lorraine and his wife Catherine's heartbreak at the death of their two sons. This example of parental lament, which has clear connections to the comparable *Flora* scenes, introduces a series of political laments foregrounding members of the Medici and Della Rovere families. Lorenzo Bianconi has identified a "mid-century vogue" for this literary-musical genre depicting political and military events (rather than classical characters), especially coming out of Rome.[4] Costa crafts her verse upon these musical models, while also drawing upon literary examples from Marino and Adimari. She includes, alongside this verse, examples of pastoral and autobiographical lament. If in her January letter to Ferdinando Costa presented herself as a victim of adverse Fate, in this volume's final poem she takes her complaints straight to Apollo himself.

In short, the voyage of Costa's epic took an unexpected turn, one to which she adapted in the poem itself and in her next two publications. Across all three works – the poem, the drama, and the elegy collection – she fulfilled her initial objective: to pay homage to her patrons while illustrating the versatility of her pen. This chapter traces that path, from the ultimately unsuccessful procreative journey of her Medici-inspired heroes to her own expedition to Parnassus. More than any of her previous publications, with the exception of the *Istoria*, Costa's texts from 1640 place her patrons, their dynastic concerns, and their memorialization at the very core of her literary efforts.

Epic Experiments, Prophetic Promises

Following Costa's successful appeal to Ferdinando, her *Flora* poem was published with a dedication and "Letter to the Reader" that reiterate her desire to symbolically join in the ongoing expressions of collective joy over the grand duchess's pregnancy and "celebrate the heights of Tuscan glory."[5] Marcello Fantoni has argued that under the grand duchy, encomiastic literature and political-historical texts were, rather than a collection of empty cliches, a litmus test of the fusion of governance and court culture. Costa was keen to show she could bridge the two though the exaltation of the birth of a new heir.[6] There was precedent for female writers composing verse on the arrival of a Medici child. Leonora Bernardi of Lucca used the prologue to her pastoral tragicomedy of 1590 to herald the birth of Cosimo II as a dawn of a great new age in Tuscany, while the earliest known work of Isabella Cervoni is a canzone composed on the same occasion dedicated to Christine of Lorraine, whom the Florentine writer likens to "glorious Flora" ("gloriosa Flora"), the mother of heroes.[7] An anonymous manuscript poem celebrates the birth of a firstborn Medici, similarly envisioned as the son of Flora and Zephyrus, while a canzone a few pages prior in the collection laments the death of Cosimino.[8] Accompanying Costa's own effort to further insert herself into the social-cultural fabric of Florence are assurances (not included in the initial letter) that her patrons will soon succeed in their procreative mission. To the original nine cantos – which correspond to the nine months of Vittoria's pregnancy – is appended a tenth in which Jove reclaims the infant for the heavens but promises future progeny to the couple in his stead.

Flora feconda blends Ovidian episodes and structure with elements of heroic epic, with explicit parallels made to the *Odyssey*, *Aeneid*, and *Argonautica*. The subject and framework are adapted from Ovid's *Fasti*, whose six books are similarly divided into calendar months: book 5 (May) recounts Flora's abduction by Zephyrus, for which she is compensated by becoming his bride and the goddess of flowers.[9] Etymologically and symbolically, "Flora" was an apt and recurrent figure for Florentine political efflorescence under Medici rule. She appeared in an array of celebratory contexts, such as the wedding festivities of the first Medici duke, Cosimo I, and Eleanora of Toledo in 1539, and in tapestries glorifying their union; the commemoration of Cosimo II and Maria Maddalena's 1608 wedding in a poetic *Dialogo* between the Arno and Flora, the "beautiful and stately queen of the Tuscan empire";[10] a poem heralding the birth of Ferdinando II himself (*La celeste Flora*, 1610); an epithalamium (a wedding poem, often sung) honouring the 1637 union of Ferdinando and Vittoria della Rovere, *Il gioco delle palle*; and assorted other works related to the continuation of the family line.[11] She also appeared in Medici-sponsored events, such as a 1613 *barriera* replete with political motifs filtered through mythological figures.[12] Most immediately relevant is the October 1628 *La Flora*, an opera with libretto by Andrea Salvadori and music by Marco da Gagliano and Jacopo Peri, performed during the nuptial festivities for Ferdinando's sister Margherita and Odoardo Farnese, duke of Parma. This was the first major political-cultural event of the grand duke's majority, one at which Costa conceivably may have performed, depending on the timing of her arrival in Florence.[13]

With her *Flora feconda* Costa thus crafted a procreation-themed short epic with explicit imperial rhetoric around one of the Medici's preferred self-referential images. Costa regularly employed the "Flora" topos with her patrons. Her poem on the grand ducal wedding anticipates *Flora feconda* by equating Vittoria della Rovere with the goddess, for example, while the poem "To the Most Serene City of Florence" personifies the court as a Flora who flourishes beneath the oak trees ("roveri," an allusion to the grand duchess's surname) and brings forth through childbirth not flowers but crowns.[14] Particularly suggestive is a *Violino* poem celebrating Margherita de' Medici. Not only does the text cast Margherita as a Flora (suggested by the meaning of her name as "daisy," as was also the case in the 1628 opera), and her husband a Zephyrus, but it specifically celebrates her fertility: she is an admired "genetrix" responsible for "new Alessandros" budding up on the fields of war, an allusion to the historical conqueror and, likely, the birth of her second son, Alessandro Farnese, in 1635.[15]

In some sense, *Flora feconda* picks up where the 1628 opera left off. As was common in operatic works of the day, Salvadori's libretto adapts the Ovidian tale, situating its expanded narrative conflict around the involvement of Venus (Zephyrus's mother, who supports his pursuit of Flora) and Cupid (who opposes their union).[16] The work concludes with the newly devoted Flora predicting that the city bearing her name will be known as the "flower of Italy."[17] Reflecting the grand duke and duchess's recent nuptials, Costa's poem begins with the couple already wed. While the 1628 opera was about marriage, the 1640 poem (and later drama) concern procreation. Despite being the very picture of fecundity, Flora laments in canto 1 that she remains without offspring. Seeing her dismay, Zephyrus promises to entreat his mother Venus to intervene on their behalf, an episode in the poem that echoes the goddess's prominence in Salvadori's libretto.

This vow initiates the couple's epic voyage. Costa had recent precedents for the composition of a mythological epic, both male-authored (most notably Marino's *Adone*) and female-authored (Lucrezia Marinella's ten-canto *Amore innamorato e impazzato* [1618]). So, too, could she point to a recent string of epics heralding a Medici dynasty: Francesco Bracciolini's *Croce racquistata* (1611) and Moderata Fonte's unfinished *Floridoro* (1581), as well as hagiographic versions in Maddalena Salvetti's unfinished *David perseguitato* (1611) and Marinella's *De' gesti heroici e della vita meravigliosa della serafica S. Caterina* (1624).[18] Notably, Costa's was not the only female-authored work of its kind printed in Florence that year. In 1640 Barbera Tigliamochi degli Albizzi dedicated to Vittoria della Rovere her *Ascanio errante*, a thirty-one-canto reworking of the *Aeneid* featuring genealogical prophecies about the Medici.

What distinguishes Costa's short epic is that the entirety of her project is fashioned around the personas of her patrons, a husband-and-wife pair that together must navigate the seas on their mission to produce an heir. Her near single-minded focus on the Medici's dynastic pursuits led her early biographer Dante Bianchi – who broadly dismissed the Seicento as an era of endless, uninspired flattery – to deem the work a case study in courtly sycophancy.[19] The tale is framed by divine backing for Medici aspirations. Venus informs her son that the couple must journey to Jove's oracle in Dodona, a forest populated by sacred oaks (a symbol for the Della Rovere). To signal her support, Venus sends with them her doves, which tradition held to be Dodonian priestesses. As in the *Aeneid*, the first encounter is therefore with a Venus who assists her son, with stakes as high as the foundation and propagation of an empire.[20] The literary inheritance of this trip is explicit, as the couple next passes over the island Aeaea where Ulysses evaded Circe's enchanting song, and the burial sites of Aeneas's nurse Caieta (Gaeta) and helmsman (Cape Palinuro).[21] After the invocation of these Greek and Roman heroes, the journey continues along other classical landmarks. Jove will grant his consent, the expecting couple will pass various tests of their epic mettle, and Flora will give birth upon their return.

This seafaring expedition places its dynastic message front and centre. The Mediterranean journey of Zephyrus/Ferdinando recalls the grand duke's own in 1628, memorialized in Costa's *Istoria*. Both the historical campaign and the fictional pursuit of fertility tie closely to Florence's political fortunes. As discussed in chapter 1, Venus's festive cave in *Flora feconda* recalls the *Istoria*'s description of the opera *Maddalena peccatrice* staged within Salzburg's stone theatre. In addition to these textual echoes, the continuous interweaving of travel and spectacle in the *Istoria* also characterizes the *Flora* poem, each canto of which incorporates music, dance, and merriment. This union of the epic quest with early modern festivity is exemplified by the couple's mode of transportation: while they return by ship, they travel east on a flying cloud that (in addition to suiting the wind god) cannot but evoke the mechanized examples that moved stage actors and singers into the air to the delight of Baroque audiences.[22] Frequently incorporated in performances, clouds (*nubes*) were etymologically tied to "nuptials" and, as a result, these machines proved "an intrinsic part of dynastic celebrations from the first Italian operas on" – including the notable example of a cloud ship in *Il giudizio di Paride* for the marriage of Cosimo II and Maria Magdalena in 1608.[23]

True to its Ovidian heroine, *Flora feconda* places alongside its heroic allusions to the *Odyssey* and *Aeneid* revisitations of episodes from the *Metamorphoses*. We turn first to three episodes in which Costa adapts these literary predecessors, instances of what she promised Ferdinando to be evidence of her literary versatility, justifying the publication of her text even after the Medici infant's death. In these encounters – with the sirens, with Arethusa and Alpheus, and with Galatea and Polyphemus – Costa experiments with genre and gender. We will then consider the other half of Costa's promised contribution: the aggrandizement of the Medici, accomplished through the genealogical prophecies by which epic poets conventionally glorified their patrons.

Sirens and Swans

The first revisitation of epic literary tradition – and the one that first risks derailing the couple's procreative mission – occurs in canto 2 as they near the carrion-covered shore of the sirens, a setting that permits Costa to reflect on the nature of skilled musical performance. As one of the sirens asks, "who among us does not enjoy performing the acts of love to the sound of sweet music?"[24] The episode evokes similar epic encounters, but rather than battle-hardened sailors who must resist the siren's lure, here it is a married couple. Indeed it is the bride Flora who falls under the spell of these monstrous women who encourage her to join Venus's amorous "empire" – and thereby forget her own role in forging a Tuscan one.[25] "Sparking" with love ("in rai d'amore scintillando") and beginning to soften ("intenerire") from their song, Flora starts to descend from her cloud.

Zephyrus blocks Flora's path by summoning a bevy of swans. Rather than model this scene on the *Odyssey*'s siren episode, in which the sailors plug their ears with wax, Costa instead adapts that found in the *Argonautica*. There the sailors, like Flora, are about to abandon ship when Orpheus overcomes the sirens' voices with his superior talents on the lyre. Costa's swans break into a joyous heavenly music that similarly vanquishes the sirens, who fall into confusion and plunge to their watery deaths. While in the *Argonautica* it is Orpheus's lyre that carries the day, in *Flora* the sirens play instruments (a harp in the poem, a variety of instruments in the later drama) that prove unequal to the sole sound of the swans' "voices." In the drama the frustrated sirens indeed smash their ultimately inferior instruments as they drown, a fate that derives from Marino's rewriting of the Homeric encounter in *Adone* (IX.43).

The *Flora* episode is noteworthy not only for its homoerotic undertones, but also for its staging of debates over musical rivalry and morality. The episode contrasts with canto 7 of the *Adone*, which (within a larger contest between Poetry and Music) weighs the salubrious and salacious potentials of song by introducing the alluring voice of the siren Flattery (La Lusinga), whose skilled performance – rivalling that of historical *virtuose* such as Virginia Ramponi – so enchants Adonis that no other swan, nightingale, muse, or siren can win him over.[26] Here instead honest swan-singers performing in harmony with the divine (later embodied in the drama as an additional chorus of gods) triumph over the seductive sirens. The "empire" of the erotic is safely dispensed with, and that of political legacy is pursued instead. Costa would dramatize this same tension in her later sacred epic devoted to St. Cecilia, patron saint of music, whose executioner vacillates between interpreting her performance as heavenly and siren-like.[27] The *Flora* contest also recalls the sort of staged rivalries between singers in which Costa herself notoriously had been involved in Rome.[28]

The *Flora* confrontation is courtly and theatrical in nature. The arriving swans are festive ("festanti"), and the sirens' dramatic deaths conclude their performance: "the rocks were the theatre and spectators of their vain pride."[29] The episode dramatizes potential distractions to the ruling couple's procreative mission, which the sirens hinder and the swans sustain. Beneath this mythological framework lies an argument for the fruitful exchange between the honest court singer and her patron. The episode recalls Ariosto's allegory of the swans who rescue their patrons' medals from the grasping talons of the crows and vultures of court and, like "rare poets" ("poeti rari"), preserve them for eternity.[30] Rather than distract or beguile, Costa's swan-singer lends support to the political-rhetorical needs of the sovereign through her performances. In turn, her musical service should be rewarded, just as Zephyrus and Flora covered the swans' shores with flowers in thanks before continuing their journey eastward.

Arethusa's Flight

If recrafting epic encounters with the sirens allows Costa to investigate musical service and decorum, in the next episode she revisits Ovidian themes of desire, flight, and lament at the site of Arethusa's Sicilian spring. Structurally canto 3 mimics the narrative nesting of both the *Metamorphoses'* book 5, in which Arethusa tells her story and that of Proserpina to Ceres (the goddess of fertility) within a narrative frame actually sung by the muse Calliope, and Catullus's *Poem 64*, in which the short "epic" story of Peleus and Thetis's marriage – from which Achilles was born – frames the tale of Ariadne's abandonment by Theseus, told through the ekphrasis of images embroidered onto a wedding bedcover. Flora and Zephyrus enter Arethusa's grotto, upon whose walls they find "alluring and pleasant" pastoral images.[31] Among these decorations, which Flora asks her hostess to interpret, is a depiction of Arethusa's near-rape. Like Aeneas, who was asked to relate the Trojan War he saw sculpted into Carthage's walls, Arethusa becomes at once image and voice. And like the Virgilian hero, with a sigh she interprets the scene, here in grieved song ("misto di cordogli il canto sciolse").[32]

Arethusa's tale counts among Ovid's most terrifying portrayals of sexual violence. One day she bathed in the waters of the river god Alpheus, unwittingly arousing his desire. Arethusa fled, but Alpheus assumed human form and gave chase. Diana shielded her with fog as she tried to escape, but when she broke into a cold sweat, her body dissolved into a stream. Delighted, Alpheus retransformed in order to mingle ("misceat") his waters with hers. Diana opened the earth, allowing Arethusa to become an underground spring that bubbled up on the Sicilian island of Ortygia.[33]

There are several explanations for Costa's emphasis on the episode. The nymph's Sicilian destination fits *Flora's* Mediterranean itinerary, but just as relevant is her provenance of ancient Pisa – a Greek city from which its modern Tuscan counterpart allegedly originated (lest the allusion go unnoticed, the later drama specifies "Pisa, from which your Pisa got its name").[34] Another means of introducing Costa's patrons into her poem, Arethusa indeed takes the time amid the breathless account of her flight to deliver an octave on her love for those "who reign among the Tuscans."[35] The subject also may have been suggested by Filippo Vitali's *Aretusa*, an elaborate and early *favola in musica* organized in 1620 by Florentines in Rome.[36]

Arethusa and Flora are suggestively similar. They are among Ovid's few female victims to narrate their attacks first-hand and maintain narrative relevance afterwards (Flora assists Juno in childbirth, Arethusa recounts Proserpina's abduction). Yet while Arethusa rejects her aggressor, Flora readily consents to marriage after her assault. Before Costa's Arethusa describes Alpheus's rapacious pursuit, Flora indeed suggests that her hostess's enjoyment of pastoral delights remains only partial if she does not have a "corresponding love object."[37] Despite their shared backstory, these two Ovidian heroines diverge in their attitudes towards love, marriage, and violence.

Costa's account is indebted to Giovanni Andrea dell'Anguillara's aforementioned *Le Metamorfosi di Ovidio* (1554–61). More than a vernacular translation, this highly successful edition was itself a transformation: Anguillara published a significantly elaborated narrative in *ottava rima*.[38] In addition to maintaining his extended length (20 and 23 octaves, respectively), Costa's version replicates his literary embellishments. While Ovid's Arethusa swims for the duration of a line and a half of verse ("I beat [my limbs], drawing them and gliding in a thousand turns and tossing my arms")[39] before fleeing, for instance, in both early modern versions the bathing scene extends to a full octave:

Anguillara:	Costa:
I bend and splash my arms and feet,	Now I strike the waves with my right hand
Now I extend, now I curl up my body,	And now I've turned my left shoulder
	into a dive,

I strike the water with my hands and
    feet,
And spray it out from my mouth.
I then delight in changing my strokes,
And turn my face, breast, and lap to-
    wards the sky,
And keeping above me the light,
I let myself be carried down by the
    river a bit.

Here I splash the current with both
    hands,
There my face emerges from the waters.
And changing the order of my strokes,
Now I have my breast extended, now
    curled up,
And turning towards the sky's light,
I let myself be prey to the violent river.

Le braccia e i piedi a tempo incurvo
    e scuoto,
disteso or tengo il corpo, or più
    raccolto,
con le mani e coi piè l'acqua percoto,
e la discaccio col soffiar dal volto.
Mi diletta dapoi di cangiar nuoto,
e 'l volto e 'l petto e 'l grembo al ciel
    rivolto
e, tenendo a l'insù drizzato il lume,
mi lascio alquanto in giù portar dal
    fiume.

Hor con la dritta man l'onde percoto,

Ed hor l'homero manco al lancio ho
    volto;
Qui con ambe le mani il flutto scoto,
La co'l corpo ne l'acque inalzo il volto;
Ed hor cangiando gli ordini del nuoto,
Ho 'l petto steso, ed hora il sen
    raccolto.
E, rivolgendo inverso il cielo il lume,
Mi lascio in preda al violento fiume.[40]

Costa's borrowing is underscored by her repetition of Anguillara's end rhymes (*sc[u]oto/percoto/nuoto, raccolto/volto/[ri]volto, lume/fiume*). She also mirrors the corporeally expressed terror found in his account of the heroine's plight. While Ovid measures the mounting likelihood of Arethusa's capture by the increasingly perceptible breath of her pursuer behind her, Anguillara shows the physical toll of her flight as her feet and bare torso grow bloodied from the bramble through which she runs.[41] In addition to foreshadowing the lacerations of sexual viola-tion should Arethusa be caught, these scratches recall those in that highly parallel encounter in the *Metaphorphoses* in which Apollo warns Daphne's skin will be marred if she flees him.[42] Anguillara has dug those imagined injuries into the flesh of Arethusa. Her bloodied body is all the more pronounced in Costa's version: "Even my breast is torn, and on every side / I receive a thousand miserable viola-tions. / And from my foot, which already falters exhausted from its flight, / I pour forth more than a river of blood."[43]

After Arethusa finishes her tale, Zephyrus and Flora look upon Alpheus em-pathetically ("compativa d'Alfeo gli amori intensi").[44] The cavern is then filled with celebratory song and dance, an unexpected response that links Arethusa's sad song to the sort of performance found within festive settings. The scene closes with Alpheus auguring the couple's success in their procreative quest and Zephyrus, Flora, and Arethusa sweetly applauding ("applauser dolcemente") his pronouncement.[45] This unexpectedly celebratory conclusion to Arethusa's saga reminds us that, as Wendy Heller has observed, "lamenting women were sources of pleasurable arousal for the viewers and listeners."[46] It also returns us to Catullus, whose poem similarly concludes with the nuptials celebrated by the gods, at whose banquet the Parcae prophesize the birth – and death – of Achilles. Alpheus similarly leaves open the possibility that the couple might still encounter an adverse Fate, a nod to Costa's source text all the more poignant after the Medici child, like his Greek predecessor, perished. Costa uses the Catullan frame to transform the *Metamorphoses* episode (by way of its elaborative Cinquecento rewrite) into an example of female complaint – one whose terror is partially displaced by revelry and Flora's encouragement of love.

Costa's relationship to classical and recent predecessors is perhaps nowhere more marked than in this episode. Nevertheless, she would reframe the encounter in the subsequent drama, distilling the Catullan imitation by adding an introductory soliloquy by Alpheus and a concluding exchange between him and Arethusa, in which the nymph demands that he "stop whining about love already."[47] His unwillingness to do so repositions the episode from female to male complaint and heightens the distinction with Zephyrus and Flora, who have already continued along their dynastic voyage.

Reconfiguring Abandonment and Lament

Costa again inventively re-elaborates a familiar episode from the *Metamorphoses* in canto 7, as Flora and Zephyrus return home from Dodona.[48] If the encounters with the sirens and with Arethusa examined desire, enchantment, and violence by way of competing musical moralities and a Catullan-inspired plaint of an assailed woman, Costa inserts into her poem on marriage and procreation an example of the lamenting abandoned woman topos that so thrilled audiences and readers of the day. She does so by rewriting the story of Galatea, her beloved Acis, and the cyclops Polyphemus. In the *Metamorphoses* Polyphemus, enamoured of Galatea, spots the two lovers together and crushes his rival Acis with a boulder. Distraught, Galatea opens the earth so that Acis's blood can transform into a spring.[49] Costa selected an episode like that of Arethusa: one involving a first-hand account by an Ovidian heroine, a Sicilian setting, and a watery metamorphosis. The myth of Galatea was especially popular in the Seicento and was seen in works by Chiabrera (*Galatea o le Grotte di Fassolo* and *Polifemo geloso*) and Marino (at length in his *Adone*, in three madrigals in his *Galeria*, and in twenty-four "Polyphemic" sonnets in *La lira*), and in Benedetto Fioretti's lament *Polifemo innamorato di*

Galatea, performed before the Accademia degli Umoristi in Rome and published in 1627.[50] Just a year before *Flora feconda* was issued, Loreto Vittori (whom Costa knew from Rome) published the libretto for his opera *La Galatea.*[51] In short, Costa adapted a myth currently in vogue.

Rather than follow Anguillara's text as she had in the Arethusa episode (and as Marino partially did in the *Adone*), Costa twists the love triangle so as to offer her own version of the popular female lament. While the Ovidian Acis died because of his love for Galatea, here he only has eyes for Flora, once he spies her sailing nearby: "a spring becomes a flower's lover."[52] Flora – newly pregnant, intent upon her procreative mission, and now unflappable in a manner distinct from her behavior in the earlier siren episode – pays him no mind. Spurned, he splashes frantically between the shore and her ship. Like Catullus's, Ovid's, and Monteverdi's Ariadne/Arianna, and like Ariosto's Olimpia, Costa's Galatea unexpectedly finds herself a woman wailing as her beloved sets off across the waves. She, too, cries out his name as she sees him depart, receiving no response but the echo of her own voice:

> No less anguished appears fair Galatea,
> Dishevelling her thick locks,
> And by her own hands, a traitor to herself,
> She passionately tears at her divine cheeks.
> Cruel to her pleas she calls each star,
> And hears it reverberate on the waves of the sea.

> Nè men dolente si vedea la bella
> Galatea scompigliarsi il ricco crine,
> E fatta con le mani a se rubella
> Ama le gote lacerar divine.
> Crudel a' voti suoi chiama ogni stella
> E n'ode rimbombar l'onde marine.[53]

The tearing of her cheeks ("le gote lacerare") recalls especially the manner in which Ariosto's Olimpia, watching her beloved Bireno's ship sail off, begins her lament by scratching her own face ("graffiandosi le gote"), as well as pulling her hair and beating her chest.[54]

But Costa does not just create a forsaken lover's lament from the original tale of mourning, she effectively triples it – for not only does Galatea deliver an anguished plaint, and Acis perform the conventional racing back and forth (here across the water instead of along the shoreline), but Polyphemus himself hears Galatea's lament and responds to it with one of his own. As seen in chapter 2, Costa had already experimented with male-voiced amorous lament in her *Il violino.*

In one lament a lover invites his cruel lady to "let me die … / kill me, / ridicule me," for instance, while in another the shepherd Tirsi exclaims that Filli "[does] not perceive my cry, /… [does] not hear my laments."[55] In *Flora*, the pathetic cries come from a once terrifying giant. While Polyphemus's song in the *Metamorphoses* transitions thrillingly from courtship to murderous rage, here he is a tearful scorned lover on the shore who only realizes eight octaves into his lament that, deaf to his words and subverting the conventions that would find her stuck alone on the shore, Galatea has departed to chase after Acis. This Ariostan twist of romance within the epic frame, with characters unexpectedly coming and going, underscores Polyphemus's continuities with Sacripante, the *cavallier dolente* who cries over Angelica's pursuit of another man; both the giant's and cavalier's heaving chests are compared to Mongibello (that is, Sicily's Mount Etna).[56]

While the lament began with Galatea echoing Olimpia, it ends with Polyphemus doing the same. Just as the Ariostan heroine's final words in that episode express the grim hope that her body be devoured by a wolf, bear, lion, or tiger ("il lupo, il leon, l'orso venga, / e la tigre") – the bear being Olimpia's variation on a similar verse in the *Heroides* in which Ariadne anticipates being consumed by wolves, lions, tigers, or seals – the cyclops concludes by imagining his death by "ferocious bears and insidious wolves" ("orse feroci, e insidiosi lupi").[57] With that, the supposedly terrifying monster faints ("languendo ei cadde"), the vestiges of his ire perceived only in the earthquake produced by the fall of his immense body.[58]

Costa experiments with lament by multiplying it, passing it from one character to another. Her decision to highlight male lament may reflect a similar move found in Vittori's *Galatea* libretto. There Polyphemus plots against the couple by spreading the false rumour that Acis has been unfaithful to Galatea, prompting the nymph to dismiss her lover and causing him, after a tearful plaint, to faint in anguish, at which point the still ferocious giant crushes him with the boulder. Costa's weepy and wilting cyclops is not her only innovation. While Galatea's female peers must find happiness in new companions (Adriana with Bacchus, Olimpia with Oberto), *Flora feconda*'s focus on coupling does not allow Galatea to remain abandoned for long. Not only has she gone after Acis but, most unusually within this tradition, he comes to his senses, returns, and pleads for her forgiveness. Festive music and dance celebrate their happy reunion. Costa's version of the Galatea myth therefore introduces a scenario conducive to female amorous lament but also resolves it in a manner harmonious to the poem's procreative focus by reinstating the couple's joy and displacing the excess of anguished emotion onto the monstrous body of the cyclops.

Prophecies of Birth and Empire

While the *Flora* works feature Costa's adaptations of epic and mythological episodes, like those seen in cantos 3 and 7, that are intended to display her literary dexterity and inventiveness, their primary narrative focus is nevertheless the couple's reproductive quest. This mission comes to a head upon their arrival in Jove's Dodonian forest in canto 5. Yet here, too, the text initially centres upon the role of female complaint.

In a work otherwise filled with music, the reader encounters utter silence in this mystical oak grove. For days Zephyrus makes offerings to Jove to no avail. An exasperated Flora finally bursts into a heated lament, incensed that the god grants fertility to all but her. Her complaint revises the female lament tradition, substituting traditional plaints about dead or double-crossing beloveds with this new procreative-minded speech delivered alongside an attentive, able-bodied husband. Her quarrel is not with man but with the highest of the gods. How is it possible, she demands, that he even grants fertility to beasts and in the wilds of Africa but denies progeny to her? "You let even monsters give birth, / such that more sterile Africa blazes," a statement that she repeats even more emphatically in the drama, charging that "You, who have made fertile / The most ferocious monsters / And granted childbirths in the forests of Africa, / Now harm me alone."[59] The passages, whose contrast between Italian and African fertility are repeated elsewhere in the works, articulates the dynastic and territorial concerns of a Europe preoccupied with maintaining and extending its supremacy, and in particular of a Tuscany entangled in economic and socio-political relationships with its Mediterranean neighbours.[60]

This figure symbolizing Vittoria della Rovere concludes her lament by calling upon the oaks to intervene on her behalf: "Oaks, if you have sound, by you let my pain / be more worthily vented to your god."[61] Behind this evocation of the Della Rovere arboreal symbol are Dodona's mythological roots: the oracle communicated through the rustling of the forest leaves, a movement and sound that Flora here describes using language ("si scioglia") often associated with the production of song. When Flora falls silent, the previously still oaks begin to shake forcefully, filling the woods with thunderous and marvellous sound. Underscoring the popularity and power of the female lament, Flora's complaint produces results where Zephyrus's faithful acts of reverence did not. From the woods a prophetic voice speaks: "FROM THE GOLDEN OAK WILL ARISE A GREAT PROGENY / THAT WILL EXTEND THE EMPIRE AS FAR AS THE SUN."[62] This declaration, printed in capital letters, was already presented to the reader in the poem's Argument and is repeated in canto 9 (upon the child's birth). It is also the longest passage retained verbatim in the subsequent drama (act 3, scene 3).[63]

These two lines are the most important of the epic and its dramatic rewrite. From this point forward, the procreation of the protagonists – and their Medici counterparts – is secured, although, as we shall see, Costa introduces various narrative obstacles. This was, of course, until the infant's death presented a new development with regard to the poem's denouement, necessitating an additional canto. Before this turn of events, the oracle's pronouncement – placed at the epic's original midpoint – not only heralds the grand duke and duchess's success in producing an heir but also predicts the realization of their "imperial" aspirations. The Medici had long sought to extend Tuscany's commercial and cultural radius in the Mediterranean and the New World, with mixed results examined by Brian Brege.[64] Militarily and politically, any Florentine hopes for a colonial project rivalling that of their European neighbours was limited by the grand duchy's relationship to Spain. Tuscany's global reach often came by both moving within other powers' imperial structures abroad and by attracting the fruits of those power's foreign investments locally. Lia Markey argues that the Medici and their circles engaged in a form of "vicarious conquest" through artistic representations of and collecting from the New World, and Nathalie Hester similarly points to a broader "poetic imagination," rather than historical reality, of "Italian global eminence" in the peninsula's New World epics.[65] In this age of conquest and colonialism, in which the Italian states generally did not (or could not) fully participate, *Flora*'s promise of a Tuscan empire is a clear example of Costa's dynastic messaging, which plays to diplomatic wishful thinking and the ways in which the Medici sought to solidify their position, especially within the Mediterranean. Costa elsewhere made sweeping claims about the future of Medici might – her opening canzone to Ferdinando in *Il violino*, for instance, anticipates that "both hemispheres" will be subject to him and other rulers will "lay down their crowns before [his] sceptre" – but the imperial prophecy is the raison d'être of the *Flora* texts.[66]

With procreation promised and "empire" foretold, Jove orders a new, properly "epic" ship built with lumber from his woods, with the golden oak serving as its mast and as a symbol of divine favour. Before the couple sets sail, Hymen sings of their love, while the Muses decorate the ship with flower garlands, the Graces dance, and swans frolic in festivities, much as in an epithalamium.[67] Zephyrus and Flora dismiss earlier false predictions of their barrenness, declaring that Jove has revealed himself "the glorious augur of our seed."[68]

Like all epic travellers, however, Flora and Zephyrus face impediments as they sail westward. Some of these echo literary tradition. Mirroring book 1 of the *Aeneid*, for example, they are first beset by angry winds before Neptune saves them from shipwreck. Elsewhere they reference historical events, most notably when in canto 8 Flora experiences pain, fever, and skin rash – an allusion to the smallpox infection Vittoria della Rovere suffered during her pregnancy.[69] To Flora's rescue comes yet another Ovidian character: Glaucus, the fisherman who became a sea god after consuming special herbs that he had witnessed bring his catch back to life.[70] He applies these herbs to Flora's chest, saving mother and child.

The medical-mythological resolution of the smallpox episode that threatened the pregnancy allows Costa to introduce the sort of genealogical prophecy required of epic, here delivered by the clairvoyant sea god Triton.[71] As noted above, an increasing number of epic works dedicated to the Medici foretold future glory for the dynasty, putting Florence in the heroic position long occupied by Ferrara and substituting the d'Este out for the Medici. Given that these predictions are professed to a gravid Flora, who has just survived a health scare, readers might anticipate the prophecy to foreground female contributions to the family line. Precedent for such a move first appeared in the *Orlando furioso*, where Ariosto's "extraordinary choice to stage a woman [Bradamante] as the depositary of dynastic prophecies" prompted poetic interest in women's multifaceted role in fostering dynasties.[72] This does not prove to be the case in *Flora feconda*, however, as no women appear in its ancestry of male heroes. Triton traces the future Medici lineage (with the occasional error) from an assumed Greek origin to Giovanni di Bicci de' Medici to Cosimo II. While papal tiaras are heavily emphasized (Triton includes even Pius IV, of the distantly related Milanese Medici), mention of the Medici's union with royal houses and Italian duchies through marriage must wait until the following canto. Some chronological flexibility permits Costa to end the prophecy with Lorenzo II, who became Duke of Urbino in 1516, and thereby present Ferdinando and Vittoria's union as the happy culmination of historical forces (never mind that Lorenzo's short-lived rule temporarily deprived the Della Rovere of power). Triton's genealogical prophecy is reinforced by the dolphin-born lyrist Arion, who sings of a coming golden age to be found upon the Arno. This prophetic solution to the dangers of pregnancy sets the stage for the transition to the ninth – formerly the final – canto, the culmination of both the gestation and the journey.

Costa had intended to end the poem with jubilation and a final genealogical prophecy. Uniting homecoming with nativity, in canto 9 the triumphant couple sails back into the Tyrrhenian. Venus glides onto the watery scene upon her pearled shell as a chorus of cherubs sing and dance in intricate weaves, leaps, and formations, "contests" ("a gara") that underscore the courtly nature of the revelry by evoking performative genres such as the tournament.[73] The canto shifts into an allegorical mode almost immoderate in its glorification of the Medici. As the Arno and the Appennini (like Arion before them) sing of a coming golden age, the gods plant Jove's golden oak on the shore. Art and Virtue construct around it a temple in which Flora gives birth, before they then found the Tuscan cities of Siena, Pisa, Livorno, and Florence.

While the fruits of this union are Tuscan, they are indebted to Flora's Marchigiano roots. A prophecy for the Della Rovere line complements that for the Medici in the preceding canto. Singled out are the Della Rovere popes Sixtus IV and Julius II, as well as the various "Leonardos and Raphaels, Giovannis and Giulianos … Francescos and Guidos" who added to the glory of Urbino.[74] Zephyrus rejoices that his descendants will be conjoined not only to that court but also to the royal houses of France and Austria. While canto 8's prophecy establishes a patrilineal legacy, canto 9's honours marriage. Once again, however, no direct mention is made of either family's women. What is more, although the later drama will dedicate more space to praising Vittoria della Rovere herself in Triton's prophecy, as discussed below, even her male ancestors will be written out of the vision in deference to the Medici.

The patrilineal focus of the composite prophecies replicates what we have elsewhere seen to be Costa's emphasis on her patron Ferdinando and her silence regarding his *tutrici*. This choice stands in stark contrast to the epic genealogy found, for example, in Barbara Tigliamochi's *Ascanio errante*, dedicated to Vittoria that same year. When Aeneas descends to the underworld in that work, he receives a joint prophecy about the glories of the Della Rovere and Medici lines. Among the Medici appear several women: the first duchess (Eleonora of Toledo), the *tutrici* (Christine of Lorraine and Maria Maddalena), and even Ferdinando II's sisters (Maria, Margherita, and Anna).[75] Because *Flora*'s narrative is wrapped tightly around the mission to produce an heir to the grand duchy, however, Costa's prophecies centre on male progeny.

Apotheosis and Parental Lament

Had Cosimino survived, the poem would have ended with celebrations and song. "Pierced by voices all around," canto 9's last lines read, "the air resounds with 'Ferdinando' and sings of this birth."[76] Drawing us to the present with the first prophetic naming of the grand duke, these verses mirror Costa's assertion that she composed this song (*canto*) to join her voice to the chorus of Tuscan joy. However, the child's death necessitated the speedy addition of a tenth canto – an addendum that upset the gravidic framework but preserved the publication's fate. Compelled to resolve this thorny narrative issue, Costa settled on apotheosis. In canto 10, the exuberance of the natal festivities prompts Jove to "see the child, who to the Earth was a loving sun, as worthy of the heavens."[77] The god resolves to carry away ("rapir") the infant, a chaste version of his more eroticized abductions of Europa and Ganymede.[78]

Poetically, perhaps the sole advantage of the new canto was that it gave Costa one additional form of lament with which to experiment. Where in previous cantos she proffered examples of scorned lovers and embittered suppliants, here she examines parental grief. The unexpected turn of events elicits cries from the bewildered couple. How can it be, Zephyrus protests, that Jove had foretold that this heroic babe would lift up Italy, wear the laurel crown, revive the music of the swans, line the Arno with flowers?[79] His dirge is amplified by that of his wife, who questions why she was saved from sirens and shipwreck if her epic voyage is to end tragically. "I moan, gasp, sigh, freeze, and expire," she cries before collapsing, her husband nearly doing so as well.[80]

To Flora's tears Jove responds that human affairs are subject to mysterious celestial forces (the fact that Flora and Zephyrus are themselves gods is conveniently overlooked). Although their son belongs to the stars, they will have as many descendants as the oak has branches. As the Olympian gods embrace the exalted infant, all gaze upon him and with harmonious plectrums ("plettri armoniosi") sing a hymn that completes his apotheosis.[81] With hope restored, tribulation turns to joy ("gioia"), the final word in the poem.[82]

Despite the unanticipated detour that Costa's epic journey takes, one that necessarily defers dynastic fulfilment, the poem concludes by substituting immortalization for procreation. Among the texts that the poet adapts as evidence of her skill and versatility – episodes drawn from epic and mythology, and reshaped according to varied gender and genre dynamics – is the *Flora* epic itself, which introduces a poetics of paternal grief. Costa would continue exploring this theme throughout the rest of the year.

Lacrimosi accenti in the *Flora* Drama

By November Costa would again revise her *Flora*, transforming it into a drama under the slightly altered title *La Flora feconda*. Among Costa's works it arguably has been the most overlooked. Even her biographers sum it up in passing as a theatrical rewrite of the poem, although Natalia Costa-Zalessow notes the inclusion of intricate scene changes, music, and dance.[83] Yet while Costa labelled *La Flora feconda* simply a "drama" in five acts, there are indications that she may have conceived of it as a *dramma in musica* – as indeed her contemporary and Vatican librarian Leone Allacci classified it in his 1666 *Drammaturgia*, the first bibliography of Italian theatre.[84] A variety of metrical structures replace the poem's *ottave*: passages of hendecasyllable and *settenario* (seven-syllable) verse that, their regular rhyming notwithstanding, are suggestive of recitative-like narrative; six-line canzonettas (ABBACC) delivered in unison by the heroic couple;[85] numerous choruses in *quinario* and *quadrasillabi* (five- and four-syllable) verse; and, in one case where the stage directions specifically mention a sung performance by King Alcinous's court poet Alauro, a six-stanza madrigal (ABBACCDD) in hendecasyllables with two *quinario* lines preceding the ritornello.[86] The prevalence of strophic material indicative of musical setting is mirrored by various textual allusions to song. We might consider, for instance, the reference by one of the work's ten choruses (in this case, of cherubs) to Venus and Cupid singing ("Canta Amor, canta la Diva") – a description that follows *quinario* and *quadrasillabi* verse delivered by the goddess and her son amid merry dances – while Cupid alludes to Zephyrus and Flora's love song ("canto amato").[87] The heroic couple is represented as singing in unison ("cantando insieme"), reflecting their numerous shared *canzonette*.[88] The original poem was similarly replete with images of music-making, dance, and festival – and of course the epic genre is imagined as the poetic song of its narrator – but these elements are literalized in the drama. While no indication has come to light that the work was ever set to music, or indeed performed (as is also the case with Costa's equestrian ballet libretto), the character of the drama is decidedly lyrical.

This time Costa entrusted her work to Vittoria della Rovere, her first female dedicatee. Given the subject matter, this selection is fitting. It bears noting that Vittoria, in addition to supporting female artists and musicians, was one of the few patronesses available to contemporary female authors. Like the aforementioned Tigliamochi, the Venetian nun Arcangela Tarabotti similarly placed her *Antisatira* under "the protective shade of [Vittoria's] most famous golden oak tree," for instance.[89] But, as noted in the Introduction, Costa was the best represented female author in the grand duchess's library. She lauds Vittoria not only in the *Flora* works but in a pamphlet poem and individual verse in *La chitarra* and *Lo stipo*.[90] These encomia for Ferdinando's spouse are especially notable when considered in contrast to Costa's textual silence regarding his regents.

The drama's dedication begins with a nod to the original poem's epic frame: "The ancient Romans used to hang the spoils of their victories [*vittorie*] on a tree trunk for immortal fame, and so, too, do I fasten to your Most Serene Highness's oak [*Rovere*] my *Flora feconda* so that it might bring victory over time and consecrate itself to eternity." While she hopes the grand duchess will safeguard her against the threats of time and envy, the true victory is not Costa's but Vittoria's own. "Since I do not have a fertile mind," Costa continues, "I at least wanted to present you with a work that bears the name 'fecund.'" [91] She anticipates Vittoria's imminently fruitful production of heirs who – drawing strength from the Rovere oak and the Medici name – shall vanquish all enemies. By the letter's end, Vittoria herself emerges as the heroic champion, immortalizing tree, and victorious symbol all in one.

Although the death of Cosimino no longer wielded the same impact as it did for the poem, *Flora*'s main trajectory remains unchanged, albeit it without the nine-month frame. However, there are numerous alterations that, coupled with the matter of the work's genre, render it worthy of more extensive consideration than it has received thus far. Here we might consider just a few examples. There are several instances in which Costa's adjustments indicate a consideration of the gender and status of her new dedicatee. Flora's parturition, for instance, is no longer observed directly by the reader and the allegorical congregation of canto 9 alike. Instead, the Arno ushers Flora off scene in the company of nymphs to deliver the child, promising in the meantime to spread the news across the Tuscan empire and leaving Zephyrus to a perform a soliloquy; the nymphs later announce the birth.[92] Another case in point is the recrafting of the siren scene, in which there is now little indication that Flora herself is enticed by their song. Instead, the chorus of salvific swans is reinforced by a chorus of gods, providing an additional buffer between the couple and inveiglement. The only hint of the sirens' previous sway over Flora is the choruses' call for her to "carry forth with your Zephyrus, / [And] follow happily your destiny," shunning the temptresses' barren ("infeconde") shores.[93] Similarly, additions are made to the Arethusa/Alpheus and Galatea/Acis episodes. As noted above, in the former case new scenes feature an opening lament by Alpheus as a scorned lover and a concluding exchange in which Arethusa reconfirms her rejection of him. In the latter episode, an entire scene is dedicated to Acis's request for forgiveness upon his return. While in the poem he attributed his abandonment of Galatea to the variability of nature, here he adopts a newly Petrarchan tone when he acknowledges his "youthful mistake" ("la colpa giovanile") and begs her "pity and … pardon" ("pietade e … perdono").[94] In place of the penitent poet we encounter a lover entreating his mistreated beloved to take him back.

Vittoria herself gains visibility in Triton and Arion's genealogical prophecies. While the epic centred on the male line, tracing the Medici up through Cosimo II and circling back to Lorenzo II as a link to Urbino, here Arion's prophecy concludes with Ferdinando II, who, "born from Austrian blood" – a rare but oblique nod to Maria Maddalena – "will be bound in love to the goddess [Vittoria] of the Metaurus … and the fertile oak (*Rovere*) will be his treasure."[95] But while such changes reflect Costa's new dedicatee, the prophecies themselves complicate what might otherwise be seen as a rewriting suited entirely to Vittoria herself. Triton's declaration centres on crowns (papal, royal) and arms (military heroes), while Arion's genealogical survey proceeds from Lorenzo the Magnificent to Ferdinando, with no further mention of Lorenzo II as a bridge between the two states.[96] There are also significant changes to the second prophecy series, which in the epic's canto 9 had turned towards Urbino and the Della Rovere. The Marchigiano popes and "Raphaels" have been replaced with promise of "Lorenzos … Mattiases … Leopoldos … Giovan Carlos" – Ferdinando's uncle and brothers – with only passing mention of "many others in Urbino."[97] Vittoria's past bonds to the Marche and its influence have slid to the back burner, her ties to the present Medici court and her maternal imperatives taking precedence.

Finally, among the notable differences between the two *Flora* works is the handling of parental grief, which takes on particular importance given its role as the *fil rouge* of Costa's 1640 publications. In the epic, Zephyrus responds to the news with initial stupor, which gives way to a lament. At approximately six stanzas, it does not match Flora's eighteen-stanza lament in length but expresses much of the same raw emotion.[98] When she collapses ("cadde Flora a tai note"), he nearly does as well ("e di cader dubbiosa / anch'esso ha l'alma").[99] By the time Costa wrote the drama, however, she had recalibrated this image of fatherly despair. When the child is taken in act 5, at first Zephyrus briefly protests that they had been promised progeny. Following Jove's explanation, however, he quickly acquiesces to the baby's apotheosis and urges Flora to keep faith: "Look how … our child glimmers equal to the sun. With your exalted delivery, you have produced the god of the Tuscan empire."[100] Zephyrus's attempts to calm Flora echo Jove's call for her to "Temper, oh Flora, your grief" ("Tempra, o Flora, gli affanni").[101] Flora, in contrast, delivers two disconsolate laments in which she does not hesitate to take aim at the god with the same tone that her literary predecessors used to accuse unfaithful lovers or bemoan a beloved's absence. "So by treacherous acts / you now divide me from my self?" she cries, this second verse an adaptation of a line from Tasso's *Rime*.[102] It is only with the promise of future heirs that Flora finally tempers her anguish ("A così eccelsi detti / Tempransi i mesti affetti") and eventually accepts Jove's promise of future Medici sons.[103]

Anticipating this final scene, Costa recrafts Flora's desire to bear children in act 1 as a lament. When Zephyrus presses her to reveal the source of her sorrows, her response adopts both the exclamations ("deh," "ahi lassa") and the "tearful words" ("lacrimosi accenti") of poetic complaint. Flora's earlier epic yearning has become a dramatic plaint from the very start. Her suffering is mirrored by her husband's in this first scene in a way that it will no longer be by the final act: "Look, Flora, how I feel pain at your pain."[104] After promising to secure Venus's assistance, he departs with a trepidation characteristic of inseparable lovers ("And yet, alas, how shall I leave without dying?").[105] A far cry from Zephyrus setting off "happier than ever" to find his mother, as seen in the poem, this scene's tonal shift reflects Costa's foreknowledge of the Medici baby's fate.[106] The tale is no longer about birth but rather ultimately about how death will be redressed.

La Flora feconda stages the kinds of lament common in poetry and increasingly in music, but refashioned to engage with the subject of the tragic loss of a child. By frontloading much of the couple's anguish, and later curtailing Zephyrus's expressions of paternal woe, Costa prevents the script from slipping into an overly tragic mode. The promise of future Medici heirs becomes reconciliatory if not fully celebratory – a framing emphasized by the work's prologue, delivered by a personified Arno, who anticipates the coming glories of his shores, while a group of merrily dancing nymphs sing: "Gay / and bountiful / [Zephyrus and Flora's] offspring / shall conquer the dawn and outshine the sun."[107]

Political and Personal Lament

Costa did not spend 1640 solely on *Flora* revisions. In June she was granted licence to publish *La selva di cipressi*, a collection of funeral and complaint *canzoni* in *ottava rima*. Her dedicatee was the Medici's distant cousin Charles of Lorraine, Duke of Guise. As others have noted, the details of the French duke's exile have not been fully established.[108] After getting caught in the crosshairs of chief minister Cardinal Richelieu, he fled to Florence in 1631. He was given apartments in Palazzo Vecchio, where he was later joined by his wife Henriette-Catherine de Joyeuse and their children. Costa composed a poem for the occasion, verse that plays on the "gioioso" [joyous, *joyeuse*] nature of the family's reunion.[109] She also included poems lauding Charles Louis and François in the "drawer" of *Lo stipo* reserved for Medici kin.[110] *La selva di cipressi*'s dedication notes Costa's gratitude for the favour the duke had long shown her, suggesting that he counted among her benefactors. Charles and Catherine had recently lost two sons: nineteen-year-old Charles Louis in March 1637 and twenty-seven-year-old François, Prince of Joinville, in December 1639, the same month as the Medici child died. The coincidence that two of her benefactors in Florence should lose a child within weeks of each other was not lost on Costa. If historical circumstances required her to reframe *Flora feconda* and repurpose its already inventive interweaving of festivity and complaint in order to accommodate political and parental lament, this volume offered an additional opportunity to display her poetic skill in further adapting the genre, and to embrace loss and mourning as literary themes.

Costa's publication followed on the heels of a comparable work by Alessandro Adimari. Her burlesque touch in her earlier texts is indebted in part to Adimari's *Tersicore*, and here her elegiac volume appears to be influenced by his *La Melpomene*, a collection of "funeral sonnets" ("sonetti funebri") approved for publication in March 1640, shortly before Costa was granted her own publication rights. Printed consecutively by Massi & Landi, they show continuities in their frontispieces, both possibly by Stefano della Bella, with comparable rows of funereal cypress trees arranged in a fashion reminiscent of period set design.[111] While Adimari's *Melpomene* (named for the Muse of tragedy) is more ambitious in terms of the number of figures represented – fifty pairs of sonnets and elegies honour as many individuals, in comparison to Costa's fourteen – she dedicates far more textual real estate to each (26–100 octaves) in a volume twice the length. Tellingly, Costa dedicates the two longest poems to her patron and to her personal woes (100 and 81 octaves, respectively), favoured themes throughout her corpus. Unlike Costa, Adimari states that he has only included figures whom he personally once served, presented alphabetically by the publishers in order to avoid thorny issues of precedence.[112] The writers share only four honorees: Cosimo II, his son Francesco, and the two Lorraine sons.[113] As she had in the *Istoria*, Costa evades any mention of Ferdinando's regents, even though their recent deaths (Maria Maddalena's in 1631 and Christine of Lorraine's in 1637) would have made them prime candidates for inclusion. While Adimari recognizes fifteen women, including Christine, Costa's sole female figures (beyond mourners) are allegorical, pastoral, or herself.

More broadly, Costa's designation of the volume as a lugubrious work ("opera lugubre") recalls the division of Marino's *Lira* into generic categories that included "rime … lugubri," a reconfiguration of the *canzoniere* structure initiated by Tasso.[114] While Costa does not maintain Marino's categorical arrangements within her collections, the subject of funeral verse may have been suggested in part by his model. Marino's first section focuses on "lugubrious-amorous" verse of a rather Petrarchan nature about the loss of his *donna* and other women before transitioning to "lugubrious-encomiastic" verse on historical personages.[115] While Costa includes no women, Marino's sequence of historical leaders, cardinals, military heroes, and cultural figures finds an analogous procession in *La selva di cipressi*. First are five poems Costa dedicated to the Guise (Charles Louis and François together), Della Rovere (Francesco Maria II), and Medici (Ferdinando I, Cosimo II, and Francesco). These are followed by five poems about non-Florentine men of note (Vittorio Amedeo I, Duke of Savoy;[116] the German general Bernard of Saxe-Weimar; Ambrogio Spinola, celebrated commander of the Spanish army in the Netherlands;[117] Albrech von Wallenstein, famed generalissimo of the imperial army; and Bertoldo Orsini, Marquis of Monte San Savino). Curiously, next come a set of three poems of a more pastoral nature, including a final autobiographical composition, reminiscent of Marino's "lugubrious-amorous" section. These latter are interrupted by a canzone for Ferdinando Saracinelli, librettist for Medici court spectacle "under [whose] care one heard Flora emulate on earth the harmonies of the heavens."[118] Saracinelli is one of the few included figures with whom Costa had a relationship; he was one of her celebrants in *Il violino* and at her daughter's baptism represented the grand duke (the girl's godfather). The placement of his canzone might be due to his death just as Costa was assembling the volume, but it also replicates Marino's arrangement, which concludes with artists and poets. As we shall see, one of Costa's idylls even suggestively echoes Marino's intermediary section on murder victims.

That Costa should open her volume with verse honouring her patronage families is hardly surprising. In contrast, her inclusion of figures acclaimed for their transalpine military feats at first might seem odd. However, not only did Florence partially participate in those wars through the figures of Francesco and Mattias de' Medici,[119] but as Ellen Rosand notes, "toward the middle of the century political events assumed a new importance as subjects for laments, adding a high-baroque dimension of actuality to the repertoire of traditional themes of pathos derived from the pastoral and from Ariostesque romance."[120] Many of these political laments responded to the wars in northern Italy and Europe. Costa could look to poetic predecessors locally, in the case of Andrea Salvadori's 1633 *Sonetti... in lode del campo imperiale, e in morte del re di Svezia*, a volume that similarly contains verse for Francesco and for Wallenstein and underscores Tuscany's political, familial, and religious connections to the imperial cause.[121] Costa also would have known the musical laments, particularly those coming out of Rome. Notable examples included Rossi's *Ravvolse il volo* for Carlo Emanuele of Turin (Vittorio Amedeo's father) and *Ferma, ferma quel volo*, attributed in at least one source to Carlo del Violino, for Wallenstein.[122]

Costa's relationship to political lament is clearly evidenced by an earlier poem, her *Lagrime della Regina di Svezia* published in *Lo stipo*'s "drawer" of complaint verse. The poem treats the celebrity case of King Gustav II of Sweden's grieving widow, Queen Maria Eleonora of Brandenburg. Salvadori, as indicated by his volume's title, had included two sonnets on the death of the Swedish king. More relevant still, however, is composer Luigi Rossi's cantata *Un ferito cavaliero* (entitled *Lamento della Regina di Svezia* in one manuscript).[123] The cantata (usually dated between 1632 and 1641 and its verse attributed to artist-poet Fabio della Corgna) and Costa's poem share the same narrative structure: a wounded cavalier rides to inform the queen of her husband's battlefield death; after hearing the news she descends into madness and mourning. The historical queen infamously refused to bury her husband's body for over a year, daily caressing and crying over it.[124] Textual comparisons reveal Costa's direct reliance on the cantata. In its first verses, for example, the dusty, sweaty, and bloodied cavalier arrives and bows before the queen ("Un ferito cavaliero / di polve di sudor di sangue asperso /…/ s'inchina"), an image that reappears nearly identically in Costa ("[un] cavalier ferito / [...] / di polve a un tempo, e di sudore asperso, / con riverente inchino … / nel proprio sangue anco sommerso").[125] In addition to establishing 1639 as the terminus ante quem for Rossi's cantata, the connection evidences Costa's relationship to Rome's musical circles and places her in the circle of poets and musicians crafting laments around political-military personages.[126]

Costa's *Cipressi* elegies employ many of the poetic commonplaces of similar sixteenth- and seventeenth-century volumes: for example, the mourning of a city figured through its river and landscape, scenes of despondency, and the ravages of envy (to which we will return in chapter 7) and misfortune. The individual components of the volume merit a more detailed analysis, but for the purposes of the present study we will focus on the first canzone, that on the Guise, and on the idylls as examples of how Costa adapts the lament mode, including autobiographically.

The framework of the poem, the rivalry between Fortune and Death, sets the tone for a collection intent on exploring suffering, aggrandizing its honorees, and articulating Costa's own woes.[127] Fortune first wreaks havoc on the Guise by compelling them to abandon France for Florence. This opening focus on exile prefigures Costa's own expatriation in the final autobiographical poem. When Death, not to be outdone, strikes down first Charles Louis, then François, the duchess Catherine cries that in escaping to Florence she changed her skies but not her fate ("Ah che cielo mutai, ma non già sorte") – a sentiment later reiterated by Costa, who laments that changing her skies did nothing to avert her destiny ("Ah che cangiar di ciel nulla mi giova, / E sempre il Fato contra me s'avanza").[128]

The tenth canto of the *Flora feconda* on parental heartbreak shapes this first poem of the *Selva di cipressi*. Tearing at her breast and her hair, Catherine wails over the cruel loss of her son, paralleling Flora's maternal plaint: "Though he fell but once," she cries, "I die every hour in his death."[129] While Catherine might rightly complain that they are playthings of the gods, Charles's response is initially measured and reminiscent of *Flora*'s denouement: he reminds her that their sons have been reclaimed by heaven and that they are already blessed with other children. Indeed, his speech initially models what would become Zephyrus's more emotionally moderated response in the revised *Flora* drama published later that year. Charles, prefiguring Jove's near identical command to Flora, urges his wife to "temper, alas, temper your pain" ("Tempra, deh, tempra il mal").[130] But his constraint soon gives way to the histrionic vacillations of the lament mode: "But, alas, where am I going? What am I thinking? … The world has become for me a cruel scene of sighs, tears, and pain."[131] Charles's paternal restraint dissolves fully into a plaint characteristic of female lament, and specifically Flora's, in not only verbal but also non-verbal expressions: just as she collapses upon her final note ("Cadde Flora a tai note") so does he ("Carlo a tai note cade"). His fall – which evokes that which the Zephyrus of the poem had risked but narrowly avoided ("e di cader dubbiosa / anch'esso ha l'alma") – only heightens his wife's anguish.[132] Shared, irremediable grief grips a couple less easily consoled than Zephyrus and Flora, to whom Jove assures future progeny. If the figure of Charles recalls the female reaction to parental grief, so too does it evoke Polyphemus's amorous lament and collapse. The duke's sorrow, however understandable, risks becoming immeasurable, unmasculine, and therefore monstrous. But just as Flora is compelled to accept her loss, the Guise, too, ultimately right themselves and carry on, albeit in "afflicted and anguished steps."[133]

Costa's final three idylls distinguish *La selva di cipressi* from Adimari and Marino's elegies. However, we again encounter a Costa who experiments with a literary tradition inherited especially from Ovid but also from contemporary predecessors like Tasso, and who offers new iterations of the lamenting woman. Costa's Ovidian reappropriations are most readily evident in a poem describing the troubled love of "Clori and Aci." Despite their shared passion, Clori elects to follow the "lying cards" ("mentitrici carte") Destiny deals her and depart for a new city, deaf to the pleas of a now deserted Aci.[134] Though Clori feigns happiness, her heart is soon secretly pierced with regret. The idyll thus bends the tradition of female lament: here the woman anguishes over a wrong she herself has committed. Yet, as if initially stuck in lament's conventional gender roles, Clori tearfully describes herself as abandoned ("abbandonata") and decries Aci's cruelty. Only after fifteen octaves of complaint does she finally perceive her own culpability: "I alone was my own undoing."[135] Just as Clori comes to this realization, she receives a letter from a distraught Aci – a clear nod to the *Heroides*, but one that inverts the gender roles of author and abandoner. Forcing herself to read this letter, whose precise contents she does not reveal, Clori launches into an increasingly agitated lament, anticipating a death that will permit her to rejoin her love. Her wish is granted in the next line: "upon these notes she fell" ("cadde a tai note"), a lexical echo that conjoins her to Polyphemus, Flora, and Charles.[136] When he learns of her death, Aci laments, faints, and then perishes. The demise of the letter writer recalls Ovid's Dido and Canace, whose suicides follow composition of their messages, but here it is the folly and remorse of a woman who abandons, rather than one who is abandoned, that prompts the demise of both lovers.[137]

The other two poems are arguably the most interesting and successful of the "lugubrious" volume, and the only ones to not end in scenes involving death. *Tirsi trafitto* (Tirsi Stabbed) begins on the shores of the Arno where Lilla plays with her children, whose resemblance to their long-departed father prompts her to lament his absence.[138] Just as she sighs his name, she hears him call out her own; he appears before her, his neck bloodied from a deep wound. The injury recalls Marino's set of homicide sonnets, decrying for example the blade that "stabbed and killed" ("trafisse e… ancise") one young man.[139] The scene is also semi-autobiographical. The year prior, Costa's companion and Medici bravo Tiberio Squilletti had been stabbed in the neck. Reportedly, the assailant's stiletto broke in two during the attack, leaving the blade dramatically embedded in Squilletti's nape, where it remained as he gave chase to his aggressor and then reported the event to the grand duke. The thrilling episode contributed to enduring interest in Squilletti's escapades. Chroniclers alleged that following this stabbing, Squilletti distracted himself during his recovery with disreputable women, at which time he met Costa and published under her name. In reality, the two already had a long-standing relationship, though this episode foreshadowed Squilletti's other near assassination in 1641 for which she would be a material witness.[140]

The poem's language is cemeterial even if its outcome is not. Upon hearing Tirsi call her name, their home transforms into a tomb and Lilla becomes "almost a living figure in marble" ("quasi di marmo effigie viva") – a line that recalls Catullus's description of Ariadne as "like some Bacchante's stone statue" (*saxea ut effigies baccantis*) as she watches Theseus's ship sail off.[141] But in a reversal of this classical theme, Lilla's anguished stoniness is not for a lover who departs but for one who arrives, seemingly at death's doorstep. Lilla fits within the lament tradition of women confronted with troubling sights: just as Ariadne cannot believe what she sees (*necdum etiam sese quae visit visere credit*), and Ariosto's Olimpia sees or believes she sees her Bireno depart ("vide lontano, o le parve vedere"), Lilla both yearns and is loath to see wounded Tirsi ("Brama vedere, e di vedere è schiva").[142]

Her lament is at first distinguished by its verbal silence, interrupted only by the sounds of her beating her chest. The narrator supplies the words she is unable to utter: "nor can she say, while dying, 'I run towards death.'"[143] Her silence gives way to wordless screaming. When she finally recovers her speech, in a twenty-eight-octave plaint, she translates his imminent death as her own: "Oh lethal steel, importunate steel, / In one with my idol you pierce and wound me."[144] Anticipating her own death, she tells her children that they will soon be orphans, a fate worse for her daughter than for her son.

Tirsi trafitto thus recounts in rustic fashion this bloody tale, official inquiries into which were still ongoing.[145] While a volume dedicated to polishing the familial legacies of the Guise, Medici, and Della Rovere, as well as other prominent men of the day, might seem an odd place for such a poem, the rationale behind its inclusion becomes clear in the final stanzas. As Lilla's lament reaches its full furor, the narrator interrupts to return our attention to Tirsi himself and, in so doing, draws the reader back to the historical present. Ferdinando II himself has taken Tirsi's/Squilletti's care under wing. The following octave thanks by name the doctors responsible for saving him: Giovanni (Nardi, court physician),[146] Antonio (most likely, Medici),[147] Battista, and (the surgeon Cesarino or Michel'Agnolo) Coverini. The poem ends with Lilla's call for justice and Ferdinando's swift response: the assailant is hanged, a justified and punitive death substituted for an unjust and prevented one.

This autobiographically tinged episode recalls *Gerusalemme liberata*'s Erminia, Tasso's pagan princess and another of Ariadne's lamenting descendents whom scholars have identified as "a powerful double for the poet himself."[148] Erminia's feverish nightmare in which the Christian hero Tancredi, injured and bleeding, calls out her name (VI.65) – as Tirsi does Lilla's – causes her to buckle on Clorinda's armour in order to go tend to him. When her plan unravels, she flees to the pastoral landscape of a shepherd, who gives her refuge and who responds to her tears with his own ("il pietoso pastor pianse al suo pianto") – a line echoed by Lilla as her children cry ("piangete al pianger mio").[149] Yet Erminia's fears are later realized when she encounters a seemingly dead Tancredi, wounded in battle with Argante; her ensuing lament nearly distracts her from curing him as only she, his faithful healer ("medica … pietosa") can.[150] Like Lilla's, Erminia's lament is premature; the injury to her beloved is not fatal, thanks to a healing intervention. But unlike Tancredi, Tirsi does not owe his recovery to the talents of the woman who loves him but instead to the medical expertise of the doctors employed in Florence and the good will of its grand duke. Costa has written Erminia's agency out of the episode, transferring it to her own patron and his court. Ferdinando uniquely forestalls death in this volume of elegies (just as he had done during the plague, according to the preface to Costa's *Istoria*).

In *Elisa infelice*, the final poem, "the author describes under the name 'Elisa' a portion of her own unlucky life."[151] This autobiographical composition revisits the theme of exile first seen in the opening poem for Charles of Lorraine: both patron and poet must wander due to their misfortunes. The poem, discussed at length in chapter 7, traces the downfall of "Elisa" – a Venus-like Roman beauty who wins votaries through her beguiling glances and sweet music. Like Clori, who fell for the lying cards ("mentitrici carte") of Destiny, Elisa lives with false hopes ("speranze mentite") until Fortune turns on her. Her beauty ignored, her songs silenced, and her name sullied, she is compelled to abandon Rome for Florence. The scene of her departure lament seems pulled straight from the stage, as she dramatically hesitates, turns, turns back again, and continually glances behind her as she leaves her native city's walls for Florence.

Though initially pacified by the Arno's pleasant diversions, Elisa (like Clori) hides her pain until finally she begs for Jove's intervention. The god sends a companion, Aminta, whose past tribulations and present passion match her own. Costa gives the reader a clue to this lover's identity, calling him "qual Tiberio" – that is, Tiberio Squilletti.[152] Aminta urges Elisa to change her circumstances through the act of writing: "You ought to gird your pen / in order to blunt heaven's scorn. / A page figured with the highest notes / can conquer the stars and subdue fate."[153] Elisa begins to write love verse, fine *scherzi*, and odes to the Tuscan kings ("re toschi").[154]

Her enthusiasm is short-lived. Misfortune returns, raining mockery and criticism upon her compositions. In response to this turn of events, to which Aminta merely resigns himself, Elisa resolves to change master and kingdom ("muterò servitù, cangirò regno").[155] She departs once more – but this time towards Parnassus to confront Apollo himself, her compositions clutched under her arm.[156] Here she encounters Italy's most illustrious poets, both male and female: Dante, Petrarch, Pietro Bembo, Giovanni Guidiccioni, Giovanni della Casa, Vittoria Colonna, Veronica Gambara, and Margherita Sarrocchi – predecessors who commiserate with her over her predicament and direct her to Apollo as one "who laments, and is tormented by, Destiny."[157] As she stands before the god, she is indeed the very picture of lament: "Elisa's lashes are heavy with pain, / And between hiccups she hides her tears, / Now she lifts her face, now she lowers / Her uncertain eyes and conceals her affliction. / At last she readies her grievous complaints."[158] Elisa declares herself the victim of Fate and Envy, who conspire to undermine her writing. Despite her tears, she also strikes a note of defiance: "I therefore snap my lyre, [...] / and pour out my inkwell."[159] Dramatizing the kind of renouncement of verse made by poets such as Petrarch, she swears off the rhymes that are her "injury and ruin."[160]

Urging Elisa to temper her sorrow, Apollo attributes her difficulties to the negligence of the present age (rather than any fault of the Arno's) and reminds her of his own tribulations. The poem ends with Elisa consoling herself that her adversities compare to those of a god ("E si consola, che se 'l Fato è rio, / Ha le sventure sue pari ad un Dio").[161] Might we detect in this final line an echo of Arianna's last verse in Rinuccini's eponymous libretto, "blessed is the heart that has its comfort in a god" ("beato è il cor che ha per conforto un Dio"), with Arianna's ultimate marriage to Bacchus over mortal Theseus here becoming Elisa's intellectual one with Apollo over Aminta?[162]

Yet Apollo cautions that the bitterness of the laurel requires his followers not to play but to weep ("più, ch'a scherzare, a lagrimare impara"), advice that speaks to the famed misfortune of poets but also urges for a pivot in Elisa's/Costa's literary style itself, from the proclamation seen in *La chitarra* that women should not write seriously to this new embrace of sober subjects, from the comic to the pathetic-tragic mode. So while Elisa's and Arianna's tales end on a similar phrase, their affective payoffs diverge: the Cretan princess calls upon all to "rejoice in my joy" ("gioite al gioire mio"), while the Roman writer emotionally girds herself for the hardship of poetic enterprise. She presents her book of funeral laments as a response to this challenge.

Conclusion

Rhetorically, Apollo's directive to "Elisa" affirms Costa's success in fulfilling the twofold objective she had outlined in her letter to Ferdinando urging the publication of her *Flora feconda*: to highlight her fealty to her patrons and to prove her poetic versatility. Interweaving political, pastoral, and personal laments, her verse considers the itinerancy of exile, mediates between the expressions of parental grief found in the two versions of *Flora feconda*, and continuously emphasizes her patrons' dynastic greatness, from their illustrious ancestors to the skilled physicians in their employ.

The volume's revisitation of the lament – which is indebted to Marino, Rossi, and Adimari, among others – echoes the original project of the *Flora* poem. Organized as a dynastically themed epic whose books correspond to the gestational period needed to produce an heir, it marries reinvestigations of familiar literary figures (the sirens, Arethusa, Galatea) with political prophecies, all set against a background of festivity. Costa takes in hand one of the Medici's long-favoured images, Florence (and its grand duchesses) as Flora, and transforms it into the stuff of epic, with the goddess's procreative mission a heroic act. As the death of Cosimino turned the celebratory work into a ultimately more tempered one, and introduced procreative disappointment into a volume envisioned for elevated patron praise, *Flora* centres lament in a manner that would shape Costa's works for the remainder of the year.

This pivot towards the sober over the salacious would be short-lived, as the following year Costa published the most burlesque of all her compositions, the ridiculous comedy *Li buffoni*. Yet her departure from Florence in 1644 also marked a move away from a literary climate that had embraced her previous brand of ribaldry. The stylistic lessons of her 1640 works – the *Flora* epic and drama, the *Selva di cipressi* verse collection, and the *Festa reale* equestrian ballet manuscript (to which the next chapter turns) – would serve her well as she sought to establish herself in print in Rome and later Paris, courts in which she would further hone her ability to meet the political messaging needs of her patrons.

Chapter Four

Starry Carousels: Equestrian Ballet and Aristocratic Astronomies

In the same period that Costa was composing her *Flora feconda* – before she knew that the immediate death of Ferdinando's and Vittoria's child would soon necessitate revisions to the poem – she was simultaneously preparing a gift manuscript for the grand duke. While presented to him together with the revised and published *Flora feconda* in early 1640, this work, a libretto for an equestrian ballet entitled *Festa reale per ballo a cavalli* (Royal Equestrian Ballet Fete), remained celebratory in nature.[1]

Equestrian ballet was perhaps the most spectacular form of Baroque musical theatre. Blending new artistic developments in opera and dance with dressage and rhetorical plotlines celebrating courtly power and harmony, the genre offered audiences an exhilarating and novel performative medium. Though not the first horse ballet crafted by a woman – that honour goes to Francesca Caccini, who composed the musical score for *La liberazione di Ruggiero dall'isola d'Alcina* (1625), which concluded with a *balletto a cavallo* – it appears to be the first, and only, female-authored libretto in the genre.[2] Costa's is an allegorical tale of good governance set against a colourful pageant of two golden chariots and sixty mounted cavaliers performing synchronized dressage moves set to vocal and instrumental music.[3] Costa's contribution to the genre places her within a select group of artists – librettists, composers, scenographers, and choreographers – who developed this exhilarating form of musical theatre at the behest of powerful patrons. While in chapter 3 we saw Costa pivot from epic grandiosity to lament, here we find her experimenting with encomiastic state spectacle in perhaps its most ambitious form.

Fascinatingly, Costa dedicated her ballet to not one but two different patrons. The libretto is therefore not merely an example of a magnificent – though puzzlingly understudied – genre, but also a clear case of how Costa rhetorically positioned herself as she manoeuvred between courts. While the Florentine grand duke was the ballet's first recipient, it is best known through its 1647 print iteration in France.[4] Then in Paris, while part of the cast of Rossi's *Orfeo*, Costa put forward her ballet as one of the season's other Carnival productions. When it was deemed too technologically difficult to stage, Costa settled for publishing it in an edition dedicated to Cardinal Jules Mazarin.[5]

The earlier manuscript has been largely overlooked. Yet the 1640 Florentine version is no scribbled, preliminary draft, but rather a fine presentation manuscript. The volume is copied out in a sophisticated hand on gilded-edged parchment, adorned with decorative details as well as an illustration likely by the acclaimed Florentine artist Stefano della Bella, and bound in a rich vellum impressed with the Medici coat of arms in gold (figs. 4.1 and 4.2). It is an elegant offering from artist to benefactor.

The text itself did not undergo substantial revisions over the intervening seven years; the plot, characters, structure, and much of the language remain the same. Costa's movement from Florence to France is dramatized, however, by a rewriting of the ballet's final scene, the most markedly encomiastic portion of the text. In this climactic moment, the characters and their horses are lifted into the heavens, becoming stars and planets, as the characters sing out praise for their respective sovereign. Incorporating astronomical debates of the early seventeenth century, Costa arranges these horsemen according to celestial imagery associated with each of her two patrons. In the manuscript for Ferdinando, they mimic the moons of Jupiter discovered by Galileo, spheres he dubbed the "Medicean Stars." No longer appropriate in France, this construction gives way in the printed text, and the horses take the shape of the fleur-de-lis and solar bodies that the French astronomer Jean Tarde identified with the house of Bourbon. Within Costa's allegorical framework, this alteration from Florentine manuscript to Parisian published libretto thus necessitates recomposing the very heavens above.

Strengthening her relationship to her patrons, Costa selected a performative genre in vogue among the aristocratic families of the seventeenth century. Staged at key state events, equestrian ballet was a vehicle for communicating the dynastic and military concerns of a court. Costa's *Festa reale* participates in such political-cultural messaging, first in Florence and then in France, by envisioning an equestrian spectacle down to its finest details, while also experimenting with its generic conventions, by incorporating important artistic collaborations, and by constructing and then refashioning her work in light of scientific debates and the propagandistic purposes to which they were adapted. Costa's relationship to horsemanship did not end with her ballet libretto. At moments spanning her literary career, she turned to forms of equestrian theatre through satire (in her *Buffoni*) and occasional poetry (most notably a broadsheet composed for the Barberini, discussed in chapter 5) as a means of showcasing the versatility of her talents and signalling her familiarity with the pastimes and aspirations of the Seicento court. Even before writing the *Festa reale*, Costa had already composed two poems celebrating Giovan Carlo de' Medici's organization of a joust and another acclaiming Cornelio Bentivoglio's performance in the 1634 *Giostra dei saraceni* organized by

Figure 4.1. *Festa reale per ballo de' cavalli di Margherita Costa romana,* first page of dedication, Florence, 1640. BNCF, Fondo Nazionale II.II.371, fol. [6]r. Printed with the permission of the Ministero della Cultura / Biblioteca Nazionale Centrale, Firenze. Further reproductions not permitted.

di globi raccogliendofi intorno alla per
fona di Gioue formeranno l'Arme de'
Sereniffimi M E D I C I, ed
à fuono di tutti li ftrumē=
ti applaude loro concor=
demente la Terra, e'l
Cielo.

Figure 4.2. *Festa reale per ballo de' cavalli di Margherita Costa romana,* final page of the *argomento,* Florence, 1640. BNCF, Fondo Nazionale II.II.371, fol. [14]r. Printed with the permission of the Ministero della Cultura / Biblioteca Nazionale Centrale, Firenze. Further reproductions not permitted.

Antonio Barberini.[6] In short, the genre represented for Costa a means of jockeying for support and clout.

Dancing War Horses

Much like Costa herself, the *balletto a cavallo* enjoyed a popularity in early modernity that has largely gone unrecognized.[7] Emerging in the late Cinquecento, the theatrical genre bridged medieval and Baroque tastes in entertainment and political showmanship. The jousts inherited from the Middle Ages, in which cavaliers competed in tests of skill, evolved into far more grandiose spectacles that paired allegorical frameworks with choreographic feats and new musical and singing practices. Expensive to produce and extensively trained for, the ballets were typically high court events. While the first documented performance took place in France in 1581, and though the ballets remained popular in Vienna until the mid-eighteenth century, during the Seicento equestrian ballet was largely the purview of the Medici court.[8] Bringing together music and movement on a grand stage, the *balletto a cavallo* emerged alongside, and extensively drew on, the two new art forms that largely defined late sixteenth- and seventeenth-century European performative culture: opera and the *ballet de cour*.[9]

Growing interest in horsemanship also contributed to the rise of ballets such as Costa's. Beginning in the early sixteenth century, first in Italy and later in France and elsewhere, noble families sent their sons to study at elite riding (dressage) academies. The masters of these riding schools published a number of training manuals.[10] In this merging of practical and theoretical pursuits, masters and pupils modelled themselves on classical predecessors such as Xenophon, whose recently rediscovered *On Horsemanship* proved foundational for the emerging equestrian schools.[11] In its idealized form, horsemanship blended utility and aesthetics. Dressage had explicit military, as well as artistic, objectives at the time. Contemporaries believed that the jumps, kicks, and turns mastered at the academies allowed them to display ferocity and dexterity on the battlefield. While more elaborate movements could prove impractical in actual combat, and while dressage and warfare required horses of different breeds and training, the equestrian schools and the performances offered useful exercises and skills in how to negotiate the tight and treacherous spaces of the battlefield through highly calibrated movements.[12] By the end of the sixteenth century, the increased use of firearms and shifting military tactics correlated with a transition from a model of cavaliers to cavalries. Drills and manoeuvres drawn from dressage, such as the caracole (left or right turn), honed riders' discipline and fostered smooth and coordinated formations.[13] Indeed, the kinds of spectatorship afforded in cities and courts could play a crucial role in developing the skills of soldiers from lower ranks, as Lodovico Melzo insisted in his 1611 *Regole militari... sopra il governo e servitio della cavalleria* (Military Rules ... for the Direction and Service of the

Cavalry), for even those men unaccustomed to handling horses themselves "will [there] have at least seen others manage them."[14]

Adding to dressage's appeal was the notion that it amplified the virtues of its practitioners. First, as with the medieval joust, the study of elite horsemanship permitted noble would-be warriors to train in times of peace and thus maintain their martial valour. This had the added benefit of allowing a sovereign to parade his forces and show off their skills through spectacle. Gracefully guiding a horse through complex, taxing movements also demonstrated a man's *sprezzatura* and refinement.[15] The rigorous footwork known as airs above the ground – manoeuvres still practised today – especially highlighted these qualities. The horse could rear up and balance on its hindquarters with its forelegs tucked in (the pesade), maintain this position while executing a series of hops (the courbette), or jump from this upright posture and, with all four legs in the air, kick its back legs out sharply (the capriole). The ability to orchestrate such technically challenging movements in tight synchrony with other riders showcased both individual mastery and collective harmony. As Kate van Orden elegantly observes, this was "a symbiosis of chivalry and civility so complete that stylized training to warfare could double as training to stylization, enough so to turn the equestrian ballet into practice for being a gentleman at large."[16]

From its inception dressage was considered not only a martial but a musical art. Riders guided their horses by counting out beats and singing commands, a musical frame that mimicked the sounds and instruments on the battlefield.[17] The master Cesare Fiaschi made this relationship explicit by including in his equestrian manual musical staves showing the rhythms required for the various movements described. Music is absolutely essential to horsemanship, he tells his would-be critics: "And since to a cavalier it might seem strange that I wanted to in-sert music into this second treatise of mine, judging it unnecessary, I will respond by saying that without measure and tempo one cannot do any of this well."[18] A decade later, Pasquale Caracciolo expressed a similar conviction in his hefty treatise, *La gloria del cavallo*. Much like tumblers, dancers, and fencers, he argues, horses require a sense of rhythm and "can never do anything beautiful or good" without music in their training; he further insists that the horse is "an animal of admirable perception that admirably delights in and moves to music."[19] Similar comparisons of horses and dancers were already to be found in Xenophon's trea-tise, which argues for a humane approach to training, stating that "what a horse does under constraint ... he does without understanding, and with no more grace than a dancer would show if he was whipped and goaded."[20] When the rider trains his steed through music, early modern masters emphasized, the horse responds in the form of dance. When executing the capriole, for instance, one sees the horse "dancing on his haunches and forearms."[21] In subsequent years, these mu-sical and balletic roots would be paired with song and storylines, creating a new performative genre. These dramatic enactments of historical battles between rival political-military powers became allegorical contests between forces of good and evil, peace and discord, with far more neatly stitched-up resolutions than possible in actual warfare.

Featuring splendid costumes and magnificent stage machinery, attended by thousands of spectators, typically performed by members of the elite houses themselves, recounted by foreign participants and ambassadors to curious publics abroad, and memorialized by lavish festival books and etchings that detailed everything from the ornate chariots to the choreography, equestrian ballet, with its marriage of dance, music, art, dramaturgy, and mechanical know-how, epitomized Baroque spectacle. The genre took special hold in the Florentine grand duchy. Regularly staged for court weddings and other important celebrations that called for a display of pageantry, equestrian ballet allowed the Medici to re-wash their mercantile origins in aristocratic colours while vaunting an image of military might, however illusory. This ennobling objective is especially evident in Costa's text, the title of which emphasizes the fete's "royal" quality. Similarly, the synchronized dances and allegorical victories of virtue over vice or discord allowed organizers (in Florence as elsewhere) to communicate both power and unity. Whether performed by equine or human bodies, courtly dance employed aesthetic devices infused with political meaning. In the words of Roy Strong, the *ballet de cour* was "the evocation by means of art – visual symbol, allegory, music and movement – of the macrocosm-microcosm analogy and through that the tuning of the aspirations of earth to the harmonies of heaven."[22] As the festival books drive home, equestrian ballet also allowed the court to measure its entertainments against those of antiquity. Comparing these ballets to the games of ancient Greece and Rome, as well as the more modern Florentine *calcio storico* (historical soccer) and Pisan *gioco del ponte* (bridge game), contests organized by wise governments for the betterment of their youth, the poet and librettist Andrea Salvadori concludes that "superior to all the other most beautiful and noble games are those done on horseback, and superior to all the others are those worthy of being done by princes."[23] By staging and starring in horse ballets, the Medici crafted their public image as classical heroes.

When Costa dedicated her manuscript to Ferdinando in 1640, equestrian ballets and the publications memorializing them were well-established at court. A booklet distributed to spectators and a subsequently published festival book record the first Medici performance, the 1608 *Ballo e giostra de' venti* (Dance and Joust of the Winds), part of the nuptial celebrations for Cosimo II and Maria Maddalena.[24] An etching by Mathiew Greuter shows the square transformed into a vast theatre seating thousands – with additional spectators peeking out of windows and down from rooftops – gathered to watch the navigation-themed dance.[25] Surrounded by two dozen musicians dressed as tritons, tempests, and sirens, and accompanied by a whale-drawn carriage, King Aeolus (played by Francesco de' Medici) executed a series of dances with the winds, represented by thirty-two mounted riders (led by

Cosimo). The distributed booklet aided literate spectators in orienting themselves in this new form of pageantry. It pairs Greuter's etching – where key elements are numbered and lettered – with a synopsis, list of participants, poetry, and choreography descriptions. Those unable to read along could still delight in the unfamiliar sight of the dancing steeds: "With great attention the entire population beheld this spectacle as a magnificent thing, since it was done with horses, and as a bizarre novelty, since animals were made to dance."[26]

The new archduchess had a passion for such equestrian spectacles, and in 1616 the Medici returned to Piazza Santa Croce with another ballet in her honour, *La guerra d'amore*, in which two exotic cavalier kings – played by her husband and his brother – fought for the hand of an Indian queen. Jacques Callot contributed splendid etchings to the festival book, portraying the ballet's sumptuous chariots, 164 soldiers and "savages," and 16 sets of choreography.[27] Though impressed by the costumes, machines, and numerous players, the spectators marvelled especially at the innovative horsemanship choreographed by Angiolo Ricci and led by the Medici: while musicians played and sang, "[the riders] made their horses dance to the delight and astonishment of all who watched ... and the horses did such varied and uniform movements that everyone's eyes battled their ears."[28] Referring the reader to Callot's choreographic grid, Salvadori describes the specific series of formations that merited such lofty praise. In this way, readers of the festival book could recall or visualize with a technical aid the feats of horsemanship displayed. Several months later, Salvadori published another festival book in anticipation of his *Guerra di bellezza*, a horse battle and ballet staged as a backdrop to the delicate negotiations for a marriage between Cosimo's sister and the heir to the duchy of Urbino.[29] The publication (with etchings by Callot) allowed young Claudia and Federico Ubaldo della Rovere, their parents, and other guests to identify the dynastic iconography incorporated into the spectacle's elaborate set of chariots, as well as to anticipate the formation of a heart across the arena stage by the ballet's 300 performers. So varied and beautiful would the *balletto a cavallo* be, Salvadori underscored, that the character Fame would conclude the spectacle by announcing to all the other cities of Italy and Europe that the Medici had achieved perfection in the genre. Buoyed by these successes, Maria Maddalena commissioned three additional ballets and musical jousts during the 1620s: *Le fonti d'Ardenna* (1623) and *La disfida d'Ismeno* (1628), both with libretti by Salvadori, and that for Caccini's *La liberazione di Ruggiero*, with libretto by Ferdinando Saracinelli.[30]

Costa may have had the opportunity to witness a ballet firsthand the following decade when the city celebrated the 1637 wedding of Ferdinando II and Vittoria della Rovere. The family staged a wildly successful opera, *Le nozze degli dei*, followed by an equestrian spectacle. Revisiting the chivalric themes from his and Caccini's earlier Ariosto-inspired work, Saracinelli now depicted the comparable liberation of Rinaldo in Tasso's *Gerusalemme liberata*.[31] Perhaps self-conscious about a narrative that may have seemed a tad stale, the festival book author emphasizes the majesty of Ricci's choreography and its aristocratic execution:

> Besting even himself, [Agniolo Ricci] has gained eternal fame. He owes a debt of gratitude to the princes and the cavaliers who brought his design to life so well. It is truly characteristic of this court, and this city, where cavaliers – dedicating themselves continuously to chivalric exercises, shifting from ballets and tournaments to real wars and battles – have at all times, by land and by sea, given proof of Tuscan valour.

> Vincendo egli se stesso s'è messo in possesso d'una eterna fama. Ben è dovere ch'ei ne professi particolare obbligatzione, & a principi & a gl'altri cavalieri, che così bene hanno colorito quanto da lui era stato disegnato. Propria prerogativa di questa corte, e di questa città, dove impiegandosi ognora i cavalieri in esercizi cavallereschi, trapassando da balli, e da tornei alle vere guerre, & a' veri combattimenti hanno in ogni tempo, e per terra, e per mare dato saggio del Toscano valore.[32]

Insisting on a partnership between artists and patrons – who command in theatre and war, respectively – the book affirms the ballet's dual role as an act of courtly entertainment and an expression of Florentine military might. An accompanying etching by Della Bella underscores these messages: in addition to sixteen choreographic schema, the image is framed by two mounted Tuscan cavaliers who survey both the arena and the territory that lies beyond (fig. 4.3).

While libretti and festival books played an important function in memorializing ballets and the political-military messages that governed them, they needed not simply record an event. We see one such example in the book that was published and disseminated in advance of the ballet *Il mondo festeggiante*, commemorating the 1661 marriage of Cosimo III and Marguerite Louise of Orléans.[33] This volume offers a detailed plot synopsis, lyrics, descriptions of the battles and livery, and etchings by Della Bella, one illustrating twenty-four different sets of choreography and two others depicting a packed Boboli theatre, stunning machinery (including a colossal Atlas that moved across the stage), and a towering archway (fig. 4.4).

Written and sketched so as to seem *ex eventu* rather than anticipatory, the book simultaneously imagined and shaped the audience's reaction of awe. In one passage, for example, author Giovanni Andrea Moniglia encourages the reader-spectators to blur the boundaries between reality and mimesis, thereby subscribing to the genre's martial premise: "Although the battle was fake, those valiant fighters showed a tenacious desire for victory, though they encountered every kind of danger and exposed themselves to every sort of risk. And, having souls of valour in their courageous breasts, in striving to win they did not care if they lived or died."[34]

Such examples suggest a fluid relationship between text and performance. This context helps situate Costa's *Festa reale*, a work twice circulated but never staged.

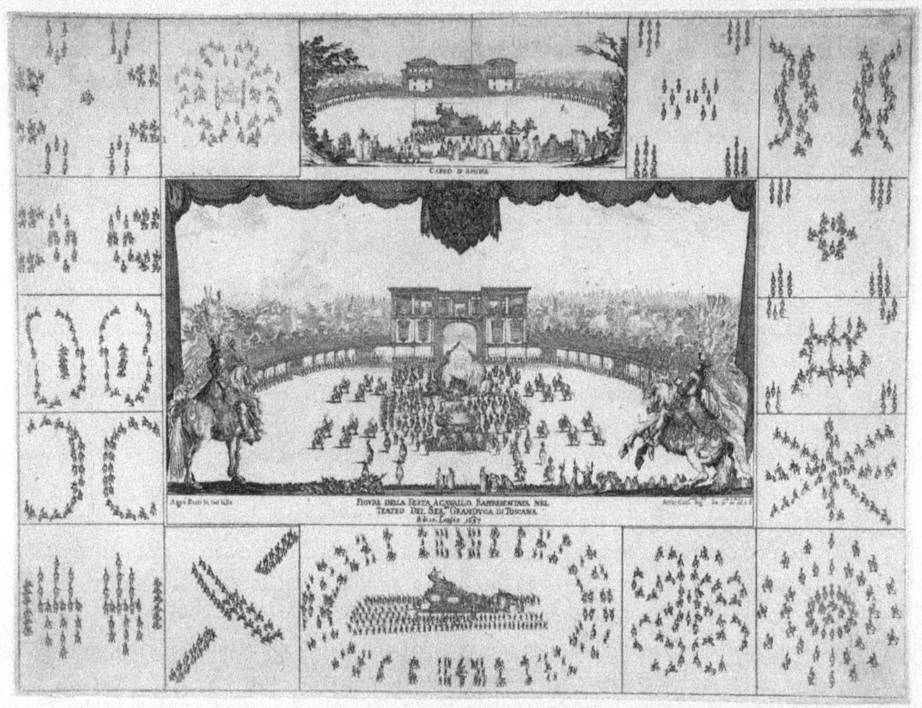

Figure 4.3. Stefano della Bella, etching of horse ballet, in Ferdinando Bardi, *Descrizione delle feste fatte in Firenze per le reali nozze de' serenissimi sposi Ferdinando II, gran duca di Toscana, e Vittoria, principessa d'Urbino*, 1637. Courtesy of The Metropolitan Museum of Art (www.metmuseum.org), The Elisha Whittelsey Collection, The Elisha Whittelsey Fund, 1967.

While the French would later forgo a performance due to the technical impracticalities the ballet posed, in Florence there seems to have been no event on the calendar suited to such a spectacle. Costa acknowledges this lack of an "opportune occasion" in her dedication to Ferdinando but urges the grand duke not to let this fact impede his patronage of her since, she argues, truly great princes enjoy their subjects' offerings regardless of when they are presented.[35] Yet this letter might also explain why a performance never materialized. After addressing the thorny issue of timing, Costa indicates that she is presenting her *Festa reale* manuscript to the grand duke alongside her *Flora feconda*. Given that the poem on the birth – and then death – of the Medici prince and the ballet are dated one day apart (26 and 27 January, respectively), and that Costa casts them as companion pieces, she may have hoped originally to stage the ballet as part of any natal festivities, plans

Figure 4.4. Stefano della Bella, etching in Giovanni Andrea Moniglia, *Il mondo festeggiante*, 1661. Digital image courtesy of the Getty's Open Content Program.

that would have been swiftly terminated. Whatever her reasons, Costa gifted her patron a libretto for a performance she clearly knew would not come to light, at least for the foreseeable future. Yet with its meticulous lists of squadron cavaliers, mottoes, and liveries, together with its exhaustive synopsis and stage directions, Costa's text in many ways presents itself as something more akin to a festival book than a mere script. Though the stage directions are composed using the future tense, the *Festa reale* reads like an event recorded as much as an event proposed but never realized. In other words, though unable to bring her spectacle to the stage, Costa equates it with other great ballets through her use of the page. In so doing, she seems to suggest that a spectacle seen in the mind's eye through the aid of a written text can stand in for an actual performance.

The *Festa reale* offers its readers an easily intelligible allegorical plotline. In the opening scene, Honour, Virtù (Virtue/Might), and Valour organize mock cavalry battles along the Arno.[36] Honour delights in the military showmanship displayed by the dancing squadrons and their "king" commanders, Mars and Apollo, and sprinkles the combatants with waters from his fountain. Unbeknownst to him, this water has been contaminated by Discord, who wreaks havoc on earth after

Jove denies her the status of celestial goddess. Instantly infected with hostility, the cavaliers erupt into actual blows, staged through a more violent dance. Honour is unable to break up the fight, and Discord, disguised as Peace, offers assistance. The three Virtues are baffled when the intervention of "Peace" further inflames the brawl. Hearing the cacophony below, Jove descends and reveals the true identity of the figure posing as Peace: Discord's veil falls away, her serpents slide out, and her telltale bloody red gown appears. As the Virtues and the chorus express their horror, the earth quakes, and from the abyss arises a dragon that shreds Discord's coverings. Virtù and Valour place her in chains, while Honour touches the combatants with fountain water freshly cleansed by the fronds of his laurel crown. As the ferocity abates, clouds emerge from either side of the theatre and lift the Virtues, the god-kings, and the cavaliers up into the heavens.

The *Festa reale*'s elemental plot provides an architectural shell upon which Costa crafts a dazzling production intended to astound her reader-spectators, as she outlines in the substantial *argomento* and concluding stage directions.[37] Within a "large and magnificent theatre," she envisions an immense archway above Honour's fountain and a basanite altar with the inscription *honori sacrum* (devoted to honor).[38] She introduces her knightly dancers into this larger-than-life setting with full pageantry. Guided by Virtù, Apollo drives a gem-encrusted golden chariot with the motto *omnia lustrat* (illuminates all) and is followed by thirty cavaliers outfitted in silver, gold, and red, representing the phases of daylight. Led by Apollo's lieutenant, Phosphorus (the Morning Star), these mounted paladins have mythological names associated with constellations and are divided into white, gold, and red squadrons. From the other side of the theatre arrives Mars's chariot, led by Valour and ridden by Honour, upon whose exterior are displayed instruments of war and the motto *omnia terret* (frightens all). The lieutenant Hesperus (the Evening Star) commands thirty cavaliers who each bear an allegorical name, such as Fear and Fury, and are cloaked in a rainbow of colours "in order to make the show more beautiful" and to reflect the "capriciousness of soldiers."[39] All sixty cavaliers are accompanied by uniformed squires holding shields painted with emblems and inscribed with mottoes, each of which Costa details. In the finale, these sixty men and their horses are to be transported by the theatre's machinery into the sky and transformed into stars. In short, what may at first read as a bare-bones libretto instead anticipates an explosion of colour, language, and images across the stage floor and into the heavens.

Music and dance would of course accompany this visual marvel. In structuring these elements, Costa demonstrates both her knowledge of genre conventions and her ability to rework them. Following a model dating to 1608, for example, she employs shifts in mood and instrumentation to highlight plot developments.[40] But Costa, perhaps in a nod to her own background as a singer, goes a step further and sets the storyline itself in motion through her characters' response to music. A symphony of "the sweetest instruments" (cimbali, lutes, theorbos) plays as the three Virtues first enter the stage.[41] Hearing these notes, Honour urges his companions to forgo such songs that "calm souls and soften hearts" in lieu of more martial pursuits.[42] Again, contemporaries took seriously the notion that dressage trained elite horsemen for armed conflict even, or especially, in times of peace and that its foundational objective was therefore military in nature. Within ballet narratives, these precepts often manifested themselves in a set sequence: a battle is quelled by an external, often divine, force and a more harmonious horse dance then concludes the spectacle.[43]

Costa inverts this pattern. In the first of two dances, the two sets of cavaliers stage a "peaceful and graceful arms dance," an equestrian tournament put on for the approval and entertainment of Virtù and Valour and set to the music of cornets, flutes, trombones, and similar instruments.[44] "Where there is no fury," Virtù approvingly declares, "the war is sweet."[45] This, adds Honour, is a war that "resembles dance and is of peace."[46] Honour rewards the riders with words of praise and water from his sacred font; the initial plot interruption is therefore not one that arrests the ferocity of combat but one that prizes the glory of horsemanship. When rancour is introduced via the polluted fountain, however, those emulated battles instantaneously transform into actual warfare between rival kings, a clash that now terrifies the Virtues even though it is still performed through dance – "un ballo di battaglia" (battle dance) that only Jove can stop.[47] The "sweet war" of courtly divertissement has become the "bitter war" of real conflict.[48] The fury of the dance is now punctuated by trumpets, drums, and lightning.[49] Through this inversion of genre conventions, Costa dramatizes the martial potential understood to be at the core of equestrian ballet. More than a battle so heroically performed as to blur the boundaries between reality and fiction – such as that described by Moniglia above – the *Festa reale*'s doubled dances suggest that only a narrow brink divides delightful spectacle and actual combat. With the subjugation of Discord, the "sound of trumpets gives way to the symphony of most sweet instruments" and the musical landscape returns to its initial state.[50] The spectacle concludes with these same instruments celebrating the concord struck between Heaven and Earth as the cavaliers, gods, and Virtues begin their starry ascent.[51] Only when peaceful resolution reharmonizes the terrestrial and celestial spheres – here through the literal passage of the combatants into the heavens – is there a return to the "sweetness" associated with force that is trained and ready but abeyant.

If equestrian ballet was a visually spectacular medium for rhetorical messages about statecraft – if it permitted a ruler to showcase his military strength while simultaneously arguing for the consonance between his earthly reign and the cosmos – then the *Festa reale* is more than just a loose but entertaining allegorical drama about peaceful governance. With this work, Costa signalled her familiarity with elite court culture and her ability to wield its symbols effectively and innovatively. Delivered alongside her *Flora feconda* – a poem that celebrates the Medici lineage – her manuscript applauds Medicean political and cultural authority. Nowhere is this strategy clearer than in the final scene, to which we now turn.

An Astronomical Finale

With Discord vanquished, the ballet's final spectacle begins as mechanized clouds lift Apollo, Mars, and the sixty mounted cavaliers into the air. It is here, in the thematic and technological climax, that the manuscript and print versions diverge. In the original manuscript, as the stage spins around to reveal a new empyreal setting, the horsemen become stars while Apollo and Mars are transformed into planets. The latter are joined by Saturn, Mercury, Venus, and the Moon, and together these six globes encircle Jove. Within extensive stage directions outlining their formation, Costa includes an illustration showing Jove seated in the heavens and orbited by these planetary spheres (fig. 4.5).

This solar system clearly assumes the shape of the Medici coat of arms. Thus positioned, the characters praise the Florentine court:

> VALOUR: Watch, as they happily form
> the emblem of the Medici rulers,
> in whose highest splendour
> Flora accepts glory, and the Appennini, honour.
>
> JOVE: The honour of these globes delights,
> and as long as my resplendence endures
> in this kingdom, so too shall that
> of the most beautiful Medicean Stars.
>
> HONOUR: Where Ferdinando reigns Discord is banished,
> and with his luminous torch and mighty stars,
> there is heavenly peace.

> VALORE: Mira, che forman lieti
> De' regnatori Medici l'insegna;
> Ne' cui sommi splendori
> Flora ha le glorie, ed Apennin gli onori.
>
> GIOVE: De' globi l'honor piace.
> E tempo fia, che in regio si belle
> Mia pompa anco saran Medicee Stelle.
>
> HONORE: Ove FERNANDO regna
> Sbandita è la Discordia, e 'n ricca face
> Con stelle di virtù v'è ciel di pace.[52]

The spectacle ends by coupling the reverberating name of Ferdinando and the sparkling image of the *stelle medicee* (Medicean Stars).

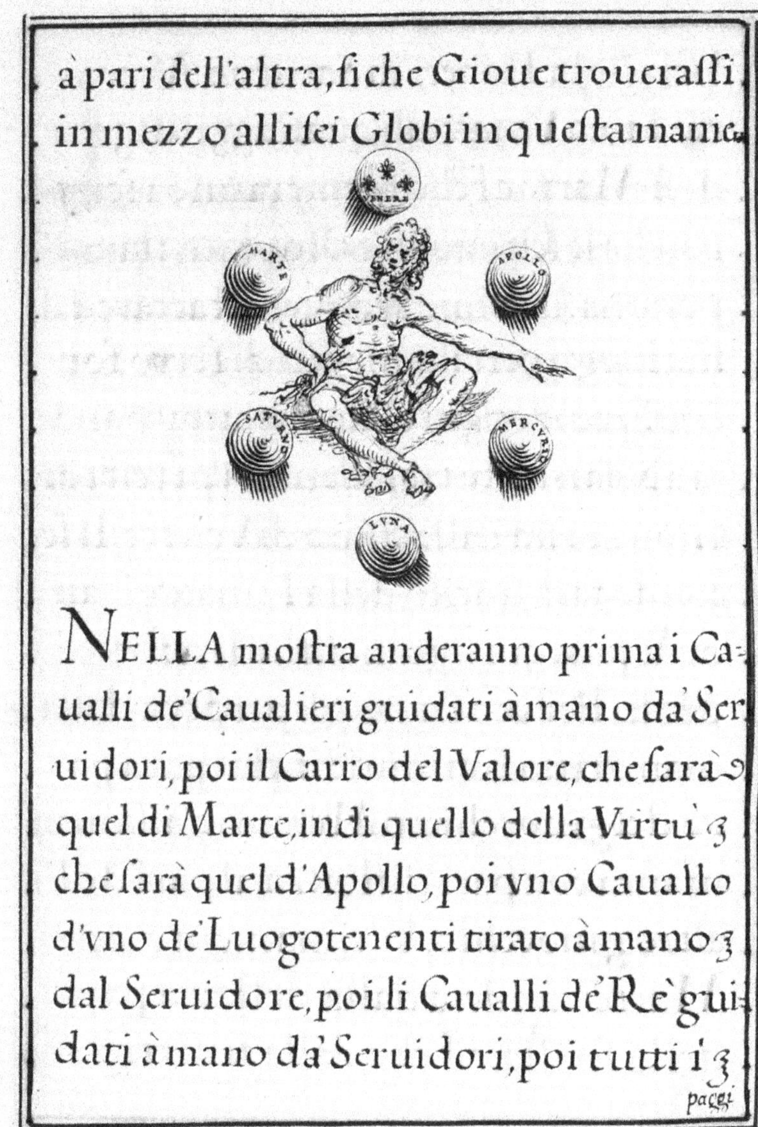

à pari dell'altra, sì che Gioue trouerassi
in mezzo alli sei Globi in questa manie⸗

N ELLA mostra anderanno prima i Ca⸗
ualli de'Caualieri guidati à mano da'Ser
uidori, poi il Carro del Valore, che farà
quel di Marte, indi quello della Virtù
che farà quel d'Apollo, poi vno Cauallo
d'vno de'Luogotenenti tirato à mano
dal Seruidore, poi li Caualli de'Rè gui⸗
dati à mano da'Seruidori, poi tutti i

Figure 4.5. *Festa reale per ballo de' cavalli di Margherita Costa romana*. Jove and the Medicean Stars, figure in stage directions, Florence, 1640. BNCF, II.II.371, fol. [36]v. Printed with the permission of the Ministero della Cultura / Biblioteca Nazionale Centrale, Firenze. Further reproductions not permitted.

"Medicean Stars" was, of course, no idle turn of phrase in seventeenth-century Florence. Looking to the heavens with his telescope in 1610, Galileo discovered four of Jupiter's moons.[53] The publication of his findings, *Sidereus Nuncius* (The Starry Messenger), provided the first concrete evidence that there were at least parts of the universe that did not move with the earth as their centre. In a bid for the patronage of Cosimo II, Galileo christened these moons the *stelle medicee*.[54] Mario Biagioli has argued in his study of Galileo-as-courtier that by connecting the celestial moons to the Medici dynasty, the astronomer tapped into an already familiar "master narrative" that likened Cosimo and his heirs to the cosmos.[55] Though rewarded by the grand duke with a choice post in Tuscany, and elevated to immediate international celebrity, Galileo initially encountered resistance from those unable or unwilling to replicate his findings. He succeeded in swaying opinion by demonstrating how to properly use the telescope for celestial observation, while his allies initiated a campaign to promote the discovery. Figures like court poet Andrea Salvadori, seen above as an author of equestrian ballet libretti, crystallized the new Medicean universe through verse.[56] The campaign also included images and illustrations, as well as state spectacles, such as a 1613 Florentine *barriera* in which Jove arrived on the scene surrounded by these Medicean Stars, "discovered by the Florentine Galileo Galilei, His Highness's mathematician of the rarest intelligence, and peerless in our times for his work with the marvellous telescope."[57] Giovanni Villifranchi, author of the *Descrizzione* and some of the poetry (alongside Alessandro Adimari, Ottavio Rinuccini, and Jacopo Cicognini, the latter composing the verse on the Medicean Stars), described Galileo's choice of nomenclature as a modern parallel to the ancient practice of "translating worthy heroes into the heavens."[58] This brand of imagery fit neatly with the Medici's long-standing efforts to align themselves with a tradition of classical heroism by inscribing them onto the cosmos and thereby making them, in all senses, stellar.

Although Costa echoed this established tribute to the grand ducal family, her timing may at first seem odd. She composed the *Festa reale* not in the wake of Galileo's 1610 discovery but rather after his 1633 Inquisition trial, when he remained under house arrest in nearby Arcetri. Attitudes towards Galileo were more tempered in Florence than in Rome, however. Ferdinando personally visited him shortly after his return to Tuscany, and the Medici family supported a posthumous publication of his collected works (excluding the condemned *Dialogue Concerning the Two Chief World Systems*) in the 1650s.[59] While explicit evocation of the *stelle medicee* re-emerged in art of the 1660s, more oblique references appeared earlier in locations such as the Sala di Giove in Palazzo Pitti.[60] The Medicean orbs also maintained a visible place in print. In the 1620s, the publisher Pietro Cecconcelli began including the phrase *alle stelle medicee* on title pages (including that of the libretto for *La liberazione di Ruggiero*), at times incorporating a device depicting Jupiter's four moons. Amadore Massi and Lorenzo Landi inherited this device, printing it on the works of Galileo's followers even into the 1630s – including

Figure 4.6. Gasparo Mola, reverse of a medal for Cosimo II de' Medici, in or after 1610. Image courtesy of Wikimedia Commons.

Costa's *Flora feconda*.[61] As Eileen Reeves aptly states, "this discreet image suggest[s] Florentine loyalty to the astronomer both before and after his abjuration and condemnation."[62] Its continued use also indicates that the Medici were fond of their celestial associations.

Of the various representations of the Medicean Stars that circulated shortly after their discovery, one in particular stands out for its continuities with the illustration in Costa's manuscript. The work in question is a commemorative medal cast by the goldsmith Gaspare Mola for Cosimo in or after 1610 (fig. 4.6). The reverse shows Jove seated in the heavens, an eagle at his knee, thunderbolts readied in his right hand and a sceptre in his left, and his crown framed on either side by the four Medicean Stars.[63] The medal predates Costa's manuscript by three decades, yet a side-by-side comparison highlights their resemblance. The position of the legs, arms, and especially the ankles is notably similar. The thunderbolts are grasped in a comparable manner, and while its position has shifted, the eagle is still represented in profile. All that has substantially changed is the presence of the sceptre and the change from the original four satellites to the new set of six inspired by the Medici emblem.

Who created Costa's illustration? The image is unsigned, making any attribution conjectural. The most likely candidate, however, is Stefano della Bella. As we have already seen, Della Bella provided the author portrait for *La chitarra* and *Lettere amorose*, as well the frontispiece for *Li buffoni* and perhaps *La selva di cipressi*. Although Costa dedicated her libretto to Ferdinando at a time when Della Bella was working in France, the same was true when he supplied the frontispiece for *Li buffoni* the following year, meaning that this distance did not prove an impediment to their collaboration. Indeed, even when Della Bella lived outside of his native Florence, as he did from 1633 to 1650, he returned periodically in order to execute works commissioned by the Medici, such as the festival book commemorating Ferdinando and Vittoria della Rovere's wedding. He was especially recognized for his ability to portray court festivals. Of particular historical and aesthetic value are his prints for equestrian ballets (see, for example, fig. 4.3), impressive for their size, detail, and portrayal of choreography. Della Bella's connections to the genre would have made him an ideal collaborator for Costa's manuscript. The artist had also already worked with Galilean themes in his frontispiece to the 1632 *Dialogue Concerning the Two Chief World Systems* (fig. 4.7). On the banner in the heavens above Aristotle, Ptolemy, and Copernicus, the Medicean balls encircle the paired names of scientist and patron – now Cosimo's son, Ferdinando II. The emblematic orbs recall the Medicean Stars, discussed in Day 2 of the dialogue, as well as the planetary spheres.[64] Here, as in Costa's manuscript, Jupiter's four moons and the Medici's six *palle* have been integrated.

Della Bella would again explore these themes in his frontispiece for the aforementioned 1656 *Opere di Galileo Galilei* (fig. 4.8).[65] This elegant etching depicts "Galileo Galilei in the act of showing the *stelle medicee* to three damsels representing three sciences [Optics, Mathematics, and Astronomy]."[66] Although the collection did not include the condemned *Dialogo*, Galileo gestures towards the heavens, where – in a clear allusion to a Copernican universe – six Medicean balls circle a glowing sun.[67] The topmost of these *palle*-planets is Jupiter, itself orbited by the four Medicean Stars. These astronomical themes again intersected with courtly spectacle in Della Bella's etchings for the 1661 *Il mondo festeggiante* (fig. 4.4). Halting the cavaliers' equestrian battle, Jove descends from the heavens through the triumphal arch accompanied by the four *stelle medicee*.[68] Beginning to dance, he executes an intricate series of courbettes alongside his starry companions (fig. 4.9).[69] If in the Trecento Dante envisioned dancing stars wheeling through paradise, by the Seicento those heavenly stars could perform an equestrian carousel.

This detail from *Il mondo festeggiante* is especially noteworthy because of its compositional continuities with both the Mola medal and the *Festa reale* illustration. Here again is Jove seated upon the clouds amid the Medicean Stars, with the zigzagged thunderbolts clutched in his right hand and his eagle in profile, though it has now returned to his left side. The commonalities between all three images

Figure 4.7. Stefano della Bella, frontispiece for *Dialogo di Galileo Galilei*, 1632. Etching. Courtesy of The Metropolitan Museum of Art (www.metmuseum.org). Bequest of Grace M. Pugh, 1985.

Figure 4.8. Stefano della Bella, frontispiece for *Opere di Galileo Galilei*, 1656. Etching. Courtesy of The Metropolitan Museum of Art (www.metmuseum.org), The Elisha Whittelsey Collection, The Elisha Whittelsey Fund, 1951 (by exchange).

Figure 4.9. *Il mondo festeggiante* (detail). Digital image courtesy of the Getty's Open Content Program.

could be explained by a Della Bella attribution for the *Festa reale* illustration; in his youth, the artist had apprenticed at Mola's workshop, where he may have seen or sketched the preparatory materials or, depending on its dating, perhaps even the medal itself.[70] While the *Festa reale* illustration moves away from the long, rough lines Della Bella often used in his drawings, its short hatching and rough facial features recall some of his prints from roughly the same period, such as an image of Jupiter from a 1644 pack of mythologically themed playing cards commissioned by Cardinal Mazarin (fig. 4.10).[71]

Della Bella's relationship to both Galilean themes and equestrian ballets makes him a promising candidate for Costa's artistic contributor. When incorporating the sublimest of the metaphors for Medicean cultural-historical predominance into her stately pageant, Costa likely turned to her primary artistic associate, the leading Florentine draftsman of the day, Stefano della Bella.[72] Though unable to stage her ballet and thus project her grand finale's tribute to the Medici into the heavens themselves, she shrewdly incorporated the visual element into her otherwise imaginative libretto through the artistic memorialization of the Medicean

Figure 4.10. Stefano della Bella, Jupiter from *Jeu de la Mythologie* (Game of mythology), 1644. Etching. Courtesy of The Metropolitan Museum of Art (www.metmuseum.org). Bequest of Phyllis Massar, 2011.

Stars. The result is an elegant presentation manuscript clearly aimed at further cultivating Ferdinando's favour. Seven years later, it was in Paris that the *Festa reale* played out its final act.

The New Constellations of the Parisian Print

In 1646, Costa received an invitation to sing at the Parisian court of Anne of Austria, queen and regent mother of France. A period of Italian opera had arrived in Paris, driven largely by the ascension of Italian-born Cardinal Mazarin to Chief Minister. The concretization of Mazarin's authority in France following the deaths of his predecessor, Cardinal Richelieu, in late 1642 and of Louis XIII a few months later allowed him to begin shaping cultural policy alongside the queen regent, an unshakeable ally happy to give him free rein and whose passion for musical theatre he shared and keenly entertained. Following performances brought to Paris of Francesco Sacrati's *La finta pazza* and Francesco Cavalli's *Egisto* in 1645 and 1646, respectively, plans began for a new work the next year: Luigi Rossi's *L'Orfeo*, the first Italian opera written specifically for a French audience.[73]

Mazarin's agents coordinated the selection and transport of Italian musicians to Paris. Included on their list were both Costa sisters, Margherita in the role of June and Anna Francesca as Eurydice.[74] When *Orfeo* premiered at the Palais Royal in March, it drew large crowds particularly excited about the superb stage machinery. The Tuscan ambassador described a theatre so packed that he was able to find a seat with his peers thanks only to the intervention of Anna Francesca Costa.[75] The production also enchanted Anne herself, resulting in six additional performances through May. During this Parisian sojourn, Costa courted her new hosts through writing as well as song. With Mazarin's assistance, she published a trio of works with the official crown publisher and director of the Imprimerie royale, Sébastien Cramoisy. Two were new volumes of poetry. She addressed *La selva di Diana* to Marie Christine, Duchess of Savoy, who had recently invited her to sing in Turin. This work is the subject of chapter 6's study of regency; for now, it suffices to say that it includes a lengthy poem lionizing Anne as the guardian of a new golden age in France. Mindful of Anne's favourable attitude towards Italian performers, Costa further dedicated to her a full volume of celebratory verse, *La tromba di Parnaso*, which panegyrizes the regent and members of her household, from ambassadors to ladies-in-waiting. A further set of three poems lauds Mazarin, including in verse honouring his support of her publishing activities.[76] Costa artfully concludes the volume with a series of poems celebrating Anne and Mazarin's recent crowning cultural achievement, the staging of *Orfeo*. Verse addressed to Rossi, the castrato Pasqualini, and the librettist Francesco Buti praise their individual and collective success on the Seine.[77] (Notably excluded is the opera's leading couple: the castrato Atto Melani, the queen's favourite who starred as Orpheus, and Costa's sister, who played his lost bride, though the volume as a whole does conclude on the word "Eurydice.") Costa thus applauds the cultural program of her hosts while also positing the activities of Italian writers, composers, and performers as a treasure for the court and a highlight of her volume.

The final sonnet, dedicated to Buti, opens with a declaration of Costa's own literary aspirations – "Buti, I too seek the revered laurel" – but goes on to insist that he has received greater gifts from the Muses than she.[78] Depending on the timing of publication, there may have been more than conventional humility behind Costa's suggestion that she trailed the librettist in achievements. Not long before this, she had aspired to an even grander entrée into Parisian theatrical circles. Word circulated at the beginning of the year that another work was to be staged after *Orfeo*. In the running were Giovan Battista Andreini's musical comedy *La Ferinda* and Costa's *Festa reale*, which she revamped for the French court.[79] The addition of the April and May performances of *Orfeo* to the calendar came at the expense of both works, neither of which was ultimately staged.[80] According to the seventeenth-century music and dance theorist Claude-François Ménestrier, the

Festa reale's technological demands proved a decisive factor in Mazarin's decision to reject the ballet. Although master stage designer Giacomo Torelli was on hand, engineering crowd-pleasing machines for *Orfeo* with the assistance of Stefano della Bella, and although Nicola Sabbatini's 1638 illustrated manual on the subject offered mechanical designs for a variety of ways to move clouds and characters through space, Costa's vision was too grand even for their great talents.[81] It simply was not feasible to lift sixty horses and their riders into the sky. Mazarin stuck with *Orfeo* but helped Costa publish her libretto, which she dedicated to him.

Following in the footsteps of Henry Prunières, several scholars have cited Ménestrier's account as evidence of Costa's failures, but without acknowledging his high estimation of her "genius and talent for poetry."[82] Reflecting back on this moment more than thirty years later, Ménestrier saw fit to include an exhaustive two-and-a-half-page synopsis of the *Festa reale* in his *Des représentations en musique anciennes et modernes* (Performances in Ancient and Modern Music) and to thereby place Costa within a constellation of noteworthy contemporary figures in musical history.[83] The detail with which Ménestrier sets out the ballet's plot and staging, down to the squadrons' various mottoes, indicates that he read her work in its print manifestation and considered it a significant enough contribution to the French musical scene for extended citation.

Costa's decision to put her *Festa reale* in the running for the French Carnival production was likely as motivated by strategy as it was by convenience. More than merely dusting off an old, unused libretto to see if this time around she could get it staged, as her few biographers have implied, she sought to capitalize on French interest in Italian musical and theatrical performance by proposing a genre with French roots but currently dominated by Italian practice. She may even have been sensitive to the fact that the last great equestrian ballet staged in France was on the occasion of Louis and Anne's engagement in 1612.[84] Presenting her libretto to these new patrons necessitated some textual repackaging, though much of this was admittedly rather minimal. Costa brazenly duplicated most of the original dedicatory letter, swapping in Mazarin's name for Ferdinando's and adjusting elements of her encomium here and there. The plot trajectory remains constant, though the battles are transplanted from the banks of the Arno to those of the Seine. The key deviation in the printed text from the manuscript occurs at the ballet's climax. The exaltation of Florence is replaced by a substantially longer passage, one that embraces the French kingdom as a haven for "afflicted heart[s]," exalts Queen Anne, and equates the young Louis XIV with the figure of Peace.[85] The celestial choreography, however, has been radically reconfigured. Gone are the six planets that orbit Jove; the elevated cavaliers and horses instead outline the shape of three fleurs-de-lis. Jove himself extols not the Medicean but the "Bourbonian Stars."[86]

Unlike the facile exchange of names in the dedicatory letters, this transition from Medici to Bourbon is no perfunctory substitution made simply to add a more French flourish to a previously Florentine text. Like *stelle medicee*, the phrase "Bourbonian Stars" alluded to a specific astronomical debate, in this case on the nature of sunspots. Astronomers in the first decades of the seventeenth century endeavoured to explain the nature of these dark marks, which the telescope made more readily visible on the sun's surface. Hanging in the balance was the Aristotelian notion of an unchanging and unblemished sun. In the 1620s the French canon Jean Tarde entered the fray. According to his diaries, he first learned of these spots from Galileo himself during a 1614 visit to Florence.[87] While Galileo believed them to be clouds in the solar atmosphere, Tarde later joined others (most notably the Jesuit astronomer Christoph Scheiner) in maintaining that they were instead bodies orbiting the sun.[88] Taking his cues from Galileo's *Sidereus Nuncius*, Tarde published his observations in a volume entitled *Borbonia Sidera* and dedicated it to Louis XIII, monarch of the house of Bourbon, in hope of securing patronage.[89] In this, and his 1623 French translation, *Les astres de Borbon*, Tarde posited that a multitude of satellites – even as many as thirty – circled the sun. His titular homage to Galileo, it should be noted, ignored the latter's insistence that comparisons between Jupiter's moons and these conjectural solar bodies were ill-conceived.[90]

In transforming her legion of dancing horsemen into Bourbonian Stars, Costa revived an astronomical phrase coined to flatter the father of the current young king. While it is not clear how Costa became familiar with the image, as the debate had cooled by the mid-1640s, when the spots largely disappeared, it is evident that she made more than simple "tweaks in form alone" (in the words of one commentator) when refashioning her ballet for a royal French audience.[91] As befits a text so concerned with courtly image-making, she chose her alterations shrewdly. The movement from Jupiter's stars to the sun's satellites ought to strengthen, not lessen, one's appreciation for the *Festa reale*'s revisions. In order to secure patronage in France, Costa had to dismantle and rebuild the universe.

A Burlesque Ballet

To prove herself attentive to the spectacle of statecraft, Costa selected the highly rhetoricized genre of equestrian ballet and filled her composition with dynastic images, first Florentine and then French. As we have seen, however, throughout her career Costa interspersed demonstrations of her courtly urbanity with reminders of her "bizarreness," and the manuscript version of the *Festa reale* was no exception. A year after its completion, she undertook her ridiculous comedy *Li buffoni* (1641). Despite the stylistic gulf that separated them, *Li buffoni* revisits several of the themes that had occupied Costa as she composed the *Festa reale* not long before.

First among these is the court itself. If as a genre equestrian ballet exalts a court and its means (military as well as monetary), this comedy counters with a satirical glimpse at the coarser amusements and preoccupations of the Medici. As we have seen in chapter 2, the dwarfs, hunchbacks, and other "freak[s] of nature" who make up the administration of the play's Moroccan principality caricature historical personages in the Medici's employ, while other visual and textual clues orient the reader-spectator to the work's Florentine subtext. Costa humorously puts on display the Medici and their entertainments, from gluttonous feasts to dwarf-led games and brawls.

While Costa's comedy mimics courtly divertissements, it also takes aim at the loftier pursuits essential to her ballet libretto. For example, the astronomical concerns in the *Festa reale* are brought back down to earth in *Li buffoni*. Amid the dancing buffoons and dwarfs, the frontispiece depicts a figure holding a telescope to his eye (see fig. 2.8). Though visually claiming this Galilean device for the Florentine court, the comedy (a copy of which Galileo owned) converts the technological innovation into a contraption of outlandish play. This component of the engraving alludes to a scene in which two characters debate which one's debauchery, arrogance, and capriciousness would make him the better buffoon. The most important requisite, they concur, is a constant state of inebriation. Masino (the secretary of state, a man "crooked in both stature and appearance") tells Tordo (the prince's adviser, a character based on Ferdinando's historic lens maker) that to satisfy this requirement he would create a telescope with a fixed bottom and a vented top to "use ... as an enema tube / so the wine wouldn't impair [him]." Into this device he could "void / and give back the drink [he] had enjoyed."[92] Rather than an instrument that brings man into closer proximity to the cosmos, the telescope is reduced to a receptacle for excreta.

As a form of theatre associated especially with the seventeenth-century Medici, equestrian ballet offered rich material for Costa's comedic talents. In act 2, Princess Marmotta orders Tedeschino to distract her from her sorrows by singing, dancing, and prancing about on a stick as though it were a horse. Despite his initial protests, she calls out specific dressage movements she wishes to see ("Oh, yes, Tedeschino, some caprioles!").[93] He succumbs – giving commands ("Ya, ya, ya, whoa, whoa, whoa"), naming the airs above ground that he performs ("a few more courbettes"), singing a tune about promenading as though before a horse tamer at the manège, and vaunting the dexterity with which he manoeuvres his hobbyhorse ("Look how well I lead him / through his voltes in pirouettes").[94] A buffoon's arsenal of skills typically included humorous, acrobatic stunts performed on horseback, ones that Costa here bends into an imitation of dressage and ballet.[95] The mimicry ends in comical disaster when the inept Tedeschino is "thrown" from his steed while executing a series of jumps and kicks. Through a burlesque reworking, Costa upsets the conventions of equestrian ballet. The aristocratic rider has been replaced by a "Cavalier of Pleasure," that is, a buffoon. Rather than presenting an authoritative military-political message before admiring audiences, Tedeschino is derided throughout the work as a "political ass" and the "dimwit of diplomacy."[96] In place of an expertly trained and extravagantly priced steed, he performs upon an inanimate wooden pole.

These inversions of custom, class, and social position reflect Costa's transition from state pageantry to *commedia ridicolosa*. The genre permits Costa to hold a mirror to the cruder pastimes of the Medici while also satirizing through carnivalesque role reversals the family's more magnificent aspirations. Since *commedie ridicolose* performances were, like equestrian ballets, largely a courtly phenomenon – typically composed and played by artists, academicians, and other members of elite cultural circles, often in prominent palaces – one may assume that the Medici were themselves in on Costa's joke.[97] As seen in chapter 2, the play's prologue in fact dramatizes how Costa permits herself to upend the symbols of a magisterial Medicean court that she herself extols elsewhere. Here Ancient Comedy verbally spars with young Buffoonery as the two heatedly compete for place of primacy in contemporary theatre. Buffoonery disparages Ancient Comedy as a decrepit and venomous old hag, while Comedy berates Buffoonery as an disgraceful hustler. Buffoonery emerges victorious from the *contrasto* only when she invokes the Medici name, insisting that within their territory there is no longer space for obsolete forms of comedy. Ancient Comedy acquiesces and departs from the stage: "To this great name, and not to your words, / I am forced to yield / ... / ... now from the aspect / of the Medicean Stars (*Medicee stelle*) I take my leave." These stars twinkle down on Costa's brand of comedic theatre alone since "without buffoonery the scene has no appeal."[98]

Costa thus composed one spectacle that exalts the Medici through majestic pomp, the allegorization of political virtues, and a dedication to the grand duke, and another that satirizes them through burlesque treatment of both their more stately and coarser forms of recreation. Arching across both her comedy's prologue and her ballet's conclusion, however, are the same Medicean skies. Through their fixed presence, Costa underscores that both the high and the low are facets of the Medici courtly cosmos and that her representation of them is sanctioned from powers above. While *Li buffoni* and the *Festa reale* manuscript are not companion pieces, as were the *Festa reale* and the *Flora feconda*, these parallels speak to Costa's attentiveness to Florentine courtly divertissement and pageantry at their most base and sublime levels. By exploring similar phenomena from the perspective of two divergent performative traditions, Costa showcased her versatility in genre, style, and register.

Conclusion

Measuring herself against the librettist Francesco Buti in *La tromba di Parnaso*, Costa professed that "I too seek the revered laurel and spur the winged steed."[99] The allusion is, of course, to Pegasus, symbol for the soaring of poetic imagination. Yet the horse was no idle metaphor for Costa but rather a figure to which she repeatedly returned through the genres of occasional poetry, satire, and ballet. In imaginatively lifting her own horses to the heavens through equestrian ballet, she mirrored the creative ascension of Pegasus – literalizing Pasquale Caracciolo's assertion in *La gloria del cavallo* that equestrianism soared thanks to its dual "wings" of the literary and military arts.[100] In sending her buffoon tumbling down from his hobbyhorse, she upended such aspirational imagery.

Equestrianism provided Costa with an emblem for and subject of literary enterprise. Throughout her career it also afforded her a rich means of courting elite benefactors invested in the pageantry and rhetoric of horsemanship. As we will see in the following chapter, she returned to these themes in her late-life work on behalf of the Barberini as well in her last known publication: a broadsheet celebrating their grand 1656 operatic carousel. Costa astutely identified equestrian spectacles as being especially dear to her aristocratic patrons as vehicles for the display of technological innovation and magnificence on the one hand, and of political-military rhetoric on the other. In contrast to opera, equestrian spectacle – like *ballet de cour* – featured young princes and dukes as not merely organizers, but as performers in their own right. In addition to fusing music, choreography, and stage engineering, Baroque equestrian ballets were thus both about and by their sponsors, allowing these noblemen to join the constellation of local talents exhibited before elite, often international, audiences. Through this medium, writers, composers, choreographers, and aristocratic patron-performers became collaborators. The centrality of equestrian themes across Costa's years of literary activity was as much about cultivating a relationship to her benefactors as participating in an elaborate and exciting form of musical theatre.

While equestrian ballet has slipped into the shadows of history – much like Costa herself – it should rightfully be placed alongside opera and *ballet de cour* as one of the great performative innovations of Baroque Europe. By trying her hand at one of the age's most spectacular genres of musical theatre, Costa drew on her identities as a performer, a poet, and, ultimately, a courtier as she fused music, dance, and poetry while contributing to dynastic image-making, collaborating with artists, appropriating scientific and propagandistic discourses, and negotiating the transition from one patronage network to another as she moved across Italy and France.

Chapter Five

The Singing Saint and the Plumed Bee: Courting the Barberini

Costa's relationship to Cardinal Mazarin, described in the preceding chapter, illustrates that, despite the risqué quality of her early publications and her less-than-spotless reputation, she was capable of forging connections to important men of the church. Throughout her career, Costa used verse to celebrate a handful of ecclesiastic figures, most notably Cardinals Francesco and Antonio Barberini (and, following his death, their uncle, Urban VIII), Camillo Pamphili, and Mazarin himself. A high ecclesiastic post did not preclude the patronage or protection of female singers, despite their reputation for sexual promiscuity and the papal ban on their performing in public in Rome. Anna Francesca Costa enjoyed the attentions of Giovan Carlo de' Medici in Florence even after his elevation to the cardinalate in 1644, for example, while Leonora Baroni and Nina Barcarola attracted Antonio Barberini's in Rome.[1] Costa's literary record is peppered with evidence of her relationships to these men, but none so long and across so many genres as the Barberini.

After the 1623 election of Urban VIII (Maffeo Barberini), the family dominated the city's political and cultural life for over twenty years. From the works of Bernini and Borromini they commissioned, to the numerous spectacles they organized, to the many publications they supported, the papal nephews – Don Taddeo (prefect of Rome), Cardinal Antonio, and especially Cardinal Francesco – played a decisive role in shaping Baroque Rome. Urban's 1644 death threw all that carefully constructed influence up into the air. Public ire was still roiling over the family's costly and fruitless War of Castro (1641–4) against Parma and, later, Tuscany, Venice, and Modena. Others in the city harboured resentments built up over the unusually long papacy.[2] While Francesco and Antonio endeavoured to preserve their position during the conclave by ultimately supporting the election of Giovanni Battista Pamphili (Innocent X), their plan proved futile and their enemies too powerful. Chased by accusations of corruption and misconduct, in the fall of 1645 Antonio fled for Paris under the protection of Mazarin. Francesco and Taddeo soon followed.[3] After years in exile, the family brokered their return to Rome through the 1653 marriage of Taddeo's son, Maffeo, to Innocent's grand-niece, Olimpia Giustiniani.

Costa's and the Barberini's paths would cross at each of these junctures. The family's importance for Costa is underscored by the fact that she was better represented in Francesco's personal library than in nearly any other.[4] While Costa's first direct dedication of a work to the Barberini dates to 1644, there is ample reason to believe that she may have belonged to their musical-intellectual circles even before this. Many of the musicians connected to Cardinal Maurizio of Savoy, including those with whom Costa was hired to sing at a 1627 dinner for the Count of Soissons, passed into the Barberini's service when Maurizio left Rome.[5] Costa's only known poem set to extant music, *Oh Dio, voi che mi dite*, was entrusted to Marco Marazzoli, a composer also in the cardinal's household.[6] Her early *La chitarra* had applauded Cornelio Bentivoglio's performance in the 1634 *Giostra dei saraceni*, financed by Antonio, who – with the rest of his family – organized innumerable operas and spectacles in the city.[7] Poems such as these recognized that such events transcended public entertainment and served to communicate their sponsors' power and authority.

Costa's return to Rome in 1644 was pivotal in terms of her historical and textual relationship to the family. As the diarist Giacinto Gigli relates, that February Costa arranged her arrival alongside the "famous thief and violent killer" Tiberio Squilletti.[8] The couple professed their desire to leave Florence to become penitents in Rome and to obtain a papal absolution for Squilletti. Costa facilitated these negotiations, thanks to her Barberini connections, and upon their arrival the pair was honourably escorted by the family's own carriages, to the astonishment and dismay of many. While Squilletti received an official post and salary, Costa quickly set about solidifying her own position with the publication of a new work on a topic far removed from those she had explored in Florence: a hagiographic epic dedicated to Cardinal Francesco on the martyrdom of St. Cecilia.[9]

In this same period, Costa composed another poem acknowledging Francesco's role in securing her return to her native city. Although *Cecilia martire* came out just before Urban's death, Costa would have to wait several years to publish this homecoming canzone.[10] Along with a handful of others for Francesco's brother Antonio, papal uncle, and mother, it would appear in her 1647 *Tromba di Parnaso*, one of the volumes she published while she – like the Barberini – was Mazarin's guest in France. Also testifying to their enduring relationship is Costa's last known publication, a broadsheet celebrating a 1656 Barberini-sponsored operatic carousel, a further example of her identification of equestrianism as a means of courting patrons discussed in chapter 4. This final work was the culmination of a long-standing literary connection to the family, in works that ranged from sacred verse to panegyric, from elegy to occasional poetry.

This chapter charts Costa's textual relationship to the Barberini, focusing especially on her *Cecilia martire*. The poem in heroic *ottava rima* offers an unusual means of approaching the hagiography of the Roman saint associated with celestial and, eventually, secular music, a martyr who died in the arms of Pope Urban I. Costa not only dedicated to the Barberini a poem on a timely, in vogue subject following the 1599 rediscovery of Cecilia's body, but also introduced their cultural restoration efforts into the framework of religious epic. In penning such a work, Costa had notable female predecessors in Maddalena Salvetti (*David perseguitato*, 1611) and Lucrezia Marinella (especially her comparable *La Colomba sacra* [1595], and her prose *Le vittorie di Francesco il Serafico, li passi gloriosi della diva Chiara* [1643], similarly dedicated to Urban VIII, the first portion of which reworks her verse *Vita del serafico et glorioso San Francesco* [1597]), among others. As Virginia Cox has noted, the field of sacred narrative in the late sixteenth and early seventeenth centuries, though dominated by the towering figures of Tasso and Marino (both key models for *Cecilia martire*), also saw "female poets ... in the vanguard."[11] Indeed, Costa's sacred turn in this work mirrors that of Marino himself and better fits the tastes of her Barberini patrons, who were not fans of Marino's amorous verse and who had placed the *Adone* on the Index of Prohibited Books in 1627.[12] This chapter traces Costa's cultivation of the Barberini through her epic on the singing saint, her praise and defence of them in her French-published encomiastic poetry, and finally her celebration of the "plumed bee" of Barberini musical-military spectacle.

The Singing Saint, Diva of the Seicento

In 1644 Costa first brought a religiously themed work to press.[13] In contrast with her *Sette giornate* manuscript, a text whose opening ribald episodes call into question the author's professed conversion in the final two cantos, *Cecilia martire* is a thoroughly sacred poem about a virgin martyr and the patron saint of music. Costa selected a suitably proper, and prominent, dedicatee: Cardinal Francesco was at the epicentre of Rome's cultural life. The volume blends homages to her patrons' spiritually infused cultural endeavours with recognition of seventeenth-century Rome's investment in early Christian heroes as well as narrative elements drawn from the religious epics of Tasso and Marino. As in Florence, Costa published with highly respected printers, in this case the Mascardi. The result is a handsome quarto volume, complete with two illustrations by an unknown artist.[14] While Costa does not date the dedicatory letter, the volume was published before Urban's death on 29 July. In his diaries Cardinal Ernst Adalbert von Harrach recorded receiving "a book of poetry about the martyrdom of St. Cecilia on behalf of its author, Margherita Costa," the day before the August conclave to select the next pontiff began. Costa's scandalous reputation, rather than her supposed newfound spiritual path, caught the Austrian cardinal's attention. This "odd *dama*" of low repute was Squilletti's mistress, and maybe his own nephew's as well.[15] As we shall see below, Costa herself was acutely aware that her choice of a sacred subject might raise eyebrows.

Sacred epic was a genre of mounting popularity in the late sixteenth and seventeenth centuries. To understand why Costa chose to try her hand at it with a composition on this particular saint – reasons that extend beyond their shared connections to music – and to appreciate her innovative hagiographic approach and its appeal for the Barberini, it is helpful to first begin with Cecilia herself. Her evolving cult was especially vibrant in the Seicento, visible not only in music and art but also in literature and theatre. We thus turn first to Cecilia's legend and its transformation over time.

Cecilia's Cult in the Seicento

St. Cecilia's legend is told in the *Passio Sanctae Caeciliae virginis et martyris*, an anonymous work first circulated circa 495 (two centuries after her purported lifetime).[16] It exemplifies what Hippolyte Delehaye has called the "epic *passio*," a narrative work featuring a heroic martyr across a variety of episodes.[17] Though much of her story is assumed to be fictionalized, it weaves together the values of filial obedience, virginity, good works, courage, and unshakeable faith. These components of her hagiography made her a prime candidate for the sort of heroicizing storytelling about Christian saints popular during the Counter-Reformation and through the first half of the seventeenth century.[18]

The *Passio* describes Cecilia as the daughter of an affluent Roman family that, despite her vow of chastity, marries her off to the young pagan nobleman Valerian. On their wedding night, before her bridegroom can so much as lay a finger on her, she warns him that her virginity is safeguarded by an angel who will strike him down should he violate her purity. A shaken Valerian asks to see this intervening angel. Cecilia directs him to first go to the Via Appia, where he is baptized by Urban I. The couple's new spiritual marriage is celebrated by the angel, who crowns them with garlands of roses and lilies. After Cecilia also converts her brother-in-law Tiburtius, the two brothers are arrested and executed by the prefect Turcius Almachius. After performing acts of charity and repeatedly converting the agents sent to investigate her, she too is seized and brought before Almachius, whom she engages in theological debate. When she refuses to denounce her faith, Cecilia is subjected to a series of torments: after she survives a boiling bath in her home with little discomfort, she faces beheading. Three sword blows by the executioner injure but do not decapitate her. She finally expires, after three days of performing charitable works, preaching, converting her fellow Romans, and giving her property over for the founding of the *titulus Caeciliae*, the church that would bear her name. Urban lays her body to rest in the Catacombs of St. Callistus.

This was not to be Cecilia's final resting place, however; twice more she was moved. In the ninth century Pope Paschal, following a dream-vision, first located her body – presumed lost – and translated it (along with the bodies of Valerian,

Figure 5.1. Stefano Maderno, *St. Cecilia*, 1600. Church of Santa Cecilia in Trastevere, Rome. Image courtesy of Wikimedia Commons.

Tiburtius, and Urban) to the church of Santa Cecilia in Trastevere, which he had rebuilt. In 1599 Cecilia's body was again "rediscovered" during renovations organized by the cardinal priest Paolo Emilio Sfondrati – conveniently just in time to make his church a highlight of the Jubilee celebrations the following year. Preparations and anticipation of the Jubilee had already been marked by heightened interest in the Church's early history, as illustrated by Cardinal Cesare Baronio's voluminous *Annales ecclesiastici* and the archaeological excavations of Antonio Bosio, each aimed at mapping and verifying holy remains; both men would participate in the examination of Cecilia's tomb.[19] Female martyrs played an important role in this project of documenting and celebrating Rome's sacred roots, as recorded in Antonio Gallonio's 1591 *Historia delle sante vergini romane*, which features seventy-nine women, including Cecilia.[20]

On 20 October, Cecilia's sarcophagus was located and opened.[21] Inside, the saint was positioned like a demure young bride merely asleep in her bed.[22] Witnesses identified her by her golden dress, the blood-soaked cloths at her feet, and the cilice that was somehow visible from under the dark silk veil that covered her. Her position was memorialized in Stefano Maderno's exquisite marble sculpture placed at the church's altar – directly above the crypt – shortly thereafter (fig. 5.1). In Maderno's sculpture, Cecilia's face is turned away from the viewer, revealing a glimpse of her neck marred by the slashes of the sword blade, from which a trickle of blood appears.

Announced with great fanfare, the news spread rapidly and drew crowds eager to see the saint's body, which was displayed for a month. On her feast day, 22 November, it was ceremoniously reinterred following a procession and high mass performed by Clement VIII. Cardinal Sfondrati would promote the discovery by continuing the new decorations of the church and commissioning theological and historical works, notably Bosio's *Historia passionis beatae Caeciliae*.[23] The search for Cecilia's sarcophagus proved highly successful, both for the discovery itself and the acclaim it brought the *titulus* at a crucial moment in the church's calendar. It also whipped up interest in her cult while lending strength to the ongoing efforts during the Counter-Reformation to verify church history.

Cecilia is most familiar to modern audiences through music and art. Her association with music is particularly strong, but it in fact originates from a single line of her *Passio*. During her wedding festivities, as the musicians played, "she sang to the Lord Himself in the depths of her heart: 'Let my heart and my body be immaculate, so that I do not fall into confusion.'"[24] Early artistic representations did not render Cecilia in the guise of musician, in keeping with her rejection of worldly music for the celestial; indeed, in these works the saint did not yet have a clear iconographic identity at all. This would change over time. Due to a misreading of the *Passio*'s reference to "instruments" (*organis*) as organs, Cecilia's later iconography incorporated the portative organ. In the most famous example, Raphael's altarpiece *The Ecstasy of St. Cecilia* (1514), the organ dangles neglected and inverted in her hands as she gazes upwards towards the angelic choir and beyond, its pipes beginning to slide out, soon to join the ensemble of broken musical instruments scattered at her feet.

As musical culture changed over the sixteenth and especially the seventeenth centuries, Cecilia evolved from a rather passive patron saint of music to a practitioner in her own right.[25] Her repertoire expanded to include other instruments: Guido Reni's 1606 *Santa Cecilia* holds the violin, Domenichino's 1617–18 saint plays the viol, and Carlo Saraceni's c.1610 version shows her strumming a lute, with a violin, recorder, bombard, and harp nearby. Notably, Cecilia also begins to sing aloud; in Antiveduto della Grammatica's *Saint Cecilia Singing with Two Angels*, for instance, she holds a part book and appears to move her lips.[26] Cecilia would also become the protectress of several academies dedicated to music: Siena's Accademia dei Filomeli (c. 1570), Florence's Accademia degli Elevati (1607), and, of course, Rome's Accademia di Santa Cecilia (originally the Congregazione dei Musici, 1585). Transformed in these ways, Cecilia lent legitimacy and dignity to musical performance – a change that mirrors the shifting social role of musicians themselves.[27]

Cecilia's connections to music and art have been the subject of numerous scholarly studies; however, the number and variety of publications about her that appeared in the seventeenth century have gone largely unnoticed until recently.[28] The 1599 rediscovery prompted a flood of literary and theatrical treatments over the coming century, assuring her place among the saints populating the period's sacred literature. This development dovetailed with wider trends in religious representation. The Counter-Reformation ushered in fresh enthusiasm for holy figures in literary and theatrical works. Yet while martyr saints played a prominent role in this surge, especially in Rome, Cecilia's inclusion in their number was not a given. She had long been a more secondary figure within the pantheon of saints, one without an identifiable iconography until the thirteenth century. Moreover, while Counter-Reformation publications of this kind emerged in the 1560s and picked up steam in the 1580s,[29] only two works fully dedicated to Cecilia (a sacred drama and a narrative poem) appeared in these decades, and only two (one dramatic, one poetic) predate this.[30] In stark contrast, nearly thirty dedicated publications appeared in 1599 and throughout the Seicento – occasionally in Latin but primarily in the vernacular, and across a variety of genres. Many of these are dramatic works, from *sacre rappresentazioni* to tragedies to opera librettos, but there are also poems, histories, and treatises. While other female saints like Agnes, Agatha, and the later Francesca Romana also enjoyed literary attention in the Seicento, Cecilia's sum of texts far outpaced theirs.[31] Nearly 65 per cent of Cecilia publications appeared in the first half of the century, suggesting that the rediscovery of her tomb spurred literary interest in her for several decades, in both sacred and secular circles. If this prompted the first wave of Cecilia publications, changing musical trends contributed to a second wave. Leaving aside oratorios, which I have not counted in the publication numbers, seven of the thirteen works published in 1637 and thereafter are explicitly identified as primarily musical or operatic in nature.[32] The heroic life of a singing saint was, it seems, an enticing argument for the new *melodrammi in musica* and their printed librettos. Cecilia's recent burst of literary popularity, backed by the Counter-Reformation fervour for martyrs and Seicento Rome's search for evidence of early church history, meant that the dedication of a handsome work on her would have pleased any patron.

Sacred Epic and Barberini Rome

The Barberini were not just any patrons, of course. In Cecilia, Costa identified a legend with glaring parallels to both her and her benefactors. Both women shared Roman origins, and, indeed, both lived in Trastevere. Cecilia's titular church stands above the reputed site of her home; Costa owned a house in the neighbourhood and, for a period, a vineyard practically under the shadow of the church's bell tower.[33] Cecilia was the patron saint of music, Costa a chamber and opera singer. Perhaps most importantly, Cecilia was spiritually guided and tended to by Pope Urban I, and Costa sought the support of Pope Urban VIII and his nephews. Urban VIII especially would have fancied a venture such as this, invested as he was in highlighting continuities with his namesakes within a broader family project of cultural and intellectual patronage.[34] This included, for example, rededicating a restored church, Santi Urbano e Lorenzo a Prima Porta, and renovating in the 1630s the ancient Sant'Urbano alla Caffarella near Via Appia Antica – the latter of which Costa highlights in both the textual and visual components of her publication.[35] In fact, Costa restructures the Cecilia legend narrative as inherited from the *Passio*, the *Golden Legend*, and the new torrent of literary-theatrical sources in order to foreground the role of Urban I.

Cecilia martire places the poet and her benefactors in the constellation of literary texts that greeted the burst of fresh interest in the saint's cult after 1599. While the publication fits within the era's religiously themed literature broadly, a few oddities about it as a Cecilia work immediately jump out. First, it is curious that Costa, a singer with three previous theatrical compositions under her belt, should choose to write a long poem rather than follow the trend for dramatic works on Cecilia. This choice can be explained partially by the fact that there was also a significant appetite for religious epic in the late Cinquecento and Seicento, "a vast and critically under-investigated body" of literature. [36] Through a broadening of the epic frame, readers could approach as "heroic" the deeds and virtues of biblical figures and saints. A hagiographic epic allowed Costa – always intent on displaying her versatility and virtuosity – to add a new literary genre to her repertoire. And though a poem, her work exemplifies many of the attributes that Robert Kendrick has identified in Roman sacred opera, of which the Barberini were prominent organizers, including the incorporation of demons and an emphasis on *romanità*.[37]

Second, and more notably, Costa forgoes many of the *Passio* episodes that were particular favourites in artistic and literary-theatrical representations of the saint. We see no wedding or earthly musicians, no spiritual union with Valerian or conversion of Tiburtius, no interrogation by the prefect Almachius, and no good works performed for the community. Costa inverts narrative convention, alluding to these parts of the legend only obliquely and in the final canto through the words of an already deceased Valerian. In place of the marital story, she centres the poem on Cecilia's martyrdom itself and the relationship between the female saint and her pope. As we shall see, this recalibrated focus is visually underscored by the volume's two illustrations.

This tale of Cecilia's death and burial is divided into four cantos, each slightly over 100 octaves: The Bath (*Il bagno*), Martyrdom (*Il martirio*), The Temple (*Il tempio*), and The Sepulcher (*Il sepolcro*). This structure imitates that of Marino's *La strage degl'innocenti* (Massacre of the Innocents), posthumously published in 1632 and in numerous later editions, which is similarly organized into four books (Herod's Suspicion [*Sospetto di Erode*], The Counsel of the Satraps [*Consiglio de' Satrapi*], Execution of the Slaughter [*Essecuzione della strage*], and Limbo), and which has the same broad narrative arc: infernal incitement, debate or hesitation, suffering, and an aftermath with otherworldly resolution.[38] This four-part division offers suggestive parallels with works like Marinella's *La Colomba sacra*, another hagiographic epic which similarly pits a female martyr against a Roman authority (in that case an emperor) who tries unsuccessfully to slay her before resorting to beheading.[39] Like Marino's work, each canto begins with an explanatory "Argument" in verse; the volume itself is introduced by another set of prose Arguments and Allegories providing spiritual interpretation. While other early modern works on St. Cecilia took the form of domestic dramas or tragedies interspersed with fantastical, humorous, or courtly elements,[40] Costa's narrative features the supernatural confrontation between good and evil, between heaven and hell, through angelic and demonic interventions.

The distance between this new publication and her previous one, the rambunctious and risqué *Buffoni* of 1641, must have been as striking to Costa as it is to modern readers. In the first stanza, she criticizes her Muse for having sung "in vain" of "light jests … and mad passions" while in Tuscany. Now she should temper (*tempra*) Costa's plectrum and "honour [her] cittern with a more thankful and melodic voice, with more beautiful songs."[41] After having "stained the ill-limned page to no avail" with her previous amorous themes, Costa now is in need of a different kind of Helicon and turns ("volgo") her songs heavenward to sing of God's triumphs.[42] The passage summons the first line of Marino's *La strage degl'innocenti*, in which the poet similarly informs his Muse that he shall no longer sing of love but instead of religious matters.[43] It also recalls the second octave of Tasso's *Gerusalemme liberata*, in which the poet dismisses a Helicon muse in preference for one drawn from the heavenly choirs ("beati cori").[44] Costa's banshee-like Muse from *La chitarra* and the *Sette giornate* has now been similarly converted, a transformation in keeping with the self-conscious shifts from secular to sacred modes characteristic of post-Tridentine religious writing.[45]

After pledging to set aside the erotic, however, Costa reflects on how a woman such as she ventured to write a sacred narrative at all. "I, a defenceless sinner in a mortal hide, / Dare to speak about eternal greatness?" she asks. "I, of lowly thoughts and weak will, / Attempt to call by name He who governs earth and sky?"[46] The question (grounded in Costa's usual professions of humility as well as Counter-Reformation concerns regarding the accessibility of sacred history) is largely rhetorical. This postured worry may have not been entirely unfounded, however, judging by the commentary of the aforementioned Cardinal von Harrach, who contrasts the subject of this publication – "heylige" (Saint) Cecilia – with its author, "not the saintliest of women" ("nicht eine aus den heyligsten").[47] Even her modern biographer Dante Bianchi bristles that a woman he holds to be of base morality and skill "should soil the image of one of the most suggestive … figures for the appeal of purity and art united together" simply by writing about her.[48]

The affirmative answer to the question of whether she should or could write a sacred poem rested on her biographical continuities with Cecilia as well as her newly professed identity (alongside Squilletti) as a penitent. In the next stanza she asks St. Cecilia herself to "guide my audacity and temper [*tempra*] my song."[49] The imperative *tempra* points back to the first stanza; Costa's transformed Muse, we realize, is now Cecilia herself. Costa's turn ("svolgo") heavenward replicates Cecilia's own when in her legend earthly music is introduced and she instead looks towards that of the divine sphere. Costa next calls on her to aid in honouring Cardinal Barberini, for if once Cecilia was baptized by a "holy" ("sacro") Urban, now Costa will lionize the nephew of a new "sovereign" ("sovrano") Urban. Should Cardinal Barberini not respond to Costa's humble song, Cecilia's celestial one may prove more persuasive.[50]

The saint will not be alone in exercising a positive, protective influence on Costa's writing. In her dedication, Costa argues that any risk posed by her efforts is mitigated by her patrons' influence. Just as daisies ("margherite") depend on the dawn's light (when their petals open), and as the Egyptian statue of Memnon is believed to "sing" at sunrise,[51] so too will Costa be illuminated and brought to song by the "Vatican Barberini sun" – the rising sun being, in addition to bees, one of the family's heraldic devices.[52] Conjoining symbols of protégée and patron, the image sequence highlights the response to radiating munificence: beauty and song.

Following this examination of Costa's role as writer of a sacred narrative and her evocation of Cecilia as Muse, the first canto opens with Cecilia already in the boiling baths of her Trastevere home. Untroubled, she continues her sacred hymns uninterrupted. The narrative then moves on to hell, surveying its seething monsters before arriving at Satan himself. Enraged that Cecilia is meanwhile "sweetly singing songs to her god / and counts herself lucky amid her misfortunes," Satan vows that infernal fires will prevail where earthly ones have failed.[53] As he concludes his harangue, he echoes the defiant threat that the pagan warrior Argante levels at the Christian Goffredo in *Gerusalemme liberata*: "Whoever does not want peace shall have war."[54] While this line comes from the two men's confrontation in Tasso's canto 2, Costa's episode is an adaptation of the infernal counsels in his canto 4 and Marino's book 1 (and of their mutual source in Vida's 1535 *Christiad*). In each, Satan stirs up a monstrous assembly over the injury they suffer at God's hand before sending his attendants to cause further suffering and mayhem. In Cecilia's case, the ire is over not only her imperviousness to pain but her vow of chastity: "she who does not value love does not merit life."[55] His forces descend upon Cecilia's house, bringing flames, winds, and storms of epic proportions. Despite the afflictions waged upon her body, she remains insusceptible and merely taunts her would-be tormentors. As Cecilia lifts her voice in joy to Heaven, they change tactics. Just as these same nefarious figures lead Herod to commit evil in Marino's poem, here they goad the prefect Almachius. Should Rome as he knows it be undone by a "foolish girl" ("stolta fanciulla"), they ask, and hell conquered by a mere woman?[56] Incited by this insult to Roman glory, Almachius sets his sights on Cecilia.

Mirroring the opening to Marino's book 2, in which the "golden chariot" of the new dawn reveals a sanguinary Herod disturbed by the infernal spectres ("larve") who had visited his bedchambers,[57] in Costa's second canto the morning's "rosy chariot" rouses an Almachius similarly riled by his own nocturnal "larve."[58] Eager to shed her blood, he dispatches his executioner to Cecilia's home. Yet when this henchman arrives, the mere sight of her disarms him and fills his now trembling breast with doubt. Cecilia, intent on her prayers, gleams with such divine beauty and dazzling light that he is overcome. As he wavers in his resolve to kill her, celestial music breaks out around them – "invisible voices in sweet accents" that "sing to her."[59] The sound – produced first *for*, rather than *by*, Cecilia – is audible to the non-Christian intruder, who participates in a divine musical experience that differs from the *Passio*'s harmony, which Cecilia alone could perceive. Music is part of the miracle.

Surrounded by this heavenly sound, Cecilia begins to play the organ: "Then across the tonewood / with its industrious row of concave pipes, / the Diva runs her fingers."[60] The appellation "la Diva" (goddess or "the divine") is a common means of referring to Cecilia's sacred status within the Church and was similarly used in earlier sacred narratives.[61] But the word's meaning was in flux during the late Cinquecento and the Seicento, and was newly appropriated as a term of praise for skilled actresses and singers.[62] Employed regularly by Costa, it appears early in canto 1 to describe a Cecilia who, undisturbed by her boiling bath, starts to sing: "Yet the Diva is not hurt by such heat, / and sweet notes fall from her tongue."[63] Other allusions to music abound, including in the last lines as accents ("accenti") and the highest applause ("sommi applausi") fill the air as the saint is finally laid to rest.[64] Imagined by a professional singer, Costa's Cecilia is an acclaimed Seicento "diva."

We see in the executioner's reaction the sort of marvel that sacred music and divine beauty were believed to stir, within a poem whose contest between infernal and celestial forces itself dramatizes Tassian and Marinist forms of *meraviglia*.[65] Indeed, the scene recalls the near-martyrdom of Tasso's Sofronia, whose courage and luminous beauty as she falsely confesses to stealing an icon in order to save her fellow Christians from the ire of Jerusalem's king nearly softens the monarch's intractable heart.[66] There (perhaps not coincidentally also in canto 2) the virgin maiden is saved from death's flames through the intervention of Clorinda. Not having, or desiring, a Clorinda of her own, Cecilia receives the fate that would have otherwise befallen fair Sofronia at the hands of an ultimately unswayable foe. While initially the executioner is won over, he experiences an abrupt volte-face. As if he suddenly remembers music's other, darker, power – to seduce rather than to awe – he reinterprets the scene before him. He has not been stirred by Cecilia's divine *canto*, he frets, but instead has been enchanted ("incantato") by her. She, under false appearances ("larve mentite"), has bewitched him.[67] Recoiling, he blocks his ears to her insidious song ("chiudi l'orecchie al suono a i canti insidi"), a passage that recalls the comparable confrontation between the sirens and swans in *Flora feconda*.[68] In other words, he has re-understood Cecilia to be not a saint but a siren – not a Sofronia but an Armida.[69] It is tempting to see in this episode a commentary by Costa on the ease with which female singers' morality was so readily called into question in her own day.

Steeled by the nefarious spirits that regain control of him, the executioner strikes her with his sword three times – the maximum permitted by Roman law – and leaves her, not yet defeated, to perish amid the torments of the infernal hordes. Canto 3 continues this supernatural contest: God sends his angels to Pope Urban to have him provide succor to Cecilia. The canto opens onto God's heavenly throne, around which – in an echo of Dante's angelic "saintly soldiery" – gather "infinite ranks of winged minds" unified in sacred song.[70] Drawing inspiration from the first stanzas of *Gerusalemme liberata* in which God looks down upon the stalled Christian armies and summons the angel Gabriel – he who, in a closing rhyme, brings to heaven ("cielo") men's prayers and zeal ("zelo") – to assist Goffredo, here God sees Cecilia (in the same rhyme) lift her prayers to heaven ("cielo") and sends his angels to Urban on the behalf of this woman who burns with Christian zeal ("zelo").[71] Just as Gabriel finds Goffredo at his morning prayers (I.xv), so too do these angels arrive at Urban's doorstep in time to overhear his words of worship: the wish that he might protect the faith for which Cecilia, Valerian, and Tiburtius are to become exemplars. In short, Urban is Costa's ecclesiastic counterpart to Tasso's epic leader who victoriously asserts Christian authority in spiritual battle.

Urban comforts Cecilia with the assurance that soon she will sing in heaven:

There, oh Virgin, you shall with sweet notes
Be able to give life to your musical melodies,
And among the ranks devoted to the Creator,
Let loose harmonious sounds of joy,
And of the highest marvels unknown on earth
sing the praises, and to the frail living
Recount with a plectrum of sweetness full,
How serene heaven bestows its gifts.
There among the angelic choirs you will be able
To temper its movements with the sounds of the dances,
And, before the sun's everlasting rays,
Praise virtues and applaud vows.
And since you know how to most sweetly enliven
golden chords, such that you could stop
The very winds in the sky with your sweetness,
With your song you will now gladden the heavens.
Let loose, oh regal damsel, your happy notes

To your beloved numen, and in a beautiful song
Give thanks to your creator.[72]

Quivi, oh Vergin, potrai con dolci note
Dar bei spirti a tuoi musici concenti,
E tra le schiere al Creator devote
Snodar di gioia armoniosi accenti,
E d'alte meraviglie al Mondo ignote
Stender' i pregi, e a' fragil viventi
Ridir su plettro di dolcezza pieno,
Qual dispensa i suoi doni il ciel sereno.
Tra gli angelici chori ivi potrai
Temprar col suono de le danze i moti,
E avanti il sol, c'ha sempiterni i rai,
Lodar i pregi, e dar applauso a' voti.
E come dar a corde aurate sai
Soavissimi spirti, ond'è ch'immoti
Rendevi in aria per dolcezza i venti,
Renderai del tuo canto i ciel contenti.
Snoda, regia Donzella, al Nume amato
Le tue note felici, e 'n vago canto
Sciogli gratie a colui, che t'ha creato.

As Urban urges her to release her soul from her body, musicality is both the consolation and the motivation.

He next guides Cecilia through her martyrdom by holding up in a lengthy discourse the example of St. Agapitus (d. c. 275), who similarly perished by the sword after wild animals failed to kill him.[73] The choice initially seems odd. Although both figures are of debated historicity, Cecilia would have lived before Agapitus, and her renown far surpassed that of this relatively minor local saint. Why, then, should a dying Cecilia look to him for reassurance in her final hours? Why should he occupy thirteen stanzas in Costa's poem when better known examples like St. Thecla and St. Felicity are addressed in just one? Costa's attention to Agapitus was no doubt motivated by the location of his cult: his relics were housed in the eponymous cathedral in Palestrina, a small Lazian principality acquired by the Barberini in 1630.[74] While Taddeo governed this territorial symbol of the family's newfound status, Cardinal Barberini was envisioning ways to reconstruct it.[75] These efforts including commissioning a history of the town from the Barberini librarian, Giuseppe Maria Suarez, a work begun in 1633 and circulating in manuscript during this period.[76] Agapitus, the pope tells Cecilia, died under one Urban (an accidental or convenient inaccuracy) but will enjoy fresh honours under "another Urban in better centuries," thanks to these Barberini heroes

("Barberini heroi").[77] In a suggestive conclusion to the passage clearly intended as a nudge to Costa's dedicatee, he affirms Cecilia will similarly enjoy their devotions, prompting others (that is, Costa herself) to sing golden odes ("canteran con carmi d'oro") about their piety and greatness.

If canto 3 first adaptively imitates epic models like Tasso's within a hagiographic framework and next circuitously introduces a political-spiritual homage to the Barberini through a territorially important religious figure, it concludes by affirming Catholic ritual. Setting aside the *Passio*'s emphasis on Cecilia's own preaching and works – her expressions of independent agency – it instead centres and magnifies her relationship to Pope Urban, here by introducing a series of sacred rites he performs when she asks him to transform her home into a church. Armed with candles, incense, and materials with which to draw red crosses on the walls, Urban first exorcises the raging infernal spirits from her home. With holy oil and smoke, in a "rite dear to the Christian faith," he then consecrates the space under the approving watch of the angelic choir.[78] At the altar he has erected he performs a mass culminating in the celebration of the Eucharist. With her final breaths, Cecilia requests of him the last rites and a Christian burial. A line from earlier in the canto – "as in life, so in death Urban shall open the gates of heaven to Cecilia" – indicates that he had also been the one to baptize her.[79] The angelic music that greets her death and the dazzling light of her apotheosis deal the final blows to the satanic hordes, who are outmatched by the combined power of holy shepherd and virgin martyr. Perhaps the most Counter-Reformation-minded portion of the religious poem, the episode effectively performs and confirms Catholic doctrine on an epic stage.

The final canto opens with Valerian and Tiburtius descending from heaven to honour Cecilia. It is only at this late stage that we encounter these two figures – previously mentioned only parenthetically – who play such central roles in other literary and especially theatrical works. In those other texts Valerian must grapple with his bride's vow of chastity before joining her in spiritual rather than carnal marriage, Tiburtius must come to the Christian faith at the urging of his sister-in-law, and the two brothers must die together after refusing to renounce their new faith – scenes that, as noted above, were particular favourites for adaptation. Costa reconfigures this narrative arc, uniquely transforming the two men into witnesses to Cecilia's martyrdom and rendering all other relationships subsidiary to that between the pope and his disciple.

Valerian's overdue appearance brings us to briefly consider an alternative version of the section on him found in a manuscript of the poem.[80] Though a good copy bound in vellum and embossed with the Barberini emblem, this appears to be an unfinished presentation manuscript, given that a page has been earmarked for a never-supplied illustration of the saint. The two versions are identical until the fourth canto. The manuscript presents a twenty-nine-stanza discourse by Valerian that was subsequently reworked in the printed version; the published rendition is included at the end of the manuscript as something of an appendix.[81] The passage in question alludes to the couple's betrothment and marriage, which Costa had initially skipped over in a manner most unusual for Cecilia texts. While most of the stanzas simply have been reordered, some with textual variations, eleven have been completely rewritten. While the printed edition's sequence suitably begins with Valerian's account of Cecilia's martyrdom, before turning to his overview of their marriage, the manuscript foregrounds Valerian's praise for his wife's "beautiful appearance," not in the celestial fashion encountered in the executioner episode but in decidedly sensual terms.[82] Reflections on her beauty appear in both versions, including in relation to his preconversion erotic desire for her, but here his words still echo the poetics of a lover bowed by his beloved's allure. Nor is this passion safely buried in the past or respiritualized. The sight of her now "renews my ardour,"[83] he states in one of the later-replaced stanzas, for example, while the published lines "You, who can extinguish the frost of death, / were able to douse my brazen desires" originally began with the more continuously carnal "You, who *still* can make me burn to ashes."[84] Valerian speaks of Cecilia in eroticized terms in other texts, but only before his conversion. Sensual articulations by a now-martyred saint are more problematic – and, as Clara Stella has noted, more characteristic of Costa's previous literary corpus, despite her canto 1 claim to have abandoned such themes altogether. One suspects that Costa decided – whether of her own accord or at another's urging – that the episode be more suitably reworked for the broader reading public.[85]

When it is Tiburtius's turn to speak (and the print and manuscript versions realign), he – like Urban in the previous canto – celebrates the musicality Cecilia will bring with her to heaven:

> In His court amid the winged choirs
> You will let loose the sweet notes of harmony
> And make beautiful double-breathed hymns
> Resound from your musical instruments.
> The starry heavens will enjoy your songs,
> And just as you were able to rope in the winds,
> So too will you captivate the souls of heaven,
> And bring forth new palms of glory.
> Come, Cecilia, come, noble virgin,
> To pleasure, to dances, to laughter, to play.

> Ne la corte di lui tra i chori alati
> Spiegherai d'armonia dolci gli accenti,
> E begli hinni farai con doppi fiati
> Risonar da' tuoi musici stromenti.
> De' tuoi canti godranno i ciel stellati

> E quale incatenar potesti i venti,
> Avvinte renderai del cielo l'alme,
> E di gloria trarrai novelle palme.
> Su, Cecilia, su su, Vergine altera,
> Al piacer, a le danze, al riso, al gioco.[86]

Costa's heavenly court is a place of delight, where, as in its earthly counterpart, singers enthral their spectators with joyous melodies. Palms, no longer exclusively symbols of martyrdom, reward these musical gifts, opening up a new form of glory to the "diva" – one to which even Costa herself might aspire.

Unlike in many other Seicento works, which reflect a post-1599 reconceptualization of the saint's entombment, Costa's Cecilia is not buried at the site of her future church. Instead, a procession of angels, Valerian, Tiburtius, and Urban transports her body along the Via Appia to the Catacombs of St. Callistus (echoing Marino's final stanza in which the patriarchs carry the slaughtered babes into Limbo).[87] Costa's use of Appia Antica does not mean that she was oblivious to Cecilia's recent reappearance. For example, she likens the complexion of the saint's thrice-cut neck to Parian marble, an allusion to Maderno's snowy white statue with its blade marks (fig. 5.1).[88] Costa's rationale for hewing closely to the *Passio* regarding Cecilia's burial, when she abridges so much of it elsewhere, becomes clear in the final stanzas, which conclude with an angelic revelation to Urban. This parting message includes details of Urban's own martyrdom, as well as an ecclesiastical "genealogy" akin to the prophesied lineages of epic. A future Urban (VIII) will share his predecessor's "urbanity," decorate the sacred and political spaces of Christian Rome, and (in an inaccurately generous reading of the pope's health and recent fate in war), "at once conquer both the rigid forces of death and his fierce enemies."[89] Together with his nephews – Antonio, Taddeo, and Francesco – he will glorify the Church and Rome.

Among their named notable works would be the "magnanimous restoration" of Sant'Urbano alla Caffarella, a second-century pagan structure later converted into a church associated with Urban I.[90] This building fell into disuse in the Middle Ages but was "rediscovered" in the early seventeenth century as part of Rome's investigation of its early Catholic roots. Part of Sant'Urbano's original, and early modern, appeal was its proximity to Christian catacombs along the Appia Antica – a short walk from those of St. Callistus – and its association with the veneration of the martyrs. In the 1630s, Francesco Barberini led a major restoration and revitalization of the structure.[91] On 24 May 1636, the church – described by Gigli as the "site where Urban I baptized St. Cecilia" – was reconsecrated.[92] By reinserting the Callistus catacombs into Cecilia's legend via the funeral procession, Costa leads her reader through Rome and into the vicinity of Sant'Urbano, thus endorsing her dedicatee's successful rebuilding project. Indeed, one senses that the poem has been building to precisely this moment, and, lest her reader overlook this key reference, she highlights the restoration in both the paratextual Allegory and Argument. This is not the first time that Costa names a Barberini-connected structure from this same area. Early on, she claims Cecilia as a descendent of the ancient Roman noble family Caecilii Metelli, referencing specifically the "memorable and stately" tomb of Caecilia Metella.[93] The allusion may simply help orient the poem along the Via Appia Antica, but Costa might also have been aware that just a few years earlier her dedicatee had saved the mausoleum from being dismantled for its materials by Bernini on papal directive.[94]

Costa's emphasis on Sant'Urbano also informs the volume's two illustrations. The Barberini projects included the restoration of the church's eleventh-century frescoes, which portrayed scenes from the lives of Christ, Urban, and Cecilia. Though they have been heavily damaged, due in part to these interventions, their visual program is recorded in watercolour copies commissioned from Antonio Eclissi (1630) and an unknown artist (mid-1630s).[95] The latter's collection, more thorough in both detail and breadth, presents four scenes from Cecilia's *Passio*: her interrogation by Almachius, distribution of alms, martyrdom, and entombment (fig. 5.2).

Particularly noteworthy is the third scene. Cecilia kneels, facing to the left as blood begins to pool by her knees. The executioner stands behind her, his arm readied for its third and final downward swing. His single-handed diagonal backstroke differs from that of the executioner in the series dedicated to Urban, who uses a simple downward cut.[96] His position is replicated almost exactly in *Cecilia martire*'s engraving of the saint at the moment of her martyrdom (fig. 5.3): Cecilia's placement with her knees outlined, hips hovering above her heels; her hairstyle[97] and dress with its square neckline; two gashes in her exposed neck; the executioner's position behind her, his right leg visible only down to the mid-thigh and his left leg bent, the heel lifted slightly off the ground; his right hand swinging the sword and his left holding its sheath; his face looking down at hers.[98] The notable difference is in the blood: in the Sant'Urbano version it pours down rather gruesomely, while in Costa's it is an almost undetectable trickle on Cecilia's neck, consistent with the Maderno sculpture. Even the Sant'Urbano guardsman is replicated in the Costa image, his helmet peeking out from the huddle of observers.

Costa's frontispiece does include elements seemingly drawn from other sources. Domenichino's *Martyrdom of St. Cecilia* in the Polet Chapel of San Luigi dei Francesi – to pick an example close to home – also has a checkered floor, a bath behind Cecilia (alluding to the first failed attempt to kill her), artistic figures in the wall niche, and the conventional angel descending with symbols of martyrdom in hand, but the two compositions otherwise differ greatly.[99] It therefore stands to reason that the artist responsible for Costa's frontispiece had studied the Sant'Urbano fresco, either in situ or via the watercolours. Through this small portion of its larger artistic program, the church restored by her patrons is evoked and – with an early modern stylistic update – replicated within her publication.[100]

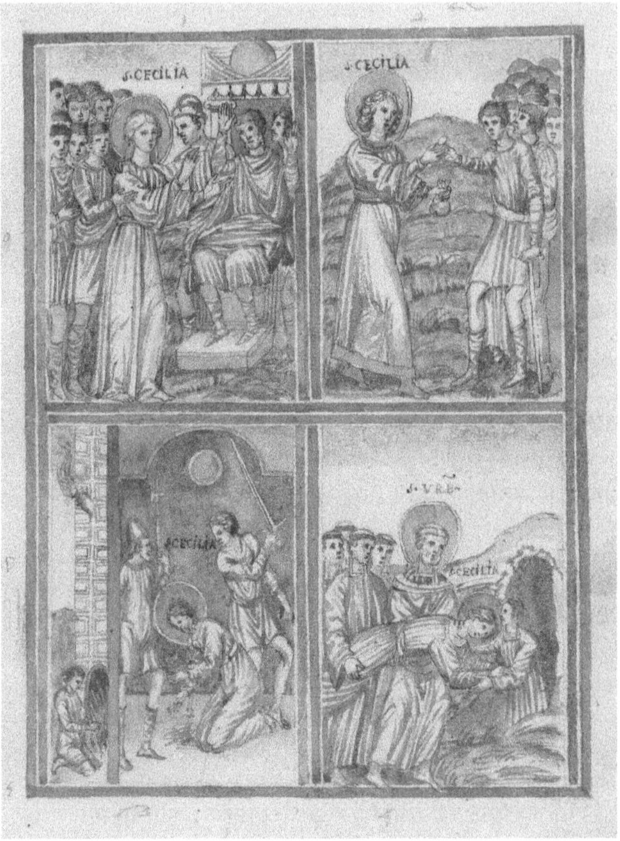

Figure 5.2. Scenes from the life of St. Cecilia, copied in watercolour from Sant'Urbano alla Caffarella, artist unknown. BAV, Barb.lat. 4408, fol. 65r.

Sant'Urbano also features prominently in Costa's first frontispiece (fig. 5.4). In the foreground, an imposing Minerva grips a shield emblazoned with the Barberini bees. Behind her sit two churches side-by-side: Santa Cecilia on the left, Sant'Urbano on the right. This juxtaposition of images visually reflects the way in which Costa has refashioned the narrative in order to focus almost exclusively on the relationship between the saint and her pope (rather than between the holy couple) – the first two cantos present Cecilia, the last two substantially expand Urban's prominence in order to place him alongside her. In short, the Sant'Urbano church makes three prominent appearances in Costa's publication: its exterior is recorded in the first frontispiece, its interior is evoked in the second frontispiece, and its restoration is heralded in the poem itself.

Figure 5.3. Second frontispiece to Margherita Costa, *Cecilia martire*, 1644. Courtesy of Houghton Library, Harvard University.

Figure 5.4. First frontispiece to Margherita Costa, *Cecilia martire*, 1644. Courtesy of Houghton Library, Harvard University.

In the poem's concluding octave, the angels, Valerian, and Tiburtius all return to heaven. Left on earth in the final verse is a pope tasked with venerating the memory of his protégé: "And Urban honours Cecilia on earth."[101] It is tempting to imagine that with this concluding line, written by a singer to a patron, the close kin of another Urban, Costa sought for herself papal guardianship. Supporting such a reading is the angel's praise for Francesco a few stanzas earlier: this "scarlet hero" shall keep the holy memory of and a deep affection for the diva Cecilia alive in his breast, an affirmation that applies to both the martyr and this sacred poem about her.[102]

From Cecilia's Rome to the Parisian Parnassus

Costa's efforts to court the Barberini paid off, judging by a poem written in thanks to Cardinal Antonio for a handsome gold chain he gifted her upon the completion of *Cecilia martire*.[103] Yet there was slim opportunity for Costa to enjoy whatever benefits she may have garnered from her text's complimentary comparison of the current pope and his holy predecessor, since the Barberini's star in Rome plummeted with Urban's death on 29 July of that year. Already a thorn in the side of rivals and critics, the papal nephews had grown increasingly unpopular during the War of Castro.[104] It was their bad luck that peace was struck only in March, mere months before they were to lose their grasp on the highest rungs of power after twenty years. As noted above, by the autumn of 1645 and early 1646 the brothers would depart for France under the protection of Mazarin. While Costa's decision to accept an invitation to the court of Marie Christine, duchess and regent of Turin, in January 1645 may have been coincidental to these political upheavals, such an engagement surely would have been appealing at a moment in which the Barberini family was increasingly isolated and eventually (albeit temporarily) exiled.[105] Fellow musicians were similarly securing employment elsewhere.[106]

Like many of the musicians in the Barberini orbit, eventually Costa would travel to Paris, in her case two years later at Mazarin's invitation to take part in the 1647 *Orfeo*.[107] In addition to making her debut on the Parisian stage, Costa swiftly published her three works with the royal French press: the *Festa reale*, *La selva di Diana*, and *La tromba di Parnaso*. We have already encountered *La tromba di Parnaso*'s concluding set of poems on *Orfeo* in chapter 4, and chapter 6 will examine its larger project of exalting the French court. Within this logic of the volume, the inclusion of another set of poems initially seems odd: the aforementioned one in thanks to Antonio Barberini, another to Francesco, and a series memorializing Urban, as well as his sister-in-law (Antonio and Francesco's mother) Costanza, whose death followed the pope's by mere weeks. Bridging the months between Costa's February 1644 return to Rome and the immediate aftermath of Urban's passing in July, this selection of poetry shows a poet caught in the middle of her patrons' changing circumstances.

The poem to Francesco centres upon Costa's arrival in Rome. While her auto-biographical poetry typically frames her as an exile, as will be discussed in chapter 7, this poem is instead about homecoming. Rather than setting the stage with a conventional reference to Ulysses, the quintessential male wayfarer, Costa begins her poem with an allusion to Astrea, the goddess of justice, who fled earth's corruption for the stars but who would reappear at the dawn of a new golden age. Such an epoch is to be found in Barberini Rome, Costa declares. And like the goddess, she too returns to her native land after many years spent "far from the paternal roof," now that "through [Francesco] the golden age is renewed in me."[108] Her re-entry is dramatized through stanzas of reseeing ("riveggio," "veggio"): she spots the Esquiline Hill, the gleaming Vatican, and the Tarpeian Rock of the Campidoglio. Finally, she bows ("inchino") before Santa Maria Maggiore, the basilica of which Francesco and Antonio were the former and current archbishops, respectively.[109] Undergirding this poetic itinerary through the Eternal City is her recent identification as a penitent, which had facilitated her and Squilletti's return. The cardinal's clemency and largesse have rewarded her contrition, she states – even as she quickly dismisses anticipated criticisms that her still flowing golden locks were hardly the shaved hair expected of penitents. Indeed, the poem highlights Francesco's various benefactions to Costa's family: her own return to Rome, the safe placement of her sister (presumably Anna) in a convent, and the employment of her ne'er-do-well brother Paolo as a soldier. The latter subject takes up a surprising five of the nineteen octaves in a poem already remarkable for the uncharacteristic glimpse it offers into Costa's familial context. Costa's oscillation between fear and pride as her brother takes to the battlefield likely dates the poem to the period around her February departure from Florence and the March conclusion of the War of Castro. Despite the acknowledgments of Francesco's generosity, these stanzas also serve to underscore the reciprocity of her family's relationship to the Barberini and her professed support for a military enterprise that was generally unpopular but dear to these patrons.

Costa addresses two further poems to Antonio Barberini. One appears to predate Urban's death, perhaps composed during the War of Castro since Costa is still able to claim that "the Lion, conquered by the bees, lies down" and that Italy kneels before Antonio's feet.[110] In this verse celebrating Antonio's military prowess, Costa's efforts to ingratiate herself veer towards the unabashed. "I desire nothing else for my own well-being than your own, and hope fervently that my fortunes will be protected by that same hand that knew how to protect Italy, which for so much of your rule enjoyed good fortune," she declares in its introductory prose letter.[111] Amid a series of poetic allusions to both of the rivers he has conquered and others famed for containing precious gold and amber sediment, she heralds his military *salute* (salvation, well-being, safety) and his munificence, claiming that the gold which rains steadily down from his hands gilds the century.

Antonio's generosity is foregrounded in the other poem, that thanking the cardinal for the golden chain he gifted Costa for her *Cecilia martire*. Predictably, the verse plays on the chain theme: just as the cardinal – himself an unbreakable chain of virtue – enchained his enemies, so too has he "chained" Costa's neck and, with it, her heart. And just as Jove once grasped a golden chain from which Juno was held pendent ("pende da catena appesa"), a scene from the *Iliad* (XV.15–22), so too does Costa depend on her benefactor ("io pendo da te").[112] Should the terms of this rather overwrought comparison not already be clear, she declares him a worthy Jove in the following line (conveniently sidestepping the reason for Juno's detention, as the goddess to whom she likens herself was being punished for her troublemaking).

Although the stated context for the poem is the presentation of *Cecilia martire*, the composition is also a response to Urban's death. The Barberini sun has been extinguished on earth, she writes, and Hercules has been felled by the Nemean Lion. Reversing the outcome of the first of Hercules's twelve labours, this image also negates the lion/bee symbolism found in the other poem for Antonio (as well as in the frontispieces for Urban's own poetry editions in which David, and later Samson, wrestles with a lion out of whose mouth the Barberini bees fly, and in the Barberini-commissioned tapestry *Constantine Fighting the Lion* representing an emperor with whom the pope self-identified).[113] Costa proposes her *Cecilia martire* as an aid to mourning, since Antonio will be able to recognize his uncle in its pages. This notably inverts the power dynamic of the epic itself, where Urban I had heartened Cecilia with the promise that that the Barberini would keep her memory alive. Costa now suggests that through her *Cecilia* poem Antonio may keep eternal his uncle's memory. Just as Cecilia derived faith, happiness, and tranquillity from her bond with the Barberini pope's ancient predecessor, now this same saint renders unto Urban VIII "sublime applause and warm welcome" ("applausi eccelsi ed accoglienze liete") in heaven – a phrase that recalls the *sommi applausi* that similarly filled the air during Cecilia's entombment in the epic's final lines. In short, Costa repositions her *Cecilia martire* after Urban's death to underscore his sanctity and to reiterate her own panegyric service to the family.

After the poems to Antonio are nine sonnets, which Costa calls *saette* (arrows), a series denouncing "the fickleness of the lowly masses upon the death of Urban VIII."[114] The titular arrows, we learn in the third sonnet, are those of God's ire at this betrayal of his vicar. They are, in other words, at once both God's and Costa's. While a *sede vacante* regularly threw Rome into upheaval, at times violently, Urban's had prompted a particularly acute reaction.[115] When Rome's citizens were blocked from destroying a Bernini statue of him safeguarded at the Capitol, for example, they settled for smashing a stucco replica to bits. Written condemnations of his papacy were especially harsh. Gigli, for instance, noted that *pasquinate* (the anonymous, typically satirical works pasted onto Rome's "talking statue" Pasquino) abounded:

The populace unleashed itself against the dead Urban and the Barberini, with insults and with the pen, writing every evil of them, so that an infinite number of texts were published, in Latin and in vernacular, in prose and in verse, to an extent that I believe I have never seen before. Some were curious and facetious, others satirical and stinging, and still others biting and unbecoming of a Christian to rip apart the reputation of a pope with false slander, as if an impious and most wicked tyrant had died. If the Christians treated the head of the Church in this way, what would the Turks and heretics do? In short, anyone who had wit and was an eloquent writer or good poet proved it by speaking ill about Urban and his nephews.

Il popolo si sfogava contro Papa Urbano morto, et i Barberini, con parole ingiuriose, et con la penna, scrivendone ogni male, onde furno publicate infinite composizioni così latine, come volgari, così in prosa, come in versi, che io non credo che fusse già mai simil cosa. Alcune erano curiose et facete, altre satiriche et pungenti, et altre troppo mordaci et indegne di huomo Christiano in lacerare la fama di un Papa, ancora con false calunnie, come se fusso morto un empio, et sceleratissimo Tiranno. Che se i Christiani così trattavano il capo della Chiesa, che faranno li turchi et li heretici? In somma chi haveva bell'ingegno, et era eloquente scrittore, o buon poeta, lo dimostrava in dir male di Urbano et de' suoi nepoti.[116]

Ameyden similarly recorded that that residents had taken to singing a serenata against "Papa Gabella" (The Taxation Pope), a nightly event with an ever-growing crowd of musicians, assemblies of the elite's carriages, and a populace that "repeated the refrain like a sing-song."[117] In the words of John Hunt in his study on papal vacancies, "based on the sheer number of pasquinades circulating, Urban VIII was the most vilified pope since Paul IV," that is, in nearly a century.[118] Costa takes explicit aim at these "sonetti … e novelle," criticizing them as she symbolically replaces them with her own verse.[119]

Her nine "arrows" progress from desolation to defiance. While during his life the pope was able to keep the Romans in check, at his passing the greatest ruin fell "upon us" ("sovra noi") – a curious use of first-person plural in the initial sonnet that could refer collectively to the city's citizens but could equally apply to the Barberini and their retinue.[120] In the poems that follow, Costa decries as traitors ("traditori") those who besmirch the memory of a pontiff who had "too much goodness, too much faith, too much honour."[121] "Rome," she laments, "oh Rome, what are you doing?"[122] But if those around her have turned on the Barberini and proven themselves to lack all fealty, she stands apart: "I shall never be like you [traitors]; ever loyal, I pray for vengeance against you."[123] (She glides over the fact that she herself had approached their Pamphili successors as potential benefactors and recipients of her verse.) By the final sonnets, Costa shifts to proclaiming the Barberini's resilience. The bee – which does not sting those who feed on its honey – is reborn after its death, and the Barberini laurels will never decline in splendour.[124]

These same themes shape the two poems memorializing Costanza Barberini, the cardinals' mother. It is unlikely that Costa would have had a relationship to this devout woman who had refused to attend comedic performances and became a nun on her deathbed, but the poetic nod to her serves to further ingratiate Costa to her sons.[125] Indeed, an elegy that recalls Costa's funereal *Selva di cipressi* frames Costanza's death within the aftermath of her brother-in-law's demise: Rome herself laments that she had been home to two complementary divine virtues, majesty and piety – that is, urbanity ("Urbanità") and constancy ("Costanza") – that have just been lost simultaneously.[126] A subsequent sonnet further conjoins the two figures: Costanza's piety, which had prevented the "King of the Bees" from stinging as he built his empire, necessarily died with him.[127]

The inclusion of these Barberini poems in a volume otherwise dedicated to a celebratory portrait of the French court is curious. Bianchi deemed the *saette* in particular "tone-deaf and unforgivably lacking any sense of opportuneness if written after a space of time."[128] But the prevalence of this subset of verse – thirteen of the *Tromba di Parnaso*'s forty poems – and the pairing of funeral poems with those dedicated to Cardinals Francesco and Antonio that slightly predate the pope's death suggest that Costa perhaps may have originally envisioned assembling a poetic volume for these benefactors. Such a project would have been disrupted by the degree of their fall from power and their departure from Italy, but it could be reworked into this context thanks to the Barberini's indebtedness to the French royal house. Meanwhile, the family's inclusion in the Bourbon-themed collection signalled the latter's magnanimity. We might hypothesize therefore that Costa opted to publish these earlier compositions when given the opportunity to do so in Paris, much as she did with her *Festa reale* libretto. The singular focus of this cluster of poems is Costa's loyalty to the Barberini (an allegiance professed with an at times inartful overtness), a family whose French connections, particularly to Mazarin, possibly contributed to her own invitation to the Palais Royale. The incorporation of this verse into the *Tromba di Parnaso* pays homage to those overlapping patronage ties and demonstrates her continued fealty in a period of political hardship for her Barberini benefactors.

The Plumed Bee

The Barberini's fortunes in Rome would eventually be restored. The marriage of their nephew Maffeo to Innocent's grandniece facilitated a rapprochement with the pope and allowed their return in 1653, although Taddeo (Maffeo's father) would die in exile. Their position would only fully stabilize after the election of Alexander VII in April 1655. By then Costa too was back in Rome.

Despite the various travails they all encountered over the intervening years, Costa's relationship to the Barberini endured. Indeed, her last known publication applauds one of their most notable cultural undertakings. This 1656 commemorative broadside poem celebrates a tournament spectacle staged by Maffeo for Queen Christina of Sweden:

To the Prince of Palestrina on the Equestrian Fete Staged by His Excellency for Her Majesty Queen Christina of Sweden:

The gold-plumed bee among golden wheat sheaves
skims the immortal frond as it does flowers,
amid the battles of honour it sweetly holds its arrow
astride a winged steed and above the animated voices.
In the century of the stars and blessed breezes,
it enjoys the magnificence its merits deserve,
it smiles upon the festivities, and spreads the wings
of its fame with full glory equal to his merit.
Here, Rome, Caesar has made of your royal roof
a Campidoglio for the great queen,
who rises and bows among your patricians.
But this great prince, whose glories I wish to raise
with a fitting quill, and whom heaven destines
to be a sun among the stars, has his leaf on Olympus.

Sonetto stampato di Margherita Costa all'ecc. principe di Palestrina per la festa a cavallo fatta da S.E. alla maestà di Cristina Regina di Svezia:

L'ape ch'ha penne d'or tra spighe aurate
Lambe qual suol i fior, fronda immortale
Ha tra pugnia d'honor dolce lo strale
Sovr'alato destrier, voci animate.
Nel secol de le stelle, aure beate
Gode de' preggi suoi pompa fatale
Tra feste arride, e de la fama l'ale
Spande carca di gloria, al merto eguale
Ecco Cesare o Roma, a gran reina,
fatto del reggio tetto un Campidoglio,
Che tra patritij tuoi erge e s'inchina
Ma che gran prence, e con qual penna io voglio
Alzar le glorie tue, il ciel destina
Il sol tra stelle, ha su l'olimpi il foglio.[129]

In December 1655, Christina arrived in Rome after having abdicated her throne and publicly converted to Catholicism. The city greeted her with an array of festivities worthy of such an illustrious proselyte, including a triumphal entry, musket salutes, concerts, fireworks, and other spectacles.[130] The Barberini took a leading role in organizing these entertainments, providing the most impressive of the already magnificent displays: three operas and an equestrian carousel (a tournament opera fusing horsemanship, music, and allegory).[131] The family's leading role in orchestrating the queen's celebrations reflected not merely their formidable experience in staging such events but also their recent reinstatement in Roman religio-political life. The performances organized for Christina so soon after their full return offered them a crucial opportunity to broadcast their renewed social and cultural prominence in the Eternal City.

Costa honoured this undertaking by her long-standing benefactors, patrons who provided assistance in Rome and whose stay in France overlapped with her own. Costa – herself a singer – commented not on any of the three operas but rather on the equestrian spectacle, yet another example of how she strategically identified equestrianism as especially dear to her patrons, as seen in chapter 4. The choice certainly would have flattered her dedicatee, Maffeo, who sponsored the event (at least on paper, Francesco having provided the bulk of the considerable funding) and performed as the leading horseman.[132] While the operas – particularly *La vita humana overo Il trionfo della pietà*, whose themes Alexander VII had selected himself – were headline events on the queen's calendar, the tournament was unmatched in its grandiosity. So hotly anticipated was the performance that many of Rome's inhabitants, as well as those of neighbouring villages, gathered around the doors of Palazzo Barberini to catch a glimpse.[133]

Historical accounts commemorated the event, as did a vibrant painting by Filippo Lauri and Filippo Gagliardi showing the ornate production and its three thousand spectators (fig. 5.5). In order to fashion this outdoor theatre, the Barberini demolished a number of buildings in their courtyard, constructed stands and a triumphal arch opposite the dais, and hung tapestries around the perimeter.[134] Elaborate lighting and costumes added to the splendour (and expense) of the event. To the crowd's amazement, the nighttime carousel was illuminated not merely by candles and torches, but also – in a "modern and never before seen invention" – by sixteen iron *stelle* (stars) suspended above the centre of the theatre.[135] So stunning were these *stelle*, echoes another contemporary, that they seemed more a work of magic than of human ingenuity.[136] In addition to magnificent chariots and a fire-breathing dragon, the performance showcased two lavishly accoutred squadrons composed of 12 combatants, 8 trumpeters, and 120 grooms each. The teams of Knights and Amazonians competed in an exhibition of their skills as horsemen and pistoleers before turning their swords against the dragon.[137] Like the illumination, the combatants' extravagant headdresses dazzled audiences. The Amazonians, led by Maffeo (seen in the centre foreground of fig. 5.5), wore red and gold headpieces containing no fewer than 600 plumes apiece, while those of the Knights glittered from the silver rosettes and silvered glass sheaves of wheat

Figure 5.5. Filippo Lauri and Filippo Gagliardi, *Carousel at Palazzo Barberini in Honour of Christina of Sweden*, 1656. Museo di Roma. Image courtesy of Wikimedia Commons.

(a symbol of the Swedish house of Vasa) nestled among their turquoise feathers.[138] Vocal and instrumental music heightened the evening's excitement and drama.

Costa's sonnet likely numbered among the commemorative materials distributed by the Barberini.[139] Printed as a large broadsheet (31.7 x 44.8 cm), it is a work made for display. The continuities between Costa's poem and the historical-visual record indicate that she saw the carousel first-hand or, barring that, received her information on good authority. Her peculiar description of a "plumed" Barberini bee flitting among ears of wheat, for example, alludes to the movement of the horsemen within the tournament arena by way of their remarkable headgear. Similarly, while the contenders primarily demonstrated their skill with pistols and swords, Costa alludes to an arrow grasped in the prince's hands, one also visible in the Lauri-Gagliardi painting. Finally, Costa's descriptions of Maffeo as a "sun among stars" and the era as the "century of stars" not only is consistent with the celestial language of her own equestrian *Festa reale* and the solar imagery conventionally associated with the Barberini but perhaps also alludes to those innovative *stelle* that illuminated the performance to the awe of spectators and commentators.[140]

This composition highlights once again the centrality of equestrian entertainments within seventeenth-century political pageantry and the degree to which Costa used such spectacles as a valuable means of appealing to patrons. The prominent attribution to Costa in 1656 of a commemorative (and perhaps commissioned) poem depicting an event of social, political, and economic importance to the Barberini also underscores the cultural weight her name still carried in Rome even at this relatively late date. It also caps a long-standing relationship Costa enjoyed with the family, and Cardinal Francesco in particular.

Conclusion

The Barberini's tournament commemorated the Catholic victory that Christina's conversion represented, but it also dramatically re-established their socio-political legitimacy in Rome and restored their primacy in the sponsorship of those courtly spectacles by which such legitimacy was then so unforgettably communicated. Costa's print relationship to the family – from the *Cecilia martire* sacred epic to the poems included in *La tromba di Parnaso* to the broadsheet lauding their equestrian spectacle – is testimony to this tumultuous decade in the family's fortunes, from when their troubles were just on the horizon to when breathless crowds again pressed against their doors eager to see one of their performances. At least in print (even if she dedicated the *Sette giornate* manuscript to their Pamphili rivals), Costa presented herself as a loyal Barberini creature throughout these years. It is at the end of this trajectory, spanning their restorations of the ancient Sant'Urbano alla Caffarella to their construction of an impressively innovative theatre, that the broadsheet poem's suggestion that the Barberini bee now "enjoys the magnificence its merits are due" ("gode de' preggi suoi pompa fatale") takes on a fuller meaning. Like Costa herself in 1644, the Barberini enjoy a "well-deserved" homecoming.

Beyond the elegiac and occasional verse that affirmed her continued support and loyalty, Costa's composition of *Cecilia martire* marks a significant undertaking in terms of both her grasp of different genres and her incorporation of patrons into her writings. Fitting neatly within burgeoning interest in both sacred epic and Cecilia herself, the poem's dual protagonists (a singing saint and her Urban protector) and a plotline carefully recalibrated from conventional narratives are crafted to strengthen her Barberini bonds. The poem also marks a turn from her burlesque Florentine works, recalling instead the more sober publications (such as the *Flora* texts and *Festa reale*) by which she had advanced Medici dynastic rhetoric. This same approach would also guide the publication to which we next turn, *La selva di Diana,* in which she pivots from celebrating popes and cardinals to exalting powerful women, namely, female regents. Yet perhaps in the figure of a Cecilia – steadfast, courageous, and self-assured in the face of contrary forces – we might detect the seeds of Costa's first full exploration of political and cultural authority as exercised by women.

Chapter Six

Hunting for Diana, or An Ode to Regents

The period of Italophilia in the French musical-theatrical scene that brought Costa to Paris and prompted the publication of her *Festa reale* and *La tromba di Parnaso* in 1647 also saw her produce a third volume, the collection of verse entitled *La selva di Diana*.[1] Each of these three texts honours a patron who facilitated Costa's performance itinerary in the mid-1640s. The *Festa reale* and *La tromba di Parnaso* celebrate the French court broadly, and Cardinal Mazarin and Queen Anne specifically (with a nod to the Barberini, as discussed in the previous chapter), for the invitation to perform in Rossi's 1647 opera *L'Orfeo* and, in the case of the cardinal, for his assistance in getting her works published. With the dedication of *La selva di Diana*, Costa looks back to Marie Christine, the regent duchess of Savoy for whom she sang in 1645 and to whom she here pays homage in a volume of poetry that champions the figure of the "regent" as a ruler, benefactress, and modern-day Diana.

Costa did not overlook the fact that her current patroness in France was also a regent. Mirroring the book's dedication and opening thirty-eight-stanza poem applauding Christine is a concluding canzone extolling Anne, who also happened to be the duchess's sister-in-law. The volume thus honours two of the most important regents in seventeenth-century Europe, women who also shared an enthusiasm for music and dance. Bridging these two pillars of the book – a duchess at one end, a queen at the other – is a set of fourteen poems lauding an assortment of women before whom Costa had sung in Rome, likely around 1644. Led by one Lavinia Lopez Buratti, this coterie included Cardinal Mazarin's stepmother, a countess, a number of women connected to the illustrious Malvezzi family of Bologna, and even Buratti's baby daughter, all of whom are addressees of individual poems. The publication reconstructs through verse a performative itinerary defined by female hosts who supported Costa's endeavours, and lent legitimacy to her pursuit of a singing career, a vocation that often left women susceptible to censure and slander.

Like the "unfamiliar woods" of Diana and her nymphs, Costa's text is largely devoid of men.[2] Unlike her other verse collections, it exclusively features women as dedicatees or as speakers. This was a notable departure from Costa's previous works, particularly given her tributes to men of influence and her neglect of Ferdinando II's two powerful female regents. Gone are the ventriloquized male voices, the haughty and indifferent *bella donna*, the burlesque characters, and the salty innuendos characteristic of Costa's Florentine verse collections. In *La selva di Diana*, women alone have a narrative voice, and the predominant theme of the amorous poetry is female suffering, due especially to lovers' departures, infidelities, and inattentions. Even the handful of religiously themed poems showcase a woman who turns to the divine only after being spurned by her beloved, as in a poem voiced by the "Beautiful Woman to Amore While Standing before Her Confessor."[3]

This focus on distance and loss may reflect empathy that Costa likely felt with her two honorees. Her 1645 Turin contract describes her as "the widow Margherita Costa."[4] Although her modern detractors dismissed this widowhood on the basis of her presumed courtesanship – Alessandro Ademollo quipped "Some widow!"[5] – Costa herself would later emphasize her status in a 1657 letter to Mario Chigi, from whom she sought assistance and patronage.[6] Costa thus shared with Christine and Anne the bond of having lost a husband (even if her will demonstrates that they were estranged) – as well as a lover, in the case of the recently imprisoned Squilletti – and of needing to strike a position of visibility and cultural authority even, or especially, as a woman on her own.

Despite the themes of loss and despair prevalent in its selection of amorous poetry, *La selva di Diana* nevertheless focuses simultaneously on the triumphs of powerful women and the opportunities they confer on those in their retinue. Tracing Costa's relationship to the three women who headline her volume – Christine in Turin, Anne in Paris, and Lavinia in Rome – through both her performance history and her literary tributes, this chapter suggests that she dramatically expanded the criteria for effective female regency, redefining the role by staking out new possible identities for the regent – ones that did not necessarily require either widowhood or aristocratic blood – and reimagining the ways in which women could use cultural capital to secure power. In so doing, Costa tackled a thorny socio-political question of the day. Early modern Europe saw the rise of a number of female regents and rulers, from the aforementioned *tutrici* in Florence to Catherine de' Medici, from Christina of Sweden to Elizabeth I. While the instatement of female rulers following the death of a husband or father was often a political necessity, the very presence of women in power could easily provoke resentment among their subjects. Objecting to the Catholic queens of mid-sixteenth-century Scotland and England, for example, the Protestant theologian John Knox famously decried this "monstrous regiment of women," which he deemed "moste repugnant to nature."[7] To allow a woman power, he blustered, was to "defile, pollute and prophane … the throne and seat of God."[8] While other commentators proved more measured in their criticisms, women's regency existed to the chagrin of many – particularly when the woman in question was foreign-born, as both Christine and Anne were.

The regent was an especially contentious figure in France and its satellites like Savoy, where Salic law forbade female succession. Although the text of the law was revealed in the mid-sixteenth century to have been forged, restrictions on female rule persisted.[9] In any case, as Katherine Crawford has argued, the acceptability of female regency hinged on the assumption that, despite her presumed deficiencies, the mother's natural maternal affection for her child ensured her faithful stewardship of his kingdom during his minority, while his right to the throne lent legitimacy to her otherwise impermissible power.[10]

At the same time, however, men were also framing female exemplars within written "galleries" of famous women, such as Cristofano Bronzini's well-known *Della dignità e nobiltà delle donne*.[11] In 1640s France, such galleries increasingly centred on the figure of the *femme forte*, a heroic woman whose strength derived from her paradoxical ability to overcome the weaknesses endemic to her sex. Drawn from ancient and biblical sources, as well as modern history, these women – typically virgins and widows – fused female virtue with "virile" approaches to military-political demands. Notably, they did so in service to religious, familial, or civic forces; the archetypal *femme forte* was the Virgin Mary.[12] Similar ideas had already circulated in Tasso's late sixteenth-century *Discorso sulla virtù feminile e donnesca*, which differentiated between female virtue (namely modesty) and womanly *virtù*; the latter was the exclusive purview of noble women who, as the inheritors of royal and imperial blood, could demonstrate manly virtues. The first "heroic woman" in Tasso's gallery is Mary of Hungary (1505–1558), a regent he extols as a valorous military captain and a wise public administrator.[13]

The portions of Costa's *La selva di Diana* addressed to historical personages similarly resembles a gallery of *femmes fortes*. In contrast with the lovesick and forlorn women who populate the section of amorous poetry, the regents are the volume's heroines. They excel at their roles by fusing maternal care with political might. To the virile traits of the *femme forte* Costa conspicuously adds cultural patronage of music and the other arts. So invested is she in the potentialities of female regents that, remarkably, she inventively presses into their ranks Lavinia – a noblewoman who remained married and lived in papal Rome. Drawing together in verse the characteristics of the ideal regent and the particular rhetorical campaigns and personas of Christine, Anne, and Lavinia, Costa signals her newfound appreciation for and, indeed, reliance on the historical women who determined the performance calendars of their courts or coteries. Consequently, imagery of performances and accolades – for both patroness and protégée – dominate the poems directed to these hostesses. Indicative of this orientation is the work's "Letter to the Reader." Alongside its stock professions of female authorial humility, common to all Costa's publications, we find what is for her a more unconventional request, one as exceptional as the regents she describes – that we overlook her gender and admit that her work merits consideration if not outright applause ("se non la vuoi stimar degna d'applauso, confessala di riguardo meritevole").[14]

Giving a Regent the Royal Treatment

In January 1645, Costa received an invitation to join Marie Christine's court as a chamber singer. Her generous salary – 1,000 lire, along with provisions of wine, bread, meat, and other foodstuffs – far surpassed those of other female singers employed by the duchess.[15] Also performing in those years was one Isabella Lessona, for instance, whose lifetime of musical service never saw an increase in her 400 lire stipend; even the occasional gift, such as a 500 lire bonus, did not prevent her from approaching Duke Carlo Emanuele II after his mother's death to augment her "meagre salary."[16] While Costa's compensation was more handsome than Isabella's, her stay was brief, since she appears to have returned to Rome later that year. The most likely scenario is that, the open terms of her contract notwithstanding, Christine invited Costa in 1645 with the intention of also having her perform in one or a series of spectacles, staged that winter and spring, that were of particular importance to her regency. And while Costa's more critical commentators point to her return to Rome as indication of a failure in Turin, archival documents from 1649 indicate that in fact she would be invited back to the city following her time in France.[17]

Christine, the French daughter of Henry IV and Marie de' Medici, had arrived in Turin for her 1619 marriage. Upon his death in 1637, her husband, Vittorio Amedeo, left behind not only a five-year-old son but also two brothers, Cardinal Maurizio and Tommaso, Savoyard princes who had nourished hopes of ascending to power, especially when the duke and duchess seemed doomed to remain without surviving male issue.[18] The absence of any instruction by Vittorio Amedeo on the future of his realm, save for a deathbed request that his wife assume the regency in lieu of his siblings, strengthened their resolve. Once Christine was confirmed, Maurizio went on a letter-writing blitz, fuming to his associates that a maternal – rather than uncular – regency would result in "the ruin of Piemonte, the desolation of its peoples, and harm to both Italy and Christianity."[19] Backed by Spanish forces, he and Tommaso commenced a military campaign against their sister-in-law, who was supported by French armies. From 1639 to 1640, Turin was the site of a double siege: the Spaniards held the city and attacked its central citadel, where Christine's supporters had retreated, while the French attacked the city's external walls. The duchess herself subsequently escaped with her children to Chambery. Eventually the warring parties agreed to a compromise, dividing the territories between them: Maurizio in Nice, Tommaso in Ivrea, and Christine in Turin.

When a peace agreement was finally struck in 1640, Christine set about restoring the city and signalling her legitimacy through patronage. The impetus to do so was all the stronger due to the continued presence of the French armies, which would remain for five more years, leaving only in March 1645. In addition to sponsoring architectural and urban development projects, such as the construction of Piazza Reale (now Piazza San Carlo), the duchess renewed the rich calendar of *feste*, ballets, and concerts that had enlivened the city before the siege.[20] Christine had shared her passion for music and especially ballet with the Turinese court prior to her husband's death, cultivating a series of annual events celebrating Carnival, the feast of Saint Nicholas, and her birthday (also the couple's wedding anniversary).[21] Her efforts complemented the campaign first begun by Duke Emanuele Filiberto (1528–1580), who, after moving his capital from Chambery to Turin, strove to transform it into a new centre of culture and learning.[22] The staging of Christine's spectacles was suspended after her husband's death , but her return to Turin led to a revitalization of the city's music and theatre scene. Through a program of "monumental opulence," the new Savoyard festivals exalted the young duke and staged collective support for his regent mother.[23]

Christine's enthusiasm for theatre was perhaps heightened by her affair with Count Filippo San Martino d'Agliè, Turin's pre-eminent poet, composer, and choreographer who produced the court's most impressive performances.[24] When Costa's contract was struck in 1645, d'Agliè was then preparing *Il dono del re dell'Alpi* (The Gift of the Alpine King), a magnificent spectacle staged at the Castle of Rivoli just outside Turin. Fusing dance, song, and impressive stage machinery, this production celebrated Christine's birthday while buttressing the authority she held over the Turinese provinces – a critical and timely message, as negotiations for the long-awaited departure of the French armies neared completion and would be executed just weeks later.

A form of elaborate dinner theatre, *Il dono del re* took place in four different halls of the castle, each decorated to resemble a province in Christine's realm: Savoy, Turin/Piedmont, Nice, and Monferrato.[25] While other seventeenth-century courts memorialized such events with printed festival books, Turin preferred the medium of the manuscript. Thirteen lavish volumes, likely prepared by the calligrapher Tommaso Borgonio in collaboration with local artists, offer detailed descriptions and brilliantly coloured illustrations, such as that in figure 6.1 showing the first hall of the *Dono del re*.[26]

As Christine and her kin feasted on delicacies from each province, from fish to fine wines, a sophisticated system of mechanical transport ushered them from room to room, where they enjoyed vocal music and dance. When they reached the final hall, dancers representing local populations performed a grand ballet. In the words of Mercedes Viale Ferrero, the event exhibited "a veritable repertory of the popular customs, traditions, and trades of the duchy."[27] A procession of Savoyard rulers followed, leading a silver chariot bearing Carlo Emanuele II in the guise of the Alpine king. Ostensibly a birthday gift from the young duke to his mother, the spectacle represented him offering his kingdom to her as the titular gift. This is, the manuscript text proclaims, a worthy reward for she who "knew how to defend and maintain [the kingdom], through arms and art, and with virtue in her heart and the marvels of her royal spirit."[28]

Figure 6.1. Illustration in *Dono del re dell'Alpi*, 1645. Turin, Biblioteca Nazionale Universitaria, q.V.60, c.4. Courtesy of the Ministero della Cultura, Biblioteca Nazionale Universitaria di Torino. Reproductions not permitted.

While the grand finale of *Il dono del re* was a ballet, vocal performance played an essential role throughout the production. Ensembles of chamber singers and a chorus of the duke's subjects sang the praises of both regent and realm. Each of the halls featured a female singer personifying one of the four represented regions of the duchy; the political symbolism of their costumes and props, from trophies to oars, visually exemplified their lyrical exultations of the duchess's victories. In figure 6.1, for example, a singer is seen performing from her perch atop a pedestal on the right, across from the ducal family; in her hand she grasps the Savoyard standard, a white cross on a red background.

The manuscript demonstrates that four individual women sang these solo pieces.[29] While there are extant part books for the ensemble ballet numbers, no musical scores remain for these pieces.[30] Neither the Borgonio manuscripts nor the newly launched gazette *Successi del mondo* name the singers, and archived household expense books detailing such information skip over the years between 1633 and the 1660s.[31] But the dating of Costa's contract – signed and paid a month before the 10 February performance – suggests that she was likely hired to perform as one of these four featured soloists. Christine's household singers regularly took part in ballets, meaning that an appearance by the newly arrived Roman performer would have been expected and in keeping with convention.[32]

Costa was not an unknown commodity at the Savoyard court. In April 1627, Ludovico d'Agliè (uncle of Filippo), court poet and ambassador to Rome, reported on the entertainments he provided for the visit of Louis de Bourbon, Count of Soissons, to that city. While d'Agliè had arranged for the famed harpist Orazio Michi "dell'Arpa" and castrato Loreto Vittori to perform before dinner, a pointed request by the count's men "to hear women's voices" prompted him to also commission Costa and another unnamed Roman woman to sing after the feast. The women provided, he underscored, a "most charming and honoured entertainment."[33] That d'Agliè names Costa so matter of factly, while leaving her peer unidentified, suggests that she already counted among the various musicians who orbited the Savoyard household in Rome.[34] There Cardinal Maurizio maintained an august presence during the 1620s in keeping with the family's regal aspirations, largely through the lavish patronage of writers, artists, musicians, and composers, and the founding of the Accademia dei Desiosi.[35] The cardinal later sought to add lustre to the Savoyard court by enticing several of these luminaries to follow him north, setting a precedent for Christine's importation of a Roman singer a few decades later.[36] Filippo d'Agliè was also then in Rome with his uncle and may have seen Costa perform at the Soissons dinner or at comparable events. Members of the ducal family kept close tabs on the cultural activities sponsored in their name. In 1623, for example, Vittorio Amedeo's brother Emanuele Filiberto, Viceroy of Sicily, wrote Ludovico with thinly veiled impatience that a requested report describing that year's Carnival festivities – infantry and horse tournaments, as well as a musical comedy – was still outstanding.[37]

In short, any singer known in the halls of Palazzo Montegiordano, the cardinal's splendid Roman residence, was also on the radar of Palazzo Reale in Turin. Christine likely invited Costa, a well-known singer with experience performing before Savoyard figures, in order to enhance spectacles, like *Il dono del re*, that were vital to her cultural campaign in the wake of the siege. While the terms of Costa's contract allowed for an annual renewal, over the course of the century Turin became a "must go" destination for distinguished female singers hired expressly for the Carnival season.[38] The reason for Costa's first departure is unclear; however, the timing, duration, and nature of her stay would soon become the norm for visiting musicians of her calibre.

Costa's exposure to the highly orchestrated demonstrations of Christine's authority – from the musical productions to ongoing artistic and architectural programs – informs her poetic overtures in *La selva di Diana*. The panegyric poem that opens the volume contains the requisite praise of Christine's beauty and feminine virtues: there are references to the *materno amore* (maternal love) upon which her regency so acutely relied, as well as eloquence, honesty, prudence, and goodness.[39] But Costa's Christine is also a heroic woman, and passages hailing her military victories serve to underscore her political legitimacy. Under her guidance, the Alps – personified as a woman with snowy-white locks crowned with an oak garland, that is, the classical *corona civica* bestowed on those who save fellow citizens from an enemy – supports the stony walls of the Italian kingdoms upon her own back ("sostien col tergo le sassose mura de regni de l'Italia"). She safeguards them from hostile swords and enemy ire ("ferro ostile e nemica arsura"), raising her brow to rebel armies ("contr'oste rubella alza la fronte").[40]

The poem mirrors and resolves an earlier one concerning her husband's death and the Siege of Turin (then still ongoing) from Costa's 1640 collection of elegiac verse, *La selva dei cipressi*, discussed in chapter 3. Christine's poem, called simply *L'Alpi* (The Alps), celebrates her triumphs and honour in the siege's wake; Vittorio Amedeo's, entitled *Le lagrime dell'Alpe* (The Tears of the Alps), is a historical lament by a personified Italy who bemoans the terror and bloodshed she endures upon his death. Echoing Ariosto's portrayal of the sixteenth-century Italian Wars in canto 33 of the *Orlando furioso*, Costa describes the infernal caverns that opened to release the Furies of war following the duke's demise.[41] In addition to scenes of combat – bodies filling the river Dora and horses marching through the river Po – the poem portrays the destruction mythologically, through repeated allusions to sobbing nymphs, and environmentally, through images of a forest razed in order to build war machines.[42] Surveying the territorial ruin, Italy bewails this "tearful spectacle" ("spettacolo lagrimoso").[43]

In presenting readers with a renewed landscape of joyous plenty, the poem dedicated to Christine revisits passages from this earlier text.[44] In *La selva di Diana* Costa reworks two full stanzas on the illustriousness of the ducal house, such that they are no longer about an extinguished light but about reignited promise.[45] She uses these moments of revision to resolve the mythological and environmental woes of the earlier poem. While there the ducal throne has "with its nymphs been abandoned to the earth, / and the waves [of the Po] are swells of war" ("con le sue ninfe abbandonata a terra, / e sono l'onde mie flutti di guerra"), here it is "to [its] nymphs the fruitful bearer of every good, / and its waves are swells of peace" ("a le sue ninfe è d'ogni ben ferace / e son l'onde sue flutti di pace").[46] The forest is reinhabited and transformed by a new Diana, while the cypress – a symbol of mourning – is supplanted by the mighty oak.

In addition to lauding her patroness's political-military success, as well as other qualities that made her a good regent, Costa strategically homes in on the question of Christine's regality, a question of great importance to the duchess.[47] In December 1632, the duke had asserted the royal status of their house, via the *trattamento reale*, on the basis of a 1485 claim to the crown of Cyprus. This act balanced the need to create a sustainable political identity for Savoy with Christine's legacy as a princess of the French crown (whose sisters, perhaps not irrelevantly, had become the queens of Spain and England). The couple next initiated an image campaign to anchor this adopted majesty, one that Christine especially sustained until her later life, "exploit[ing] in the quest for Sabaudian royalty a wide range of court culture, particularly court art, court theater, and court erudition."[48] A 1634 thesis frontispiece by artist Giovanni Boetto, for example, shows Victory crowning Teucer the first king of Cyprus; Teucer has the duke's features, while the deity who endows him with the closed golden crown indicative of royalty bears those of Christine.[49] Perhaps with French precedent in mind, Christine filled the city and its cultural products with this symbol. Crowns are to be found throughout the *Dono del re* manuscript, for instance, in both costumes and decorative elements, culminating in a scene in which four court pages emerge bearing the crowns proper to the family: those of count, marquis, duke, and king.[50] This imagery would come to a head in the *Theatrum Sabaudiae*, a monumental two-part illustrated atlas of Savoy; in the first volume alone, no fewer than seventy-four closed crowns appear on the folios depicting the various Savoyard lands, impressing a stamp of royalty across Piemonte.[51]

While the desired recognition of the house's royal status had not proven forthcoming – Italian states like Florence and Venice were in no hurry to strengthen a rival, and Cardinal Richelieu resisted acknowledging the Savoyard claims in France – shifting tides in Paris now aided Christine's ambitions.[52] As the new chief minister following Richelieu's 1642 death, Cardinal Mazarin proved more receptive than his predecessor and began addressing the duchess with royal titles.[53] Though full political recognition remained elusive, the gains were not insignificant. As Toby Osborne reminds us, courtly investment in titles was not a "matter of antiquarian interest" during a period in which new claims to sovereignty (such as the Medici's transition from merchants to grand dukes) heightened competition between peninsular states.[54] With the *trattamento reale*, Vittorio Amedeo and Christine demanded the use of royal titles in official correspondence and royal protocol in the reception of their ambassadors. Mazarin complied in part, and others in the Parisian court dutifully followed suit.[55]

The fact that the frontispiece to *La selva di Diana* – a work printed in France by the official publisher "of the king and regent queen" – would announce its dedication to "l'Altezza Reale," Her Royal Highness, was thus not a negligible detail but rather would have been a source of satisfaction to Christine, who had been explicitly denied the title *reale/royale* by Richelieu. Costa's volume is one of the few published outside of Turin to address her in this fashion, and its direct poetic reference to the duchess's high titles ("titoli ... primieri") indicate that this was no happy accident but instead a strategic choice.[56] Given Christine's protracted efforts to unite her natal bond to the French royal house with the dynastic ambitions of her adopted family, reinforced by the artistic programs in her various residences, she may have been pleased to see the queen of France bookend the volume with her; her keen eye would have approvingly noted her more prominent position with respect to her sister-in-law.[57]

Costa gives Christine this "royal treatment" throughout her poem, showing her rule to be legitimated by blood and deed. In one stanza, the Savoy are adorned with crowns of laurel, olive, and gold; another similarly traces Christine's ancestry to both the French fleur-de-lis and the papal tiara (through her Medici lineage) before concluding with an image of her own golden crown ("corona d'oro").[58] Elsewhere Costa portrays Christine as lifting her "immortal sceptre" ("scettro immortal") above the Alps.[59] She directly references Cyprus, the origin of Savoyard assertions of kingship; within a series of comparisons of Christine to legendary women and divinities, Costa calls upon the Cypriots to abandon their cult of Venus (born from the island's seafoam) and to shift their devotion to her new fair rival.[60] In praising Christine's beauty, Costa affirms through mythological symbolism her patroness's territorial claims.

Costa's presentation of Christine's Olympian qualities echoes the imagery then circulating in Turin. The inscriptions and ornaments lining the city's streets for her son Carlo Emanuele's triumphal entry into the city in April, for instance, portrayed her as Minerva, Alcmene (mother of Heracles), and an Amazon.[61] Costa's identification of Christine as a Diana allowed her to bridge her two poems about the siege and its aftermath, those dedicated to the duke and the duchess, respectively, within a sylvan setting. But the goddess also happened to be a family favourite. Hunting was a beloved pastime at their court, as well as an artistic and theatrical topos at their various residences, known collectively as the "crown of delights."[62] This program is evident in the Castello di Valentino, a riverside hunting palace given to Christine upon her marriage, one she refashioned as her *maison de plaisance*, with her apartments completed in 1644.[63] In addition to two rooms whose decorations depict her as a Flora, receiving the bounty of the Muses and the offerings of the city, a *sala della caccia* features Diana with her nymphs and hounds; its imagery associates hunting with the art of governance.[64] In Christine's later residence, the Vigna di Madama Reale, Diana appears repeatedly in the dozen paintings gracing a room dedicated to the "delights of the hunt" ("delitie della caccia").[65] Carlo Emanuele later constructed a magnificent hunting palace, the Venaria, whose internal decorations centred on Diana and whose gardens featured an elaborate temple dedicated to her. Its architect, Amedeo Castellamonte, termed it "Diana's realm" ("reggia di Diana").[66] While Costa would not have seen the Vigna or the Venaria, she would have performed in the Valentino after her patroness relocated there from the Rivoli castle in March, allowing her to observe both the family's attraction to the goddess and Christine's preferred modes of self-representation.[67]

By positioning Christine as a new Diana, and her court as a sylvan sanctuary, Costa invites the question of who might emerge as the new Actaeon. She offers an answer in her dedicatory letter, explaining that she selected her title to ward off anyone who might endanger the publication itself: "I wished to entitle it *Diana's Forest* so that any envious eye that might insidiously yearn to obscure it would become to the regal name of Your Royal Highness a new Actaeon."[68] Christine becomes not merely the protectress of her child's realm but also of the writers and singers who there seek haven. Costa repeatedly praises her welcoming nature, and portrays Turin as an inviting, bejewelled paradise:

> On its mighty banks
> the Po binds its chilly locks with a ruby garland
> and exalts amid its crystal magnificence,
> nourishing the flowers and making fronds bud.
> It has a diamond heart and its frosts are pearled,
> it has golden sand and silver waves,
> it turns according to fine turning of the propitious heavens
> and its shores harbour delightful swans.

> Con serto di rubbin l'algente crine
> Il Po s'annoda su le forti sponde
> E vanta tra le pompe christalline
> Nudrire i fiori è germogliar le fronti
> Ha di diamant' il sen perle ha per brine
> D'oro ha l'arene, et ha d'argento l'onde
> Rota, al vago rotare de' i ciel benigni
> E serbano i suoi lidi ameni cigni.[69]

Gliding along the Po – the glassy pool in which the goddess bathes – are her swans, that is, singers, who enjoy her benign protection and in return enhance the beauty of her surroundings.

While the gem imagery is reworked in part from another *Selva di cipressi* lament, for Francesco Maria della Rovere,[70] the mention of a diamond heart alludes to Christine's personal device: a diamond accompanied by the motto "plus de fermeté que d'éclat" ("more firm than brilliant"). As Costa was doubtlessly aware, given the duchess's proclivity for buying, wearing, and being depicted with fine jewels, the diamond was a symbol of her persona.[71] Her motto's consonance with the *femme forte* topos – uniting feminine and masculine virtues – suits Costa's dual focus on Christine as beautiful mother and fierce defender. D'Agliè would later draw a similar comparison in his *Le delitie,* a description of the Vigna di Madama Reale that offers a warm posthumous defence of Christine and her regency. This "great heroine" had, he declares, a "heart of diamond," the firmness of which permitted her to withstand the pressures of regency, ones that would cause even "athletes to sweat, bronze columns to shake, and marbles to sway."[72] The frontispiece (fig. 6.2) pictures Christine (again in the guise of Flora with the

Figure 6.2. Jean Baptiste Girardin after Tommaso Borgonio, frontispiece to Filindo il Costante (Filippo San Martino d'Agliè), *Le delitie, relatione della Vigna di Madama Reale Christiana di Francia*, 1667. Courtesy of the Ministero della Cultura, Biblioteca Nazionale Universitaria di Torino. Reproductions not permitted.

residence behind her) being crowned with garlands and presented with her realm's bounties, surrounded by a classical colonnade of marble. The female identity of the statues points to this as a gallery of heroic women who honour the regent, a representation akin to those made in the 1640s for Queen Anne in France, as we shall see below.

Like this later frontispiece, Costa's poem ends with Christine (now both a Diana and a Flora) figuratively encircled by admirers. In addition to Costa herself – depicted as joyously taking up a pen ("impennare") in praise of her patroness – the Muses lavish her with their favours while the poets, accompanied by a choir of "melodious voices" ("voci canore"), sing for her. The final verses anticipate that "Phoebus will immortalize your glories in song, / for you the air will shower down roses and violets, / and the sun will be crowned with an even finer gold."[73] This superlative golden crown that outstrips even the sun's own splendour is the culminating image with which Costa gives Christine the royal treatment.

Applauding a Golden Age in Paris

La selva di Diana concludes by turning to Christine's sister-in-law. The Spanish-born Anne was wed in 1615 to Louis XIII, with whom she had a chilly relationship.[74] At the time of the king's death in 1643, Louis XIV – the couple's first child after nearly two decades of stillbirths – was a mere four years old. The immediate political scenario Anne faced differed from that of Christine, whose transition to power was uncodified but secured by her husband's deathbed decree. Perhaps wary of regency due to his repeated conflicts with his own regent mother, Marie de' Medici (whom he had twice exiled), and general distrust of his wife, in his will Louis restricted her authority by establishing a voting council able to undermine her wishes. Only by quietly convincing the Parliament to overrule these arrangements did Anne solidify her position.

While Marie had struck a bold leadership persona that at times overshadowed her son, Anne distanced herself from this precedent by emphasizing her child's authority and rhetorically assuming the role of an ancillary, obliging mother.[75] She placed her trust unwaveringly in Cardinal Mazarin, who guided the regent in policy and political strategy and saw to the education of the young king, his godson. This relationship, largely unexpected given the cardinal's connections to Anne's nemesis Richelieu and the continuation of his anti-Spanish policies, caused her opponents to lament and, later, to more strongly condemn what largely became a governing partnership (and, according to rumours, an affair).[76] Even in the event of civil unrest, Anne generally deferred to the cardinal's judgment rather than chart her own course, though she remained intent on preserving her son's position. In her study of French regency, Crawford observes that the seamless transition of power from mother to child upon Louis's majority in 1651 was unusual in that "no regent before her slipped so entirely from view."[77] In this regard, at least, Anne played the role of the ideal regent.

Though Anne opted for a tamer persona than that of her Medici mother-in-law, her regency witnessed a surge in artistic and literary images of heroic women. The *femme forte* topos, which had begun to circulate during Marie's reign, expanded in the 1630s and especially the 1640s, casting Anne and her ladies in these inspired roles.[78] In 1645 Anne herself commissioned Simon Vouet to decorate her Palais Royal apartments with paintings depicting the deeds of illustrious women. One of the most important written texts, Pierre Le Moyne's *La gallerie des femmes fortes*, was published in 1647, the same year Costa sang in Paris. Twenty biographies of Hebrew, Greek, Roman, and Christian women, each paired with a modern parallel, explicitly invited comparisons with the queen mother. Le Moyne admits to having had reservations about female rule but declares that he sees instead "a regency managed with vigour."[79] He imaginatively restages the crowning of this "heroic and royal" queen – this time at the hands of her valiant female peers:

These are sovereign and illustrious women, who, like you, have been the most beautiful sights of their ages. They are victorious women whom virtue and glory have crowned with their own hands. And it should be a sweet satisfaction to you that so many sovereign and illustrious women have descended from their thrones and theatres to become your spectators. The sound and acclamations of so many victresses who clap for you should be a pleasing concert. The important thing, Madam, is that this applause is not for show, that these acclamations are not flatteries compelled or bought. They are serious and legitimate tributes that the vanquished render to their victress.

Ce sont des souveraines et des illustres, qui ont esté comme vous, les plus beaux spectacles de leurs siècles: ce sont des victorieuses, que la vertu et la gloire ont couronnées de leurs propres mains. Et ce vous doit estre une douce satisfaction, que tant de souveraines et tant d'illustres, soient descendues des leurs trônes et de leurs théâtres, pour estre vos spectatrices: ce vous doit estre un agréable concert, que le bruit et les acclamations de tant de victorieuses, qui vous applaudissent de leurs palmes. L'importance est, Madame, que ces applaudissemens ne sont pas des ieux de théâtre; que ces acclamations ne son pas des flatteries contraintes ou achetées. Ce son des tributs sérieux et legitimes, que des vaincues redent à leur victorieuse.[80]

The passage dramatizes the work's frontispiece by Charles Audran (following a design by Pietro da Cortona), in which a statuesque Anne receives a laurel garland to accompany her royal diadem, while these women watch approvingly from their niches (fig. 6.3).

The image suggestively recalls the Hall of Fame in the Forum of Augustus, whose colonnade with honorific statues of *viri illustres* (illustrious men) has been

Figure 6.3. Charles Audran (after Pietro da Cortona), frontispiece to Pierre Le Moyne, *La gallerie des femmes fortes*, Paris, 1647. Call number 192680. Photograph by Jessica Goethals, from the collection of the Folger Shakespeare Library.

regendered as female.[81] Below, Arts and Letters complete the tableau by carving into the pedestal – adjoining the *femme forte* title – "Anne of Austria, the Regent Queen of France and Mother of Her People" ("reyne regente de France mère du peuple").[82] This type of visual campaign, a later iteration of which we saw in the frontispiece of d'Agliè's *Le delitie* (fig. 6.2), would reappear the following year with a work by Jean Puget de La Serre showcasing all of Anne's Austrian ancestors of the same name; the frontispiece, which also appears in an exquisite manuscript version made for Anne herself, depicts the queen in a "temple of glory" ("la temple de la gloire"), a raised sword in one hand and a portrait of her son in the other, she and her female predecessors evoking classical sculptures on pedestals but shown in motion as if come to life.[83]

Anne's ability to faithfully serve as mother to both her son and France would come under attack that year. The factionalism, fiscal concerns, and contempt for Mazarin that contributed to the Fronde (a period of civil war) initiated an "open season on Anne's reputation."[84] The *frondeurs* lambasted her for taking a back-seat approach to rule and giving carte blanche to an unpopular foreigner. The polemical, often satirical pamphlets (*mazarinades*) that circulated in this period articulated anger over her perceived divided loyalties, accusing her – at times graphically – of fornicating with their enemy.[85] Anne nevertheless stayed steadfast in her support of Mazarin, and he remained chief minister even after Louis XIV reached his majority.

Whatever the cause of Anne's allegiance to Mazarin, outside the arena of policy-making they shared an enthusiasm for Italian opera and theatre. Despite her woes, from her unhappy marriage to civil unrest, the queen consistently sought pleasure in the performances staged at court. She covertly continued to watch plays during her mourning, staged and performed in her own ballets, and even went against her normally devout nature by rejecting clerical admonitions that she cease hosting weekly French and Italian comedies.[86] Mazarin had long cultivated similar interests and swiftly issued invitations to Italian singers and specialists of all varieties under the name of the new regent, burnishing the cultural reputation of the court while ingratiating himself to its sovereign. His efforts met with success, initially in private chamber performances and then expanding into the more elaborate operas *La finta pazza*, *Egisto*, and *L'Orfeo*. So charmed was Anne by Leonora Baroni, invited in 1644–5, for instance, that the soprano was given nearly the same liberties as the *femmes de chambre* and could freely enter the queen's quarters.[87] Anne replicated such intimacies with the castrato Atto Melani, who reported being asked to sing for her hours each day and, later, to participate in her morning *lever*.[88] While allowing for a bit of grandstanding on Melani's part, such accounts highlight the queen's enthusiasm for Italian performers. It is unclear to what degree, if at all, Costa may have penetrated this inner circle. However, Alberto Ghislanzoni suggested that the Costa sisters were among a select group of *Orfeo* cast members that the queen requested remain in France for an additional few weeks after the final performance on 8 May 1647.[89]

In recognition of such "honours received in Paris by Her Majesty the Queen of France," Costa lionizes her patroness in both *La selva di Diana* and *La tromba di Parnaso*.[90] The latter is dedicated to Anne herself, and it is worth briefly considering its function before returning to the issue of regency contemplated in the former. If to Grand Duke Ferdinando II Costa had dedicated the *Chitarra* and the *Violino*, to Queen Anne she lifts her *tromba* (trumpet), heralding her as the guardian of a new golden age in France. In keeping with the astronomical themes of the *Festa reale*'s grand finale, in which riders and steeds ascend into the sky to become Bourbonian Stars, two poems dedicated to Anne in *La tromba di Parnaso* place her firmly within the heavens. Lifting her song up to the stars ("passin le voci mie sovra le stelle"), and acknowledging that her own star rose thanks only to the two watching "stars" of the queen's gaze ("e tua mercede sollevata sia / da le due stelle tue la stella mia"), Costa depicts her benefactress as France's guiding light:

> Anne, you take your great name from the year [*anno*],
> and whatever the year, your fine rotations are delightful,
> With your rays you illuminate friendly stars,
> And breathe into us the air of spring.
> You pass the hours placidly, and sweetly make
> The days happy amid gentle souls,
> And of the whole universe you alone
> With your countenance deserve to rule.

> Anna da l'anno il tuo gran nome prendi,
> Ed hai vaghi qual l'anno i tuoi bei giri,
> Di amiche stelle le tue luci accendi,
> Ed aura a noi di primavera spiri;
> Placide hai l'hore, e dolcemente rendi
> Felici i giorni fra soavi spiri,
> E sola poi de l'universo intero
> Col tuo sembiante meritar l'impero.[91]

This octave largely replicates one introducing a poem that Costa had addressed to another Anne, Anna de' Medici, in her *Lo stipo*; in that earlier verse, the princess was a celestial ornament but still a "virginal Rose" awaiting her future marriage.[92] Here Costa unequivocally affirms regent Anne's legitimacy and fitness to govern, while also lauding the merits of her household. As the "new sun" ("novo sol") that animates the Parisian court, she – like the starry horsemen of the *Festa reale* – adorns the heavens with the golden fleur-de-lis ("di aurati gigli vagamente adorna / cielo").[93]

Classical allusions appear amid this celestial topography. Costa compares the queen's beauty to that of Dido, Semiramis, and Cleopatra, for example – a trio who, in addition to their allure, also all happened to be powerful ruling widows.[94] As in the *Selva di Diana* poem for Christine, Costa credits Anne with a renascence figured through pastoral imagery, incorporating elements drawn from performative culture: the rivers bubble festively ("festanti"), the nymphs dance to pleasing songs as they decorate their chariots, and the trees merrily ready themselves to dance while daisies ("margherite") crown the forest floor – the latter an allusion to Margherita herself, one of the sources of this courtly music.[95] Anne is credited especially for cultivating a worthy future ruler in Louis XIV. So great are her successes, Costa professes, that France's glory now surpasses even that of Rome.[96]

Memorializing that glory, *La tromba di Parnaso* showcases Anne's retinue while also reflecting Costa's intersecting debts to her, Mazarin, and the Barberini.[97] The poems for the cardinals are discussed at greater length in chapter 5; here it suffices to note that by including the Barberini, Costa acknowledges their presence in France as exiles from Rome following Urban VIII's death, and signals her continued loyalty to them. Nor are they the only displaced figures appearing in these pages; also featured are Anne's sister-in-law Henrietta Maria, Queen of England, who had returned to France during her husband's travails during the English Civil Wars. Joining her, both in Saint-Germain and in Costa's volume, was her son, the future king Charles II. *La tromba di Parnaso* functions as a gallery of illustrious and notable figures connected to Anne's court: members of the royal family (Gaston, Duke of Orléans; his daughter, Mademoiselle de Montepensier; Louis II, Prince of Condé); *maréchals* (marshals) and other military men of distinction (Charles de Schomberg, for example, and Rupert of the Rhein, then in Anne's employ); political figures (such as François du Val, Marquis of Fontenay, France's ambassador to Rome); and notable Italians responsible for the successful *Orfeo* production (Rossi, Pasqualini, Buti).[98] The poems dedicated to Mazarin notably include verse in thanks for his role in facilitating the publication of her three works by the crown press. More intimate figures are not overlooked; Costa even applauds the beauty of Anne's ladies-in-waiting. The resulting portrait suggests political stability, military strength, and a flourishing cultural scene.

Costa followed the model of Isabella Andreini, who similarly published a collection of verse while performing for Henry IV in 1603. Though she repurposed poems addressed to the king and queen from her first 1601 edition of poetry, and while her posthumous 1605 edition would include additional verse about French personages, Andreini's Parisian *Rime* paused her experimentations with poetic genre in order to prioritize extolling the influential men and women of Henri's court through encomiastic verse.[99] Imitating this predecessor, Costa paid homage to her benefactress while also currying favour with desired allies and current admirers. Her flattery of Anne's *femmes de chambre*, for instance, not only added further lustre to an already gleaming portrait of the French kingdom, it also opened doors to additional patronage opportunities; these ladies were conduits to their mistress and patronesses in their own right, and their good favour was widely sought.[100] Two of her other addressees, the maréchal of Gramont and the duke of Mortemart, are named (rather scornfully) by Madame de Motteville, memoirist and member of the queen's household, as examples of those who vociferously and sycophantically heaped praise on Mazarin for *l'Orfeo*: the marshal "set this comedy among the great wonders of the world," she noted, while the duke, as a "great amateur of music and great courtier, seemed enchanted with the mere name of the lowest actors."[101] One imagines that Costa would identify such votaries as useful associates. Notably absent among her array of dedicatees is Louis XIV; the nine-year-old king appears only obliquely as a satellite of his regent mother.

The decision to include prominent personages like Henrietta Maria – a patroness in her own right – was a natural one, but arguably the general visibility of exiles in this volume contributes to Costa's broader portrait of France under Anne's watch as a sanctuary for worthy but fate-battered figures. Indeed, this is the prevailing theme in the nineteen-stanza poem dedicated to her in *La selva di Diana*. While the queen may not have been getting rave reviews from the members of Parliament, in the space of the poem she fosters an Edenic era of artistic activity worthy of gratitude at home and envy abroad. The opening stanza praises Anne's hospitable approach to the arts:

> You who in the name of honour nourish in your breast
> The favourable winds of studious endeavours,
> And amid musical trills devise accents,
> And plait your hair with sacred fronds,
> Flee at last the century of ignorance
> And at the golden shores of the Seine
> Proudly dock your song
> If you desire honour, riches, and acclaim.

> Voi che nel seno a pro d'honor nudrite
> Di studiose fatiche aure seconde,
> E tra musici groppi accenti ordite,
> E il crin trecciate di sacrate fronde:
> Secolo d'ingnoranza [*sic*] homai fuggite
> E de la Senna a le dorate sponde
> Approdate fastosi il vostro canto,
> Se desiate honor, richezza, e vanto.[102]

The octave may entreat the attention of the Muses, but it functions equally as a call to Costa's fellow musicians and writers, alerting them that an oasis amid their travails is to be found in France, where talent and effort are still met with respect and reward. The discerning, generous spirit of the queen – repeatedly referred to as the "great soul" ("grand'alma") – ensures that applause greets the performance of music and that laurel crowns the brows of poets.[103]

Costa takes care to acknowledge the legitimacy of Anne's regency, as she did with Christine. She lauds the stability and prosperity of her realm, for example, and optimistically suggests that under the *femme forte*'s watch France is protected from both European and Ottoman threats. Young Louis's position is unassailable, as he holds Fortune firmly by her forelock. Like the efforts of the artists assembled in her court, the sovereign honour of her kingly son is greeted by resounding applause ("d'applauso rimbomba honor sovrano").[104] Costa also re-employs a language of fecundity, deploying frequent allusions to germination and nativity that reflect the regent's dual role as the progenitrix of the future ruler and the wellspring of cultural policy.

But if the poem for Christine is replete with images of dominion and rank – the golden crown central to her cultural campaign – that for Anne is defined by musicality, symbol of her new golden age. Dozens of references to voices lifted together in song give this text a performative air. We might take as example the lyrical exultation of the queen by the Muses – here addressed as divas ("dive"), again uniting the term's original meaning of "divinity" with the emerging concept of the *prima donna*.[105] Costa's own crafted persona of a performer, beleaguered by obstacles and misfortune, in search of a more hospitable climate dovetails neatly with these themes. In a rare moment in which she addresses the difficulties faced by singers writ large, she engages and intensifies the image of serene swans already utilized in the poem to Christine in order to depict Anne's court as an uncommon sanctuary: "And in the company of melodious voices, pleasing swans / shall, apart from the horrors below, enjoy benignant skies."[106]

The poem concludes by pairing traditional symbols of authority with Costa's new patronage-centred criteria for effective regency. As the queen wields her sceptre and mantle ("scettro… manto"), she uses her command to permit ("premise") singers such as Costa to break into melody. The true mark of her regality – and, Costa implies, legitimacy – is not just the material instruments of power. Rather, the final lines conclude, it is the ability to match virtuosity with its due reward that reveals her royal soul ("alma reale"). While Christine's heroism could be more obviously tied to her victory in the Siege of Turin, and the glorifying spectacles that followed, Costa places as her other pillar of regency in *La selva di Diana* the more halcyon – but, in her eyes, just as mighty – act of munificent cultural sponsorship, in this case through Anne's support of opera.

Fashioning a New Regent

So appealing did Costa find it to celebrate the regency of her patronesses in the *Selva di Diana* that she took poetic licence in order to extend the same honour to Lavinia Lopez Buratti, the noblewoman who had invited her to sing before an assembly of ladies in Lazio. In the poem dedicated to her (the first in the lyrical series commending members of this coterie), Costa poetically stages a scene of musical patronage and performance. During a summer harvest, Lavinia gathers her "nymphs," that is, her female companions in Rome, to her pastoral grounds in nearby Albano. Desiring music to accompany their bacchanalian festivities ("bacanari giochi"), she summons Costa – who here calls herself Artigemma – to sing before them.[107] As the assembled women applaud her "beautiful harmonies" ("bei concenti"), with a heavenly voice Artigemma breaks into improvised song.[108] The remainder of the poem becomes an encomiastic melody addressed to Buratti. The *canzoni* dedicated to the other ladies also reiterate musical themes, such that taken together they might be read as a veritable concert.

While it may be impossible to know whether such a performance took place, or if Costa took a bit of artistic licence, the setting is nevertheless apt for the purposes of both this poetic series and the volume as a whole. Nestled in the lakeside hills to the southeast of Rome, Albano Laziale was an idyllic spot, so much so that Urban VIII had recently established a papal summer residence there (Castel Gandolfo); the painter Claude Lorrain would celebrate its construction in a 1639 pastoral landscape that included a cluster of pipe-playing shepherds in the foreground.[109] In addition to her appropriately bacchic themes – Albano was and is known for its superior wines – Costa was surely aware that these hills once also housed an important cult of Diana.[110] Along the shores of Lake Nemi, a temple devoted to Diana Nemorensis, or Diana "of the woods" (from the Latin *nemus*), had stood; the Romans attributed sacred qualities to its lush sylvan surroundings.[111] Interest in her cult was heightened in Costa's day thanks to the first excavations of the site in 1637.[112] We may thus surmise that Costa chose a setting that was simultane- ously *du jour* and suitably pastoral, one that may have even inspired her to entitle her volume "Diana's Forest."

Appropriately, Costa begins the lyric series by exploring ancient Roman themes. Artigemma's song first celebrates her hostess through a favourable but surprising comparison with ancient Lavinia, the Latin princess for whose hand Aeneas had battled and killed Turnus. We catch but glimpses of her in the *Aeneid* – the fiery combustion of her hair that portends both the glorious fruits of her marriage and the bloodshed it will necessitate, her abduction to the countryside by her mother, her famous deep blush at the news of her broken betrothal and new engagement, her anguish over her mother's suicide – but never hear her speak nor witness her act.[113] Through prophecy, however, we understand her important (albeit passive) role as the unifier of the Trojan and Latin lines and the progenitrix of the Romans, although these acts of marriage and childbirth fall beyond the epic's temporal scope.

Yet Virgil's is but one of several depictions offered in classical and medieval literary traditions. The Lavinia of Ovid's *Fasti*, for example, is a jealous wife who, when Aeneas invites Dido's sister Anna to their home, plots the woman's demise, proving herself a marital adversary rather than an ally.[114] Dante encounters Lavinia twice in the *Divine Comedy*: first in Inferno, where she sits at her father's side among the illustrious classical figures in Limbo; and again as he ascends Purgatory, where in a vision she finally speaks in order to tearfully condemn her mother's suicide.[115] Composers and choreographers were similarly interested in developing her "tantalizing brief and mute role" in Virgil's poem.[116] Like Dante, Monteverdi gave her voice in his 1641 opera *Le nozze d'Enea e Lavinia*, for instance, a "tragedy with a happy ending" whose final scene depicts her felicitous marriage and newfound love.[117]

An altogether different Lavinia – one endowed with courage and power – is to be found in another strand of the classical tradition leading back to Livy. In his history, she is a regent, and a highly successful one at that. "Aeneas' son was not yet ripe for authority," he states, "yet the authority was kept for him, unimpaired, until he arrived at manhood. In the meantime, under a woman's regency, the Latin state and the kingdom of his father and his grandfather stood unshaken – so strong was Lavinia's character – until the boy could claim it."[118] Boccaccio later picked up this thread. Though he begins his *vita* of Lavinia in *On Famous Women* by dismissively attributing her fame to her passive role in provoking the war between Aeneas and Turnus, in the second half he swaps the Virgilian account for the Livian, envisioning a pregnant Lavinia who must confront the death of her husband. Fearing the threat posed by Aeneas's eldest son Ascanius, she hid in the forest to give birth to Justus Silvius Postumus. Ascanius willingly withdrew, however, to found Alba Longa, leaving mother and infant alone. Boccaccio confirms both the office and the achievement described by Livy: "She carried the spirit of the ancient nobility in her breast and so lived honourably and virtuously, administering the realm with the utmost care until she turned it over intact to Silvius."[119] Boccaccio's regent Lavinia is beautifully represented in the illustration accompanying a fifteenth-century French translation (fig. 6.4). Here Ascanius kneels before his stepmother, extending the crown to her as she in turn holds her infant child upon her knee. Boccaccio would later reiterate and amplify the identification of Lavinia as regent in his commentary on the *Divine Comedy*, justifying Dante's inclusion of her among the elite company of Limbo.[120]

Boccaccio's *vita* also acknowledges other versions of the tale in which Lavinia remarried and Ascanius raised her son. Christine de Pizan flatly refutes this charge in her *City of Women*, where Lavinia appears as the last of the historically "foundational" women upon whom Christine's titular city is built. Although drawing on the Boccaccian narrative, she insists that

> this lady did not wish to marry ever again, and during her widowhood she acted most prudently and ruled the kingdom with her considerable intelligence. She knew

Figure 6.4. Boccaccio, *Le livre de femmes nobles et renomées,* c. 1440. © British Library Board, Royal 16 G V, f. 47v.

how to cherish her stepson so that he harbored no evil against her nor against his brother; therefore, after building the city of Alba, he went there to live. Lavinia governed very wisely with her son until he was grown. From this child descended Romulus and Remus who founded Rome, as well as the great Roman princes who came later.[121]

The Lavinia of Livy, Boccaccio, and especially Christine emerges as an ideal regent: through a combination of maternal love, unimpeachable character, and a refusal to remarry, she faithfully and skilfully maintained her son's state before peacefully turning over the reins of power. Christine further affirms her regency as the cornerstone of Rome.

It is to this Lavinia – a powerful mother guided by inner nobility, rather than a blushing pawn or jealous wife – that Costa turns in her song:

> On the proud Quirinal hill Lavinia once
> Hoisted Trojan arms, and magnificently
> erected the Campidoglio to the Tiberine empire,
> And was a rock of faith and steadfastness.
> With sovereign skill she laid the foundations
> Of Alba, on whose royal throne she reigned as queen,
> And in tribute gave a kingdom
> as her nuptial token of faith.

> Lavinia già sul Quirinale altero
> Vantò l'armi Troiane, e il Campidoglio
> Fastosa eresse al Tiberino Impero
> E fu di fede e di fermezza un scoglio.
> In Alba con sovrano magistero
> I fondamenti porse, c' il reglio soglio
> Calcò reina, ed in tributo diede
> Un regno d'immeneo pegno di fede.[122]

Aeneas is notably absent in this account of Rome's origins, alluded to only obliquely as the recipient of his wife's immense territorial dowry. Setting him aside – and also dispensing with Romulus, traditionally viewed as the founder of the Capitoline – Costa attributes to Lavinia alone the foundation and construction of Rome and the defeat of the city's would-be invaders. No faint damsel, she is instead the bedrock ("scoglio") of her realm.[123] Also notably missing is any reference to her son or stepchild. Costa expands the narrative inherited from Boccaccio and Christine de Pizan, in which the threat posed by Ascanius is diffused by his relocation to and founding of Alba Longa; she instead makes Lavinia the founder and queen of that town as well. Lavinia becomes the first regent of Rome, one whose dowry is given less to a husband than to a people. The bestowal of her lands is an act of regal generosity by a *materfamilias*.

The geographic proximity (and common misidentification) of Albano Laziale and Alba Longa invited Costa to amplify Lavinia's role in this way – she uses both names to refer to her performance setting – and permitted her to draw parallels between the ancient and modern towns, between epic foremother and lauded descendant. Still in song, Artigemma turns to her modern-day benefactress to suggest that she can become a "new Lavinia":

> She erected the honour of a Campidoglio,
> And you erect a Campidoglio of study,

She beat back the wrath of others with arms,
And you subjugate others with your illustrious acts.
She had a kingdom as her dowry, and you a heart
endowed with a thousand kingdoms and a thousand ornaments.

Quella d'un campidoglio er[e]sse l'honore
E tu di studi un campidoglio ereggi.
Co' l'armi ella abattè l'altrui furore
E tu soggioghi altrui con atti eggregi.
Ella un regno ebbe in dote, e tu d'un core
Ricca ch'ha mille regni e mille fregi.[124]

If this earlier paragon wielded power through arms, courage, and property, Costa insists, so too could her patroness obtain authority by promoting intellectual pursuits, performing great deeds, and exercising her generosity. While the Latin sovereign was tasked with securing the future of Rome, her Seicento namesake enjoys the advantages of a period of comparative peace ("ingrembo della pace il regno godi"); patronage becomes the comparable foundational act of her generation. A friend to virtue, beauty, and study, she calls on Artigemma to memorialize her victories in song.[125] While epic poets exalted the heroic deeds of the ancients, Costa becomes the rhapsode of the modern patron.

This envisioned role for Lavinia is, of course, symbolic – all the more so from within the papal states, where regency is impossible and female rule unthinkable. Lavinia Buratti does not appear to have been a widow at the time, if her delivery of a child in December 1647 is any indication.[126] Moreover, Costa makes no reference to her son, of which she had at least one; in a volume dedicated to women, she instead opts to conclude this section with a poem admiring Lavinia's baby daughter. The comparison with ancient Lavinia nevertheless underscores the importance Costa placed on the figure of the regent as an example of womanly authority as well as (and perhaps most pertinently) a benefactress able to make her own patronage choices. It is in the realm of cultural influence that Costa declares Buratti can become "a new queen that rules over Lazio"[127] – an assertion that does not seem too farfetched when we recall the exceptional leverage that Olimpia Maidalchini exercised during the papacy of Innocent X. In contrast to men like John Knox, who would like to be rid of regents, Costa imaginatively adds to their numbers. In Costa's poetic imagination, the heroism of regency requires neither actual widowhood nor concrete political authority but rather – in a vision that returns to another facet of the word's etymology – the will to exercise control, in this case over cultural activity and artistic production. Through patronage, women of the social upper crust could emulate both ancient exemplars and their royal contemporaries.

Conclusion: A Royal Audience

The characteristics that Costa exults in Lavinia place her in the company of the two regal women alongside whom she appears in *La selva di Diana*. Just as Lavinia is a "friend to studies" ("di studii amica"), Anne's court is cast as a haven for those dedicated to "studious endeavours" ("studiose fatiche") thanks to the queen's "soul friendly to study" ("alma di studi amica"), while Costa's own "long studies and industrious endeavours" ("lunghi studii e … fatiche industri") prove futile without Christine's assistance.[128] While Costa repeatedly insists upon the unworthiness of her own capabilities, as she does in all her works, here we encounter a Lavinia who "request[s] the voices of my rough song," ("chiedi le voci del mio rozzo canto"), a Christine who "welcome[s] the song of my rough style" ("accogli il canto del mio rozzo stile"), and an Anne celebrated throughout her entire poem for nourishing otherwise beleaguered artists.[129] Within Costa's rhetorical posture of humility, these three ladies do not merely tolerate her unpolished voice but in fact magnanimously call her to them and transform her into a swan.

Costa's fictional women vary widely in the degree of autonomy they seek – from the disdainful *bella donna* to the compliant sexual object – but the historical women she encountered in the latter part of her career held both their respective realms and her career in their hands. "Your grace alone can open the heavens to me / and relieve me from wicked blows," she writes to Christine, so "let bitter fate now submerge me at her will; / the fall will be all the sweeter because you will lift me up."[130] In the case of her patronesses, Costa did not simply buttress their social and political programs, as she did with her male patrons. In addition to lending support to their claims of legitimacy, Costa refashioned the heroism of the *femme forte* regent (or, in Costa's rendering, her new non-aristocratic counterpart), measuring her success not merely by her maternal care and skilled execution of political duties but also her enthusiastic embrace of patronage.

Chapter Seven

"A Change of Sky Does Me No Good": Envy, Rivalry, and Other Courtly Criticisms

Until recently, Costa's biography – already hazy – was especially uncertain following her 1647 performance in *Orfeo*. In 1654 she published her final full-length work, *Gl'amori della luna*. Little was known about its context, beyond its dedication to the German dukes of Brunswick-Lüneburg, which led scholars to hazard that Costa may have travelled to northern Europe. Slowly but surely, however, new details are emerging about her later life. Most notable is the addition of Venice to Costa's post-Parisian itinerary in the early 1650s, possibly in several of the city's operas. The years she spent in the Serenissima also explain her relationship to the German dukes, opera enthusiasts with close ties to the city.

With its new public opera houses and flourishing performance calendars, Venice offered professional singers a stimulating but demanding scene. Personal correspondence indicates that Costa's time there was not without its obstacles; letters by her daughter Giovanna Vittoria suggest that the Venetian "swamps" afforded Margherita little pleasure and numerous worries.[1] It is perhaps little coincidence, then, that her *Gl'amori della luna* revolves around issues of competition and jealousy and, despite its pastoral trappings, leaves a lingeringly grim picture of city and courtly life.

Although Costa paints these themes with a heavy brush in this drama, laments regarding her station and treatment pepper all her works. In part this was strategic. As this book has argued throughout, she savvily courted patrons through her publications, referencing their interests and advancing their rhetorical campaigns. The inclusion of passages reflecting negatively on previous courts allowed her patrons to measure themselves favourably against their predecessors. "Other" courts fostered misfortunes and mistreatment, while each "current" one offered a comparatively idyllic environment – a rhetorical manoeuvre that recalls similar ones made by the Cinquecento master of courtly politics, Pietro Aretino.

However, Costa's works also contain implicit and even explicit criticisms of courtly life and the patronage system. While it would distort her record to classify Costa as a writer of anti-courtly literature per se – she dedicates far too many pages to celebrating them – nevertheless she taps regularly into that tradition. Paola Ugolini has defined early modern anti-courtliness as the diffuse "sentiments of dissatisfaction, regret, negativity, scepticism, and mockery aimed at the court as an institution, at the kind of life one might lead at court, and at those who inhabit it."[2] One readily locates all three iterations of anti-courtly rhetoric in Costa. Voicing frustration over a system that pits performers against each other before the eyes of inconstant audiences and benefactors – a system that its participants are wont to game – and over a literary environment that questions women's aptitude for writing, Costa punctuates her oeuvre with critiques of the courtly milieu and the figure of the courtier (even if musicians such as she counted as courtiers). These tensions boil over in Costa's final work, a pastoral brimming with the kinds of clashes, rivalries, and even violence highlighted by anti-court literature. Ostensibly its publication in Venice – a city without a court as such – allowed Costa a bit more freedom of expression, though the city maintained a relatively strict musical patronage system that could also feel court-like.[3]

In this final chapter, we turn from Costa's intrepid efforts at cultivating and winning over her benefactors to her decidedly less rosy picture of what it meant to be a professional performer – particularly a woman with literary ambitions – forced to traverse the circuits of early modern patronage. Viewed from this angle, her corpus offers a more cynical view of the costs of survival within this system. While Costa's autobiographical allusions should be taken with a healthy grain of salt, it is nevertheless also true that when considered together, these poems, dedicatory letters, and self-portraits offer an extended commentary on the potential pitfalls of serving at the behest of elite patrons or competing for limited attention and resources. Like her more adulatory gestures, these critical passages comprise an integral a part of Costa's authorial persona; indeed, all but two of her poetry collections conclude with a poem of complaint and her dedicatory letters hit on many of these same notes.[4] Also illustrative of this more critical assessment are several fictionalized poems concerning courtly life, as well as the comedy *Li buffoni*, which turn the tables on the performance of courtly belonging. This chapter first examines Costa's final publication, her surprisingly cutthroat *Gl'amori della luna* libretto, published in Venice, before considering the role of envy and exile throughout her corpus, and concluding with her unflattering assessment of courtiership.

Envy's Deadly Game

In December 1652, Desiderio Montemagni received a letter of complaint from Venice. As Cardinal Giovan Carlo de' Medici's secretary, Montemagni was accustomed to mediating between the cardinal and the performers and artists who received his patronage. Even a man thus familiar with the rivalries endemic to both court and stage may have been surprised to receive a plea from a daughter on behalf of her mother. Giovanna Vittoria Costa complains that "la Campaspe" (soprano Anna Maria Sardelli) had sent letters encouraging "Signor Nicoletto Vendramin" to halt his attentions to her. Montemagni should entreat Giovan Carlo (Giovanna's godfather) to intercede, she states, since these messages could prove disastrous to the Costas: "Thanks to what she has written, [Vendramin] might decide to no longer come by, and that would do us great harm, since he is a cavalier who delights in music and brings other gentlemen to come hear my lady mother sing."[5]

This was not the first time that Giovanna voiced concern over her family's fate to the cardinal from Venice, a city she was anxious to leave, or that the Costa women called upon him to settle their other rivalries.[6] A few years earlier Anna Francesca had him sent a letter of her own in which she fretted that Margherita not only had taken possession of clothing she had left in Rome but, worse still, had written messages to Leopoldo de' Medici discrediting her. To remedy these wrongs against her property and her patronage – which Anna Francesca attributed to Margherita's envy, greed, and scheming – Giovan Carlo ought to ensure the return of her dresses and recognize the "evil ends of this woman" should he too receive such letters from her.[7] While not about sisterly rivalry or apparel, Giovanna's letter points to a comparable clash between singers contending for elite support. A fellow prima donna and Medici creature then active in Venice, Sardelli was threatening to cut off Margherita's access to the city's musical patronage scene.[8] Her machinations posed no idle threat; the Vendramin were major players and had built a theatre (Teatro San Luca, or Vendramin) in 1622 that first housed comedies and, later, operas.[9] Rivalries between singers could also provoke scandal and shame, as shown in an infamous incident in 1639 in which Leonora Baroni's home in Rome was smeared with excrement by contenders for Antonio Barberini's attention.[10]

Venice was, of course, a republic, one where Europe's first public opera had been staged in 1637. Theatre here was becoming a commercial, rather than courtly, enterprise.[11] But the spectrum of singers active in this period typically relied on both internal and external patronage networks, such that the city often adopted courtly paradigms even if it did not have a court proper.[12] "When one's reputation is blackened, all life is lost," Giovanna wrote in an earlier letter to Giovan Carlo, and in Venice "the nobleman is god; a mother without any other guide but a passing recognition of worldly miseries is a target for extraordinary mishaps."[13] Complicating the dynamic of patrician figures in Venice itself was the web of interested, invested patrons from elsewhere. The Medici brothers extended their impresarial activities to the Serenissima, sending their *virtuosi* as cultural calling cards and attentively monitoring their activities; a well-known case involved Sardelli herself, whose attempt to renege on a contract by joining a convent raised alarm in both cities.[14]

Costa had returned to Venice in 1650 with the Medici's assistance, as evidenced in an August letter from their ambassador Francesco Maria Zati (who had only just finished putting out the Sardelli fire) to Montemagni pledging that he would provide her all the support she might require.[15] Costa would soon appear as a leading heroine in Cavalli's *Rosinda* and possibly his *Calisto* and *L'Eritrea* in 1651–2. While a sonnet by Paolo Abriani would laud Costa's virtuosity as the sorceress Nerea in *La Rosinda*, none of these works was a commercial success.[16] Costa's position was thus far from guaranteed. She could not afford to have spectator-patrons like the Vendramin driven away by a competitor – even if his interest in her voice seems to have depended at least in part on his attraction to her daughter. While staged rivalries of the sort initially anticipated by the 1626 opera *Catena d'Adone* (in which Costa and Cecca del Padule were to vocally spar so that listeners might compare their skills) raised the stock of both performers, having one's access to benefactors jeopardized was an altogether different matter.

It is not clear what, if any, action Montemagni took to quell the dispute between the Costas and Sardelli. Two years later Costa would seek to better secure her standing with her last full-length publication. *Gl'amori della luna* is a three-act pastoral about the infatuation of Diana (i.e., the Moon) with Endymion, a subject perhaps fresh in Costa's mind following *La Calisto's* exploration of the same myth. Costa does not state the work's genre on the cover page, in the dedication, or elsewhere, raising the question of whether this is a theatrical script that includes musical elements or an opera libretto. Scholars have been divided in their classifications, but most take it to be a *dramma in musica*, and it is listed in Claudio Sartori's authoritative *Libretti italiani*.[17] As was the case in with *La Flora feconda*, discussed in chapter 3, the work has metrical elements and strophic material, such as the inclusion of almost a dozen *ariette*, indicative of musicality. The identities of the work's publisher and the dedicatees also suggest it may be a libretto, though there is no indication it was ever performed. Costa once again secured an important printer, in this case Andrea Giuliani – then the most prominent Venetian publisher of opera libretti, including *La Calisto* and *L'Eritrea*.[18] She dedicated it not to one of her Venetian contacts but rather to the three brothers of Brunswick-Lüneburg: Georg Wilhelm, Ernst Augustus, and Johann Friedrich. Here again, Costa was forward-looking. The German dukes developed a taste for Venetian opera over the century, visiting the stages of the Serenissima and eventually importing performers to their respective courts in the north.[19] Italian librettists responded to this promising source of support by dedicating more than thirty works to them in as many years, between 1654 and 1688.[20] With her own 1654 dedication, Costa was at the forefront of this wave.

Gl'amori della luna stands out within Costa's oeuvre not merely for its northern dedicatees. It is her only publication in duodecimo, rather than quarto, format. It is also her sole work (including subsequent single poems and letters) whose byline reads "Maria Margherita Costa," rather than her customary "Signora Margherita Costa romana."[21] Furthermore, it is the only work whose dedication directly addresses the trajectory of her literary career. On both the Tiber and the Arno, she recounts, she "employed not a needle but a pen."[22] Spurred by the protection of Ferdinando II early in her career, she published fourteen volumes.[23] But while she enjoyed accolades in Florence during her youth, she was unable to establish herself there over time: after her "quill was plucked and tongue silenced, they did not know how to make any other sound than to shriek at my misfortunes."[24] The forces of ignorance see women's letters as monstrous, she laments. Consequently, despite her every toil across the great distances she travelled, she saw her gifts obscured, discouraged, even oppressed, and herself dimmed into silence by "envious beaks" ("invidi rostri").[25] By transporting Diana from the chaste forest (an allusion to her *Selva di Diana*) to her lovers (in *Gl'amori della luna*), Costa will surely incite those scandalmongers again, and so she turns to the German brothers for their protection. After all, she promises, "where there are patrons, one doesn't lack for Virgils."[26] Given this promise to make them "Augustan" through her poetry, it bears noting that the letter makes no reference to any of her prior benefactors other than the Medici, now immersed in the impresarial work of opera. Implied is an invitation to the German dukes to supplant these Tuscan rivals on the field of musical sponsorship.

Costa revisits these themes in her letter to the reader. Although she had abandoned her pen over the previous four years, she states, the vicissitudes of Fortune compelled her to "employ [her] skills under a foreign sky in defence of an enemy tongue."[27] Her meaning is not readily clear, and not only because her previous publication dates from seven years prior, not four. Does this indicate that she writes from Germany itself? (If so, in what way has she upheld the German language?) It is conceivable that Costa travelled north sometime between her daughter's 1652 letters from Venice and 1656, when she published a pamphlet poem for Ferdinando in Florence.[28] Johann Friedrich in particular was becoming a fixture in Venice, reserving several opera boxes and eventually luring away top talent for his court in Hanover.[29] However, the first Italian production in northern Germany was staged only in 1662, Giovanni Andrea Bontempi's *Paride*, meaning that a trip by Costa in the early-to-mid-1650s would fall rather early in this time frame and would predate any major performances.[30] Other Venetian libretti were dedicated to the dukes in this period, such as Giulio Cesare Sorrentino's *Ciro* (1654) and Francesco Maria Piccioli's *L'incostanza trionfante ovvero il Theseo* (1658, published by Giuliani), without raising the question of whether their librettists had journeyed to Germany. Likely the "foreign skies" ("cieli stranieri") are those of the Serenissima. This seems especially probable given other instances of the phrase in Costa's autobiographical poems; in *La selva di Diana*, she uses it to describe leaving Rome for either Venice or Paris, while in *La selva di cipressi* it refers explicitly to her departure for Florence.[31] All the skies that do not stretch above her native Rome are foreign, the phrase "cieli stranieri" becoming shorthand for her itinerancy. The question of whether Costa ever travelled north is for now unanswered, but it seems unlikely.

The "Letter to the Reader" issues Costa's customary apology for her rough style, attributed here to her having been compelled to compose the libretto in a mere fifteen days. She had, she states, been "constrained by the cords of envious beaks [*invidi rostri*]."[32] She does not delve further into the identity of these jealous "beaked" figures who sought to provoke, hinder, and, as stated in the dedication, eclipse her, but one may imagine that the interference of personages such as Sardelli or other detractors continued to trouble her.

Perhaps with these concerns in mind, Costa selected the figure of Envy (Invidia) to deliver the prologue. An enemy of liberty, joy, and love, Envy announces that she will conceal herself among the play's goddesses in order to bring anguish to Diana (a structure that calls to mind the prologues to Tasso's *Aminta* and Andreini's *Mirtilla*, in which Amore similarly announces his intention to disguise himself in shepherd's garb to interfere with the other characters).[33] So that the reader may identify her hand even while she is camouflaged – Envy will not explicitly reappear as a character – she describes herself to the spectators:

> I, the bitter child of ire and spite
> Against those who claim the luck of joy,
> A wicked minister of tortuous troubles,
> Spread pain and dole out sobs.
> I am Envy, a shadow of myself,
> And wherever there is the fairest clear sky,
> In opposition I extend my frosty steps,
> And a winter of barren shadows encumbers the world.
> My bushy hair threatens the air,
> I tinge my face with squalid pallor,
> And while I have fire in my eyes,
> I turn others' hearts to ice.[34]

> De l'ira, e del dispetto acerbo parto,
> Contra chi vanti fortunata gioia,
> Ministra ria di tormentosa noia,
> Pene diffondo, e gemiti comparto.
> Io son Invidia, di me stessa un'ombra,
> Ch'ove più vago il suo sereno ha 'l Cielo
> Contraria stendo i passi miei di gelo
> E 'l verno di secch'ombre il mondo ingombra.
> Con gl'hirti crini miei l'aria minaccio,
> Di squallido pallor tingo il mio volto;
> E se ben foco ho nelle luci accolto,
> Fo gl'altrui cori divenir di ghiaccio.

This self-description of Envy echoes the opening stanza of a poem "To Jealousy" in *La selva di Diana*, for instance, in which an enamoured woman is overcome by – and thereby assumes the appearance of – Gelosia:

> With black wings and serpentine hair,
> An icy-handed monster grips my heart
> And, with trembling frosts, scatters with blood
> And colours with fear my dear ardour.
> My spirit remains entangled in pain,
> The soul in my breast is reborn and dies,
> And my face gives off such mortal pallor
> it seems already lifeless among the living.[35]

> Con ali nere e crin di serpi avvinto
> Mostro c'ha man di gel mi stringe il core
> E con tremanti brine il caro ardore
> Sparge di sangue, e di timore tinto.
> Resta lo spirto nel dolor convinto,
> L'anima dentro il sen rinasce e more:
> E sparso il volto di mortal pallore
> Sembra tra vivi già di vita estinto.

These depictions draw on conventional literary depictions of Envy, departing from Ovid's depiction of her frigid, sunless lair where she chews on snakes:

> Pallor o'erspreads her face and her whole body seems to shrivel up. Her eyes are all awry, her teeth are foul with mould; green, poisonous gall o'erflows her breast, and venom drips down from her tongue. She never smiles, save at the sight of another's troubles; she never sleeps, disturbed with wakeful cares; unwelcome to her is the sight of men's success, and with the sight she pines away; she gnaws and is gnawed, herself her own punishment ... Wherever she goes, she tramples down the flowers, causes the grass to wither, blasts the high waving trees, and taints with the foul pollution of her breath whole peoples, cities, homes.[36]

In both instances, Envy is identifiable both by her cadaverous flesh and shadowy bearing and by her desiccating impact. Costa was not the first to feature Envy, or her close cousin Jealousy, in a prologue (other examples include Giovan Battista Della Porta's *Fantesca* and Ludovico Dolce's *Marianna*), but the repeated emphasis across her self-referential dedicatory letter, letter to the reader, and the prologue is more emphatic.[37] It suggests a heightened concern with the pitfalls of rivalry and spite.

The loosely woven plot of *Gl'amori della luna* in fact opens with Love (Amore, i.e., Cupid) and Slumber (Sonno) in contest over fair Endymion. Their desire to win him over to either ardour or languor, respectively, motivates the storyline: Love strikes Diana, who then pursues Endymion, while he – succumbing to one of Slumber's elixirs – rejects her advances.[38] In an exchange that recalls the power of the Medici name to settle the dispute between Ancient Comedy and Buffoonery in *Li buffoni*, Diana succeeds in winning Endymion over to the cause of Love only after invoking the three German dukes; impressed by her knowledge of these great and wise warriors, he (rather implausibly) abandons his lethargy. Diana and Endymion are not the only pair of figures who face off in this libretto. In addition to the primary contest between Love and Slumber, secondary plotlines feature a parallel competition between Feeling (Senso) and Reason (Ragione) as well as pastoral's requisite clash between nymphs and a satyr. Simply put, all parts of the story are powered by rivalry and even violence, with the occasional exception of tangential elements such as a scene featuring a randy old woman in search of young love (Costa's humorous take on *commedia*'s conventional *Vecchio* and a rare later-life echo of her earlier burlesque style).[39]

Costa's libretto offers an unusual take on the pastoral tradition. First there is the manner in which she revisits genre precepts. The pastoral mode is *of* the court, city, or academy in its production and, at the same time, it presents an appealing bucolic alternative *to* those spaces and to the problems they engendered. In this regard, it translated positive urban values into the rustic landscape while simultaneously cracking open the door to expressions of anti-courtly sentiment, particularly by liminal characters such as the satyr.[40] Curiously, the figure who most illustrates this tension in *Gl'amori della luna* is not a seemingly marginalizable satyr but instead Reason, who delivers an impassioned monologue on how little today she is valued. The idyllic forest ought to be her domain, she begins, a space where intellect reigns – an unexpected twist on Costa's part of the pastoral tradition, and its emphasis on the importance of restorative leisure, *ozio*. Yet Reason laments that Endymion has fallen prey to that bucolic leisure ("a l'otio in preda") to the point of dormancy, and in fact the shepherd's devotion to his own *ozio* becomes an obstacle to be overcome in the play. Reason further bemoans the fact that many have abandoned her path in today's "age of Love" ("età d'Amore"):

> How far from Reason
> [people] live in opinion.
> Feeling counts above all else,
> and today one vain thought
> can rule over every mortal being.
> …
> A soul accustomed to leisure
> no longer cares about

the mortal quest for glory,
and no longer values fame.
And whoever lies conquered in Love's grip
is extinguished by leisure.
Oh, bitter and harmful fate,
For where Reason is lacking, there deceit lies.

Quanto fuor di Ragione
Vivon d'opinione.
Su tutti il senso vale,
E puote un van pensiero
Hoggi l'Impero haver d'ogni mortale.
…
La gloria più non ama
Dei mortali la brama,
La fama più non prezza
Alma ne gli otij avvezza
Ed è da l'otio estinto
Chi tra pugne d'Amore rimane vinto.
O sorte aspra di danno,
Ove non è Ragione, ivi è l'inganno.[41]

Reason's complaint – that the proper pursuit of values that we might identify as "epic" has been supplanted by unseemly amorousness and repose – recalls the rescue of Ariostan and Tassian heroes from pleasure gardens. Reason laments that urban life subjects one to fickle public opinion. However, she similarly critizes the excessive leisure engendered by pastoral landscapes that hampers one's wider ambitions. She thus creates a tension between country *ozio* and courtly aspirations. It is not that the quest for fame and glory is misplaced, she suggests, but that the fleeting call of opinion and sentiment undermines rational assessment. This monologue is followed by the arrival of Feeling, and the two engage in a *contrasto* again reminiscent of that between *Li buffoni*'s Ancient Comedy and Buffoonery. But while a vanquished Ancient Comedy leaves the stage, Reason later returns to remind her audience how poorly things stand: she herself has been undone by fickle Fortune, Love and Feeling have prevailed such that mortals are rendered irrational, and chaste Diana has abandoned her virtue. Love may win, but at the cost of Reason being "extinguished."[42] Costa's critique of *ozio* is novel and surprising within the pastoral tradition; furthermore, her call to reason is unexpected within a literary corpus that long emphasized the indomitability of the passions. By associating both city and country with the mutable influence of Feeling, rather than Reason, Costa breaches the fictive boundaries between Arcadia and Court in the pastoral mode. The play's "happy" resolution is tarnished by the intrusion of deceit.

Second, Costa disrupts conventional rustic play.[43] The inhabitants of an ideal pastoral landscape should be free from the clutches of jealousy and vicious contests. Pastorals typically feature friendly or "amused" Arcadian contests, Ugolini has argued, that are "intriguingly structured as mirroring the competitiveness of the court, yet depriving it of its innate aggressiveness." These encounters are "cleansed of all the intrinsic violence and deception" of their urban counterparts, presenting the reader-spectator with a happy and neat "accord [that] is antithetical to the cutthroat competition among peers of the courtly world." [44] Indeed, punctuating Costa's narrative are a series of scenes featuring nymphs and shepherds who together sing arias and play games. But the recreation of choice for Costa's brigade turns out to be the decidedly urban genre of parlour games, and the resolution of those divertissements is in both cases quite literally cutthroat.

The first entertainment is the *gioco della staffetta*. The band of companions play this card game on stage, describing their hands as they proceed. We get a glimpse of this game's social role in Vincenzo Nolfi's 1631 conduct manual for his future wife, *Ginipedia*; in his section on social pastimes, Nolfi lists the *gioco della staffetta* as one of the parlour games beneficial to women.[45] Such diversions teach ladies how to not to be duped by others, he states, and also promote moderation and composure, since effective card-playing strategy requires maintaining a poker face.[46] The nymphs' and shepherds' merriment in *Gl'amori della luna* is interrupted by the arrival of a satyr, who plans to snatch the nymph Ermilla. The brigade's playful mimicry of competition in cards is immediately redirected and played out with this intruder. The moment the satyr comes on the scene – before he speaks or acts – Ermilla, abandoning the pretence of inscrutability, shouts for her companions to "kill, wound him."[47] Her companions join this bloody "massacre" ("strage"), assailing the satyr with darts and arrows and then urging the spectator to behold him bleeding out on stage.[48] With this grisly ending to act 1, the libretto introduces a direct spectatorship of violence unusual in early modern theatre and opera. The scene evokes the dismemberment of Orpheus by the brutal Maenads.[49] The Orphic ending is avoided or disrupted in works like Castiglione's *Cortigiano*, in which the Duchess signals to the ladies attending *that* courtly game to rise up after Gaspare oversteps in his verbal assault of them, "and [to rush upon him] laughing ... as if to assail him with blows and treat him as the bacchantes treated Orpheus," a violent tension that is diffused through civilizing laughter.[50] In contrast, the pretence of civility is dismantled in Costa's first game.

As Karen Raizen reminds us, "the pastoral stage, despite its happy resolutions, is by no means a carefree locus ... darkness and death tinge every scene, displaying the morbid underbelly of the pastoral surface and the shadows that lurk in the hillsides."[51] But Costa draws this morbidity from the wings to centre stage. The randy satyr intent on violating his chosen nymph is a familiar, expected face in the pastoral landscape. His rape attempt is typically – though not always – fought off. Tasso's shepherd Aminta, for example, saves Silvia by arrows and stones; the satyr runs off, thwarted but unharmed.[52] The satyr of Guarini's *Il pastor fido* holds Corisca by her hair, threatening to snap her neck if she does not yield; she escapes because the locks he clutches are actually a wig.[53] Andreini's satyr in *Mirtilla* is duped by Filli, who saves herself by convincing him that she shares his desires; she ties him up with the promise of kisses before pinching him, pulling his beard, and leaving him strung up like a "laughingstock."[54] One of the scenes most similar to *Gl'amori della luna* is found in *La Calisto*. Here a young satyr (*satirino*) tries to abduct Linfea with the help of two fellow satyrs, all of whom she fends off with the help of other nymphs; these figures spar in a ballet number, the women trying to wound the assailants and the satyrs brandishing swords before beating a retreat.[55] A parallel scene can also be found in *Diana schernita*, Giacomo Francesco Parisani and Giacinto Cornacchioli's 1629 tragic Roman *boscareccia* opera, in which Amore conspires with Pan to defeat his nemesis Diana by disguising Endymion as Actaeon, leading to his death.[56]

Costa's satyr appears on stage only twice: first to announce his libidinous intentions, and next to die. He does not intersect with the Diana/Endymion (or Love/ Slumber) storylines; a conventional pastoral figure, he is included to incorporate a spectre of violence that in other works is threatened but that here is realized. Almost as though she has memory of the near escapes of her textual female predecessors, Ermilla leaps to action as soon as he appears. In so doing, she loses entirely the self-control exercised in the *gioco della staffetta*. Primed by the seemingly friendly game of cards, the brigade erupts – as if to demonstrate the real competition that was already pulsing under the surface (akin to the transformation of the "sweet" dance of equestrian ballet to real combat in the *Festa reale*, discussed in chapter 4). Recreational rivalry gives way to real conflict. The satyr has been slaughtered by figures whose urban games belie their supposedly pastoral identities.

At their next gathering (in Feeling's enchanted grove) this group plays the *gioco delli spropositi*. The shepherd Fileno explains the rules of this women's parlour game. Each player whispers a word or phrase to the person sitting next to her, who then whispers a related word or phrase to his neighbour, and so forth; once everyone in the circle has gone, the players repeat their words out loud. Anyone who had failed to utter something logically associated with what she herself was told must pay the forfeit.[57] In the first round, the libretto provides stage directions to guide the imagination of the game:

ERMILLA: Jealousy – – – – – *softly*

CELINDO: Great torment – – – – – *softly*

DORI: And portent – – – – – *softly*

FILENO: Wicked pain – – – – – *loudly*

ERMILLA: Jealousy – – – – – *loudly*

CELINDO: Great torment – – – – – *loudly*

DORI: And portent – – – – – *loudly*

FILENO: Wicked pain
ERMILLA: Jealousy
ALL TOGETHER: Jealousy

ERMILLA: Gelosia – – – – – piano
CELINDO: Gran tormento – – – – – piano
DORI: E portento – – – – – piano
FILENO: Pena ria – – – – – forte
ERMILLA: Gelosia – – – – – forte
CELINDO: Gran tormento – – – – – forte
DORI: E portento – – – – – forte
FILENO: Pena ria
ERMILLA: Gelosia
TUTTI ASSIEME: Gelosia[58]

After this fourth and final round, Ermilla proclaims that they all must pay the forfeit, in this case by weighing the relative strengths of Love and Jealousy. They do so by together singing an arietta on the ferocious powers of Jealousy, who is both the "daughter" (*figlia*) and "monster" (*mostro*) of Love. Under her bestial and icy influence, all things are exterminated, a description that echoes the prologue. Just as the *gioco della staffetta* concludes act 1 with the slaying of the satyr, so too does the *gioco delli spropositi* end act 2 with the bloody and patricidal final line of the brigade's song: Jealousy "kills [her 'father'] Love and becomes a chimera."[59] The lines echo closely the opening to *Adone*, canto 12 ("O di buon genitor figlia crudele / che 'l proprio padre ingratamente uccide"), which compares Jealousy to an array of mythological monsters.[60] Costa was not the first to introduce game playing into a musical work – there are a few other examples, beginning in the mid-sixteenth century – and Tasso's pastoral *Aminta* describes a similar circle game in which nymphs and shepherds whisper to one another.[61] While these other instances might feature breaches of decorum through players' angry outbursts (or in the case of Aminta, murmured sweet nothings), the games in *Gl'amori della luna* take particularly violent turns, pointing to the dangers that underlie competition.[62]

By act 3, Love appears victorious and Envy seems thwarted in her attempt to disrupt Diana's story. Endymion now shares the goddess's affections, Reason has surrendered to Feeling, and even the nymphs have reversed their earlier disapproval of amorousness. Following a celebratory ballet, the work ends with a horse-drawn chariot drawing Diana and Endymion into the sky as Love sings a last aria, the final lingering word of which is *amore*. And yet, while Love has defeated his adversary Slumber, and his ally Feeling has overcome Reason, the arietta sung by the nymphs and shepherds in their game forewarns that nevertheless he is powerless against his child, monstrous Jealousy, who can readily slay him. As Envy herself telegraphed in the prologue, she continues to lurk in the shadows of the drama without being challenged or extracted. Never routed, she remains a latent but lethal force.

Considering that Love's good turn of fortune in Costa's plot is due to the weight carried by the names of Georg Wilhelm, Ernst Augustus, and Johann Friedrich when Diana names them to her beloved, why might a shadow – however slight – be cast across Love's final victory? If Endymion surrendered to Diana's ardour only after her evocation of these dukes, the reach of patrons' authority can be undone by jealousies and risks being curtailed by such "envious beaks" as those that threatened Costa's reputation and livelihood. The greatest threat to the love shown by patrons is Envy and the dark rivalries she breeds if left unchecked. If the pastoral mode offers its authors "a way to safely deal with potentially troublesome topics," through *Gl'amori della luna* Costa confronts the problem of envy and rivalry through the secure filter of a fictionalized landscape that is itself anything but safe.[63]

The Gales of (Mis)Fortune

Envy is a recurring concern throughout Costa's oeuvre. Her sole text that does not explicitly address it in some capacity is the *Festa reale*, a work that nevertheless features a sweetly simulated war that devolves into real blows due to Discord's competitive hatred for Jove. Often envy manifests in Costa's lovers and beloveds gripped with erotic jealousies.[64] Costa's autobiographical verse and her portrayals of historical addressees also point to backbiting, spite, and rivalry as endemic to the professional music scene and life at court.

The historical figures to whom Costa turns her pen are alternately praised for their ability to rebuff others' jealousies or (particularly in funeral and exile verse) sympathetically cast as victims of those same forces. Of the former we might take as an example Lorenzo de' Medici, who is praised in the opening dedicatory poem of *Lo stipo* for disregarding "envy's bitter wars."[65] Similar approbation peppers the rest of the volume's honorees, from Ludovico da Verrezzano, general of the Tuscan Galera, who "over Envy and death triumphs," to academies such as the Ruginosi, whose members "subdue every dark onslaught of Envy."[66] Patrons who curb, rather that permit, jealousies and rivalries are elsewhere warmly applauded. In addition to holding the ire of invidious destiny ("l'ira dell'invido destin") at bay for herself and for Turin through prudent governance, for instance, Marie Christine will save Costa's *Selva di Diana* from "all envious eyes" ("ogni invido lume").[67] The dedication to *La Flora feconda* expresses the similar hope that Vittoria della Rovere will guard the work against the ravages of time and envy.[68] *La selva di Diana*'s poem to Queen Anne inviting performers to her tranquil shores promises that there "one needn't fear the treachery of an envious beak [*invido rostro*]";[69] one of the *Tromba di Parnaso* poems for Mazarin similarly proclaims that envy is vexed to find itself turned away from the Seine ("da la Senna l'invidia ange smarrita").[70]

For those undone by Invidia, we might consider the example of France's Achille d'Étampes de Valencay, captain and cardinal, whose premature demise Costa attributes to the "harmful beak [*rostro*] of the envious Parca" who snips the threads of men's lives.[71] Francesco de' Medici's death similarly results from the envy that Enyo, goddess of war, harbours towards the supposedly great military hero; she makes an infernal voyage to procure the help of Plague – a viper-haired, pallid, Medusa-like woman – that mirrors Juno's enlistment of Allecto in the *Aeneid*, Minerva's of Envy in the *Metamorphoses*, and Costa's descriptions of Envy/Jealousy seen above.[72] The poem for Francesco's father, Cosimo II, traces the wandering of Virtue from realm to realm, battered by "the bitter offences of Envy" until she arrives at his Tuscan shores.[73] The epic Flora attributes the loss of her child to the envy of the stars ("e Invidia han de' miei beni anco le stelle"); in the dramatic revision, Jove decrees that, though she and her husband suffer this loss, they will be spared "Envy's glances" ("de l'Invidia gli sguardi").[74]

In short, the presence or absence of envy and its effects is a frequent, almost insistent, means by which Costa measures her universe. And although two of her male celebrants congratulated her early in her career on her ability to evade its perils – Alessandro Adimari declaring that for she "who conquers envy and tames time, / the world is a theatre and the universe a scene,"[75] and Ottavio Tronsarelli similarly proclaiming that she bests both time and envy[76] – Costa presented her own career as one plagued by doubts and hardships. As this book has shown, in many regards such passages strategically permitted her to cast a recently departed city or court in shadows while shining a happy light on a welcoming new patron. The *Lettere amorose*, for instance, opens with a distraught Costa lamenting her unhappy fate. Yet the Arno, overhearing her cries, appears before her to confirm that while "the winds of envy are against you," she should replace horror with play, sorrows with sweet joys, by writing of love.[77] A metonymy for the Florentine court, the Arno welcomes, restores, and nourishes her, while elsewhere she had suffered Fortune's gales. But Costa also continually reminds her readers of the hardships that writing brought upon her. In *La chitarra*, she foresees being criticized as rash or foolhardy for "wishing to sing" ("voler cantar") on the Arno when she was born on the Tiber – that is, for being an itinerant performer and a foreign writer.[78] She raises concerns (even if to brush them aside) that she inappropriately addresses erotic themes or that she will be considered a "poetessa ... di buon mercato" (cheap poetess).[79] Here, and in *La selva di Diana*, she defends herself against those who maintain that her texts are actually the work of another, accusations that she attributes to the ignorance of the age.[80] These explicitly autobiographical moments – which are almost always tied to Costa's itinerancy, the underserved instabilities of her musical career, her "misfit" identity as a member of court and as a poet – lend a picaresque quality to her literary persona.

Perhaps there is no more telling case than the autobiographical poem with which she concludes *Lo stipo*, which we have already encountered in chapter 2.

Having been urged by Benedetto Guerrini to burn some of her poetry, she does so with an anguished lament, not of a lover but of a poet. Across forty-seven octaves, as she feeds the papers to the fire, she pronounces over 100 curses on elements of her literary career: from the verse itself ("maladetti i sonetti, e madrigali / maladette l'ottave, e le sestine") to her days of study ("maladette giornate ch'in studiare io dimorai") to the jealousy that proved her undoing ("maladetta sia la gelosia, che mi condusse in così gran follia").[81] How could she have believed that her frail plectrum's song would please and that where patrons abound she might obtain the laurel?[82] Now her ink is tinged with blood drawn by an enemy beak ("nemico rostro").[83] In a theatrical outburst she denounces her previous volumes and renounces her literary career, vowing never again to cross into Parnassus. But the canzone appears in a printed work, rendering its protests performative rather than proscriptive. Costa would again resume her poetic journeys, including to Parnassus itself. Indeed, as the following section outlines, the act of travel was one means by which she reframed her troubles and levelled criticism at the court, especially that of Rome.

Imagined Exiles

Costa directly confronts her movements as a singer-writer in *La selva di Diana,* with a concluding poem on "the author's departure from Rome in 1647."[84] In this Parisian publication, she addresses Rome as an adored but negligent parent – alternatively a mother and a father who, despite her child's tears, "scorns ... and casts [her] away."[85] Reappropriating the tone of the *bella donna* or jealous Marmotta, Costa complains that her position as a native daughter is undermined by Rome's interest in an unfamiliar rival: "you deny to me that which you don't dare deny to a foreign beauty."[86] The language confuses filial anxieties with the erotic tensions articulated elsewhere in Costa's oeuvre. This disorienting turn is heightened by the poem's reliance on images of rising, falling, and spinning. The target of Fortune's wheel, Costa is a "new Icarus" ("Icaro novel"), permitted to soar only to come crashing down. But unlike that predecessor, who hubristically discounted the paternal cautions of Daedalus, her misfortune derives from her Roman parent's disregard.[87] Here "honours are immersed in horrors," flowerbeds veil snakes in wait, and she, holding on to nothing of her earlier acclaim, now spirals downward and begs for recognition.[88]

Already she has left the Tiber's shores once before; she finds herself again heading to "foreign skies" ("vado al cielo straniero").[89] Now poor, defenceless, and destitute, she departs even while her heart remains in Rome: "I leave without leaving" ("parto senza partire").[90] In short, Costa depicts herself to the French court as an exile, a daughter disinherited, compelled by mistreatment and hardship to abandon her native walls. Such characterizations were often at odds with reality. The portrayal of herself as arriving in Paris an émigré from an inimical Rome is confuted in large part by the fact that the French royal house invited her – without her prompt acceptance.[91]

Nor was this the first time that Costa cast herself as an exile. A poetic exchange in *Lo stipo* with the writer, theologian, and member of the Umoristi Paganino Gaudenzi offers an illustrative example. Gaudenzi addresses Costa in two parts: first, a Latin elegy *De di[s]cessu Margharitae Costae* (On the Departure of Margherita Costa) and, second, an "extemporaneous *scherzo* translation" in Italian.[92] In these poems, which he would later reprint (without Costa's response) in a volume defending Marino's poetry, Paganino asks how Rome could let Costa go and, conversely, how she could bear to leave her "cherished" Rome.[93] In departing, she forsakes Venus, mother of Aeneas, whose beauty she shares; at the same time, her obstinate fatherland dismisses her "with an irate countenance: 'away, oh Costa, go away from me.'"[94] Rejected by this fatherly Rome so "cold in love," she turns towards Flora, mother to the Medici.[95] Gaudenzi's question is tinged with irony, since in 1628 he too left Rome after one of his publications caused him to fall out of the Barberini's favour; he departed for a professorship in Pisa, from where he would unsuccessfully attempt to re-establish ties with Rome.[96] This poetic dialogue is therefore between two personages both distanced from their Eternal City.

Costa responds by identifying Rome as a city known for expelling its citizens. She compares her own departure from its walls to that of Scipio, Cicero, and Camillus. Though she does not mention Ovid by name, taken together her autobiographical poems recall in tone and thrust his *Tristia*, verse on his exile from Rome. Her retreat is due not to the political or military machinations that undid these ancestors, however, or the depiction of a "wanton muse" ("lascivia musa") but to jealousy and competition.[97] In response to Gaudenzi's claims that she surely set the Romans' hearts ablaze, Costa retorts that while she indeed may have sparked a few short-lived and superficial passions, she was no match for the Venus to whom he compares her, since the goddess "wishes no other woman to reside there" and "refuses to share her spoils with other women."[98] Moreover, she continues, Rome offers little fertile ground for the musical and literary ambitions of her "frail plectrum" since it "is the only realm to a thousand Apollos."[99] Beyond Costa's familiar self-deprecating posture of "frailty," the stanza casts her predicament in the light of competition. In the first half, she is bested in a contest she did not seek with an unbeatable rival, Venus's jealous territoriality driving her away. In the second half, she confronts a Rome overrun with would-be Apollos, the surplus of whom drown out her own song. Under the poem's light mythological wrapping, we come to the crux of her response to Gaudenzi: she has confronted too much competition from women in the realm of love and from men in the realm of lyric. Yet Costa does not yet rise to the same level of indignation seen in her complaint poem in *La selva di Diana* of a decade later; as she discusses her first departure from Rome, she concludes on a more hopeful note as she looks towards her new "royal patrons" in Florence. In order to enjoy a more Edenic environment, and "in order to drink in true eternity from the Arno, Costa is pleased to leave the Tiber."[100]

Costa revisits the same themes in the final poem of *La selva di cipressi*, discussed in chapter 3. Concluding this volume of laments, verse dedicated to historical and pastoral figures, is the eighty-one-stanza autobiographical poem in which "the author, under the name Elisa, describes part of her unlucky life." Initially Costa likens "Elisa" to a mortal-born goddess, another Venus, esteemed by the inhabitants of Olympus and adored by her "scores of lovers" for her beauty and music.[101] Abruptly, however, her star plummets. Among the ignorant masses her name is brought low and stinging poems ("pungenti carmi") defame her.[102] No longer able to endure having become in her native city "sorrow's dupe and the world's laughingstock," she resolves to leave Rome for Tuscany's "foreign sky" ("ciel straniero").[103] After a dramatic departure from the city, Elisa arrives in Florence still burdened with misfortunes. This sequence concludes with her fear that "in region *straniera* / È ben folle colei ch'*aita spera* (in a foreign land / she is mad who hopes for help), an end rhyme that foregrounds the vulnerability of itinerancy.[104]

In response to Elisa's continual woes, Jove sends her a kindred and loving spirit in Aminta. At his urging she first begins to write: penning love poetry, playing *scherzi* on her lyre, and immortalizing the Tuscan kings ("re toschi").[105] But adversity soon takes aim at her once more; as was true for Costa's Guise dedicatees, whose exile in the volume's first poem was soon followed by heartbreak and death, Elisa soon discovers that "a change of sky does [her] no good."[106] When her poems are mocked, when praise is heaped on other's inferior work, when circumstances suggest Apollo himself despises her songs, her pen falters. To Aminta she bemoans that they have lost money and she her mind. Yet when he discourages her from contesting her turn of fortune, she recoils, declaring her intention to leave both him and Florence: "I'll change where I serve, I'll switch realms / … / I'm leaving you, Aminta, and going to a land / more foreign [*ciel straniero*] to me than this … / Perhaps far from the Arno / to me the heavens will be less severe and fate less wicked."[107] Exiting Florence's walls, she heads not for another Italian court but for Mount Parnassus, clutching her best works – poetry and prose composed in Rome and Florence. She enters Apollo's abode, intent on confronting him. There she encounters an illustrious but select coterie of writers who embrace her as one of their own: Dante, Petrarch, Bembo, Guidiccioni, Della Casa, Colonna, Gambara, and Sarrocchi.

This is the sole passage in Costa's oeuvre that directly references literary predecessors, male or female, other than her own interlocutors. Costa places herself in the company of Italy's poetic giants – an assembly noteworthy for its near gender parity of five men and three women. Also suggestive is their number: Elisa brings their company to nine, like the Muses themselves. Commiserating with Elisa, these poetic gatekeepers lead her before Apollo. To him she directs a lengthy lament in which she blames Envy for her adversity, vowing to smash her lyre and pour out her ink in bitter defiance of a laurel she now despises. If she writes as well as her peers ("s' a par d'ogni altro il foglio / Vergato rendo de' miei puri inchiostri"), why must she alone be picked apart by injurious beaks ("punta da crudi, ingiuriosi rostri")?[108] Reminding her of his own tribulations in love, Apollo ascribes her sorrows not to Florence itself but to the injuriousness of the age and the suffering endemic to literary enterprise. Poetry, he professes, is the arena of teary lament and not of jest. Elisa concludes with the somewhat consoling thought that "if Fate is wicked / at least her own misadventures resemble those of a god."[109] Apollo's recommendation to switch from lighthearted verse to lament traces Costa's movement from her earlier "bizarre" and burlesque volumes to the elegiac *Selva di Diana*, the last of her poetry collections published in Florence.

Costa populates her Parnassus with exemplars with whose subjects and style she had little in common; she leaves out writers whose impact on her compositions was pronounced (Ovid, Ariosto, Tasso, Andreini, Marino). Of this group, only one – the Roman Margherita Sarrocchi (d. 1617), academician and author of the epic *Scanderbeide* – was a close contemporary of Costa's. Virginia Cox has rightly observed that, with the exception of her two temporal outliers, Dante and Sarrocchi, Costa selects members of the Petrarchan canon – Petrarch himself and his poetic retinue from the first half of the Cinquecento. In so doing, Costa points to a literary tradition by now largely past, one that coincided with an era of flourishing women writers, from the foremother Colonna to the last generation represented by Sarrocchi.[110] Costa does not express nostalgia for Petrarchism itself – despite Apollo's suggestion that poetic inspiration teaches one to weep rather than to jest – but Elisa does profess to be taken aback by the animosity she experiences specifically as a female writer in this new era: "In my folly, I had believed as a woman that every noble heart would rejoice at my frail plectrum and would from my works derive pleasure equal to their worth." [111] Instead she encounters envy and hostility. Elisa's mistake, it seems, was believing that the social norms of Cinquecento women's writing still applied to her. Costa's poem ends with bittersweet resignation to the tribulations she will necessarily confront as a writer, particularly in the face of rancour and jealousy in those she had hoped to be her audience.

The Condemnable Courtier

Costa's vulnerabilities as a woman are especially on display in her *Sette giornate* manuscript, which also criticizes courtiership. As outlined in chapter 2, the first five cantos of the poem feature divertissements, such as "The Hunt" and "The Game," before the protagonist "Margherita" experiences a conversion in the final two cantos and renounces all facets of courtliness, determined to live a life of respectability (a change of heart that does not, however, appear to have required a rewriting or reframing of her initial audaciousness). The first canto, "The Banquet," tells the story of the grabby cardinal whom Margherita fended off, hitting him over the head with a bed warmer and sending him tumbling. While she recounts the episode with a Boccaccian flourish, her humour is perforated by the blame she lays at the feet of her dedicatee, Camillo Pamphili: she hints that it was with his "help" that her would-be aggressor "put me in danger / so that I was almost like a lamb in the hands of bear."[112] Costa thanks him – presumably with irony – for exposing her to such a risky entanglement. "I obeyed you," she underscores, "because I valued your love."[113] Now, however, she (at least momentarily) calls into question his attention and affection, which seem "misleading and feigned":[114]

> You told me clearly
> That I should expect that service [of love]
> And I took you at your word,
> And you saw my believing in you as a sign
> That I judged you to be a cavalier
> And a person of good faith.
> But I feel that you're wearing me out,
> And I see that, changing your true name,
> You come close to that of "boy,"
> And truly I do not understand
> How someone so well born
> Doesn't don his word atop his locks.

> Voi mi dicesti senza impedimento
> Ch'io dovessi aspettar per quel servitio
> Et pigliai la parola per strumento
> Et il credere a voi vi è stato inditio
> L'esser tenuto voi cavalierazzo
> Et persona di fede a mio giuditio
> Ma provo, che di me fate strapazzo
> Et vedo, che cangiando il vero nome
> Voi v'accostaste a quello di ragazzo
> E veramente non comprendo come
> Un che ben nato sia, la sua parola
> Non porti sempre in cima delle chiome.[115]

Though she is but a silly little woman ("son fra le donne donnicciola"), Margherita is not one to be easily won over by sweet nothings uttered by deceitful men. She is worldly enough to recognize and deflect the strategies of those at court:

> By now I know and have experienced the court
> With those that are called courtiers.

Putting faith in them is akin to death.
They have big mouths and tight fists,
They fill your ears up more
Than do charlatans with their false testimonials …
I don't say this to reflect on you,
Though pardon me if inadvertently it does;
It is not my intention that everyone who
Fires me up with their promises
Will receive similar blows by my hand.
I made a promise, I kept it, I withheld
My part for a while, and as you well know,
I was, and am, and will be Margherita.

Hormai conosco e provato ho la corte
Con quei che sono chiamati cortegiani
Che lo sperar in lor è una morte
Questi c'han' larga bocca o strette mani
T'empion l'orecchie più con le parole
Che non fan di spergiuri i ciarlatani …
Non dico ciò per far la conseguenza
Sopra di voi, ma se pur fatta fosse
Scusatemi, ch' è stata inavvertenza
L'intention mia non è che chi si mosse
A farmi con promesse tanto ardita
Riceva sotto man simil percosse
Io promessi, io mantenni, io la partita
Trattenni un pezzo, e voi pur lo sapete
Ch'io fui, et sono, et sarò Margarita.[116]

Costa redirects her complaint from Pamphili – whom by the canto's end she partially exculpates – to the courtier. Loud, stingy, false, and jealous, he would pose the real threat were she not well practised in thwarting him. The lecherous cardinal in her tale is one such figure; Costa assures Pamphili that she does not intend to subject him to the same fury she rained upon his companion. Nevertheless, he ought to have recognized the well-known faults of the courtier and not exposed her so to one of their number. The terms of patronage, which should afford her protection, have been tested and proven worse for wear. In the passage's final lines, Costa signals that she – always Margherita – knows how to play the game but also that she can draw a firm line against those who pose a risk to her.

Just as substantial passages of the *Sette giornate* replicate Costa's earlier depiction of her wild, untameable muse, so too does this description of courtiership derive from *La chitarra*.[117] Reordered and revised, these verses reproduce lines from a poem in which the *bella donna* – a woman who, like Margherita, "by now recognize[s] the courtly style" – "complains about the court when her lover, who serves it, leaves her while she is ill."[118] An innovative take on romantic jealousy, in which the woman fumes over the attentions paid not to a female rival but to the court itself, this poem lambasts the falseness, iniquity, and baseness of the court. Speaking to her beloved, the *bella donna* permits herself even greater liberty than Margherita does in condemning the court, that cruel space where great promises are made but little materializes, a place where "they, pretending to speak about you as a game, / bring you to ruin," "envy has a sure seat," and "every faithful heart is derided."[119] Begging her paramour to break free, she ultimately warns that "no one succeeds at court who doesn't know how to playact."[120]

Costa takes equally pointed aim at the court and its creatures in the poem *Cortegiano ravveduto* (The Reformed Courtier), found alongside the similarly themed *Zerbino ravveduto* (Reformed Dandy) and *Giocatore ravveduto* (Reformed Gambler) in *Lo stipo*'s "drawer" of fake gems. In this satirical work, the rehabilitated courtier addresses his former peers.[121] "What worse thing can be said (oh the anguish!)," he cries, "than 'courtier' (oh woe!), than 'court' (oh alas!)?"[122] Across sixty-two stanzas, he unreservedly condemns the court as a place of discord, fraud, lies, dissimulation, and above all else, jealousy – for there "envy was born and roosts."[123] At the courtly palace

> Wicked tongues, lying hearts and souls,
> Perfidious entrails of sharpened minds,
> Culpable scammers of offences to faith,
> Have their highest seat under its roof.
> A thousand hearts, a thousand souls, a thousand lives,
> A thousand faces, a thousand eyes, and a thousand feet
> Does that ungrateful monster, the courtier stripped of truth,
> Wish to have at court.

> Le male lingue, i cor, l'alme mentite
> Hanno sotto il suo tetto altera sede,
> Perfide entragne di menti scaltrite,
> Macchinatori rei d'onte di fede.
> Mille cori, mill'alme, mille vite,
> Mille volti, mille occhi, e mille piedi
> Vuol haver nella Corte il mostro ingrato
> Del finto corteggian del ver spogliato. [124]

The tenor of the attack is all the more remarkable for appearing in a volume "intent on enriching" the Florentine court, with verse dedicated to the Medici, their political and military allies, academies enjoying their sponsorship, and so forth.[125]

The poem ends on a note reminiscent of the *Sette giornate*'s final conversion: the reformed courtier has vowed to flee this wayward environment forever. Though he condemns himself to poverty, he departs pleased to escape the "infernal scum" that is the court, his diatribe strikingly ending on the formidable word "hell."[126]

Costa's swipe at courtiership is nowhere more memorable than in her *Buffoni*, a play that revises the portrait of a harmonious Florence painted in her *risposta* to Gaudenzi and elsewhere.[127] As noted in chapter 2, this burlesque comedy satirized the Medici court and its pastimes by using historical figures in the employ of the grand ducal family for its cast of misfits and "freak[s] of nature."[128] These personages became the titular buffoons of Costa's fictional court. Verbal and physical comedy is staged through their many conflicts: Act 1 opens with a scene of warring spouses; acts 1 and 2 end with wild fisticuffs as the members of the household staff (including the prince himself) pummel each other; and the court's two rival buffoons, Tedeschino and Baldassare, face off in an acrimonious contest of insults.

First, however, the comedy begins with the heated *contrasto* between Ancient Comedy and Buffoonery. In addition to disputing the merits of their respective performance styles, they offer competing visions of contemporary courtly life. Just as Love in *Gl'amori della luna* triumphed against Slumber but remained haunted by the dangers of Envy, Buffoonery ultimately wins this war of wits (by proclaiming herself the Medici's preferred theatrical genre), but Ancient Comedy, while acquiescing, offers a critique of courtliness that colours the remainder of the play. Always lurking in the wings of this "ridiculous" sketch of princes and princesses, cooks and hunters, secretaries and buffoons – a comedy likely performed in the setting of a Medici or associate palace – is the ambiguous figure of the courtier. The prologue opens with Ancient Comedy cataloguing the disreputable male figures she spots in the courtly audience before her: the adulterer, the imbiber, the gambler, the thief, the playboy, the miser, the pillaging soldier. Concluding this inventory of rogues is the courtier:

> And the courtier, who like a snail,
> wears his entire wardrobe on his back,
> with a parched mouth withdraws into his chamber.
> In order to skimp, he stows in his shell
> what's left of his wages (or in truth of himself)
> and lives off his master's sneers.

> E 'l cortegian, ch'a guisa di lumaca
> Tutta la guardarobba indosso porta
> Co' denti asciutti in camera se n' torna
> Né, per spender, avendo entro lo scrigno
> L'avanzo del salario, o ver del suo,
> Si pasce ch'il padron l'ha fatto un ghigno.[129]

These lines – delivered before Buffoonery interrupts to assume the place of primacy on the Medicean stage – present the courtier as starved for all but his prince's disdain. Satisfied by scraps and scant shows of attention, he worms his way through the court.

Of the men Ancient Comedy decries, the courtier alone re-emerges in the comedy as a figure of derision. Costa places these criticisms in the mouth of Tordo, the state adviser (and, historically, the supplier of Ferdinando's telescope lenses) and the sole male figure – aside from the buffoon Tedeschino – not included on the comedy's paratextual list of fools and grotesques. It is he who is tasked with voicing complaints about the nature of the court and its retinue, saying of the mad German Michelino, for instance:

> Even in madmen pride has its place.
> He has no brains,
> and yet that too lends itself
> to the style of the court, to the courtier
> who's always arranging for his fellow
> to be sent off to the bordello.

> Fino ne' pazzi ha la superbia il loco:
> Costui non ha cervello
> E pur s'adatta anch'esso
> A lo stil de la corte, al cortegiano,
> Ch'è di procurar sempre, ch'il compagno
> Sia mandato in bordello.[130]

Tordo reiterates this characterization when debating Masino (the deformed secretary of state) over which of the two would make the better buffoon:

> What's so hard about
> getting laughs, cracking jokes,
> twisting your face into a scowl,
> grabbing a guitar and hacking away at it,
> telling a couple tall tales in the Spanish style,
> always bending to another's whims,
> saying yes twice over if that one says yes,
> letting it all go with a laugh if he says no,
> and showing off your gallows humour?
> At court such are the courtiers,
> who make the others look like suckers.

> Che fatica si sente
> fare una risata, in motteggiare,

> Far con una boccaccia un viso arcigno,
> Pigliare una chitarra, e schitarrare,
> Dir quattro sfiondature a la spagnola,
> Accomodarsi sempre a l'altrui voglie,
> Se quegli dice sì, dir sì due volte,
> Se no, non sia; e sempre su lo scherzo,
> Mostrar di piccardia aver bei motti:
> Questi son ne la corte i cortegiani,
> Che fan gli altri merlotti. [131]

In the functions of the buffoon – jocosity, mimicry, vagary, extemporization, sycophancy – Tordo sees the silhouette of the courtier. These facile entertainments diminish the standing of those charged with more sober administrative duties. Masino ironically concurs that "truly it is a blessed art," but the two men ultimately agree that their inability to imbibe vast quantities of wine disqualifies them from becoming courtier-buffoons. [132] And yet Tordo himself does not emerge unscathed from this exchange, since in the repartee he confesses to selling as his own knockoff lenses made by the Armenians. [133] Thus the character who through his professions as state adviser and lens crafter should be associated with foresight and scientific precision – the character therefore most equipped to clearly see and comment on his peers – turns out to be a fraud.

Tordo's criticism of the buffoon might be equally applied to any of the other ridiculous figures who make up Prince Meo's principality. Until the final scene, none among them is interested in effective governance, least of all the reigning monarchs. Professing his intention to dedicate himself entirely to his erotic and culinary appetites, Prince Meo initially abdicates his administrative responsibilities to his wife, who is appalled at the prospect. [134] Administration of the court is left to the ragtag group of men in Meo's employ, individuals who largely share his predilections and replicate his negligence. The sole character invested in the questions of state is the buffoon Tedeschino. Were it not for the unflattering figure he cuts as a bombast and an oblivious blowhard, he might well satisfy Castiglione's call in the *Cortigiano* for the courtier-adviser. This political interest, coupled with Masino's allusion to the "blessed art" of buffoonery, directs our attention once again to Bernardino Ricci's dialogue – a work, we will recall, that offers an ironic defence by the comic actor Ricci (the historical figure behind the Tedeschino character and Costa's dedicatee) of the "art" of buffoonery and that likely inspired Costa's composition of the *Buffoni*.

Perhaps in response to complaints like that of Tommaso Garzoni in his *La piazza universale di tutte le professioni del mondo* that buffoons had become so powerful and honoured in the courts as to replace the poets, orators, and philosophers (the true courtiers) at their master's table – such that "one can no longer find the lord without his buffoon, nor the buffoon without his lord" – Ricci instead makes his buffoon the victim of the parasitical courtier.[135] If the buffoon's station has crumbled since its noble origins, he insists, it is due to the usurpation of his position by courtly pretenders. These figures disdain the title of buffoon – taking offence when it is applied to them – even while using the very same "roads and means" to approach their prince.[136] Because the straightforwardness of the buffoon's profession reveals the dissimulated nature of their own, they are consumed by hatred and rancour for these competitors. Explicitly modelled after Plutarch's *How to Tell a Flatterer from a Friend*, the dialogue suggests that the courtier is but an amateur lackey, the buffoon a true companion.[137] It concludes with Tedeschino's wish that his readers will "honour the good and true buffoons and disgrace the false and infamous ones," that is, the courtiers.[138] Separated only by training and forthrightness about their objectives and methods, these figures would otherwise occupy the same role at court. Courtiers are buffoons without the art and title.

An anonymous celebratory poem introducing the dialogue argues that through humour Ricci/Tedeschino reveals "quel ver, ch'è nelle corti al fondo" – the truth that, depending on one's translation, is to be found at the heart or at the bottom of the court.[139] Arguably Costa's comedy has the same objective, showing through its cast of administrators and entertainers an underbelly of princely attendance. Despite Ricci's playful attempt to favourably distinguish the buffoon from the courtier – reversing Castiglione's efforts to save the courtier from any accusation of clownishness – for Costa, the courtier is merely a buffoon and the buffoon just a courtier. While only two of her characters are trained "buffoons," nearly all of the members of the Moroccan court, from servants to secretaries, appear on her list of ridiculous roles and therefore share in the pointedly plural title *Li buffoni*.

Unlike Ricci's idealized interlocutor who sits at his sovereign's hand, Costa's Tedeschino remains continually at a remove from Prince Meo. The two characters appear together only twice: first when Tedeschino is dressed as the prostitute Ancroia and falls into the prince's groping hands, next in the finale when he is thrust into a birdcage. He never laments his unfulfilled relationship to his prince, focusing instead on his amorous pursuit of Marmotta, but arguably he suffers as much from Meo's inattention as she does, since both are inhibited from performing their social functions – hers marital, his recreational. Deprived of the opportunity to perform for his monarch, Tedeschino is subject to Marmotta's demands for absurd entertainments, at which he bristles. "You've got it all wrong," he laments, "I'm no jack-of-all-trades clown. I am a performer of quality, a man of skill … Even though I play the buffoon, I came into this world a cavalier."[140] These knightly affectations echo ironically the grandiose claims made in Ricci's dialogue, but they also gesture towards the debasement required for courtly service. Faced with her threat that he should never dare show his face again if he refuses her requests, the buffoon must consent and perform the various antics his mistress calls out, be he cavalier or comedic actor.[141] While Tedeschino (who, like Costa, is an exile from Rome)[142] prides himself on being able to flow with the changing tides of patronage, "switch[ing] out my livery / to suit my needs" in a quest for doubloons, Marmotta replies that Tedeschino does not know how to do "what … one does at court" – to bite one's tongue and please the prince.[143]

In the final lines of the *Sette giornate* manuscript, after Margherita's supposed conversion, she renounces the tools of beauty and courtiership, imaginatively restoring them to their rightful owners (her makeup brushes to painters, for example, and her curses to card players). To the court itself – where the courtiers live in futile hope until their deaths ("con le lor speranze / vivon i cortigian' sino alla morte") – she returns falsity and envy ("falsità," "invidia").[144] The conversion is not merely one from vice to virtue; it is also an abandonment of the courtly lifestyle, its exigencies, and its entertainments. The work concludes with Margherita's intention to live henceforth as a "solitary handmaid … in a narrow cloister, a narrow cell" – hidden away, that is, from city and court.[145] Yet her dedication to a Pamphili prince and the inclusion of divertissement-like cantos belie her abandonment of those spaces and follow instead the conventions of patronage. To a degree, this move replicates that of the *Buffoni*, a comedy that ridiculed courtiership before a courtly audience and that offered an unflattering portrait of princely service; it is a work that claims to have been sanctioned by just such a sovereign – just as pastoral, too, critiques courtly life to an often courtly audience. In each case, Costa brings her benefactors in on the joke, so to speak. At the same time, these passages underscore the degree to which she remained beholden to her patrons throughout her career, risking the buffoonishness that came with attending them and enduring the envies and rivalries endemic to their retinues. Her encomiastic portraits of her courtly benefactors themselves are counterbalanced by a sardonic assessment of what it meant to be a courtier – something of which, as a professional early modern singer, she had first-hand experience.

Conclusion: A Lonely Coda

Among the last known records of Costa are two letters penned from Rome in 1657. The first is a plaintive message to Don Mario Chigi in May. She grounds her pleas for Chigi's assistance in her identity as both the proverbial needy widow and the professional but aging female performer. She was, she writes, "without help … and with no one on my side," a "widow and poor *virtuosa*" with two daughters to support.[146] Costa likely did find herself immersed in "infinite woes" ("infinità di miserie") at this late stage in her career, but this letter also suggests a move to position herself within the new currents of Roman power. Chigi's brother was the recently elected Alexander VII, and he himself had newly arrived in the Eternal City as the commander of the papal army. As evidence of her talents, and as a means of attracting her recipient's eye, Costa included a sample of her poetry. In this sonnet, Costa professes that amid her ruinous affairs she will pour out her ink in Chigi's honour ("tra le ruine mie gl'inchiostri io dono"). After first venerating him, she then pivots to dwell on her own unhappy state:

> Amid studious endeavours, I am she
> Who passed her best years on vain aspirations,
> And now, laid low, the symbol of every sorrow,
> I echo death's resounding howl.
> Of two unhappy *parti* [offspring/products], the tomb and the cradle,
> Made the injurious mother by an iniquitous star,
> I succumb to the disgrace of horrid fortune.

> Tra studiose fatiche io quella sono
> Che trasse i più begl'anni a van disegno,
> Et hor depressa, e d'ogni danno il segno,
> Di latrato di morte eco risuono.
> Di due parti infelici e tomba, e cuna
> Fatta madre nocente a stella ria
> Soggiaccio all'onte d'orrida fortuna.[147]

Having dedicated her life to enterprises now proven empty, she finds herself dispirited and plagued with misfortunes in her later years. As she had before, Costa again plays with the dual meaning of *parti* as both her offspring and her works. She does not name the cause of her travails, but the reader is invited to consider the chasm between her efforts and their fruits. Yet, in accord with her other poetic addresses to benefactors, her final tercet raises the hope that through the two watching stars (eyes) of this potential patron, her own star might be reanimated ("a me dato sia / avvivata mirare... / dalle due stelle tue la stella mia"); the stellar imagery of this concluding line replicates exactly one with which Costa had courted Queen Anne a decade earlier.

With this final line of her literary oeuvre, Costa reminds us that her fate – and that of professional performers and members of court like her – rose and fell depending on the attentions of patrons. It is not clear what inroads Costa may have made with Chigi, but a month later she picked her pen back up to ask help of Mattias de' Medici. Having already approached him about her adverse financial and social circumstances several times over the prior year and a half (apparently without the desired results), in this letter Costa pleads that without his intervention she and her daughters have been stuck in Rome "with no one on our side ("senzza nessuno per noi") and amid people who would like to utterly annihilate and strip away the little that we have recovered."[148] In what appears to be Costa's final known letter, a missive to Mattias without a city or date but likely from early 1658, she once more describes herself as a foreigner ("straniera") in need of aid.[149]

With this, the trail runs cold. As was so frequently the case with performers, artists, and writers dependent on patronage structures to flourish, her late life culminated (if we may take her at her word) in worry and perceived isolation. Surely the road was far from smooth for an aging singer who had indeed been a widow for over a decade, who long carried the weight of her paramour's debts and imprisonment, and who perceived herself as the target of rivals and slanderers. While lament was central to her literary record, often for strategic ends, these final papers show us a Costa far removed from the defiance with which, in a poem published in her very first volume, *La chitarra*, a *bella donna* reminiscent of Costa's early audacious persona declares that "I am my own my own mistress … I live as a genteel lady, and Envy cannot obscure my name, for, with a steadfast mind and solid footing, I care little about what others say."[150] Tempered by past difficulties, but hopeful for the future, this extraordinary woman would long and increasingly decry the tribulations of courtly life.

Conclusion

Margherita Costa counts among the most prolific of the women writers active in early modern Italy. The number of her works, and their variety in genre and style, rival those of her acclaimed contemporary Lucrezia Marinella. Born several decades before Costa, in 1571, Marinella published her first texts in the final years of the Cinquecento, when the peninsula's literary climate was still relatively hospitable to female poets, playwrights, and authors. By the time Marinella published her final work, the *Essortationi alle donne et a gli altri*, in 1645, the cultural landscape had shifted, leading her to discourage her female peers from taking up the pen at all, after previously having argued so memorably for women's intellectual parity in her *La nobiltà et eccellenza delle donne* (1600).[1] These were the very years – the 1630s, 1640s, and 1650s – of Costa's literary enterprise, making her feat all the more impressive. Nonetheless the Seicento saw a number of remarkable women who have increasingly drawn the attention of historians: artists like Artemisia Gentileschi, composers like Francesca Caccini, actresses like Virginia Ramponi, and sopranos like Leonora Baroni, among others. Costa's extraordinary and often novelistic life, her musical career during the first generations of opera, her astute cultivation of desirable patrons, and especially her varied literary and theatrical output place her in the company of these more familiar names.

Costa's own contemporaries agreed. Men like Giovan Francesco Loredan and Giambattista "Titta" Valentino placed her in their "galleries" of illustrious women, while fellow female writer Isabetta Coreglia applauded and imitated Costa's style. Costa's celebrants extolled her virtuosity as both a musician and a poet, as did subsequent critics such as Antonio Magliabechi and Giovan Mario Crescimbeni. The latter praised her as a "woman no less wise than learned, and very well-versed in letters" such that "she not only surmounted the condition of the female mind but also that of more than a few even renowned male poets of her day, so that quite rightly she was universally applauded."[2]

Needless to say, Costa did not paint her own story with these same rosy tones. Casting herself as battered about by fate, she cultivated her patrons in part by presenting them as saving her from an inimical situation endured at a previous court and as being able to appreciate her unusual, often unconventional, talents. "After long embattling my life with various mishaps," she wrote to the grand duke in the dedication to *La chitarra*, "my adverse fortune is finally sated – or, better, has tired of tyrannizing me – and has allowed me the peace and quiet on the Arno that it had always denied me on the Tiber."[3] Finally enjoying the tranquillity required for poets, she births a work that is monstrous and dwarfish. In the accompanying "Letter to the Reader," Costa anticipates that some might criticize her audacity in "wanting to sing on the Arno" when she was born on the Tiber. "But because my soul is stripped bare of presumption, and utterly removed from wishing to equal the virtuosic and praiseworthy manner in which one writes [in Florence], I dared to bring this little (*picciolo*) volume to light." Her poems should be "pitied if not enjoyed" and protected "as a woman's *parto* [offspring/work]."[4] But that *picciolo* collection runs nearly 600 pages, and the male-authored celebratory poems with which she next opens the volume (in several cases by prominent Florentine literati) hail Costa precisely as a *virtuosa* and a swan ("cigno") able to swim gracefully to any shore. Alessandro Adimari calls the Muses to Florence to crown her, since none such as she is to be found at the Roman Capitoline. The pages of her volume, he adds, are but a pygmy-sized sample of her giant poetic knowledge ("un pigmeo del suo saver gigante").[5] If burlesque forms of the sort embodied by her book attracted the attention of the Medici in Florence, so could an epic about their procreative mission or an equestrian ballet libretto highlighting their newfound dominance in that performative genre. So too could the martyred St. Cecilia and her connection to an earlier Pope Urban win the support of the Barberini in Rome, a celebration of regency please the Duchess Marie Christine in Turin and Queen Anne in France, or a Venetian opera libretto whose plot turns on the mention of their names appeal to the Brunswick-Lüneburg dukes. While Costa's publications often acknowledged the rivalries, backbiting, and envy that risked undermining the courtly patronage system, she knew how to skilfully adapt her pen to each of her benefactors in turn, changing out her literary "livery" just as her buffoon Tedeschino did to secure his own position at court.[6] Although she likened herself to an ugly, indomitable muse and the mother of monsters, Costa understood how to make herself a publishing diva by adapting the aesthetics of the Baroque court.

Her nineteenth- and early-twentieth-century critics, such as Alessandro Ademollo, Benedetto Croce, and her biographer Dante Bianchi, would hardly agree. To their eyes, her pages evidenced only her immorality and inelegance. Croce offered as definitive proof that the works "scribbled" by Costa (a woman he found to be of "bad reputation") lacked in culture and quality a passage cited from the first poem in *La chitarra* in which Costa herself disparages her verse.[7] He neglected to mention that this is the very canzone describing that wild muse of Costa's, "Simona of Elicona," on whom the poet facetiously blames the "poor quality" of her verse but by means of whom she deftly demonstrates the burlesque and Marinist nature of her writing.

Following in Croce's footsteps, some scholars analysing Costa have taken to opening their studies with a caveat that she is not a "good writer" or that her works fall short of a certain standard. This type of devaluation is often seen in treatments of women writers, who are at times unreasonably held up to the implicit or explicit yardstick of a Dante, a Petrarch, or a Tasso and necessarily found wanting. This seems an unproductive frame, however, and not only because those canonical poets' own oeuvres can reveal variations in quality. Costa is a prolific author whose volumes and poems are sometimes more, sometimes less, technically successful, but together they offer a fascinating view on how a seventeenth-century performer navigated an itinerant professional career through a literary and theatrical engagement that saw her grapple with prevailing tastes and textual history, often with skill and almost always with innovativeness.

This book has explored the life of this unusual woman by tracing the ways in which she moulded her literary persona and the contents of her works to the various courts and cities in which she lived, fashioning a poetic and patronage itinerary from her rich bibliography. It places a spotlight on a life long cast in shadows due to presumptions about women's literary activity in post-Tridentine Italy and antipathy towards Baroque poetics. It does not pretend to be exhaustive, however, not least because so few of Costa's works or activities have been previously explored in depth. The fact that she strung together such an extensive network of benefactors across multiple cities means that the scholar is confronted with a vast quantity of materials to consult, and additional clues to her connections and performances surely await discovery in various Italian, French, and perhaps even German archives. Similarly, the sheer number of individual poems she composed – over 200 in *La chitarra* alone, and over 500 total, few of which have received previous scholarly analysis – necessarily means that the present study has considered just a few exemplary compositions, leaving many undiscussed for reasons of space and focus. Costa's textual adaptations of figures such as Ovid, Ariosto, Tasso, Andreini, Marino, and Adimari offer fertile ground for further exploration. Finally, this book takes a primarily literary approach to Costa's publications (reflecting the training of its author), but a musicological study would surely reap fruits. Steps in this direction are found in chapter 3, which traces Costa's relationship to the lament tradition in both its erotic and political forms and demonstrates her adaptation of exemplars from composers such as Luigi Rossi. In addition to following the musical themes prevalent across her corpus, future scholarship might connect her verse to the cantatas and madrigals that she would have heard performed and herself sung.

As Alessandro Metlica has observed in his comparable study of Marino's relationship to Baroque courts and their patrons, "The court represents the place of performance par excellence, and therefore literature about it, from Castiglione's

Cortegiano to Torquato Accetto's *Dissimulazione onesta*, frequently resorts to metaphors of acting and theatre."[8] As a performer Costa knew how to play her part savvily, incorporating the pleasures (and pitfalls) of the courts she knew into her pages while still carving out space for her own peculiar poetic voice. Her willingness and ability to adapt her literary persona, pivot between registers and genres, and embrace the sardonic and the stately as circumstances required recalls not only Marino himself but also the sixteenth-century career of Pietro Aretino, although certainly she never risked becoming a "scourge of princes" in his fashion. It is difficult to speculate whether Costa gained support and notoriety in spite of her identity as a woman writer and professional performer, or whether it was the very novelty of a woman daring to embrace Baroque aesthetics in her fashion that secured her place at the printing presses. Like both Marino and Aretino, however, she knew how to modulate, where to be unconventional, and when to attune her voice to a new cultural climate.

Notes

Introduction

1 Brosius, "*Il suon, lo sguardo, il canto*," 24–5.

2 Primarosa, "I volti della musica," esp. 63–4.

3 Turner, *Roman Baroque Drawings*, 158; Sani, *La fatica virtuosa di Ottavio Leoni*, 62–6, plate #92.

4 There is some informal hypothesis that Vouet's sitter may be his wife, Virginia da Vezzo, who was a singer as well as a painter herself. See Brosius, "*Il suon, lo sguardo, il canto*," 24n41. For a comparison of this portrait with that the artist did of Artemsia Gentileschi, see Solinas, "Simon Vouet, suonatrice di chitarra." Vodret and Strinati suggest that the image should more accurately be titled "Singer Playing the Guitar" ("Painted Music," 106).

5 The Biblioteca Civica di Padova possesses a copy whose cover page has been reprinted with a date of 1648; the volume contains various printing errors (blank and misordered pages) but the text is unchanged.

6 "la Chitarra… se bene è istromento vile, viene quasi da tutti esercitato"; Costa, *La chitarra*, dedicatory letter. Translations are my own unless otherwise indicated.

7 Coelho, "The Baroque Guitar," 169.

8 Alfonso de Oviedo Spinosa, in Costa, *Lettere amorose*, 14.

9 "in tale altezza di stima e in Italia, e di là da' monti"; Crescimbeni, *L'istoria della volgar poesia*, 3:323.

10 The landmark study to redress these assumptions is Cox, *Women's Writing in Italy*.

11 For an overview, see Minor, *The Death of the Baroque*.

12 See, for instance, the contributions to Strappini, *I luoghi dell'immaginario barocco*; and *I capricci di Proteo*.

13 Cox, *Women's Writing in Italy*, 214.

14 See the translations Costa, *The Buffoons*; Costa, *Voice of a Virtuosa and Courtesan*; Kaborycha, *A Corresponding Renaissance*, 179–82. For recent studies, see Robarts, "Challenging Male Authored Poetry"; Robarts, "Marinism and Macrotextuality"; Goethals, "The Patronage Politics of Equestrian Ballet"; Goethals, "The Bizarre Muse"; Goethals,

"Worth Its Salt"; Megale, "La commedia decifrata"; Megale, "Sorelle, cantanti, rivali"; Díaz, "L'opre del Zerbinar"; Di Maro, "«Ogni bizzarro humore e bizzarria…»"

15 Ray, "Renaissance of Women," 288–9.

16 Ross, "Weird Humanists," 348–9, quote on 351.

17 Bianchi, "Una cortigiana rimatrice," 1924 and 1925.

18 Costa, *The Buffoons*, 2–24; Costa-Zalessow, "Margherita Costa"; Costa, *Voice of a Virtuosa and Courtesan*, 19–48; Carter, "Costa."

19 On writers, see especially the chapter "Backlash (1590–1650)" in Cox, *Women's Writing in Italy*, 166–227. On women in music, see Gordon, *Monteverdi's Unruly Women*; Heller, *Emblems of Eloquence*; Rosselli, *Singers of Italian Opera*, 56–114; Glixon, "Private Lives of Public Women." Also see Cusick, *Francesca Caccini at the Medici Court*; Harness, *Echoes of Women's Voices*.

20 Compare this to the thirty or fewer women publishing in other national contexts. See Cox, *Women's Writing in Italy*, xiv and 245n11, based on the catalogue in Erdmann, *My Gracious Silence*.

21 Marinella, *Exhortations*, 57.

22 Cox, *Women's Writing in Italy*, 213.

23 Kerr, *The Rise of the Diva*. See also Brown, *The Diva's Gift*, esp. 1–63.

24 Comedy and music were intersecting enterprises, as we are reminded by MacNeil, *Music and Women of the Commedia dell'Arte*; and Wilbourne, *Seventeenth-Century Opera*.

25 McClary, *Desire and Pleasure in Seventeenth-Century Music*, 81.

26 See Newcomb, "Courtesans, Muses or Musicians?"

27 Franco, *Poems and Selected Letters*, 1. Also see Rosenthal, *The Honest Courtesan*; Migiel, *Veronica Franco in Dialogue*.

28 "Con la musa farommi il fatto mio"; "non inarcate di grazia le ciglie"; Costa, *La chitarra*, 4, 568.

29 "ne' servigi amorosi"; Costa, *Lo stipo*, 208.

30 As in, for instance, Costa, *Voice of a Virtuosa and Courtesan*, 19 and passim; Marongiu, "Margherita Costa"; De Liso, "Le *Lettere amorose*," 54. See a similar argument regarding Franco in Migiel, *Veronica Franco in Dialogue*.

31 Costa, *Il violino*, 55–61.

32 Scholarship on early modern patronage is vast. See, to start, Cole, *Music, Spectacle and Cultural Brokerage*; Fosi, *All'ombra dei Barberini*; Harness, *Echoes of Women's Voices*; Kettering, "Patronage in Early Modern France"; McIver and Stollhans, *Patronage, Gender, and the Arts*.

33 ASR, Notai dell'A.C Testamenti 82, fol. 343r.

34 "suavissimam vocem"; "Pleurae notissimae meritricis patrem"; Erythraeus, *Eudemiae*, 169–70. A bilingual translation is available from Nelsen (*Gian Vittorio Rossi's Eudemiae*), 258–61, although here "lyre" is translated as "flute." On Erythraeus (Gian Vittorio Rossi), whom Cox describes as a member of the "seventeenth-century misogynistic canon" (*Women's Writing in Italy*, 183), see Giachino, "Cicero Libertinus."

35 ASR, Notai dell'A.C Testamenti 82, fol. 343v. On this obligation, see Storey, *Carnal Commerce*, quotation on 21; Camerano, "Donne oneste o meretrici?," 637–40. Camerano includes select transcriptions from Costa's will.

36 Costa purchased the vineyard (which included a house) in September 1633 and sold it on 27 August 1636 at a slight loss; ASR, Trenta notari capitolini, Officio 9, settembre 1636, 122r–126r. Also see Maoro, *Descrittione della chiesa parocchiale del Santissimo Salvatore*, 84–5. For points of comparison with other courtesans' wills, see Storey, *Carnal Commerce*, 162–87; Camerano, "Donne oneste o meretrici?"

37 Erythraeus's speaker states that he was currently in exile after having killed the rival in combat (*Eudemiae*, 2021, 258–9). Also see Costa's poem to Francesco Barberini in Costa, *La tromba di Parnaso*, 61–7.

38 It may well be that these were actually daughters. Unlike two children baptized in Florence, however, Costa never mentions them again elsewhere.

39 See Megale, "Il principe e la cantante"; Megale, "Altre novità su Anna Francesca Costa"; Rosselli, *Singers of Italian Opera*, 62; Besutti, "Costa, Anna Francesca."

40 ASR, Notai dell'A.C Testamenti 82, fol. 345v. Confirmation is found in her "Le sette giornate," 288v, where "Giovanni mio" has been replaced with "al marito mio."

41 ASR, Notai dell'A.C Testamenti 82, fol. 345v. For the baptismal record, see below. Papirio Capizucchi was prior of the *caporioni* in 1620, and a *caporione* several times in the late 1640s and early 1650s. See De Dominicis, *Membri del senato della Roma pontifica*, 102, 110–11. My thanks for this reference to Laurie Nussdorfer. A history of the family of the family was later published (Armanni, *Della nobile & antica famiglia de' Capizucchi*), but Papirio goes unmentioned.

42 Gianturco, "Nuove considerazioni su 'Il tedo del recitativo'"; Santacroce, "'La ragion perde dove il senso abonda'"; Giles, "Giambattista Marino's *L'Adone*."

43 Erythraeus describes Costa as "famous less for her singing than for her shameful ways" (non magis canendi artificio, quam turpi quaestu famosa); Erythraeus, *Pinacotheca*, 3:150–1.

44 Capucci, "Costa, Margherita" suggests that the scandal drove Costa from Rome, but there is no clear evidence yet to this effect.

45 See chapter 6, 172.

46 Courtesans could also be present. Barbara Strozzi and Leonora Baroni were both connected to publications emerging from *veglie: Veglia prima de' Signori academici Unisoni* (1637) and *L'idea della veglia* (1640). Rosand, "Barbara Strozzi"; Brosius, "*Il suon, lo sguardo, il canto*"; Robarts, "Challenging Male Authored Poetry," passim; Storey, *Carnal Commerce*, 209–10.

47 Bianchi, "Una cortigiana rimatrice," 1925, 29: 10–11; Costa, *Voice of a Virtuosa and Courtesan*, 21.

48 "Modo enim ab Anthimo rege revenimus, qui nos ad nuptias sororis suae maximis praemiis accitos, menses apud se continuos octo detinuit"; Erythraeus, *Eudemiae*,

2021, 258–61. Harness (*Echoes of Women's Voices*, 176–9), details the recruitment of Loreto Vittori up from Rome but notes that the other hired singers (including two women) go unnamed in the records.

49 Erythraeus, *Eudemiae*, 2021, 591.

50 Registro delle fedi di battesimo di San Giovanni, Reg. 262, c. 116v; Reg. 263, c. 173r.

51 Giovanna Vittoria's record (here adjusted from the Florentine calendar) oddly reads "Margherita di Stella di Cristofaro Stella." The reason for this error is unclear, but Capizucchi is named as Giovanna Vittoria's father in one of her own notary documents of 1677; ASV Notarile, Atti, b. 3551, fol. 107v–108r. My thanks to Beth Glixon for this latter information.

52 A 1652 letter from Giovanna Vittoria to Leopoldo de' Medici suggests that the cardinal himself performed her baptism. ASF Mediceo del Principato (hereafter MdP) 5561, 919r–v

53 Costa, *Istoria*. On the dating, see chapter 1, 30–1.

54 Costa, *Lo stipo*.

55 The name Daniel Wastch appears elsewhere only once, Girolamo Fantini's *Modo per imparare a sonare di tromba,* also dedicated to Ferdinando in 1638.

56 Robarts, "Challenging Male Authored Poetry," 80–4. Also see Callard, *Le prince et la république*, 101–3. Supporting this hypothesis is the publication of a *Stipo* poem, addressed to Giovan Carlo, as a pamphlet by Massi & Landi (c. 1638). On Massi and Landi, see Bruni, "Editori e tipografi," esp. 386 on Costa.

57 Callard, *Le prince et la république*, 98–10.

58 "[la] diversità de' miei carmi"; see chapter 3, 80.

59 Costa, *Flora feconda*.

60 Costa, *La Flora feconda*.

61 Costa, "Festa reale," 1640.

62 Costa, *La selva di cipressi*.

63 Costa, *Li buffoni*. Citations will be to the bilingual edition, Costa, *The Buffoons*. Also available in Ferrone, *Commedie dell'arte*, 2:235–359.

64 Costa, *Voice of a Virtuosa and Courtesan*, 22. Other hypotheses included the death of Ricci, incorrectly believed by some to be Costa's husband (who died two decades later).

65 See chapter 2, 67.

66 "questi Signori sentiranno con non poco disgusto la mancanza della Signora Margherita Costa per questi teatri. Ne doveranno però incolpare se stessi e i mali trattamenti che gli avevano esibiti. [...] non posso se non lodare la sua resoluzione." 30 November 1641 letter from Venice; Mamone, *Mattias de' Medici*, 71 (#125). Rinuccini does not name the opera, but a good contender might be *Bellerofonte*, to which Mattias had lent his singer Michele Grassechi and with whose composer (Francesco Sacrati) he was in frequent correspondence. See the assorted relevant letters in Mamone's volume, and Rosand, *Opera in Seventeenth-Century Venice*, 98–101.

67 Likely in 1630, based on a 26 August 1636, letter from Ferdinando acknowledging his six years of service; ASF Misc. Medicea 504, Ins. 30, c. 137.

68 On the stabbing and poem, see chapter 3, 104–5. On the 1641 plot, see ASF Misc. Medicea 504, Ins. 5, fols. 1–2, 7, 8; Ins. 6, fol. 9.

69 "Bisdosso overo Diario di Francesco Bonazini," fols. 281–93; "Vita, carcere, et azioni e morte del capitano Tiberio Squilletti." These and other accounts follow a shared narrative. A similar claim is found the documents concerning the stabbing (ASF Misc. Medicea 504, ins. 28, c. 3v), but here Squilletti is linked to "Checca Costa," that is, Anna Francesca.

70 ASF Misc. Medicea 504, Ins. 29, c. 1.

71 "Margarita Costa famosa meretrice, la quale anco era amica di uno, il quale poteva assai con i Barberini." Gigli, *Diario di Roma*, 1:413.

72 "Venne a Roma Fra Paolo famoso ladrone, et assassino facinoroso, et fu ricevuto con incontro di carrozze, et menò cariaggi, et andò ad alloggiare in casa di D. Taddeo Barberino al Monte della Pietà, et quivi fu honorato, et andava in carrozza con D. Taddeo con maraviglia di tutti. [...] Tutto il popolo sta in aspettatione per vederne la fine, perchè niuno può credere che costui, avvezzo a fare tradimenti et ricatti et assassinamenti, sia per essere huomo da bene." Gigli, *Diario di Roma*, 1:413–14.

73 "mostruoso"; Ameyden, "Diario," Biblioteca Casanatense MS 1832, fol. 25.

74 See chapter 5, 158.

75 Costa, *Cecilia martire*.

76 "E donna del resto di puoco buon affare, dama e mantenuta di Fra Paolo." The cardinal kept separate Italian and German diaries. von Harrach, *Die diarien und tagzettel*, 2:538 (Italian); 5:31 (German). See also Keller and Romberg, "The Tagzettel and Diaries."

77 Costa, "Le sette giornate." The first reference to the manuscript was by Roberto Ciancarelli, who transcribed canto 3 in "Roma capitale," 104–10.

78 "donne assai difamate e publiche in q[uest]a corte"; "[la Signora d. Olimpia] le ha permesso che mettino li arme di S.E. sopra la sua porta, e le ha concedutto che vadino in carrozza senza riguardo alcuno." 20 August 1645. Avvisi, BAV Capponi 63, fol. 286r.

79 Letter of 22 December 1644, from Raffaello Staccoli to Giovan Carlo de' Medici, "quella sua donna"; ASF Misc. Medicea 504, Ins. 17, c. 8r. In this and subsequent letters, Costa is never directly named.

80 Letter of 7 February 164[5] to Raffaello Staccoli, ASF Misc. Medicea 504, Ins. 27, c. 3v–4r.

81 "passione amorosa"; 9 May 1645 letter to Raffaello Staccoli, ASF Misc. Medicea 504, Ins. 26, c. 5v.

82 For details of the contract, see chapter 5, 169.

83 Costa, *La selva di Diana*.

84 On Mazarin's life and influence, see, for example, Treasure, *Mazarin*.

85 See Murata, "Why the First Opera Given in Paris Wasn't Roman"; Bianconi and Walker, "Dalla *Finta pazza* alla *Veremonda*"; Zaslaw, "The First Opera in Paris";

Ademollo, *I primi fasti*; Hammond, *The Ruined Bridge*, 153–89. On Anna Francesca's activities, see Megale, "Il principe e la cantante."

86 The full *Orfeo* cast list is found in BAV Barb. Lat. 4059, fol. 131v, and is transcribed in Hammond, *The Ruined Bridge*, 182–9.

87 Costa, *La selva di Diana*, 86–95.

88 "Havendo la Maestà della Regina risoluto di volere havere in Parigi quest'inverno una buona mano de musici tanto per la camera quanto per il theatro, si scrive alla S.ra Francesca Costa et alla Sig.ra Margherita sua sorella, che si ritrova in Venetia, di venire in Francia con altri musici, che si potranno havere costì et in Venetia" (29 September 1646); Monaldini, *L'orto dell'Esperidi*, 5–6 (#14).

89 Rosand, *Monteverdi's Last Operas*, 126n121.

90 "con tanto avantaggio quanto grande è la differenza dall'età di 17 a quella di 47"; 29 October 1646. Presumably these ages were estimated for effect. Monaldini, *L'orto dell'Esperidi*, 9 (#22). Also see his letters of 20 October (8, #20) and 5 November (11, #24).

91 1 December 1646; Monaldini, *L'orto dell'Esperidi* 11 (#30).

92 See chapter 4, 131–2. Daniela De Liso asserts, on unspecified grounds, that Costa and Mazarin were likely lovers; De Liso, "Margherita Costa a Parigi," 28.

93 Martin, "Un grand editeur parisien."

94 Costa, *Festa reale*, 1647.

95 Costa, *La tromba di Parnaso.*

96 "per gl'honori ricevuti in Parigi dalla Maestra della Regina in Francia"; Costa, *La selva di Diana*, 79.

97 Rossi and Melani were exceptions; Freitas, *Portrait of a Castrato*, 56–8.

98 17 May 1647; ASF MdP 4653, c. 116v.

99 22 May 1647, BNF Dupuy 775, fol. 80r; 23 July 1647, AMAE Aff. Etr. Toscane, 128CP/5, fol. 346. Costa dedicated a sonnet to Du Val; *La tromba di Parnaso,* 41.

100 16 February 1648, ASF MdP, fol. 844r, cited in Megale, "Il principe e la cantante," 219.

101 Milan, Archivio di Stato, Cancelleria Spagnola, XXI.33 (*olim* 469), c. 230v, cited in Bianconi and Walker, "Dalla *Finta pazza* alla *Veremonda*," 404n118.

102 "una tale cortegiana famosa chiamata Margherita Costa"; 7 February 1650, Av[v]isi diversi italiani, 1646–51, BAV Barb. Lat. 6366, fols. 131r–132v. I have yet to locate any corroborating legal documents.

103 "Per la Sig. Margherita Comica rappresentando Isifile nel Giasone." Coreglia, "Raccolta," Biblioteca statale di Lucca MS 205, 24v.

104 Michelassi, "Balbi's Febiarmonici"; Bianconi and Walker, "Dalla *Finta pazza* alla *Veremonda*," 445. Alexandra Coller hypothesized that Coreglia alludes instead to Marco Marazzoli's 1642 Venetian *Gli amori di Giasone e d'Isifile*, but Medea is not a character in that work and, as discussed above, Costa had refused to perform in Venice for the 1641/42 season. Coller, *Women, Rhetoric, and Drama*, 53.

105 ASF MdP 1503 (unnumbered); also transcribed in Mamone, *Serenissimi fratelli principi impresari*, 442 (#919).

106 "quel diavolo del Capitano Tiberio"; "palludi"; "debiti del Capitan Tibero fatti mentre vi si era in casa tenute a forzza"; "mentre noi eravamo schiave"; "Mi liberi dal
percipitio che mi se appresta nel letto del mio funerale'; 16 March 1652 letter from
Venice; ASF, MdP 5320, fols. 291r–92r.

107 ASF MdP, fol. 290r–v.

108 28 December 1652. ASF MdP 1505 (unnumbered); also transcribed in Mamone,
Serenissimi fratelli principi impresari, 464–5 (#971).

109 "Alla Signora Margarita Costa nel teatro di S. Apollinare Nerea la Maga"; Abriani,
Poesie, 20. On Abriani's verse about singers and performances, see Badolato, "Cantanti,
librettisti e impresari nelle *Poesie*," esp. 18–19; Fantappié, "'Angela Senese'," 262.

110 ASV Scuola Grande San Marco, b. 112. See Glixon and Glixon, *Inventing the
Business of Opera*, 195–8, 345–8. The contract for both sopranos (the other being
Caterina Giani) was for 1860 lire. For varying views on which woman was the *prima*
and *seconda donna*, see Jennifer Williams Brown's introduction to Cavalli, *La Calisto*,
xxiv, xlv n65, xlvi n66; Glixon and Glixon, *Inventing the Business of Opera*, 197; and
Álvaro Torrente and Nicola Badolato's introduction to *La Calisto*, xx.

111 Archivio Storico del Patriarcato di Venezia, S. Vidal, Registro dei morti, Libro VII
1627–65, f. 149 (1653). I thank Beth Glixon for sharing this record with me. These
details, not contained in her *Inventing the Business of Opera* – which argues that this
was not our Margherita Costa (195n102) but does so before Costa's presence in
Venice was clear – necessarily soften the firmer identification I made in Costa, *The
Buffoons*, 19–20.

112 Personal correspondence with Glixon.

113 For a similar assessment, see Cavalli, *La Calisto*, 2011, xx.

114 Costa, "Sonetto... All'ecc. Principe di Palestrina." Costa-Zalessow has attributed the
anonymous *Doralinda amazzone ai detrattori del valor delle dame disfida* to Costa
as a posthumous publication ("Una poesia femminista del 1672") but the evidence
seems conjectural.

115 BAV Chigi I.VII.273, fols. 125r–126r. The accompanying poem, *Prence, a te, che
di Quirino al trono*, is also transcribed in Crescimbeni, *L'istoria della volgar poesia*,
4:202.

116 A few years later Anna Francesca Costa also approached Chigi, bearing a recommendation from Mattias de' Medici. Mamone, *Mattias de' Medici*, 814–15 (#1626).

117 "al nostro nido"; "l'oppressioni de' malevoli"; 29 January 1655 letter from Rome;
Mamone, #929. ASF MdP 5458, 255r; also transcribed in Mamone, *Mattias de'
Medici*, #929.

118 17 June 1657. ASF MdP 5466, c. 341r–v; also transcribed in Mamone, *Mattias de'
Medici*, 557 (#1167).

119 ASF MdP 5465, c. 679r; also transcribed in Mamone, *Mattias de' Medici*, #1093.
Mamone notes that the document is included in a volume of letters dating from
June 1656, but it actually appears in a small, final subset dating to January–March
165[8].

120 See Bianchi, "Una cortigiana rimatrice," 1924, 23; Costa, *Voice of a Virtuosa and Courtesan*, 24. On 1 May 1677, from Venice Giovanna Maria Costa secured legal assistance to retrieve all property belonging to her then departed aunt; the document also lists her mother as deceased. ASV Notarile, Atti, b. 3551, fol. 107v–108r.

121 "Vittoria Costa nipote della gia Checca Costa, qual canta assai bene e di bellissima apparenza […] a cantato a Fiorenza tre anni nelle opere fattesi nel teatro di via del Cocomero di Fiorenza in compagna del Ottonaina et ha piaciuta assai." October 8, 1664; Monaldini, *L'orto dell'Esperidi*, 211 (#77).

122 See Michelassi, "Il teatro del Cocomero"; Vittoria's payment (of 240 lire) is noted on 178n125. Also see Weaver, *A Chronology of Music in the Florentine Theater*, 133.

123 These celebrants were Alessandro Adimari, Andrea Barbazza, Bernardino Biscia, Alfonso de Oviedo Spinosa, Ferdinando Saracinelli, Ottavio Tronsarelli, and the prince of Gallicano (typically identified as Pompeo Colonna), and anonymous poets, writing in Italian, Latin, Spanish, and Portuguese. On academies, see, for example, Everson, Reidy, and Sampson, *The Italian Academies*.

124 D'Addario, "Adimari, Alessandro."

125 *Teatro delle glorie della Signora Adriana Basile* (1628); *Applausi poetici alle glorie della Signora Leonora Baroni* (1639); and *Le glorie della Signora Anna Renzi* (1644).

126 Fontanella, *Nove cieli*, 247.

127 "Alla Signora Margherita Costa animato miracolo della poesia"; "fra nove armoniche donzelle, / La decima più chiara"; Morassini, *Rime*, 108.

128 "dolci incanti"; "magiche note"; "sdegno, amor, crudeltà, pietade, e zelo"; Abriani, *Poesie*, 20.

129 Cox, *Women's Writing in Italy*, 215–16.

130 "Ma poi che del mio Serchio al bel sereno / gionta la miro, hor sì, che dir poss'io / qui di Pindo è traslato il fonte ameno"; Coreglia, "Raccolta," Biblioteca statale di Lucca MS 205, 20v.

131 Coreglia, "Raccolta," Biblioteca statale di Lucca MS 205, 129v–32, 102r–4. On Costa's autobiographical poem, see chapters 3 (106–7) and 7 (208–9). Noteworthy in Coreglia's "Elisa del Tebre" verse are poetically unusual terms such as *rostri* (beaks), which appears frequently in Costa's corpus (see chapter 7). The poems explicitly about Costa and one of the three "Margherita" poems are transcribed in Coller, *Women, Rhetoric, and Drama*, 247–8 (discussion at 51–2).

132 "Ammirabili… le donne… infinite le Teani, le Sofipatre, le Zenobie, le Aspasie, le Corinne, le Saffi, le Coste, le Marinelle, le Tarabotti"; Loredano, *Delle bizzarrie academiche*, 47. See Robarts, "Challenging Male Authored Poetry," 164. On the Incogniti's complex relationship to women and opera, see, among others, Heller, *Emblems of Eloquence*, 48–81; Muir, *The Culture Wars of the Late Renaissance*.

133 "tanto bello compose, e tanto scrisse"; Valentino, *La Cecala napoletana*, 127.

134 Pentolini, *Le donne illustre*, 229.

135 On Ovid in early modernity, see Barkan, *The Gods Made Flesh*; Cerbo, *Metamorfosi del mito classico*, 189–213.

136 Cochrane, *Florence in the Forgotten Centuries*, 237.

137 Inventory of Vittoria Della Rovere's Books, BNCF Magl. X.44. These were six full works and two pamphlet poems (while not in the main Costa list, *La selva di cipressi* appears under "Poesie sacre e profane"). Among Costa's Florentine works, the *Istoria* and *Buffoni* are not included. On Vittoria's patronage, see Modesti, *Women's Patronage and Gendered Cultural Networks*; Benadusi, "The Gender Politics of Vittoria Della Rovere," (esp. 274–5 on the inventory); Benadusi, "Carteggi e negozi"; Cox, *Women's Writing in Italy*, 207, 220, 222. Also see Straussman-Pflanzer, "Court Culture in 17th-Century Florence."

138 Costa is also inventoried in Giovan Carlo's library; ASF. Misc. Medicea 31.10, c. 89; see Barocchi and Gaeta Bertelà, *Collezionismo mediceo e storia artistica*, 3.Pt. 1, 111.

139 Holstenius, *Index bibliothecae qua Franciscus Barberinus*, 2:310.

140 ADP, Archiviolo 106, Miscellanea, 325v, 326r, 345r, 352v. Stephanie Leone located the entries; I thank her for alerting me to them.

141 Favaro, Antonio, *La libreria di Galileo*, entries 394 and 438. The inventory does not specify which *Flora* text.

142 Piantoni, "Le *Lettere amorose* di Margherita Costa," 37; Díaz, "Exceptional Bodies and Ludic Lovers." Also see the selection in Kaborycha, *A Corresponding Renaissance*, 179–80.

143 Bergalli, *Componimenti poetici*, 2:149–54; Ronna, *Parnaso italiano*, 2:1025–7; Gianni, *Anch'esse "quasi simili a Dio*,*"* 89–90 (with an error-prone introductory biography); Morandini, *Sospiri e palpiti*, 114–24. Morandini includes two other *Chitarra* poems.

144 De Blasi, *Antologia delle scrittrici italiane*, 334–41.

145 Garella, *Li buffoni*. See Goethals, "Worth Its Salt," 377–9.

146 Costa, *Love Letters*; Costa, *Voice of a Virtuosa and Courtesan*.

147 "Della Signora Costa," date unknown; BAV, Chigi Q.VIII.177.9, fols. 15v–18r. For a reproduction and transcription, see Witzenmann, *Cantatas by Marco Marazzoli*, 138–43, 280. Also see Jeanneret, "Gender Ambivalence and the Expression of Passions," 93–4, 98.

148 Herissone, "Daniel Henstridge," 176, 185n36, 185n37.

149 Mandosio, *Bibliotheca romana*, 2:26–27. There is no evidence that Costa knew Latin.

150 Bianchi, "Una cortigiana rimatrice," 1925, 2.

151 Amati, *Bibliografia romana*, 1:107.

152 Letter to P. d'Aprosio, 22 October 1680; transcribed in Arlia, "Un bandito e una cortigiana letterati," 165. Magliabechi attributes Costa's early courtesanship to poverty or family need.

153 "Le poesie varie che sotto il suo nome vanno per istampa, non sono di essa, ma per sentimento del Magliabechi, di ... Fra Paolo"; Marmi, "Miscellanea," fol. 51r–v. Transcription in Arlia, "Un bandito e una cortigiana letterati," 165.

154 "si sa che fu disteso da Benedetto Guerrini"; Marmi, "Miscellanea," fol. 40r. Transcribed in Arlia, "Un bandito e una cortigiana letterati," 166. Contrast with Magliabechi's comments; BNCF Magl. IX.14.

155 Croce, *Nuovi saggi*, 161. Also see Croce, *Storia della età barocca*.

156 Capucci, "Costa, Margherita"; Costa-Zalessow, "Margherita Costa," 118.

157 Costa-Zalessow has revised her initial position in 1982 that Costa "was certainly not a great writer and negative assessments of her are deserved," finding most recently in 2021 that she was "a versatile, original, [and] truly Baroque writer who had the courage to tackle new themes on the difficulties in women's lives and to compete with or contest her contemporaries, Marino included"; Costa-Zalessow, *Scrittrici italiane*, 148; Costa-Zalessow, "Alla scoperta di Margherita Costa," 15.

158 "Avoit du genie et du talent pour la poësie"; Ménestrier, *Des représentations*, 232. Cinelli Calvoli, *Biblioteca volante*, 2:205–6.

159 Tiraboschi, *Storia della letteratura italiana*, 10–13:366–7.

160 Quadrio, *Ragione e storia d'ogni poesia*, 2:310.

161 Canonici Fachini, *Prospetto biografico delle donne italiane*, 149.

162 *Vita, azioni e morte di Tiberio Squilletti*, published in Lucca, unspecified date; Bizze, "Un avventuriere e Margherita Costa," 261.

163 Marcotti, "Fra Paolo," 227.

164 Montazio, "Letter to Alessandro Ademollo, 29 December 1882," 131. The prolific dramatist Francesco Antonio Avelloni (1756–1837) penned a work about Squilletti; Liborio, *La scena della città*, passim.

165 "Squilletti, the Celebrated Bandit"

166 Grifi, *Saunterings in Florence*, 235.

1 Editing History

1 A recent example is found in the introduction to Costa, *Voice of a Virtuosa and Courtesan*, 25. Costa-Zalessow further suggested (p. 26, and in "Margherita Costa," 115) that it was the high quality of the writing that prompted these accusations on stylistic grounds, but I have not encountered examples of this sort. Discussions of the volume also found in Bianchi, "Una cortigiana rimatrice," 1925, 160–1; Costa, *The Buffoons*, 5–6, 64–5.

2 Th. Van Veen, "Keeping Sight of the Piazza." Notably this was a period in which Ferdinando and his brothers often sought out non-Florentine artists.

3 Lazzeri, *Il principe e il diplomatico*, 9–14; Angiolini, "Il lungo Seicento," 70–3.

4 See *Sustermans (Exh. Cat.)*, 45.

5 "raccolto dunque dagli scritti del Signor Benedetto Guerrini hoggi Segretario di Camera di S.A."; Costa, *Istoria*, 5.

6 See Martelli, *Il viaggio in Europa di Pietro Guerrini*, 1:xlv.

7 As discussed in the Introduction (12–13), those publications have demonstrably false imprints with cities listed as Frankfurt and Venice but were instead surely published in Florence by Massi & Landi. Moreover, an identical watermark can be found on copies of the *Istoria*, *Lo stipo*, and *Lettere amorose* held at the BNCF – an encircled sun with waved rays – which, though an imperfect assessment tool, lends

credence to this supposition. See an example of the watermark in Woodward, *Catalogue of Watermarks*, 99.

8 "picciola istoria"; Costa, *Istoria*, 5.

9 "debole penna"; "povero ingegno"; Costa, *Istoria*, 6.

10 "un prencipe di sì gran nascita, ricco di tanta magnanimità, dotato di tanto merito, un vero esempio di lodevoli costumi, uno specchio di bontade, un nido d'ogni virtude, ed infine una copiosissima fonte di verdadiera e sincera pietade"; Costa, *Istoria*, 6.

11 Costa alludes especially to the Thirty Years' War embroiling much of Europe.

12 Henderson, *Florence under Siege*; Calvi, *Histories of a Plague Year*.

13 "quasi novello David"; Costa, *Istoria*, 7.

14 Calvi, *Histories of a Plague Year*, 15.

15 "virtù eroica"; Rondinelli, *Relazione del contagio*, 6–8.

16 "nella quale si loda la pietà del serenissimo gran duca di Toscana ne' tempi calamitosi dell'anno 1630" (†3r–††2r); "eroica benificenza" (109), in Rondinelli, *Relazione del contagio*.

17 Costa, *Lo stipo*, 78–80.

18 For discussion of this historic obligation, see Capponi, "Le palle di Marte." See also Lazzeri, *Il principe e il diplomatico*, 31–56.

19 Costa, *Istoria*, 3–4.

20 Strozzi, *I cinque fratelli*; Capponi, *Amore prigioniero in Delo*.

21 *Relatione della venuta a Roma del Gran Duca*. Copies are held, for example at the Folger Shakespeare Library (W.b.132 (142), fol. 140r–175v) and the Bibliothèque National de France (MS. Italien 346, fols. 25r–47v; MS Italien 901, 186r–206v; and MS Italien 1337, fols. 9–32).

22 "Al serenIssimo Ferdinando Secondo," BNCF II.II.277. Despite the coincidence of the poet being a Roman singer, it is an *autore* (not an *autora*), so unlikely to be Costa.

23 AST–Castello, Lettere Ministri, Roma, N.1, Registro delle lettere di Ludovico d'Agliè, fol. 61.

24 Costa, *Istoria*, 390–1.

25 Costa, *Istoria*, 392. Dell'Antella was a member of the regency council.

26 See Chiarini, *Pitti Palace*, 89–91; Campbell, "Medici Patronage and the Baroque"; Bertelli, "Palazzo Pitti dai Medici ai Savoia," 11–24. In reality, the regency council continued to exert considerable political power for some years to come. Angiolini, "Il lungo Seicento," 71–2.

27 ASF, MdP, 6380; ASF, MdP, 6379. On these, also see Barocchi, "Ferdinando II da Firenze a Praga"; and Bardazzi, "'Istoria del viaggio'," who each transcribe a selection of these documents; both note but do not substantially discuss Costa's volume.

28 "sono stracco"; ASF, MdP, 6380, letter from 16 March 1628, fol. 577r.

29 Settimanni, "Memorie fiorentine," ASF Manoscritti 134, fols. 396v–536r. A lengthy block of pages for entries between 8 June and 14 July (the dates when Ferdinando left Prague and arrived in Florence) was left blank.

30 "ebbe una buona parte"; BNCF Magl. IX.14, c. 7r. As was his wont, Antonfrancesco
   Marmi went a step further, writing that "it's known that [the *Istoria*] was written by
   Benedetto Guerrini" (si sa che fu distesa da Benedetto Guerrini); Marmi,
   Miscellanea, BNCF Magl. VIII.16, c. 39r.

31 Compare, for example, the text and images in Costa, *Istoria*, 237–51 and ASF MdP
   6379 fols. 174r–78r (which in turn overlaps with the *avviso* of fols. 224r–29r, as
   well as the BNCF *avviso* noted below), in the cited case pp. 237–8 and fol. 174r;
   Costa's 251–79 with fols. 180r–88r; 278–316 with fols. 189r–198v; and Costa's
   369–74 and 376–81 with ASF MdP 6380 1121r–22r and 1130r–31r, respectively.
   The *Istoria* shows more textual additions in these later examples, but the main
   narrative remains that seen in Bocchineri's letters.

32 Costa, *Istoria*, 237; ASF MdP 6379 fol. 174r.

33 One of the *relazioni* that is replicated in the *Istoria* has been attributed to Guerrini
   ("Relazione degli onori fatti da [...]"; compare to Costa, *Istoria*, 219–36), but this
   seems to have been on the basis of Costa's preface allusion to him. The *relazione* has
   been separated from the similar documents at the ASF but is of a kind with them.

34 Settimanni's eighteenth-century account largely replicates these materials, though
   with more grammatical and stylistic interventions. His section on the grand duke's
   crowning is identical to the *Istoria*'s. Settimanni may have accessed the same documents Costa used, but it is also possible that he relied on her publication and
   that, consequently, the *Istoria* had an unspoken afterlife in his later manuscript
   compilation.

35 Cox, *Women's Writing in Italy*, 219.

36 See, among others, Robin, *Publishing Women*; Richardson, *Women and the
   Circulation of Texts*; Campbell, *Literary Circles and Gender*; Cox, "Members, Muses,
   Mascots."

37 On the possible exception of an Antonio Bruni poem, potentially written by him
   for Costa, in *La chitarra*, see below, 242n121.

38 On the family's circumstances, see Martelli, *Il viaggio in Europa di Pietro Guerrini*,
   xxxvii–l.

39 The Medici also kept close tabs on such protocols maintained at their own court.
   See Fantoni, *La corte del granduca*, 36–7; Bertelli, "Palazzo Pitti dai Medici ai
   Savoia," 39–43.

40 "Hoggi, ch'ogn'un s'inchina / Agli tuoi piedi (o Sire) / E con dovuto dono /
   Ubidienza ti rende"; Costa, *Il violino*, 1.

41 Casini, "La corte, i cerimoniali, le feste," 478–9.

42 Stampino, "A Regent and Her Court"; Harness, *Echoes of Women's Voices*; Cosentino,
   "Allegorie del potere femminile," 146–63.

43 See Wainwright, "The Fair Warrior in the City of Florence"; Cox, *The Prodigious
   Muse*, 84–5.

44 Barocchi, "Ferdinando II da Firenze a Praga," 305. Barocchi points to the brothers'
   heightened interest in art collecting in comparison to the *tutrici*, but theatre and

festival were also an important fixture of the Medici court. See Nagler, *Theatre Festivals of the Medici*; Blumenthal, *Theater Art of the Medici*; Harness, *Echoes of Women's Voices*.

45 "per una buca come di caverna"; "comparse in scena tutta ornata con amoretti intorno, godeva delle sue bellezza"; Costa, *Istoria*, 281.

46 "dove archeggia antro frondoso"; Costa, *Flora feconda*, 1.xxv.i (p. 9).

47 "cosa ridicola"; Costa, *Istoria*, 71.

48 "fu una ridicoliissima [*sic*] festa"; Costa, *Istoria*, 323.

2 *Bizzarria*, Burlesque, and Buffoonery

1 "La buffoneria è vita e anima de la corte"; Aretino, *Operette politiche e satiriche*, 137.

2 Costa, *Lo stipo*. Bendinelli and Tosi, "Stipo."

3 "burlesca composizione"; Costa, *The Buffoons*, 74–5. On the comedy, see this edition's introduction, 35–69; Megale, "La commedia decifrata"; Goethals, "Worth Its Salt"; Coller, *Women, Rhetoric, and Drama*, 41–53; Aguilar, "Margherita Costa y la comedia bufonesca"; Strappini, *La tragedia del buffone*, 239–71.

4 "inventar scioccherie, rappresentar balordagini ed imitar stoldidezze"; Costa, *The Buffoons*, 74–5.

5 Diaz, *Il granducato di Toscana*, 375. See also Casini, "La corte, i cerimoniali, le feste," 464–6. For re-evaluations of the *tutrici*, see, for example, Cusick, *Francesca Caccini at the Medici Court*; Harness, *Echoes of Women's Voices*.

6 See a similar observation in Angiolini, "Il lungo Seicento."

7 Mamone, "Most Serene Brothers-Princes-Impresarios"; Mamone, *Serenissimi fratelli principi impresari*; Mamone, *Mattias de' Medici*; Michelassi, "'Regi protettori' e 'virtuosi trattenimenti'"; Barocchi and Gaeta Bertelà, *Collezionismo mediceo e storia artistica*.

8 Baudi di Vesme and Massar, *Stefano della Bella*; Massar, *Presenting Stefano della Bella*, 1971; Massar, "Presenting Stefano della Bella," 1968; Johnson, "Stefano della Bella." Della Bella shared many of Costa's same patrons in Florence, Rome, and Paris.

9 A "ritratto al naturale di Margherita Costa"; Baldinucci, *Notizie de' professori del disegno*, 1:619.

10 Brosius ("*Il suon, lo sguardo, il canto*," 32) attributes their removal to disapproval over the Sappho comparison, but this was a conventional image for female writers, on which see below. Also see Bellesi, "I ritratti delle sorelle Costa," 70–1.

11 Bellesi, "I ritratti delle sorelle Costa," 70–1.

12 Brosius, "*Il suon, lo sguardo, il canto*," 29.

13 Brosius, "*Il suon, lo sguardo, il canto*," 32–3; Primarosa, "I volti della musica."

14 "istromento vile"; Costa, *La chitarra*, dedicatory letter. See Introduction, 3.

15 See Coelho, "The Baroque Guitar"; Tyler and Sparks, *The Guitar and Its Music*, 51–99; Eisenhardt, *Italian Guitar Music*.

16 "Pigliare una chitarra, e schitarrare"; Costa, *The Buffoons*, III.ii.44.

17 "viene quasi da tutti esercitato… non sdegnerà tal volta fra il numeroso concento di variati istrumenti servirsi anco di essa"; Costa, *La chitarra*, dedicatory letter.

18 See Goethals, "Worth Its Salt," 369.

19 See Goethals, "Worth Its Salt." Danielle Vianello sees this as Buffoonery's dispute with *commedia dell'arte* (*L'arte del buffone*, 36), but multiple references are made to Ancient Comedy's ties to Greek and Roman predecessors.

20 Megale, "Sproporzioni," 71.

21 "Ti duole ch'io ti tolga la tua parte. / Almen facciamo a mezzo, e amica godi / che sia mio l'esercizio, e tua sia l'arte"; Costa, *The Buffoons*, 90–1.

22 "i detti arguti / Di più faceti e più giocondi ingegni"; Costa, *The Buffoons*, 92–3.

23 "Qui non ad altro / ch'a bersi in su 'l mattino è buono il greco"; Costa, *The Buffoons*, 90–1.

24 "de' principi Medici a la cura / Dal cielo è dato"; "A sì gran nome, e non a' detti tuoi, / Ceder m'è forza"; Costa, *The Buffoons*, 92–3.

25 Costa, *The Buffoons*, 93, line 123. Also see chapter 4, 135.

26 "di grave suon voci malgrate"; *The Buffoons*, Costa, 92–3, line 129.

27 "buffoneschi amori"; Costa, *The Buffoons*, 92–3, line 133.

28 Costa, *The Buffoons*, 94–6, lines 144–5. See Goethals, "Worth Its Salt."

29 Langdon, *Salvator Rosa*.

30 On artistic representations, see Bisceglia, Ceriana, and Mammana, *Buffoni, villani e giocatori*; O'Bryan, "Grotesque Bodies, Princely Delight"; Cheng, "Parodies of Life"; Ghadessi, *Portraits of Human Monsters in the Renaissance*, 53–98; Viatte, "Allegorical and Burlesque Subjects by Stefano della Bella."

31 "in atti e gesti sì nuovi, e sì bizzarri, che non è chi abbia veduto ancora cosa simile"; Baldinucci, *Notizie de' professori del disegno*, V:32.

32 "ridicolosi quanto mai dir si potesse"; Baldinucci, *Notizie de' professori del disegno*, V:31.

33 Costa, *The Buffoons*, 34. Also see Brown, "The Mirror and the Cage," 137.

34 Jonson, *Volpone*, III.iii.14. See Brown, "The Mirror and the Cage," 144–5.

35 Wind, *"A Foul and Pestilent Congregation,"* 19–48, citation on 27.

36 Megale, "Sproporzioni," 70; Cheng, "Parodies of Life," 132.

37 On this intersection in the Florentine context, see Gregori, "Nuovi accertamenti in Toscana."

38 See especially Longhi, *Lusus*; Rodini, *Antonfrancesco Grazzini*; Parker, *Bronzino*; Zanrè, *Cultural Non-Conformity in Early Modern Florence*.

39 Grazzini, *Primo libro dell'opere burlesche*, dedication.

40 Grazzini, *Tutti i trionfi, carri, mascherate o canti carnascialeschi*.

41 For an overview, see Rosa and Nigro, *I poeti giocosi dell'età barocca*, 163–87. For more general studies on the period's literary aesthetic, see, for example, *I capricci di Proteo*; Battistini, *Il barocco*; Corsaro, *La regola e la licenza*; Getto, *Il barocco letterario in Italia*; Snyder, *L'estetica del barocco*.

42 Conrieri, "La cultura letteraria e teatrale"; Th. Van Veen, "Keeping Sight of the Piazza."

43 Conrieri, "La cultura letteraria e teatrale," 368–71.

44 Marino, *Lettere*, 366.

45 Croce, "Introduzione al barocco," 39.

46 See, for example, Martini, "Le nuove forme del canzoniere."

47 Costa, *La chitarra*, 176–7. Di Maro ("Il cor si finge un ghiaccio," 67n24) suggests that the *Stipo*'s structure is modelled on *Adone*, canto 12.

48 Cox, *Women's Writing in Italy*, 178.

49 Getto, *Opere scelte*, 2:22.

50 See Robarts, "Challenging Male Authored Poetry," 96–7 and passim. Also see Di Maro, "Una poetessa del XVII secolo."

51 Bettella, *The Ugly Woman*, 128–64.

52 Turner, *Schooling Sex*; Muir, *The Culture Wars of the Late Renaissance*; Spini, *Ricerca dei libertini*, 61–108.

53 Cox describes the academy as "one of the fulcrums of Seicento misogyny" (*Women's Writing in Italy*, 191).

54 Robarts, "Challenging Male Authored Poetry," 147–52.

55 Adimari, *La Tersicore*. Also see Bettella, *The Ugly Woman*, 125–64.

56 These reflect differences in the 1612, 1623, 1691, and 1863–1923 editions of the *Vocabolario della Accademia della Crusca*

57 Marino, *Lettere*, 167.

58 Holzer, "'Sono d'altro garbo'," 268–76, citation on 268. On *bizzarria* in this period, also see Giles, "The (Un)Natural Baroque," 16–19; Goethals, "The Bizarre Muse."

59 Minor, *The Death of the Baroque*.

60 Quatremère de Quincy, *The True, the Fictive, and the Real*, 90–3. Costa's contemporaries would not have recognized such a distinction. For a survey of the terms *bizzarria* and *baroque*, see Hills, "The Baroque," 11–36.

61 See Asor Rosa, *La lirica del seicento*.

62 "Il solito è sempre quello, l'insolito è più nuovo"; Costa, *The Buffoons*, 73–4. Such language also commonly introduced comedies, however; the opening lines of Bernardo Dovizi da Bibbiena's *Calandra* and Ariosto's *Cassaria* similarly promised a "new comedy" ("nova commedia").

63 Costa, *Lo stipo*, 292.

64 "maledetto lo stil, che fu prezzato"; Costa, *Lo stipo*, 296.

65 DeJean, *Fictions of Sappho*, 20; on Sappho in early modernity, see 29–115.

66 Tylus, "Naming Sappho," 17. Emphasis is mine. On early modern examples, see Cox, *Women's Writing in Italy*, esp. 48–9; Campbell, *The Cabinet of Eros*, 191–204. On classical portrayals, see Campbell, *Greek Lyric*, 1:2–51.

67 Boccaccio, *Famous Women*, 193.

68 "plettro d'oro" and "plettro placido e canoro" (Spinosa); "plettro… di virtù fecondo" (Tronsarelli); "cangia in plettro ancor arco e faretra" (Biscia); "fatta Musa gentil Saffo novella" (Biscia); "favolosa Diva / Su Greca cetra" (Tronsarelli); Costa, *La chitarra*.

69 "plettro ruginoso"; Costa, *La chitarra*, 1.

70 Costa, *La chitarra*, 1.

71 "dalle muse imposto"; Costa, *La chitarra*, 6.

72 Costa, *La chitarra*, 5; Grazzini, *Primo libro dell'opere burlesche*, dedication.

73 "Ma so che vi saranno più di sei / e le dozine intiere che diranno / che se i versi son buoni, non son miei"; Costa, *La chitarra*, 4–5.

74 "Ed io, che dal principio al fin dell'anno / tengo lesta la musa, e su le dita / ho 'l verseggiar, non me ne prendo affanno"; Costa, *La chitarra*, 5.

75 "Con la musa farommi il fatto mio / ... / Cantirò dunque senza haver paura, / ch'il mondo, il ciel, l'inferno, o fati rei / facciano contro me mala congiura"; Costa, *La chitarra*, 4.

76 "quando la tocco comincia a cantare"; Costa, *La chitarra*, 572.

77 Costa, *La chitarra*, 572.

78 Costa, *La chitarra*, 569.

79 "non inarcate di grazia le ciglie, / ne mi burlate"; "non perturbare il mio cantar sereno / ch'è bello ogni mal detto in una dama"; Costa, *La chitarra*, 568, 573. *Sereno* could also mean "bright" or "cheery," and here might also offer a homophonic pun on *sirena*. My thanks to the reviewer for this observation.

80 "pura"; "nuda"; "oscuri" "foschi… mal vergati e neri"; Costa, *Il violino*, 3, 7. Robarts, "Challenging Male Authored Poetry," 78, notes similar language in the publisher's sonnet, Adimari's *Tersicore*, and Marino's *Lira*. Costa also published separate, undated pamphlet poems for the feast day (*Al serenissimo Ferdinando II*; *Alla serenissima Vittoria Della Rovere*), and other occasions (*Alla serenissima Margherita de Medici*; *Al serenissimo Principe Gio. Carlo*; *Per l'incendio di Pitti*.)

81 Costa, *Il violino*, 7.

82 "sia la mia fragil penna / nunzia delle tue gioie"; Costa, *Il violino*, 6.

83 "D'un nano, gobbo, zoppo, e mal composto /… ti fo dono"; "O sia Nano, o sia Chitarra"; Costa, *La chitarra*, 6.

84 "partorito un sconcio e biasimevole mostro"; "uno storpio e malformato nanno"; Costa, *La chitarra*, dedication.

85 "mostruoso parto"; "nelle corti di gran prencipi sono anco ammessi, e per scherzosi e faceti"; Costa, *La chitarra*, dedication.

86 On Florentine academies, their connections to (and, in some cases, dependence on) the Medici, and Costa's verse honouring them, see Michelassi, "'Regi protettori' e 'virtuosi trattenimenti'."

87 Th. Van Veen, "Keeping Sight of the Piazza."

88 "Scrivere letter d'Amor su verde alloro"; Costa, *Lettere amorose*, 6.

89 Costa had already written two poems on the appointment in *Lo stipo*, one of which she also printed as a pamphlet; before this she had celebrated in *La chitarra* his organization of a joust.

90 Costa, *Lettere amorose*, 8.

91 Goethals, "Worth Its Salt"; Costa, *The Buffoons*, 47–53; Mariti, *Commedia ridicolosa*; Ciavolella, "Text as (Pre)Text"; Cope, "Bernini and Roman *Commedie Ridicolose*."

 92 *Sustermans (Exh. Cat.)*, xx. On Tuscany's relationship to northern Africa, see Brege, *Tuscany in the Age of Empire*, 211–29, of which 227–9 on Morocco. On theatre, see Jaffe-Berg, *Commedia dell'Arte and the Mediterranean*.

 93 Megale, "La commedia decifrata." Reference to the Uffizi at I.vii.48, II.ii.89; to the telescope at II.ii.105. Some of these figures reappear in other works; see Wilbourne, "Little Black Giovanni's Dream."

 94 "pazzi, buffoni e nani"; "italianato"; "un scherzo di natura, che al nano somiglia, ma gobbo"; "un pazzo tedesco italianato"; "è nato scimunito"; Costa, *The Buffoons*, 75–6.

 95 "con la varietà de' linguaggi l'inconformità dello stile"; Costa, *The Buffoons*, 76–7.

 96 Scala, *Il teatro delle favole rappresentative*, Giornata XLI.

 97 *Sustermans (Exh. Cat.)*, #39; Megale, "Su un dipinto buffonesco di Sustermans"; Costa, *The Buffoons*, 40–1.

 98 "politico al suo tempo il più stimato." Vesme and Massar, *Stefano della Bella*, cat. 55.39.

 99 Ricci, *Il Tedeschino*. On its relationship to *Li buffoni*, see Megale's introduction (7–63); Costa, *The Buffoons*, 42–3 and passim.

100 See Goethals, "Worth Its Salt."

101 "lo sciocco di politica"; Costa, *The Buffoons*, III.i.24.

102 Squilletti does not name *Li buffoni*, but the dating makes it clear. ASF MdP 5561, fol. 606, also transcribed in Barocchi and Gaeta Bertelà, *Collezionismo mediceo e storia artistica*, Pt. 2: 380.

103 "le materie inoneste, le parole oscene, e gl'atti schifi"; Cecchini, *Frutti delle moderne comedie* (1628), available in Marotti and Romei, *La professione del teatro*, 77–92, citation on 80.

104 Julie Robarts's dissertation "Challenging Male Authored Poetry," explores as length Costa as a female Marinist.

105 Costa, *Il violino*, 34–40, 62–8, 55–61. See also Costa, *Voice of a Virtuosa and Courtesan*, 29–30.

106 On lament in *La chitarra* and *Il violino*, see Di Maro, "Il cor si finge un ghiaccio," 61–3. On gender and lament, see Refini, "'*Parole tronche et imperfette*,'" 443, and chapter 3.

107 Costa, *Voice of a Virtuosa and Courtesan*, 32.

108 "Iniquo Sesso frodolente e rio!"; "Oh Sesso horror del Mondo! / Sesso perverso, ed empio, / Sesso nido d'inganni"; Costa, *Il violino*, 10, 11.

109 Costa, *Il violino*, 14.

110 Marino, *La lira*, II:98–102.

111 "Violamento di Lilla narrato dall'istesso amante"; Costa, *Il violino*, 17–26. See Cox, *Women's Writing in Italy*, 214; Costa, *Voice of a Virtuosa and Courtesan*, 29; Robarts, "Challenging Male Authored Poetry," 112–23.

112 "Vincitor guerriero"; Marino, *La lira*, II:98. "O mostro d'impietá … / … / E della morte mia / sazia tua voglia dispietata e ria?" Costa, *Il violino*, 26.

113 Costa, *Il violino*, 114–19.

114 "ogn'altro bello io nel tuo brutto adoro"; Costa, *Il violino*, 45, 47. Also see Costa, *Voice of a Virtuosa and Courtesan*, 29.

115 Costa, *Il violino*, 153.

116 "Segua ogni cor l'ardor d'amore"; Costa, *Il violino*, 168.

117 "Una scheggia in un dito di bella donna"; "stella di cristallo sul crine di bella donna"; "Bella donna all'amante trattenuto in letto per la podagra"; Ferrero, *Marino e i marinisti*, 729, 730, 734–5.

118 Bettella, *The Ugly Woman*, 130.

119 "Mi finisi, ch'in amor mille catene / mi cingessero il cor, l'alma, e la vita / … / Fingei gelar nel gelo, arder nel foco, / e nel gel non gelai, ne in foco ardei, / ma sol lo feci per spassarmi un poco"; Costa, *La chitarra*, 570–1.

120 "non creda a questi finti ardori / … / E come ne' Teatri hor Donna, ed hora / Huom fei rapresentando in vario stile"; Andreini, *Selected Poems*, 30–1. Ovid, *Tristia*, 2.355. See Robarts, "Challenging Male Authored Poetry," 126–9.

121 Costa, *La chitarra*, 44–9, 50–6. Wladyslaw travelled through Italy in 1624–5. In a later poem, Costa expresses regret at not having accepted the future king's invitation to Warsaw (*La tromba di Parnaso*, 32–4). Robarts shows that the second of two poems for the Venetian ambassador to Rome, Angelo Contarini, is the work of Marinist poet Antonio Bruni and likely describes Costa herself; Robarts, "Challenging Male Authored Poetry," 101–4.

122 "non amar un sol amor per volta"; "il pensiero e il desire / [volgete] al filare e al cucire"; Costa, *La chitarra*, 181, 518.

123 For a discussion of the Tirsi figure, though without autobiographical connections, see Robarts, "Challenging Male Authored Poetry."

124 *I Caramogi, palio e mascherata*; Salvadori, *Poesie*, 488–92 (which incorrectly dates the *palio* to 6 August). See Cheng, "Parodies of Life," 132.

125 "mezzi huomini"; "mostri dell'Affrica"; Costa, *La chitarra*, 546–7. Robarts suggests that this may be a version rewritten by Costa ("Challenging Male Authored Poetry," 215), but she faithfully reproduces the 1629 original.

126 "sgrignuto mostro e contrafatto"; Ariosto, *Orlando furioso*, XXVIII.xxxv.5.

127 *Risposta de begl'Imbusti a Caramogi*; Solerti, *Musica, ballo, e drammatica*, 196n3.

128 "manchevolezza della natura"; *Risposta de begl'Imbusti a Caramogi*; "mancamento di natura"; Costa, *La chitarra*, 553.

129 "Aquile"; "scimmiotti"; Costa, *La chitarra*, 554–5.

130 Costa, *La chitarra*, 560.

131 "membra contrafatte, afflitte, e dome"; "l'inanellate chiome"; Costa, *La chitarra*, 564.

132 Costa, *La chitarra*, 566.

133 See Spinelli, "Temi edificanti e scelte licenziose."

134 Costa, *Lettere amorose*, 9.

135 "Or Venere sembravo, ed or' Alcide"; Costa, *Lettere amorose*, 7.

136 See Díaz, "Exceptional Bodies and Ludic Lovers"; Piantoni, "Le *Lettere amorose* di Margherita Costa"; De Liso, "Le *Lettere amorose*,"; Robarts, "Challenging Male

Authored Poetry," 129–38. See also Díaz's forthcoming translation (Costa, *Love Letters*).

137 Parabasco and Costa's letters appear together in the *Scelta di lettere amorose*.

138 Ray, *Writing Gender*, 157–81. On the letterbook, see Quondam, *Le "Carte messag-giere."* On the relationship to musical culture, see Bianconi, *Music in the Seventeenth Century*, 219.

139 Ray, *Writing Gender*, 181–2, citation on 181.

140 See Robarts, "Challenging Male Authored Poetry," 139–78.

141 Ovid, *The Art of Love*, I.437–40; Robarts, "Challenging Male Authored Poetry," 147–52.

142 "Amante alla sua diva bramoso di magior godimento"; "non dalla vostra fanciullesca volontade dipendeva, ma dal mio assoluto volere"; Costa, *Lettere amorose*, 86, 88.

143 Costa, *Lettere amorose*, 55–60.

144 "In tal disaventura è ventura il far preda di più prede, l'aver coppia di amanti, il vestirsi variati panni, … ed in fine lo spacciar sua bellezza a non conformi e numeroso prezzi!" Costa, *Lettere amorose*, 283.

145 Adimari, *La Tersicore*.

146 Sempronio, *La selva poetica*.

147 "le perfezioni imperfette delle donne"; Adimari, *La Tersicore*, 5.

148 Bettella, *The Ugly Woman*.

149 "a donna brutta" (234–40), "a donna spergiura" (195–201), "a donna zoppa" (215–17); "ad un balbettante" (244–7); Costa, *Lettere amorose*.

150 "Donna sciatta ad amante ciarlone" (298–302), "Amante muto a donna sorda" (219–226), "Amante cieco d'un occhio a donna di naso lungo e curvo" (248–51); Costa, *Lettere amorose*.

151 "bella donna a un nano" (201–10, citation on 207); Costa, *Lettere amorose*.

152 "Donna a troppo giovanetto amante: frasca da lusignuol, non da civetta"; Costa, *Lettere amorose*, 318.

153 "Vivemo però più d'ogni altro lieti, havendoci nostra fortuna sì bene accoppiati"; Costa, *Lettere amorose*, 243; for the "Bella donna ad un nano" exchanges, see 192–5 and 203–10.

154 The confrontation between Morocco and Fez may be inspired by the civil war in Morocco in the early seventeenth century, as well as the disharmony between Ferdinando II and Vittoria della Rovere. Costa may also have had in mind Jacques Callot's *commedia*-inspired *Balli di Sfessania*; see Rasi, *La caricatura*, 33–4; Strappini, *La tragedia del buffone*, 269n35.

155 "A te tocca a badare / A le cose del regno / E non saper s'io caccio o voglio amare"; Costa, *The Buffoons*, I.i.125–7.

156 "Signorsì, a me tocca / Di governar lo stato? / … / … oh povera Marmotta!"; Costa, *The Buffoons*, I.i.128–31.

157 "Son superbi i palazzi, e perch' il luogo / Ha de l'umido alquanto, han gran puntelli. / Questo lo fan perche s'attengan sodi"; Costa, *The Buffoons*, I.viii.148–50.

158 "Lo ricevono in casa volentieri / E di quanto ne puon gli fanno parte"; Costa, *The Buffoons*, I.viii.141–2.

159 "Son coltivate meglio le pianure / Che di questi paesi le colline"; Costa, *The Buffoons*, I.viii.224–5. Salvi, "Il solito è sempre quello," takes the opposite view on the contrast between an orderly Fessa and Moroccan mayhem.

160 "Si fa l'amor con tutti a la scoperta. / Ma sai: modestamente"; Costa, *The Buffoons*, I.viii.177–8.

161 "Gli uomini se ne stanno, e lasciano fare. / Se la donna rinova un bel vestito, / Una bella collana, un bello anello, / Non ha da darne conto al suo marito"; Costa, *The Buffoons*, I.viii.169–71.

162 Costa, *The Buffoons*, I.viii.138.

163 Costa, "Le sette giornate," fols. 268r–97v. The manuscript has a number of corrections in the copyist's hand and does not contain a dedication or other paratextual materials and is unlikely a finished product.

164 See also Stella, "Il *Cecilia martire*," 90–3.

165 "io fui, et sono, et sarò Margarita"; Costa, "Le sette giornate," 274r.

166 "furfante in cremisino"; Costa, "Le sette giornate," 272r.

167 Costa, "Le sette giornate," 271v.

168 "cominciaron senza discrezione / una commedia sì ridicolosa / che crepavan di risa le persone"; Costa, "Le sette giornate," 279r.

169 See, for instance, Andrews, *Scripts and Scenarios*.

170 "Ond'io con quegli pensai far un patto / e giro pel mondo, e nella loro scena / et rider, e burlar, e far il matto"; Costa, "Le sette giornate," 280r.

171 Costa, "Le sette giornate," 296r–v; Costa, *La chitarra*, 567–8.

172 Costa, "Le sette giornate," 277r–v; Costa, *La chitarra*, 571–2.

173 Costa, "Le sette giornate," 280v–82v. Emphasis mine. Costa, *La chitarra*, 1–3.

174 "restarai senza voce e senza moto"; Costa, "Le sette giornate," 292v.

175 "rinuntio il mondo"; Costa, "Le sette giornate," 295r.

176 "Arabici odor' nelle mammelle"; Costa, "Le sette giornate," 295r.

177 "La mia pazzia a musici et poeti, / La penna della piuma alli scholari"; Costa, "Le sette giornate," 296r.

178 Costa, "Le sette giornate," 297v–98r.

179 Leone, *The Palazzo Pamphilj in Piazza Navona*, 145.

180 "fui stato felice"; Costa, *All'altezza serenissima di Ferdinando Secondo*, VII.

181 "due parti infelici"; "E se sacrai miei Parti à l'alta imago / Hora a' tuoi piedi i Parti miei consacro"; Costa, *All'altezza Serenissima di Ferdinando Secondo*, XI.

182 See Introduction, 20.

3 From the Golden Oak to the Weeping Cypress: Epic, Lament, and Dynastic Messaging

1 Tondini, *Delle lettere di uomini illustri*, 2:49.

2 Costa, "Festa reale," [6]v.

3 See Lipking, *Abandoned Women and the Poetic Tradition*, 1–31; Cusick, "'There Was Not One Lady Who Failed to Shed a Tear'"; Holford-Strevens, "'Her Eyes Became Two Spouts'"; MacNeil, "Weeping at the Water's Edge"; Refini, "Echoes of Ariadne"; Refini, "'*Parole tronche et imperfette*'"; Bianconi, *Music in the Seventeenth Century*, 204–19; Rosand, "The Descending Tetrachord"; Carter, "Lamenting Ariadne?"; Heller, *Emblems of Eloquence*, 82–5; Porter, "Lamenti recitativi da camera"; Wilbourne, *Seventeenth-Century Opera*, 51–91. On English sources, see Ross and Smith, *Early Modern Women's Complaint*.

4 Bianconi, *Music in the Seventeenth Century*, 211.

5 "celebrar l'altezza delle glorie toscane"; Costa, *Flora feconda*, dedication.

6 Fantoni, *La corte del granduca*, 25–6. Metlica (*Le seduzioni della pace*, 22) describes a similar "osmosis between princely ceremonies and poetic topoi" in Marino's works.

7 On Bernardi, see Wainwright, "The Fair Warrior in the City of Florence," 138. The pastoral, *Clorilli*, is forthcoming in a new English translation by Wainwright and edited by Virginia Cox and Lisa Sampson. Cervoni, "Canzone," BNCF Magl. VII.138, 2r. I thank Anna Wainwright for generously sharing her transcription of the Cervoni poem with me.

8 *Nella nascità del Ser[enissi]mo gran principe primogenitor di Toscana*; *O Cosmo, o caro nome al mio bel regno*. BNCF II.II.295, unnumbered pages.

9 Ovid, *Fasti*, V.195–275. Costa may also have taken some inspiration from Chiabrera's nine-canto epic poem *Firenze* (1615, with subsequent editions in 1616, 1628, and 1637), a work that similarly exalts the grand duke (Cosimo II) through a hero modelled on him (Cosmo). See Th. Van Veen, "Keeping Sight of the Piazza," 106–10.

10 "bella e pomposa / del tosco impero… / regina"; Talenti, *Dialogo*, unnumbered pages.

11 Harness, *Echoes of Women's Voices*, 175n3; Th. Van Veen, *Cosimo I de' Medici and His Self-Representation*, passim; Langdon, *Medici Women*, 245n67.

12 Villifranchi, *Descrizzione della barriera e della mascherata*, 90–105.

13 See Harness, *Echoes of Women's Voices*, 174–207; Cosentino, "Allegorie del potere femminile," 161–3.

14 Costa, *La chitarra*, 7–15; Costa, *Lo stipo*, 130–4.

15 "genitrice"; "novi Alessandri"; Costa, *Il violino*, 126.

16 Solomon, "The Influence of Ovid in Opera."

17 "Fior d'Italia"; Salvadori, *La Flora*, V.x.99.

18 Cox, *The Prodigious Muse*, 154, 158–9, 178.

19 Bianchi, "Una cortigiana rimatrice," 1925, 189–91.

20 In book 6 of the *Aeneid*, Venus also sends her doves to help Aeneas find the golden boughs needed to descend to the underworld and receive his genealogical prophecy.

21 Costa, *Flora feconda*, 31.

22 See Nicola Sabbatini's *Pratica di fabricar scene e machine*, Cap. 43–9.

23 Piechocki, "Clouds, Nuptials, Nubifications," 163.

24 "E chi non fia, ch'a musica dolcezza / non ami essercitare gli atti d'amore?"; Costa, *Flora feconda*, II.xxxvii.1–2.

25 Costa, *Flora feconda*, II.xxxix.2. On *amor impossibilis* between women in epic, see DeCoste, *Hopeless Love*.

26 Marino, *Adone*, VII.84–95.

27 See chapter 5, 147–8.

28 See Introduction, 10.

29 "De lor vani orgogli / furono teatro e spettator gli scogli"; Costa, *Flora feconda*, II.[xxxxvii].7–8. For the reader's ease, Costa's system of numbering has been maintained.

30 Ariosto, *Orlando furioso*, XXXV.xxiii.1.

31 "Imagini… vaghe, e gradite"; Costa, *Flora feconda*, III.xxii.3.

32 "vaghe e gradite"; Costa, *La Flora feconda*, III.xxii, p. 3; xxvi, p. 8.

33 Ovid, *Metamorphoses*, V.635.

34 "Pisa a la vostra Pisa il nome diede"; Costa, *La Flora feconda*, II.iii, p. 45.

35 "chi fra Tosci ha 'l regno suo disteso"; Costa, *Flora feconda*, III.xxxviii.5.

36 Franchi, "L'Aretusa."

37 "li corisponde amico ogetto"; Costa, *Flora feconda*, III.xx.6.

38 Bucchi, *Meraviglioso diletto*, 129–48.

39 "quas dum ferioque trahoque / mille modis labens excussaque bracchia iacto"; Ovid, *Metamorphoses*, V.596–7.

40 Dell'Anguillara, *Le Metamorfosi*, V.203; Costa, *Flora feconda*, III.xxxi. Also see Modolo, "Metamorphosis of the Metamorphoses," 72–124, esp. 122.

41 Dell'Anguillara, *Le Metamorfosi*, V.210.7–8.

42 "auctaque forma fuga est"; Ovid, *Metamorphoses*, I.509.

43 "Lacero ho fin il petto, e in ogni lato / Provo mille nel corpo offese ingrate; / E dal piè, ch'in fuggir stanco già langue, / Spando nel campo più d'un rio di sangue"; Costa, *Flora feconda*, III.xxxvi.1–4.

44 Costa, *Flora feconda*, III.[xxxxvii].2.

45 Costa, *Flora feconda*, III.lv.2.

46 Heller, "Ovid's Ironic Gaze," 209.

47 "pon freno homai / Al tuo lagnar d'Amore"; Costa, *La Flora feconda*, II.iv, p. 51.

48 On this episode, see Goethals, "Cadde a tai note."

49 Ovid, *Metamorphoses*, XIII.735–895.

50 See Mazzoleni, "Aci e Galatea." Marino compares Acis's beauty to the whiteness of the Dodonian doves and the flowers of May (*Adone*, XIX.128.5–8).

51 Vittori, *La Galatea*. The opera was staged in Naples five years later. On Vittori's intersection with Costa, see chapter 6, 172.

52 "un fonte d'un fiore è fatto amore"; Costa, *Flora feconda*, VII.x.8.

53 Costa, *Flora feconda*, VII.xiii.1–6.

54 Ariosto, *Orlando furioso*, X.xxii.1. There are also echoes to XLIII.clxviii, when Fiordiligi pulls her hair and tears at her *belle gote* upon learning of Brandimarte's death. My thanks to Kate Driscoll for the observation.

55 "Fammi morir … / Uccidemi, / Deridemi"; "S'il mio pianto tu non senti, / se non odi i miei lamenti"; Costa, *Il violino*, 143 and 137. Also see Di Maro, "Il cor si finge un ghiaccio," 63–4.

56 Costa, *Flora feconda*, VII.xxv.1; Ariosto, *Orlando Furioso*, I.lx.8. My thanks to Kate Driscoll for suggesting a possible Sacripante parallel.

57 Ariosto, *Orlando furioso*, X.xxxiii.3–4; Costa, *Flora feconda*, VII.xxxiii.3; Ovid, *Heroides. Amores.*, X.84–7.

58 Costa, *Flora feconda*, VII.xxxiii.7. Kate Driscoll discussed epic male lament in epic in her talk "Curse, Bark, Wail, Hiss: What Do Furious Men Sound Like?" at the 2021 Renaissance Society of America conference.

59 "Tu pur hai dato il parturire a' mostri / ov' Affrica più sterile fiammeggia"; Costa, *Flora feconda* V.xxvii.1–2. "Tu, che fecondi festi / I mostri più feroci, / E d'Africa a le selve i parti desi, / Hora a me sola noci"; Costa, *La Flora feconda*, III.iii, p. 79.

60 See Brege, *Tuscany in the Age of Empire*, 211–29.

61 "Quercie, s'havete il suon, da voi mia doglia / Più degnamente al vostro Dio si scioglia"; Costa, *Flora feconda*, V.xxxvii.7–8.

62 "DA QUERCIA D'ORO SORGERÀ GRAN PROLE / CHE STENDERÀ L'IMPERO A PAR DEL SOLE"; Costa, *Flora feconda* V.[xxxi].7–8.

63 Hall, "Margherita Costa."

64 Brege, *Tuscany in the Age of Empire*.

65 Markey, *Imagining the Americas*, 159; Hester, "Baroque Italian Epic," 287.

66 "l'uno e l'altro emisfero"; "soggiaccia al scettro tuo la sua corona"; Costa, *Il violino*, 5–6.

67 On Seicento epithalamia, see, for example, Carter, "Epyllia and Epithalamia."

68 "auspice glorioso al germe nostro"; Costa, *Flora feconda*, VI.xii.8.

69 Costa, *Flora feconda*, Argomento; Acton, *The Last Medici*, 25.

70 Ovid, *Metamorphoses*, VIII.905–65.

71 See Quint, *Epic and Empire*; Stoppino, *Genealogies of Fiction*; Fichter, *Poets Historical*. Cf. *Adone*, XIX, in which Venus searches for Glaucus to procure this herb for Adonis.

72 Stoppino, *Genealogies of Fiction*, 12.

73 Costa, *Flora feconda*, IX.x.4–5. On Medici birth celebrations, see Sanger, *Art, Gender, and Religious Devotion*, 62–7.

74 "i Leonardi, e i Rafaelli, / Ed i Giovanni, et i Giuliani /… / Franceschi e… Guidi"; Costa, *Flora feconda*, IX.lix.

75 Tigliamochi degli Albizi, *Ascanio errante*, IX.47–71. Also see Marongiu, "*L'Ascanio errante*," 236–8.

76 "E l'aria da le voci intorno franta / Ferdinando risuona, e 'l parto canta"; Costa, *Flora feconda*, IX.lxiv.7–8.

77 "degna del ciel vide la prole / ch'era a la terra un amoroso sole"; Costa, *Flora feconda*, X.v.7–8.

78 Costa, *Flora feconda*, X.vii.7.

79 Costa, *Flora feconda*, X.xii.

80 "gemo, anhelo, sospiro, agghiaccio, e manco"; Costa, *Flora feconda*, xxxi.8.

81 Costa, *Flora feconda*, X.xxxxiv.

82 The canto's return to song and festivity had precedent in *Adone*, XX, dedicated to festivals following Adonis's funeral.

83   Costa, *Voice of a Virtuosa and Courtesan*, 32. Bianchi inexplicably dismisses *La Flora feconda* and *Gl'amori della luna* as only negligibly different than the *Festa reale*. Bianchi, "Una cortigiana rimatrice," 1925, 207.

84   Allacci, *Drammaturgia*, 457. Also see Weaver, *A Chronology of Music in the Florentine Theater*, 115; Kutsch and Riemens, *Großes Sängerlexikon*, 924.

85   Costa, *La Flora feconda*, III.ii.

86   Costa, *La Flora feconda*, II.ix.

87   Costa, *La Flora feconda*, I.ii, pp. 14–15.

88   Costa, *La Flora feconda*, 65, 114, 104–5, for example.

89   Tarabotti, *Antisatire*, 32, and on letters between the two women, 22–3. Also see Introduction, 22.

90   Introduction, 22–3.

91   "Solevano gli antichi Romani in un tronco all'immortalità sospendere le spoglie delle loro vittorie, ed io Sereniss[ima] Sig[nora] all'Altezza della sua Rovere appendo questo mio componimento di Flora feconda, perché dal tempo riporti vittoria, ed all'eternità si consagri.... Per non esser in me fertilità d'ingegno, almeno le ho voluto porger opera che di feconda habbia il nome"; Costa, *La Flora feconda*, dedication.

92   Costa, *La Flora feconda*, V.vii, pp. 167–8.

93   "[…] riprendi homai/ col tuo Zeffiro il cammino; / Segui lieta il tuo destino"; Costa, *La Flora feconda*, I.viii, p. 32.

94   Costa, *La Flora feconda*, IV.v, p. 121. See Goethals, "'Cadde a tai note.'"

95   "Dal sangue austriaco nato / A la Dea del Metauro / Giungesi in laccio amato/ […] E Rovere feconda il suo tesauro"; Costa, *La Flora feconda*, IV.x, p. 141.

96   "L'Arno gioisca, e l'Apennino goda"; Costa, *La Flora feconda*, IV.x, pp. 138–41.

97   "I Lorenzi […] Matthij […] Lopoldi […] Gian Carli […] e quanto altri in Urbino"; Costa, *La Flora feconda*, V.x, p. 82. Cf. the Flora-themed *Chitarra* poem on the grand ducal wedding (pp. 7–15).

98   Costa, *Flora feconda*, X.x–xxxiv.

99   Costa, *Flora feconda*, X.xxxii.5–6.

100   "Mira come ... / Chiara la nostra Prole / Scintilla a par del sole; / E nel tuo parto altero / Hai il dio prodotto del Toscano impero"; Costa, *La Flora feconda*, V.x, p. 181.

101   Costa, *La Flora feconda*, V.x, p. 181.

102   "Ove con atti infidi / Qui me da me dividi?"; Costa, *La Flora feconda*, V.x, p. 179. Tasso, *Rime*, 302.

103   Costa, *La Flora feconda*, V.x, p. 182.

104   "Mira qual Flora, io sento / Dolor del tuo dolore"; Costa, *La Flora feconda*, I.i, p. 2.

105   "E pur, ohime, partire / Dovrò senza morire?"; Costa, *La Flora feconda*, I.i, p. 10.

106   "Lieto più che mai suol"; Costa, *Flora feconda*, I.xxiii.1.

107   "E gioconda / E feconda / La lor prole / Vinca l'Alba, avanzi il sole"; Costa, *La Flora feconda*, prologue.

108 Spangler, "Mother Knows Best," 135. Also see Ranum, *Portraits around Marc-Antoine Charpentier*, 353–8.

109 Costa, *La chitarra*, 18–19.

110 Costa, *Lo stipo*, 66–75.

111 Alexandre de Vesme attributed the work to Della Bella, noting the similarities with the *Melpomene* frontispiece, while Phyllis Dearborn Massar questions the attribution based on stylistic points. Vesme and Massar, *Stefano della Bella*. Tempesti, *Mostra di incisioni*, 40, also notes the continuities between the two (both taken to be Della Bella's).

112 This choice may have reflected Adimari's inability to attend to the volume's production due to "sinister" circumstances. Adimari, *La Melpomene*, 102.

113 On Florentine grand-ducal funeral rites, see Menchini, "Funeral Oratory at the Medici Court"; Casini, "La corte, i cerimoniali, le feste," 472–73. Virginia Cox discussed sixteenth-century volumes in her talk "Mourning the Medici: The Social World of a Funerary Collection" at the 2022 RSA conference.

114 Russo, *Marino*, 58.

115 See the introduction to Marino, *Rime lugubri*, 9–43.

116 Also see chapter 6, 173.

117 Spinola is alluded to in *The Buffoons*, I.xii.97.

118 "E sotto la sua cura, a l'armonia / Flora in terra emulare il Ciel s'udia"; Costa, *La selva di cipressi*, 207.

119 Angiolini, "Il lungo Seicento," 50–1.

120 Rosand, "Barbara Strozzi," 266.

121 Salvadori, *Sonetti*.

122 Ghislanzoni, *Luigi Rossi*, 56; Caluori, "The Cantatas of Luigi Rossi," 2:58 (no. 160); Porter, "Northwestern University's Seventeenth-Century Manuscript," 100, 112.

123 See Ghislanzoni, *Luigi Rossi*, 55–6; Porter, "Northwestern University's Seventeenth-Century Manuscript," 100–1, 111; Caluori, "The Cantatas of Luigi Rossi," 71–2; Arecchi, "Six Political Lament-Cantatas," 47, 49, 52–3, 96–7. On attribution debates, see Holzer, "Music and Poetry in Seventeenth-Century Rome," 270n110. The variant title is found at the Biblioteca Casanatense, ms 2479, fols. 5–18v.

124 Persson, *Women at the Early Modern Swedish Court*, 268–80.

125 Transcription in Ghislanzoni, *Luigi Rossi*, 209–10; Costa, *Lo stipo*, 279–80.

126 This presumes that Costa relied on Della Corgna's verse and not he on hers. He also moved in Barberini circles in Rome (his portrait of Leonora Baroni was praised in her *Applausi* volume) and wrote other verse set to music by Rossi. See Galassi, *Ritratto di una virtuosa canterina*, 51–79, esp. 68. See also Brosius, "*Il suon, lo sguardo, il canto*," 33–5.

127 On this, and the Clori/Aci idyll, see Goethals, "Cadde a tai note."

128 Costa, *La selva di cipressi*, 26, 242.

129 "S'egli cadde una sol volta, io moro / Ogni hor nel suo morir"; Costa, *La selva di cipressi*, 27.

130   Costa, *La selva di cipressi*, 28.

131   "Ma (lasso) ove mi volgo, e che ragiono? / [...] E 'l mondo è fatto per me cruda scena / Di sospiro, di lagrima, e di pena"; Costa, *La selva di cipressi*, 30–1.

132   Costa, *Flora feconda*, X.xxxii.1; Costa, *La selva di cipressi*, 31. On verbal and non-verbal components of lament, see Refini, "'*Parole tronche et imperfette.*'"

133   "mesti, e addolorati i passi"; Costa, *La selva di cipressi*, 36.

134   Costa, *La selva di cipressi*, 214.

135   "Io fui sola il precipitio mio"; Costa, *La selva di cipressi*, 221.

136   Costa, *La selva di cipressi*, 226.

137   Ovid, *Heroides. Amores*, VII and XI.

138   Costa, *La selva di cipressi*, 189.

139   *Per un giovane ammazzatto*; Marino, *Rime lugubri*, 128.

140   See Introduction, 14. Costa-Zalessow also sees an autobiographical parallel but incorrectly identifies Tirsi with Bernardino Ricci; Costa, *Voice of a Virtuosa and Courtesan*, 21, 33.

141   Costa, *La selva di cipressi*, 189; Catullus, *The Poems of Catullus*, 64.61. Also compare this to Ovid, *Heroides*, X.49–50; Ariosto, *Orlando furioso*, X.xxiv.7–8.

142   Catullus, *The Poems of Catullus*, 64.55, 100–1; Ariosto, *Orlando furioso*, X.xxiv.1; Costa, *La selva di cipressi*, 189.

143   "nè può dir, morendo, io corro a morte"; Costa, *La selva di cipressi*, 191.

144   "Oh ferro micidial, ferro importuno, / Ch'in un co' l'idol mio mi feri e pungi"; Costa, *La selva di cipressi*, 195.

145   ASF Misc. Med. 504, ins. 1 and 4.

146   Nardi accompanied Ferdinando to Prague; Costa, *Istoria*, 16.

147   Costa dedicated a poem to Antonio Medici, "a champion against death" ("contro morte campione") in *Lo stipo*, 137–8.

148   Tylus, "Imagining Narrative in Tasso," 46; Migiel, "Tasso's Erminia."

149   Tasso, *Gerusalemme Liberata*, VII.xvi.8; Costa, *La selva di cipressi*, 198. This echo is also noted in Costa, *Voice of a Virtuosa and Courtesan*, 185n164.

150   Tasso, *Gerusalemme liberata*, XIX.cxiv.2. Erminia's lament was set to music in the Seicento. Porter, "Lamenti recitativi da camera," 91–3.

151   "Qui l'autora sotto nome di Elisa descrive parte della sua sventurata vita"; Costa, *La selva di cipressi*, 229.

152   Costa, *La selva di cipressi*, 243.

153   "... la penna accinta / Ti serva a rintuzzar del Ciel lo sdegno. / Può foglio d'alte note effigiato / Vincer le stelle, e soggiogar il fato"; Costa, *La selva di cipressi*, 243.

154   Costa, *La selva di cipressi*, 244–5. Compare to Costa, *Lo stipo*, 99.

155   Costa, *La selva di cipressi*, 247.

156   The episode seems inspired by Traiano Boccalini's 1615 satirical *Ragguagli di Parnaso*, in which Apollo receives assorted complaints.

157   "Chi del destin si lagna e si tormenta"; Costa, *La selva di cipressi*, 249.

158 "Elisa ha di dolor ciglia gravose, / E fra singulti lagrime nasconde, / Hora inalza l'aspetto, hora dubbiose / Le luci china, e 'l suo martir confonde. / Querele alfin appresta tormentose…."; Costa, *La selva di cipressi*, 250.

159 Costa, *La selva di cipressi*, 254.

160 "danni e ruine"; Costa, *La selva di cipressi*, 252.

161 Costa, *La selva di cipressi*, 256.

162 Rinuccini, *Arianna*.

4 Starry Carousels: Equestrian Ballet and Aristocratic Astronomies

1 Costa, "Festa reale," 1640.

2 Cusick, *Francesca Caccini at the Medici Court*, 191–246; Harness, *Echoes of Women's Voices*, 152–62; Harness, "'Nata à maneggi & essercizii grandi,'" 104–6.

3 There is no extant musical score; while the Fondazione Giorgio Cini catalogues one, this is instead a modern transcription of the *scenario*.

4 Costa, *Festa reale*, 1647.

5 The nineteenth-century commentator Émile Mignot de Lyden called Costa a choreographer on the basis of this libretto but believed she merely reworked a 1581 French *ballet à cheval*, the first documented example of the genre. The two works have different narratives, however, and Lyden seems unaware that she composed the work in Florence, where the equestrian ballet tradition was especially strong. Lyden, *Le théâtre d'autrefois et d'aujourd'hui*, 17.

6 Costa, *La chitarra*, 44–9, 410, 428. Giovan Carlo's joust is possibly, though not definitively, the 1625 *La precedenza delle dame*. On the *Giostra dei saraceni*, see, for instance, Nussdorfer, "Print and Pageantry in Baroque Rome," 443; Norman, "In Public and in Private," 234–6. On this subject matter, Costa could again find a model in Marino; on the latter's relationship to spectacle, see Metlica, *Le seduzioni della pace*.

7 Studies include Nettl, "Equestrian Ballets of the Baroque Period"; Watanabe-O'Kelly, *Triumphall Shews*, 97–103; Watanabe-O'Kelly, "The Equestrian Ballet in Seventeenth-Century Europe"; van Orden, *Music, Discipline, and Arms*, 235–84; Harness, "'Nata à maneggi & essercizii brandi'"; Harness, "Habsburgs, Heretics, and Horses."

8 For a comparative analysis of equestrian ballet in Germany, France, and Italy, see Béhar and Watanabe-O'Kelly, *Spectacvlvm Evropævm*, 600–1, 605–6, 616–18. On Florentine festival more broadly, see Nagler, *Theatre Festivals of the Medici*; Blumenthal, *Theater Art of the Medici*; Treadwell, *Music and Wonder at the Medici Court*; Saslow, *The Medici Wedding of 1589*; Bacherini, *"Per un regale evento."*

9 On *ballet de cour*, see McGowan, *L'art du ballet de cour*; McGowan, *Dance in the Renaissance*; Nordera, "Ballet de cour."

10 Early modern dressage is generally more studied by scholars of France than of Italy, despite its strong Italian roots. For an introduction, see Marcigliano, "Cavallerie a

Ferrara"; Tobey, "The Legacy of Federico Grisone"; Tucker, "Early Modern French Noble Identity"; Franchet d'Espèrey, "L'équitation italienne"; Barry, "Les airs relevés et leur histoire."

11 The Giunti press printed the work in Greek in 1516; an Italian translation appeared in 1580. On its impact, see, for example, LeGuin, "Man and Horse in Harmony."

12 van Orden, *Music, Discipline, and Arms*, 235–45; van Orden, "From *Gens d'armes* to *Gentilshommes*," 201–4; Tobey, "The Legacy of Federico Grisone," 157; Harness, "Habsburgs, Heretics, and Horses"; Adami, "Sham Fights and Mock Sieges." Also see a similar comparison in Xenophon, "On the Art of Horsemanship," xi.2 (353).

13 Delbrück, *The Dawn of Modern Warfare*, 123–34.

14 "hanno almen veduto maneggiarli ad altri"; Melzo, *Regole militari*, 3.

15 On the concealment of effort in dressage, and connections to civility, see van Orden, *Music, Discipline, and Arms*, 213; van Orden, "From *Gens d'armes* to *Gentilshommes*," 204–6; Tucker, "Early Modern French Noble Identity," 282; Schiesari, "Pedagogy and the Art of Dressage," 380.

16 van Orden, *Music, Discipline, and Arms*, 264.

17 van Orden, *Music, Discipline, and Arms*, 239–49.

18 "Et perché potrebbe forsi parer strano a qualche cavaliero che io habbia voluto inserir in questio mio secondo trattato musica giudicando forsi essi non esser necessaria, rispondendo dico che senza misura et tempo non si può far cosa buona"; Fiaschi, *Trattato dell'imbrigliare, maneggiare, et ferrare cavalli*, 88.

19 "non potrà farsi cosa bella, ne buona mai, se non si servino gli ordini, e le misure musicali"; "essendo il cavallo animale di mirabile senso che mirabilmente prende diletto della musica, e se ne muove"; Caracciolo, *La gloria del cavallo*, 421.

20 Xenophon, "On the Art of Horsemanship," xi.6 (355).

21 "ballando sopra l'anche e le braccia"; Grisone, *Gli ordini di cavalcare*, 208.

22 Strong, *Art and Power*, 43.

23 "ma sopra tutti gl'altri bellissimi, e nobilissimi, so quell che si fanno a cavallo, e sopra tutti gl'altro son degni d'esser da principi"; Salvadori, *Guerra d'amore*, 5.

24 Franceschi, *Ballo e giostra de' venti*; Rinuccini, *Descrizione delle feste*. See Carter, "A Florentine Wedding of 1608"; Harness, "'Nata à maneggi & essercizii grandi,'" 92–96; Ghisi, "Ballet Entertainments."

25 The etching was first produced for the booklet and later incorporated into the second edition of the festival book alongside other plates showing the various ceremonies and a naval battle staged on the Arno.

26 "Fu questo spettacolo, come una cosa magnifica per esser di cavalli, e come invenzion bizzarra per far ballare animali, rimirata di tutto il popolo con molta attenzione"; Rinuccini, *Descrizione delle feste*, 62.

27 Nagler, *Theatre Festivals of the Medici*, 126–28; Blumenthal, *Theater Art of the Medici*, 95–102.

28 "Fecero ballare i loro cavalli con diletto e stupore di chascheduno che gli vide…
e varii e regolati moti facevano i cavalli, onde contendeva la vista di ciascuno con
l'udito"; Salvadori, *Guerra d'amore*, 49.

29 Blumenthal, *Theater Art of the Medici*, 102.

30 For an overview, see Harness, *Echoes of Women's Voices*, 147–66.

31 Decroisette, "L'Armida trionfante"; Harness, *Echoes of Women's Voices*, 142–74.

32 Bardi, *Descrizione delle feste fatte in Firenze*, 50–1.

33 Ghisi, "'Il mondo festeggiante'"; Decroisette, "Les fêtes."

34 "Mostrarono, benché in una finta battaglia, un ostinato desiderio della vittoria, che
però incontravano ogni pericolo, s'esponevano ad ogni rischio, ed avendo ne corag-
giosi petti il valore per anima, purché cercasser di vincere, non si curavano di viv-
ere"; Moniglia, *Il mondo festeggiante*, 45.

35 "oportuna occasione"; Costa, "Festa reale," 1640, fol. [1]v.

36 The thorny issue of translating "virtù" is a familiar one. I have opted to leave it in
Italian.

37 The 1647 publication does not include the manuscript's concluding stage directions,
though it does incorporate the lists of mottoes.

38 "si farà un grande e superbissimo tehatro"; Costa, "Festa reale," 1640, fol. [7]r.

39 "far più bella la mostra"; "la bizarria de' soldati"; Costa, "Festa reale," 1640, fol.
[10]v.

40 Harness, "Habsburgs, Heretics, and Horses," 271–7, discusses this convention.

41 "dolcissimi stromenti"; Costa, "Festa reale," 1640, fol. [7]v.

42 "rattemprar l'alme e raddolcir i cori"; Costa, "Festa reale," 1640, fol. [14]v.

43 On these conventions, see Harness, "'Nata à maneggi & essercizii grandi'"; Franchet
d'Espèrey, "The Ballet d'Antoine de Pluvinel," 124.

44 "a gara un ballo placido e gratioso"; Costa, "Festa reale," 1640, fol. [11]v.

45 "ove non è furor, dolce è la guerra"; Costa, "Festa reale," 1640, fol. [21]r.

46 "qui dunque guerra fia / che danza rassomigli e pace sia"; Costa, "Festa reale," 1640,
fol. [21]r.

47 Costa, "Festa reale," fol. [13]r.

48 "aspre guerre"; Costa, "Festa reale," fol. [23]r.

49 Costa, "Festa reale," 1640, fols. [12]r–v.

50 "convertesi il suono delle trombe in sinfonie di dolcissimi stromenti." Costa, "Festa
reale," 1640, fol. [13]r.

51 Costa, "Festa reale," 1640, fol. [14]v.

52 Costa, "Festa reale," 1640, fols. [34]v–[35]r.

53 The literature on Galileo is vast. One may start with the recent biographies by
Heilbron, *Galileo*; Wootton, *Galileo*.

54 Galilei, *Sidereus Nuncius*.

55 Biagioli, *Galileo, Courtier*, 110.

56 See Salvadori's canzone *Per le stelle medicee temerariamente oppugnate* (For the
Medicean Stars Rashly Repudiated) in Galileo, *Opere*, 9:233–72. Extant manuscript

copies are in Galileo's hand, with his corrections, suggesting his editorial involvement (cf. 233–6).

57 "ritrovate dal Signor Galileo Galilei Forentino, Mathematico di Sua Altezza ingegno rarissimo, e singolare a' tempi nostri per opera del maraviglioso occhiale." Villifranchi, *Descrizzione della barriera e della mascherata*, 32, also discussed in chapter 3, 84. See Alberti, "Le 'barriere' di Cosimo II."

58 "gli antichi traslatavano in cielo gl'eroi meritevoli." Villifranchi, *Descrizzione della barriera e della mascherata*, 32.

59 On reactions to Galileo's trial over time, see Finocchiaro, *Retrying Galileo*.

60 Langedijk, *The Portraits of the Medici*, vol. 1, passim; Biagioli, *Galileo, Courtier*, 143–9.

61 Reeves, *Evening News*, 235n3. Also see Biagioli, *Galileo, Courtier*, 143, on continued references to the stars in Florentine court culture.

62 Reeves, *Evening News*, 1.

63 Langedijk, *The Portraits of the Medici*, 1:cat. 28, 104a–b. Also see Biagioli, *Galileo, Courtier*, 139–40.

64 Galileo, *Dialogo*, 111–12.

65 Galileo, *Opere di Galileo Galilei*. See Rutgers, "A Frontispiece for Galileo's *Opere*."

66 "Galileo Galilei in atto di mostrare le stelle Medicee a tre donzelle"; Baldinucci, *Notizie de' professori del disegno*, 250. Astronomy's tiara is also topped with the four stars.

67 On the inclusion of this heretical detail, see Panofsky, "More on Galileo and the Arts," 285; and more recently, Rutgers, "A Frontispiece for Galileo's *Opere*," 10–11.

68 Moniglia, *Il mondo festeggiante*, 46, 49.

69 Moniglia, *Il mondo festeggiante*, 65.

70 Baldinucci, *Notizie de' professori del disegno*, 242. Baldinucci claims the goldsmith paid his pupil little attention, but he is keen to present the printmaker as a self-made genius. It is unlikely that Mola did the illustration, not least because he died in Rome the month Costa delivered the manuscript. Both artists incorporate conventional aspects of Jovian iconography – the lightning, the eagle – but the placement of the body and the incorporation of the Medicean Star imagery are more particular.

71 My thanks to Mary Vaccaro for bringing these to my attention.

72 The calligraphy and floral ornamentation may be the work of Della Bella's collaborator and imitator Valerio Spada, recognized especially for his opulent manuscripts. While his first known manuscripts of the kind are from the 1640s, his earliest work in Florence dates as early as 1636. Costa's manuscript would therefore fall early in his career; nonetheless, its calligraphic hand and lavish foliage are stylistically consistent with some of his later works; see Massar, "Valerio Spada," 273–4.

73 See Introduction, 16–18.

74 On the sisters' recruitment in 1646, see Introduction, 16–17.

75 Letter of 8 March 1646, ASF MdP 4653, c. 11v. Also see Megale, "Il principe e la cantante," 218.

76 Costa, *La tromba di Parnaso*, 21–31.

77 On these poems – albeit in an assessment largely coloured by distaste for Costa's presumed sexual activity – see Ademollo, *I primi fasti*, 36–9.

78 "Buti anch'io cerco i riveriti allori"; Costa, *La tromba di Parnaso*, 90.

79 Much like Costa, Andreini dedicated a manuscript edition of his work (already published in 1622) to Mazarin, dated March 28, 1647; Andreini, "La Ferinda."

80 Ghislanzoni, *Luigi Rossi*, 152–53; Prunières, *L'opéra italien en France avant Lulli*, 129–30. Contributing to the decision not to show either work were the early delays in the staging of *Orfeo*. While some scholars describe all three works as having been in competition for a single production spot, *Orfeo* was already programmed and word about its setbacks circulated in January. See a letter by Stefano Costa in Monaldini, *L'orto dell'Esperidi*, 13; Ghislanzoni, *Luigi Rossi*, 126–7 and 153.

81 Sabbattini, *Pratica di fabricar scene e machine*, 127–56.

82 "Avoit du genie et du talent pour la poësie"; Ménestrier, *Des représentations*, 232. See, for example, Ademollo, *I primi fasti*, 59–60, which cites Ménestrier's praise but nevertheless raises unfounded doubts about the work's authenticity.

83 Ménestrier, *Des représentations*, 232–5.

84 This ballet, organized by equestrian master Antoine de Pluvinel, was the last major example at court until the 1660s. See Franchet d'Espèrey, "The Ballet d'Antoine de Pluvinel"; van Orden, *Music, Discipline, and Arms*, 265–81; Metlica, *Le seduzioni della pace*, 158–81.

85 "il core afflitto"; Costa, *Festa reale*, 1647, 33.

86 "Borbone stelle"; Costa, *Festa reale*, 32.

87 Baumgartner, "Sunspots or Sun's Planets"; Lewis, *Galileo in France*. For reasons that remain unclear, Tarde crossed out – but left legible – his account of this conversation.

88 Galileo and Scheiner, *On Sunspots*. Ariew, "Theory of Comets," discusses responses in France.

89 Tarde, *Borbonia sidera*.

90 Galileo and Scheiner, *On Sunspots*, 101–4.

91 Costa may have encountered the image in France or while still in Florence; Tarde's book was in Galileo's library, for example. Favaro, *La libreria di Galileo*, 37, 81. For assertions about the differences between the two versions, see Megale, "Il principe e la cantante," 217n24.

92 "Acciò ch'il vino non mi fessi male, / Di quel [occhialone] mi servirei per serviziale. / Così vacuerei / E se bevuto avessi il renderei"; Costa, *The Buffoons*, III.ii.110–13.

93 "Oh così, Tedeschino, in capriole"; Costa, *The Buffoons*, II.iii.94.

94 "Ap, ap, ap, ga, ga, ga, ga"; "quattro curvette su"; "Come ben su le volte / Gli do le giravolte"; Costa, *The Buffoons*, II.iii.42–139.

95 Vianello, *L'arte del buffone*, 61; Henke, *Performance and Literature*, 51, 55.

96 "de la politica / il maghior asino ch'haia nel mundo"; "lo sciocco di politica"; Costa, *The Buffoons*, I.xii.136–7; III.ii.24.

97 See chapter 2, 64–6.

98 A sì gran nome, e non a' detti tuoi, / Ceder m'è forza ... / ... / ... or da l'aspetto / De le Medicee stelle altrove io parto"; "Senza buffonerie sciocca è la scena"; Costa, *The Buffoons*, prologue, lines 116–17, 122–3, 145.

99 "Buti anch'io cerco i riveriti allori / E 'l volante destrier tal'hora sprono"; Costa, *La tromba di Parnaso*, 90.

100 Caracciolo, *La gloria del cavallo*, vii.

5 The Singing Saint and the Plumed Bee: Courting the Barberini

1 On the Barberini and these two women, see Hammond, *The Ruined Bridge*, 86–8; Brosius, "Singers Behaving Badly"; Brosius, "Courtesan Singers as Courtiers." On the family's musical patronage broadly, see Hammond, *The Ruined Bridge*.

2 On the war and the *sede vacante*, see Nussdorfer, *Civic Politics*, 205–53.

3 Hammond, *The Ruined Bridge*, 157; Magnuson, *Rome in the Age of Bernini*, 2:8–10.

4 See Introduction, 22–3.

5 Also see chapter 6, 172; on Barberini "inheritance" of these musicians, see Murata, *Operas for the Papal Court*, 17.

6 Introduction, 24.

7 See chapter 4, 110, 113, and Hammond, *The Ruined Bridge*; Magnuson, *Rome in the Age of Bernini*, 1:245–52; Murata, *Operas for the Papal Court*, 13–47.

8 "famoso ladrone, et assassino facinoroso"; Gigli, *Diario di Roma*, 1:413–14. See also Introduction, 14.

9 Studies include Goethals, "The Singing Saint," 58–60; Stella, "Il *Cecilia martire*"; Stella, "Tra 'infiammate stille' e 'lacci cari'"; Quaintance, "Singing Women, Saint Cecilia, and Self-Fashioning."

10 Costa, *La tromba di Parnaso*.

11 Cox, *The Prodigious Muse*, 130.

12 See, to start, Asor Rosa, *La lirica del Seicento*, 142–3.

13 A copy at the Biblioteca Giovardiana in Veroli (Lazio) has a pasted-in title page whose handwritten publication information gives the incorrect title and date for reasons that remain unclear ("La Santa Cecilia, poema sacra... 1630"). The text itself is identical.

14 On the press, see Franchi, "Mascardi, Giacomo." Lincoln, "Printers and Publishers," 554–6, notes their work with artists, from Francesco Villamena to Guido Reni, on illustrations. Costa's text is printed in a single, rather than double, column, a more costly and unique choice among religious epics; see Chiesa, "Il poema sacro secentesco," 296.

15 "Ein seltzambe dama"; von Harrach, *Die diarien und tagzettel*, 2:538 and 5:31. Also see Introduction, 15.

16 Delehaye, *Étude sur le légendier romain*, 194–220; Lapidge, *The Roman Martyrs*, 138–64.

17 Delehaye, *Les passions*, 171–226; Lapidge, *The Roman Martyrs*, 18–34. The *Legenda aurea* gives an abridged version; de Voragine, *Golden Legend*, 704–9.

18 On sacred epic, see Cox, *The Prodigious Muse*, 129–63; Cox, "Re-Thinking Counter-Reformation Literature"; Faini, "La poetica dell'epica sacra"; Selmi, "'Inchiostri purgati,'" Brazeau, "The Better Fortitude Unsung?"; Brazeau, "'Defying Gravity'"; Quondam, *Paradigmi e tradizioni*; and Maggi's introduction to Marinella, *Vita*, 7–30.

19 See Lirosi, "Il corpo di Santa Cecilia," 7–11. Bosio's *Roma sotterranea* was published posthumously in 1632 with Cardinal Barberini's assistance.

20 Gallonio, *Historia delle sante vergini romane*, 212–26.

21 On sources, see Lirosi, "Il corpo di Santa Cecilia."

22 Baronio, *Annales ecclesiastici*, 9:862.

23 Goodson, "Material Memory," 26–33; Festa, "Representations of Saint Cecilia," 85–131; Bosio, *Historia passionis*.

24 "cantantibus organis, illa in corde suo soli Domino decantabat, dicens: fiat cor meum et corpus meum immaculatum ut non confundar"; Lapidge, *The Roman Martyrs*, 146.

25 Staiti, *La metamorfosi di Santa Cecilia*, 64–118; Meine, "Cecilia without a Halo," 104–12; Trinchieri Camiz, "Santa Cecilia," 59–68; Vodret and Strinati, "Painted Music."

26 Festa, "Representations of Saint Cecilia," 220–2; Staiti, *La metamorfosi di Santa Cecilia*, 100–2.

27 Staiti, *La metamorfosi di Santa Cecilia*, 72–6.

28 See Goethals, "The Singing Saint." See a partial compendium of dramatic works in the 1755 edition of Allacci, *Drammaturgia*, 175; and a few additions in Bianchi, "Una cortigiana rimatrice," 1925, 192n1.

29 Cox, "Re-Thinking Counter-Reformation Literature."

30 Spezzani, *Rappresentatione di S. Cecilia* (1581); and Castelletti, *La trionfatrice Cecilia* (1594, reprinted in 1598 and 1724). The sixteenth-century works are *La rappresentatione di Santa Cecilia vergine & martire* (1517, reprinted roughly a dozen times through 1617 in Florence and Siena) and Battista Spagnoli's Latin *De sancta Coecilia carmen*. The latter, overlooked in Goethals, "The Singing Saint," was located by Stella, "Tra 'infiammate stille' e 'lacci cari'," 113n4.

31 A rough count suggests that Cecilia had twice as many publications as Agnes and Agatha, and four times as many as Francesca Romana.

32 The 1637 work *La S. Cecilia, drama musicale* was staged at the wedding of Wladyslaw IV in Poland, but it is an example of Italian imports to Warsaw, with an Italian librettist, composer, and singers. See Goethals, "The Singing Saint," 51, 56–8.

33 Introduction, 9.

34 Barker, "Pasquinades and Propaganda," 87–8.

35 Noreen, "Recording the Past," 20.

36 For an overview, and a catalogue of works (including Costa's), see Cox, "Re-Thinking Counter-Reformation Literature"; Chiesa, "Il poema sacro secentesco." Also see Cox, *The Prodigious Muse*, 129–212 (citation on 129).

37 Kendrick, "What's So Sacred about 'Sacred' Opera?"; Murata, *Operas for the Papal Court*; Lamothe, "The Theater of Piety"; Aercke, *Gods of Play*, 116–38.

38 The three earliest editions varyingly divide the poem into two books (Naples, 1632), six cantos (Rome, 1633), or four books (Venice, 1633), the latter of which became the standard. See Russo, *Marino*, 230–5; Marino, "Strage de gl'innocenti," 601–8; Mirollo, *The Poet of the Marvelous*, 94–7. On the comparison between Costa and Marino, see Goethals, "The Singing Saint," 59; Stella, "Il *Cecilia martire*," 87–8. Bianchi, "Una cortigiana rimatrice" (1925), 191, also sees a Marinist echo here but points instead to *Il tempio*; however, Costa's continuity with this encomiastic work is fairly limited to the title of canto 3.

39 Marinella, *La Colomba sacra*. See Cox, *The Prodigious Muse*, 143–8; Benedetti, "Saintes et guerrières"; Brazeau, "The Better Fortitude Unsung?," 300–54.

40 See Goethals, "The Singing Saint."

41 "invano" "lievi scherzi… e folli ardori"; "e con voce più grata, e più canora / Di più bei carmi la mia cetra honora"; Costa, *Cecilia martire*, 1644, 1.

42 "macchiasti indarno il mal vergato folio"; Costa, *Cecilia martire*, 1644, 2.

43 "Musa non più d'amor, cantiamo lo sdegno / del crudo re…" Marino, "Strage de gl'innocenti," I.i.1–2, 467.

44 Tasso, *Gerusalemme liberata*, I.ii.2.

45 Cox, "Re-Thinking Counter-Reformation Literature." Stella ("Il *Cecilia martire*," 93–3) makes a similar contrast between Costa's muses. Also see discussion of a similar case in Marinella in Cox, *The Prodigious Muse*, 145.

46 "Io peccatrice inerme in mortal spoglia / Oso parlar de la grandezza eterna? / Io, c'ho basso il pensier, debil la voglia / Tento nomar ch 'l mondo e'l ciel governa?" Costa, *Cecilia martire*, 1644, 3.

47 von Harrach, *Die diarien und tagzettel*, 5:31.

48 Bianchi, "Una cortigiana rimatrice," 1925, 194.

49 "Reggi l'ardire mio, tempra il mio canto"; Costa, *Cecilia martire*, 1644, 4.

50 Costa, *Cecilia martire*, 4.

51 One of the two colossi of Amenhotep III; associated with Memnon, an Ethiopian warrior killed by Achilles and son of Eos (goddess of the dawn).

52 "Vaticano sole Barberino"; Costa, *Cecilia martire*, 1644, dedicatory letter.

53 "canti al suo Dio soavemente scioglie / e ne' suoi mali fortunata gode"; Costa, *Cecilia martire*, 11.

54 "Habbia la guerra, chi non vuol la pace"; Costa, *Cecilia martire*, 1644, 14. Compare to "Chi la pace non vuol, la guerra s'abbia"; Tasso, *Gerusalemme liberata*, II.lxxxiii.5. Also see Marino's Satan declare "Vo' quella guerra / Che non mi lece in Ciel"; Marino, "Strage de gl'innocenti," I.xxxii.7, 478.

55 "Vita non merta chi l'amore non prezza." Costa, *Cecilia martire*, 1644, 14.

56 Costa, *Cecilia martire*, 1644, 30. Brazeau suggests, in private correspondence, that the passage winks towards Marinella's *La Colomba*, where the emperor ultimately knees before the female saint, stating "son vinto"; Marinella, *La Colomba sacra*, 43v.

57 "carro d'or"; "quai larve io sento"; Marino, "Strage de gl'innocenti," II.i.1 (p. 489), II.viii.3 (p. 491).

58 "carro di rose"; "con larve di furie"; Costa, *Cecilia martire*, 1644, 37–8.

59 "invisibil voci in dolce accento … a lei cantare"; Costa, *Cecilia martire*, 1644, 50.

60 "La Diva all'hor su risonante legni, / C'han di concave canne ordini industri, / Con le dita trascorre"; Costa, *Cecilia martire*, 1644, 50. *Legno di risonanza*, "resonant wood" or tonewood, refers to a variety used to construct musical instruments.

61 Cox, *The Prodigious Muse*, 152.

62 Kerr, *The Rise of the Diva*.

63 "Pur la Diva non duolsi a tanti ardori / E la lingua discioglie in dolci note." Costa, *Cecilia martire*, 1644, 7.

64 Costa, *Cecilia martire*, 1644, 151.

65 On the *meraviglioso sacro* in religious epic, see Faini, "La poetica dell'epica sacra."

66 Virginia Cox has described Sofronia as "prototypical for later Counter-Reformation representations of the female martyr"; Cox, *The Prodigious Muse*, 292n245. Also see Yavneh, *Dal rogo alle nozze*; Benedetti, "Saintes et guerrières." For a comparable reading of Marinella's St. Colomba, see Brazeau, "The Better Fortitude Unsung?," 326–32. For another reading of Cecilia as a Sofronia-like figure on different terms, see Stella, "Tra 'infiammate stille' e 'lacci cari'," 102–3, 107, 111.

67 Costa, *Cecilia martire*, 1644, 54. This echoes Petrarch's accusation in *RVF* 89.7 that Amore deceived him through disguise ("quel traditore in sì mentite larve").

68 See chapter 3, 86.

69 On similar misinterpretations of Cecilia, see Goethals, "The Singing Saint," 55–7. Tasso repeatedly likens Armida to a siren, most memorably when she first seduces Rinaldo by emerging from a river, naked and singing: "Così dal palco di notturna scena / o ninfa o dea, tarda sorgendo, appare. / Questa, benché non sia vera sirena ma sia magica larva…."; Tasso, *Gerusalemme liberata*, XIV.lxi.
1–4. See Gough, "Tasso's Enchantress"; Driscoll, "'La donna di poche parole.'"

70 "milizia santa"; Dante, *Paradiso* XXI.2. "Schiere infinite di pennute menti"; Costa, *Cecilia martire*, 1644, 78.

71 Tasso, *Gerusalemme liberata*, I.xi.7–8; Costa, *Cecilia martire*, 1644, 79. Also compare this scene to Marino's divine counsel, which culminates with celestial messengers urging Joseph to flee to Egypt.

72 Costa, *Cecilia martire*, 1644, 94–5.

73 Butler, *Lives of the Saints: August*, 171.

74 Castiglione, *Patrons and Adversaries*, 24–5.

75 He tasked Pietro da Cortona (who also painted *The Founding of Palestrina* in Palazzo Barberini) with drawing up early plans. Mertz, *Pietro da Cortona*, 31–41.

76 On this work, *Praenestes antiquae libri duo*, ultimately published in 1655, and a discussion of its place in Costa's allusions to Agapitus, see Stella, "Il *Cecilia martire*," 97.

77 "sotto'altro Urbano in secoli migliori"; Costa, *Cecilia martire*, 1644, 99.

78 "rito amico / de la christiana fè"; Costa, *Cecilia martire*, 1644, 104.

79 "Urban, come in vita, hor anco in morte / A Cecilia del Cielo apra le porte." Costa, *Cecilia martire*, 1644, 81. This detail comes from Urban's own *Passio*; Lapidge, *The Roman Martyrs*, 526–50.

80 Costa, "Cecilia martire," BAV Barb. lat. 4069.

81 The impacted sections are pp. 119–20 (printed text) and fols. 63r–68r (manuscript). For additional commentary, see Stella, "Tra 'infiammate stille' e 'lacci cari'," 106–11. Also see Costa, *Voice of a Virtuosa and Courtesan*, 35.

82 "sembianze belle"; Costa, "Cecilia martire," 63v. For a similar observation, and an extended textual comparison, see Stella, "Tra 'infiammate stille' e 'lacci cari'," 106–16.

83 "in me l'ardore / Rinovi"; Costa, "Cecilia martire," 64r. Valeriano perhaps echoes Dante upon seeing Beatrice in *Purgatorio* XXX.48 (*conosco i segni de l'antica fiamma*), itself a reprisal of Dido's amorous reawakening in *Aeneid* IV.23.

84 "Tu, che 'l gel de la morte estinguer puoi, / Spegner potesti le mie voglie audaci"; Costa, *Cecilia martire*, 1644, 127. "Tu, ch' in cenere *ancora* ardir mi puoi / [...] "; Costa, "Cecilia martire," 66v. Emphasis mine.

85 Stella, "Tra 'infiammate stille' e 'lacci cari'," 112.

86 Costa, *Cecilia martire*, 1644, 133.

87 Marino, "Strage de gl'innocenti," IV.118.

88 Costa, *Cecilia martire*, 1644, 119. Also see Costa-Zalessow, "Margherita Costa," 117.

89 "E sian le forze rigide di morte / E de i fieri nemici a un tempo dome"; Costa, *Cecilia martire*, 1644, 148.

90 "magnanimi ristori"; Costa, *Cecilia martire*, 1644, 148.

91 Noreen, "Recording the Past"; Noreen, "Lay Patronage and the Creation of Papal Sanctity."

92 "loco dove S. Urbano Papa Primo battezzò S. Cecilia"; Gigli, *Diario di Roma*, 284–5.

93 "memorabile e pomposo"; Costa, *Cecilia martire*, 1644, 5.

94 Nussdorfer, *Civic Politics*, 184n50.

95 Eclissi, "Forma della chiesa di S.to Urbano," BAV Barb.lat. 4402; "Pitture della chiesa di S. Urbano alla Caffarella"; BAV Barb. lat 4408. See Williamson, "Notes on the Wall-Paintings"; Noreen, "Recording the Past." Francesco had similar reproductions made in other Roman sites, including Santa Cecilia in Trastevere.

96 Some artistic renderings do have similar compositions: one of Guido Reni's Cecilias is also on her knees before her executioner, for instance, but she faces the viewer head-on while looking heavenward, arms extended, as he pivots behind her with his sword gripped in both hands for the backstroke; Pepper, *Guido Reni*, cat. 12 (altarpiece, Santa Cecilia in Trastevere, Cappella del Bagno).

97 She elsewhere often wears a turban.

98 A similar observation is also made in Stella, "Il *Cecilia martire*," 87.

99   https://www.wga.hu/html_m/d/domenich/3/polet1.html.

100   On poetic responses to religious art in the Counter-Reformation, see Treherne, "Pictorial Space and Sacred Time." Marino also represents his poem as a response to a painting.

101   "Ed Urbano Cecilia in terra honora"; Costa, *Cecilia martire*, 1644, 151.

102   "Heroe purpureo"; Costa, *Cecilia martire*, 1644, 150.

103   Costa, *La tromba di Parnaso*, 68–72.

104   As Laurie Nussdorfer notes, the war "fatally disfigured the image of authority and magnificence [Urban] had so carefully cultivated." Nussdorfer, *Civic Politics*, 203.

105   As noted in the Introduction, 15–16, in this tumultuous period Squilletti was also arrested by the Medici.

106   Hammond, *The Ruined Bridge*, 159–60.

107   There is some question over the Barberini's role in selecting musicians. Prunières notes that Mazarin would have been familiar with their musicians from his time in the family's service, including Costa "whom he had no doubt known in Rome"; Prunières, *L'opéra italien en France avant Lulli*, 106n3 and 138. But also see Megale, "Il principe e la cantante," 214–15, on Antonio's involvement in singers' rehearsals for the 1645 *Finta pazza*.

108   "lunge dal paterno tetto"' "per voi 'l secolo d'oro in me rinova"; Costa, *La tromba di Parnaso*, 62, 66.

109   Costa, *La tromba di Parnaso*, 62–3.

110   "Hor vinto il Leon da l'Api giace"; Costa, *La tromba di Parnaso*, 76.

111   "Altro per mia salute desiderar non devo che la tua salute, e ambir la protetione della mia fortuna da quella mano, che ha saputo proteggier l'Italia, ov' ebbe gran tempo il suo regno la fortuna"; Costa, *La tromba di Parnaso*, 72–3.

112   Costa, *La tromba di Parnaso*, 69.

113   Based on designs by Bernini, Rubens, and Cortona, respectively. See Rietbergen, *Power and Religion in Baroque Rome*, 129–30; Harper, "Tapestry Production in Seventeenth-Century Rome," 304–10. Harper notes that the tapestry was likely inspired by the contest between Hercules and the Nemean lion (p. 306).

114   "la volubilità del basso volgo nela morte di Urbano VIII"; Costa, *La tromba di Parnaso*, 77. Also see Costa, *Voice of a Virtuosa and Courtesan*, 38; Bianchi, "Una cortigiana rimatrice," 1925, 180–1.

115   Hunt, *The Vacant See*.

116   Gigli, *Diario di Roma*, 2:429. See Hunt, *The Vacant See*, 200–201; Barker, "Pasquinades and Propaganda," 70–2.

117   Ameyden, "Diario," Biblioteca Casanatense MS 1832, 131r.

118   Hunt, *The Vacant See*, 201.

119   Costa, *La tromba di Parnaso*, 82.

120   Costa, *La tromba di Parnaso*, 77.

121   "Troppo ben, troppa fede, e troppo honore"; Costa, *La tromba di Parnaso*, 82.

122   "Roma, Roma, che fai?"; Costa, *La tromba di Parnaso*, 81.

123 "Io qual voi non fia mai: qual sempre fui / fida contro di voi prego vendetta"; Costa, *La tromba di Parnaso*, 79.

124 Costa, *La tromba di Parnaso*, 85.

125 Waddy, *Seventeenth-Century Roman Palaces*, 26–7; Scanzani, "Camilla e Costanza Barberini."

126 Costa, *La tromba di Parnaso*, 47–50.

127 Costa, *La tromba di Parnaso*, 60.

128 Bianchi, "Una cortigiana rimatrice," 1924, 187.

129 Costa, "Sonetto… all'ecc. Principe di Palestrina," BAV Archivio Barberini, Indice 1, 1088. Also transcribed on the website *Scritture di donne (secc. XVI–XX): Censimento degli archivi romani:* http://212.189.172.98:8080/scritturedidonne/Vaticana _ArchBarberini/scritturedidonne.jsp.

130 Bjurström, *Feast and Theatre*, 9–37, surveys these celebrations.

131 See Hammond, *The Ruined Bridge*, 207–43. On Baroque tournament opera, see Béhar and Watanabe-O'Kelly, *Spectacvlvm Evropævm*, 616–22.

132 Hammond, *The Ruined Bridge*, 233; Masson, "Papal Gifts and Roman Entertainments"; Norman, "In Public and in Private." One contemporary assessed the cost of the spectacles at 25,000 scudi; "Racconto istorico del trionfo in Vaticano," BAV Urb. lat. 1681, fol. 214.

133 Priorato, *Historia*, 304. Also see Piccinini, "Carnevale di Roma del 1656."

134 Bjurström, *Feast and Theatre*, 34; Hammond, *The Ruined Bridge*, 235.

135 "moderna, e non più veduta inventione"; Priorato, *Historia*, 303. Priorato notes that the illumination alone cost over 1,000 scudi.

136 "Ragguaglio della festa de' caroselli," BAV Barb. lat. 4913, fol. 106r.

137 Other commentators (including my "The Patronage Politics of Equestrian Ballet") typically translate the *Amazoni* as Amazons, but this risks implying that they were female warriors, whereas the dark skin of the combatants in the Lauri-Gagliardi depiction suggests Amazonian Indians.

138 Masson, "Papal Gifts and Roman Entertainments," 259; Hammond, *The Ruined Bridge*, 236.

139 For examples, see Hammond, *The Ruined Bridge*, 236n71. See also Nussdorfer, "Print and Pageantry in Baroque Rome."

140 Costa replicates the phrase "secol delle stelle" in her 1657 poem to Chigi.

6 Hunting for Diana, or An Ode to Regents

1 For an overview, see De Liso, "Margherita Costa a Parigi."

2 Ovid, *Metamorphoses*, I.III.165, 136–7.

3 *Bella donna ad Amore mentre è avanti il confessore*; Costa, *La selva di Diana*, 77.

4 "la vedova Margherita Costa"; AST-Piave, Patenti Controllo Finanza, mazz. 124, fols. 59–60.

5 Ademollo, *I primi fasti*, 30n1.

6 See Introduction, 20.

7 Knox, *The First Blast of the Trumpet*, 12. Studies of female governance in this period include Cruz and Suzuki, *The Rule of Women*; Jansen, *The Monstrous Regiment of Women*.

8 Knox, *The First Blast of the Trumpet*, 18 and 48.

9 Hanley, "The Salic Law"; Hanley, "Configuring the Authority of Queens."

10 Crawford, *Perilous Performances*, 7, 23.

11 On "galleries" in which Costa herself appeared, see Introduction, 22.

12 Maclean, *Woman Triumphant*, 64–87; Garrard, *Artemisia Gentileschi*, 154–71.

13 Tasso, *Discorso della virtù feminile e donnesca*, 62–8.

14 Costa, *La selva di Diana*, Aiii r.

15 The 7 January document specifies that Costa would receive an annual salary to be paid out quarterly, for the period of the duchess's pleasing; AST-Piave, Patenti Controllo Finanza, mazz. 124, fols. 59–60, and, on her food allotment, fol. 62. On the contract, see Claretta, *Storia della reggenza di Cristina*, 2:536; Ademollo, *I primi fasti*, 38n1; Bianchi, "Una cortigiana rimatrice," 1924, 187.

16 "povero stipendio"; Letter from (Laura) Isabella Lessona to Carlo Emanuele II on 19 June 1665, AST-Castello, Lettere, principi diversi, L., mazz. 25. Also see the records for payments in, for instance, AST-Piave, Patenti Controllo Finanza, mazz. 123, fol. 70 (9 November 1643); fol. 119 (gift of 500 lire); mazz. 125, fol. 25r (6 January 1646). While relevant financial records are spotty after 1633, in the period 1625–30 Christine employed five female singers; Bouquet, *Il teatro di corte*, 1:21.

17 See Introduction, 17.

18 Christine's eldest son, Francesco Giacinto, died a year later and was succeeded by four-year-old Carlo Emanuele II.

19 "alla ruina del Piemonte, alla desolatione di cotesti popoli, a' danni dell'Italia e della Christianità"; Letters from 27–29 March, 1639 AST-Castello, Lettere, Principi Diversi, m. 18, fols. 159–64.

20 Pollak, *Turin, 1564–1680*, 122–33; Scott, "Fashioning a Capital," 141–70. Christine also commissioned a history of her regency, an unfinished work lacking the final chapter covering 1644/45; Castiglione, "Historia della reggenza," AST-Castello, Storia della Real Casa, m. 17.

21 On Christine's Torinese spectacles, see Viale Ferrero, *Feste delle Madame Reali*, esp. 23–4; Arnaldi di Balme and Varallo, *Feste barocche*, 83–4; Defabiani and Devoti, "La corte, la festa, la città"; Varallo, "Le feste da Maria Cristina a Giovanna Battista," 483–96; Bouquet-Boyer, "Les états de Savoie et Christine de France"; Cosentino, "Allegorie del potere femminile," 163–6.

22 See, for instance, Doglio and Guglielminetti, "La letteratura e la corte."

23 Citation from Viale Ferrero, *Feste delle Madame Reali*, 40.

24 De Felice, "Agliè, Filippo San Martino Conte di."

25 Viale Ferrero, *Feste delle Madame Reali*, 43–4 and tables; McGowan, "Deux fêtes en Savoie"; Arnaldi di Balme and Varallo, *Feste barocche*, 95–7; Defabiani, "Una 'metafora attuosa,'" 54–65.

26 "Dono del re del'Alpi," BNUT q.V.60. On festival works in print and manuscript, see Varallo, "Le feste sabaude," 20–1.

27 Viale Ferrero, *Feste delle Madame Reali*, table VI.

28 "seppe difenderlo, e serbarlo e dall'armi e dall'arti, con la virtù del petto e con le meraviglie dell'animo reale"; "Dono del re del'Alpi," c. 2.

29 While named noblemen performed the female roles in the ballets (per convention), the manuscript explicitly states that (unnamed) women sang these parts.

30 "Arie del balletto" for soprano, contralto, tenor, and bass; "Dono del re dell'Alpi," BNUT, qm.II.84 (A–D).

31 The gazette provides a short synopsis of the production's "royal magnificence"; *Successi del mondo*, 15 February 1645, 1. The gazette mentions the arrival of other singers, such as Leonora Baroni later that spring, but because Christine founded it three weeks after the start of Costa's contract, it is necessarily silent about her arrival. See Caratti and Ordano, "'Successi del mondo' (1645–1669)."

32 Bouquet-Boyer, "Musical Enigmas in Ballet," 36.

33 "sentir la voce di qualche dama"; "gratioso et honorato trattenimento"; letter from Ludovico d'Agliè to Cardinal Maurizio, 7 April 1627, AST-Castello, Lettere Ministri, Roma, m. 37, n. 2, fol. 10. The letter is also mentioned, with an incorrect date, in Rua, *Poeti della corte di Carlo Emanuele I*, 105.

34 Like Costa, these performers had connections to the Barberini.

35 On Maurizio's efforts to elevate the family's status, see Osborne, "The House of Savoy," 166–7.

36 See a 20 September 1627 letter from Maurizio to d'Agliè, AST-Castello, Lettere Ministri, Roma, m. 38, n. 1, fols. 122–3, and a 28 December 1628 letter from d'Agliè to the cardinal regarding a desired Carnival performance in Turin in m. 39, n. 1 (Registro di lettere), fols. 593–6.

37 1 May 1623 letter from Prince Emanuele Filiberto, AST-Castello, Lettere Ministri, Roma, mazz. 35, n. 2, f. 4.

38 Bouquet-Boyer, "Musical Enigmas in Ballet," 36.

39 Costa, *La selva di Diana*, 9.

40 Costa, *La selva di Diana*, 12.

41 Costa, *La selva di cipressi*, 119. Costa substitutes Furies for Ariosto's Harpies. Ariosto, *Orlando furioso*, XXXIV.ii.1.

42 Costa, *La selva di cipressi*, 119, 125, and 131. For a similar ecological interpretation, see Costa, *Voice of a Virtuosa and Courtesan*, 177n154.

43 Costa, *La selva di cipressi*, 123.

44 Costa, *La selva di cipressi*, 124.

45 Costa, *La selva di cipressi*, 121–2; Costa, *La selva di Diana*, 12–13.

46 Costa, *La selva di cipressi*, 119; Costa, *La selva di Diana*, 11.

47 Costa, *La selva di cipressi*, 9.

48 Oresko, "The House of Savoy," 310.

49 Oresko, "The House of Savoy," 304–6; Osborne, *Dynasty and Diplomacy*, 97.

50 "Dono del re dell'Alpi," fols. 44–5.

51 *Theatrum Sabaudiae*. Also see Oresko, "The House of Savoy," 277.

52 However, Osborne shows that while there had been "tacit recognition" of Savoyard royalty before 1632, the *trattamento reale* had the opposite of the intended effect by prompting other courts to restrict their use of royal honorifics. Osborne, "Language and Sovereignty," esp. 33.

53 Oresko, "The House of Savoy," 309–10.

54 Osborne, "Language and Sovereignty," 16.

55 Oresko, "The House of Savoy," 309–11.

56 Costa, *La selva di Diana*, 15.

57 Di Macco and Romano, *Diana trionfatrice*; Caresio, *Residenze sabaude*.

58 Costa, *La selva di Diana*, 11, 15.

59 Costa, *La selva di Diana*, 9.

60 Costa, *La selva di Diana*, 16–17.

61 Castiglione, *Le pompe torinesi*.

62 See, for example, Di Macco and Romano, *Diana trionfatrice*, 107–8, 339–40.

63 Dameri and Roggero, "Il Castello del Valentino"; Bernardi, *Il Castello del Valentino*.

64 Cammarata and Testa, "Castello del Valentino," 47. On Christine as Flora, see Griseri, *Il diamante*, 113–36.

65 See the descriptions in D'Agliè, *Le delitie*, 121–31.

66 Castellamonte, *Venaria reale*, 24.

67 Christine's movements are reported in the 11 March edition of the *Successi del mondo*.

68 "Ho voluto intitolarlo la Selva di Diana perch'ogni invido lume che insidioso ardisse oscurarlo resti al reggio nome di Vostra Altezza Reale un novello Atteone"; Costa, *La selva di Diana*, dedication.

69 Costa, *La selva di Diana*, 9.

70 Costa, *La selva di cipressi*, 48.

71 See Emanuele Tesauro's poem explicating Christine's device in Tesauro, *Panegirici*, 1–126. Also see Kolrud, "The Gem and the Mirror of Heroic Virtue"; Griseri, *Il diamante*, 35–52.

72 "grande eroina," "cuore di diamante," "sudano gli atleti, treman le colonne di bronzo, vacillano i marmi"; D'Agliè, *Le delitie*, 16–17.

73 "Febo de le tue glorie eterni il canto / grandini l'aria a te rose e viole / ed or più fino s'incoroni il sole"; Costa, *La selva di Diana*, 19–20.

74 On Anne's life, see Kleinman, *Anne of Austria*.

75 Crawford, *Perilous Performances*, 98–112.

76 Mazarin's role in Anne's regency is outlined in Kleinman, *Anne of Austria*, 144–57.

77 Crawford, *Perilous Performances*, 131.

78 Maclean, *Woman Triumphant*, 76–7.

79 "une regence qui est conduite avec vigueur"; Le Moyne, *La gallerie des femmes fortes*, A3v. The work enjoyed numerous editions and English and Italian translations.

80 Le Moyne, *La gallerie des femmes fortes*, A3v.

81 My thanks to Kelly Shannon-Henderson for the comparison.

82 The frontispiece re-adapts one Audran produced for Jean-François Nicéron's *Thau-maturgus opticus (1646)*. Garrard, *Artemisia Gentileschi*, 165. A later 1665 version replaced the queen mother with an image of her son circled by male busts.

83 Puget de La Serre, *L'isthoire [sic] et les portraits*; "Temple de la gloire," Bibliothèque Mazarine MS 2212.

84 Kleinman, *Anne of Austria*, 225.

85 On these *mazarinades*, see Merrick, "The Cardinal and the Queen," 667–99; Kleinman, *Anne of Austria*, 221–3. For attacks on Anne, see Crawford, *Perilous Performances*, 126–31.

86 Motteville, *Memoirs*, 1:109, 168–9. Also see Freitas, *Portrait of a Castrato*, 47.

87 Ademollo, *I primi fasti*, 13–14.

88 See Melani's 2 November 1644 and 2 February 1657 letters in Freitas, *Portrait of a Castrato*, 47, 151–2.

89 Ghislanzoni, *Luigi Rossi*, 155.

90 "Per gl'honori ricevuti in Parigi dalla Maestra della Regina di Francia"; Costa, *La selva di Diana*, 79–85. On patronage in France, see Kettering, "Patronage in Early Modern France"; "The Patronage Power of Early Modern French Noblewomen"; "Favour and Patronage."

91 Costa, *La tromba di Parnaso*, 3.

92 "vergine rosa"; Costa, *Lo stipo*, 51 and 52; quotation on 54.

93 Costa, *La tromba di Parnaso*, 8.

94 Costa, *La tromba di Parnaso*, 6.

95 Costa, *La tromba di Parnaso*, 11.

96 *Costa, La tromba di Parnaso*, 9. Some of this material, like the Dido and Rome comparisons, also appears in Christine's poem in *La selva di Diana*, 17.

97 Also present is a poem to Wladyslaw IV (pp. 32–4), to whom Costa previously dedicated a pair of poems in her *Chitarra* and whose invitation to Poland she here regrets declining. The year prior, the king married the French princess Marie Louise Gonzaga.

98 See chapter 4, 131, 135.

99 Andreini, *Rime*. See Campbell, "Marie de Beaulieu and Isabella Andreini."

100 Mallick, "Clients and Friends."

101 Motteville, *Memoirs*, 1:173.

102 Costa, *La selva di Diana*, 79.

103 Costa, *La selva di Diana*, 80.

104 Costa, *La selva di Diana*, 80.

105 Costa, *La selva di Diana*, 80. Kerr, *The Rise of the Diva*.

106 "E tra voci canore ameni cigni / godano tra bassi horrori i ciel benigni"; Costa, *La selva di Diana*, 84.

107 Bianchi identifies Artigemma as an anagram of Margherita. Bianchi, "Una cortigiana rimatrice," 1924, 28.

108 Costa, *La selva di Diana*, 21. The section recalls Chiabrera's *Vendemmie di Parnaso* series, which includes a poem summoning beautiful ladies to the harvest; Chiabrera, *Canzonette, rime varie, dialoghi*.

109 Claude Lorraine, *Pastoral Landscape with Lake Albano and Castel Gandolfo* (1639), Fitzwilliam Museum, Cambridge, UK.

110 My thanks to Carmen Nocentelli for bringing this connection to my attention.

111 Green, *Roman Religion and the Cult of Diana*; Vincenti, *Diana*.

112 On the excavations by Mario Frangipane, see Picozzi, "Orfeo Boselli and the Interpretation of the Antique," 103–14.

113 Virgil, *The Aeneid*, VII.71–80, VII.385–406, XII.64–9, and XII.604–7.

114 Ovid, *Fasti*, III.601–57.

115 Dante Alighieri, *Inferno*, IV.124–6; *Purgatorio*, XVII.31–9.

116 Virgil, *Aeneid Book XII*, 34. A dozen operas and ballets take Aeneas and Lavinia as their subject.

117 Rosand, *Monteverdi's Last Operas*, 66, 114–73, 385–91. "Lavinia" was also the stage name of a famed recent *commedia dell'arte* actress, Marina Dorotea Antonazzoni (1593–1639), whose repertoire included *La pazzia di Lavinia*. See Wilbourne, *Seventeenth-Century Opera*, 71–2.

118 Livy, *Ab urbe condita*, I.III.1 (15).

119 Boccaccio, *Famous Women*, 166–7. He instead echoes the Ovidian tale in Boccaccio, *Genealogy of the Pagan Gods*, 2:284–5.

120 Boccaccio, *Boccaccio's Exposition on Dante's Comedy*, 211.

121 de Pizan, *City of Ladies*, I.xlviii.1.96–7.

122 Costa, *La selva di Diana*, 22.

123 Given the classical and geographical context, Lavinia's rocklike faithfulness contrasts with the treachery of Tarpeia, the vestal virgin who betrayed Rome to the Sabines before being crushed to death; her body was flung from a cliff on the Capitoline Hill, later called the Tarpeian Rock (Costa references the rock in a poem to Francesco Barberini, on which see chapter 5, 158). My thanks to Kelly Shannon-Henderson for the comparison.

124 Costa, *La selva di Diana*, 22.

125 Costa, *La selva di Diana*, 22.

126 This daughter, Maria Isabella, was one of the "beauties" painted by Jacob Ferdinand Voet. Petrucci, *Ferdinand Voet*, 236, cat. 187a; Benocci, *Le belle*, 121.

127 "nuova reina ch' al Latio imperi"; Costa, *La selva di Diana*, 23.

128 Costa, *La selva di Diana*, 8, 22, and 79.

129 Costa, *La selva di Diana*, 9, 22.

130 "Sol puote la tua gratia aprirmi il polo, / e sollevarmi da la ria percossa: / Fato acerbo a sua voglia hor mi sommerga / Dolce mi fia il cader, purché tu m'erga." Costa, *La selva di Diana*, 8.

7 "A Change of Sky Does Me No Good": Envy, Rivalry, and Other Courtly Criticisms

1 "palludi"; ASF, MdP 5320, fols. 291r–92r.

2 Ugolini, *The Court and Its Critics*, 5. See also Snyder, *Dissimulation and the Culture of Secrecy*, 68–105.

3 Rosselli, "From Princely Service to the Open Market." See a comparable discussion regarding Veronica Franco in Rosenthal, *The Honest Courtesan*, 31–4, 60–2.

4 The two exceptions are *Il violino* and *La tromba di Parnaso*.

5 "lui si potrebbe con il tanto scrivere di lei risolvere a non ci venir più et a noi sarebbe di grandissimo danno, poiché è cavaliero che si diletta di musica e conduce gli altri gentilomeni a sentir cantar la signora madre"; ASF, MdP 1505 (unnumbered); also transcribed in Mamone, *Serenissimi fratelli principi impresari*, #971 (464–5).

6 On Giovanna's complaints, see, for example, ASF, MdP 5561, 919r–v.

7 "li cativi fini di questa donna." 18 July 1645; ASF, MdP 5349, f. 375r–v. See Megale, "Il principe e la cantante," 213.

8 On Sardelli, see Besutti, "Sardelli, Anna Maria ('La Campaspe')."

9 See Talbot, "Vendramin."

10 Brosius, "Singers Behaving Badly."

11 Glixon and Glixon, *Inventing the Business of Opera*, esp. 3–16.

12 Rosselli, "From Princely Service to the Open Market."

13 "dove annotta la riputatione muore la vita, qua il nobile è nume, una madre senza altra scorta che il poco conoscimento delle mondane ruine è bersaglio a favolosi accidenti"; 16 March 1652 letter from Venice; ASF MdP 5320, fols. 291r–92r.

14 Mamone, "Most Serene Brothers-Princes-Impresarios."

15 Introduction, 18–19.

16 See Introduction, 19.

17 Sartori, *Libretti italiani a stampa*, 1:188. For identifications of the work as a play, see Capucci, "Costa, Margherita"; Costa, *Voice of a Virtuosa and Courtesan*, 24; Cox, *Women's Writing in Italy*, 220. As an opera, see Pirrotta, "Costa, Margherita"; Carter, "Costa"; Ferrone's introduction to Costa, "Li buffoni," II.238; Strappini, *La tragedia del buffone*, 256; Merola, "Il mito in scena," 81; Amati, *Bibliografia romana*,1:107.

18 Glixon and Glixon, *Inventing the Business of Opera*, 120.

19 Rosand, *Opera in Seventeenth-Century Venice*, passim; Bianconi and Walker, "Production, Consumption, and Political Function," 267–70; Stein, "How Opera Traveled," 250–1; Warrack, *German Opera*.

20 Stein, "How Opera Traveled," 251. Also see Costa, *The Buffoons*, 21.

21 The addition of "Maria" has led to speculation of a spiritual conversion, but the contents of the work point away from that hypothesis.

22 "esercitai in vece dell'ago, la penna"; Costa, *Gl'amori della luna*, A3v.

23 These include her previous thirteen full-length publications. It is unclear whether the fourteenth refers to *Gl'amori della luna* itself, the *Sette giornate* manuscript, or if she has another text in mind.

24 "dispennata la penna, amutita la lingua, altro suono non hanno saputo formare, che dolorose stride a miei infortunii"; Costa, *Gl'amori della luna*, A4r.

25 Costa, *Gl'amori della luna*, A4r.

26 "ove sono i mecenati, non mancano i Vergilii"; Costa, A4r. Compare with Lelio Guidiccioni's dedicatory statement to Antonio Barberini (to whom he would

dedicate his 1642 *Eneide toscana*) that the cardinal "sempre fu mecenate, et supplirà un giorno i Virgilii, et di presente è mio Augusto"; Guidiccioni, *Rime*, A4v.

27 "Mi è stato forza sotto cielo straniero esercitare l'ingegno a diffesa di lingua nemica"; Costa, *Gl'amori della luna*, 5Ar. Costa-Zalessow instead interprets this to mean that Costa had stopped writing in Italian. Costa-Zalessow, "Margherita Costa," 117; Costa, *Voice of a Virtuosa and Courtesan*, 38.

28 On Costa's possible trip to Germany, see Introduction, 19.

29 Vavoulis, "A Venetian World in Letters." For selected transcriptions, see Rosand, *Opera in Seventeenth-Century Venice*, appendix 3.

30 Warrack, *German Opera*, 29. Stein, "How Opera Traveled," 851, lists the first in Hanover as Cesti's *Orontea* (1678).

31 Costa, *La selva di Diana*, 90; Costa, *La selva di cipressi*, 235.

32 "avvolta tra ritorte d'invidi rostri"; Costa, *Gl'amori della luna*, 5Ar.

33 Tasso, *Aminta*, prologue, line 51.

34 Costa, *Gl'amori della luna*, 11.

35 Costa, *La selva di Diana*, 71.

36 Ovid, *Metamorphoses*, II.775–82, 789–94.

37 See Refini, "Prologhi figurati," 74–9. See also Cherchi, "A Dossier for the Study of Jealousy"; Milburn, "D'Invidia e d'Amor figlia sì ria."

38 The story offers intriguing parallels to Chiabrera's *Il rapimento di Cefalo* (1600), on Aurora's love for and abduction of the hunter Cephalus, part of Amore's display of power; see Carter, "Rediscovering *Il rapimento di Cefalo*"; Sampson, *Pastoral Drama*, 232–3.

39 See, for instance, Costa, *Lo stipo*, 243–59. See also the discussion in Merola, "Il mito in scena," 88–9.

40 Sampson, *Pastoral Drama*; Clubb, "The Pastoral Play"; Ugolini, *The Court and Its Critics*, 145–80; Gerbino, *Music and the Myth of Arcadia*.

41 Costa, *Gl'amori della luna*, 45–6.

42 "estinta"; Costa, *Gl'amori della luna*, 47, 88.

43 Ugolini, *The Court and Its Critics*, 158–9. For a discussion of pastoral's attempts to move away from ancient and contemporary violence, and how the genre undermines those goals, see Tylus, "Colonizing Peasants."

44 Ugolini, *The Court and Its Critics*, 178, 156.

45 George McClure argues that early modern parlour games fell into two categories: the edifying and the more "flirtatious" entertaining types; Costa selects examples of the former. McClure, *Parlour Games*, 13–28.

46 Nolfi, *Ginipedia*, 424–5. See Evangelisti, "Vincenzo Nolfi's *Ginipedia*," 63–80.

47 "Uccidete, ferite"; Costa, *Gl'amori della luna*, 40.

48 Costa, *Gl'amori della luna*, 41.

49 While Poliziano's *Orfeo* included the scene, it was excluded from more contemporary operas.

50 "e ridendo tutte corsero verso il signore Gasparo, come per dargli delle busse, e farne come le Baccanti di Orfeo"; Castiglione, *Il cortigiano*, II.xi.30; *The Book of the*

Courtier, II.96. See Scalabrini, *Commedia e civiltà*, 13–16. On associations of courtiership with gameplaying, see Ugolini, *The Court and Its Critics*, 104–5.

51 Raizen, "Monsters of the Pastoral Stage," 423.

52 Tasso, *Aminta*, III.i.

53 Guarini, *Il pastor fido*, II.vi.

54 Andreini, *Mirtilla*, III.ii; citation at line 1502.

55 Cavalli, *La Calisto*, 2007, II.ix.

56 See Curnis, "Novelli Endimioni e falsi Atteoni"; Lattarico, *"Lo scherno degli dei,"* 20.

57 Costa, *Gl'amori della luna*, 61. A contemporary description is found in Mascardi, *Dell'arte historica*, 620. Merola, "Il mito in scena," 90, similarly notes Mascardi's gendered description.

58 Costa, *Gl'amori della luna*, 62.

59 "Occide Amore e, fassi una chimera"; Costa, *Gl'amori della luna*, 64.

60 Marino, *Adone*, XVII.i.1–2. Russo, citing Giovanni Pozzi, notes that the identification of Jealousy as the daughter of Love originates in Petrarchism.

61 Tasso, *Aminta*, I.ii.177–80.

62 See "Competition and Conversation: Games as Music" in Schleuse, *Singing Games*, 176–245.

63 Ugolini, *The Court and Its Critics*, 158.

64 See discussions in Di Maro, "Il cor si finge un ghiaccio"; De Liso, "Margherita Costa a Parigi," 36–7.

65 "dell'invidia acerba guerra"; Costa, *Lo stipo*, 19.

66 "Dell'Invidia trionfi, e della Morte"; "Dell'invidia domare ogn'atro scempio"; Costa, *Lo stipo*, 84, 114.

67 Costa, *La selva di Diana*, 14, dedication.

68 Costa, *La Flora feconda*.

69 "De l'insidia non teme invido rostro"; Costa, *La selva di Diana*, 79.

70 Costa, *La tromba di Parnaso*, 24.

71 "Invida Parca di nocente rostro"; Costa, *La tromba di Parnaso*, 44.

72 Costa, *La selva di cipressi*, 97, 100.

73 "de l'Invidia aspre l'offese"; Costa, *La tromba di Parnaso*, 86.

74 Costa, *Flora feconda*, X.xx.189; Costa, *La Flora feconda*, III.i, p. 70.

75 "A chi vince l'invidia, e 'l tempo doman / Teatro è 'l Mondo, e l'Universo è scena"; Costa, *La chitarra*.

76 Costa, *Lo stipo*, 10.

77 "Sien pur invidi venti a te contrari"; Costa, *Lettere amorose*, 6.

78 Costa, *La chitarra*, "Ai lettori."

79 Costa, *La chitarra*, 567, 572.

80 Costa, *La selva di Diana*, 60.

81 Costa, *Lo stipo*, 293, 296, 300. Also see chapter 2, 59–60.

82 Costa, *Lo stipo*, 299.

83 Costa, *Lo stipo*, 299.

84 "Partenzza [*sic*] di Roma de l'autora del anno 1647"; Costa, *La selva di Diana*, 86. Costa-Zalessow also notes the centrality of Costa's theme of exile from Rome, which she finds merits greater discussion; Costa-Zalessow, "Alla scoperta di Margherita Costa," 19.

85 "mi sdegni e mi discacci"; Costa, *La selva di Diana*, 87. De Liso ("Margherita Costa a Parigi," 38) notes a parallel with Marino's autobiographical verse in the *Lira* that describe his own departure from his "paternal roof" ("paterni tetti," that is, Naples) and arrival in Florence. Marino, *La lira*, I:233–4.

86 "neghi a me quell che negar non osi / a straniera vaghezza"; Costa, *La selva di Diana*, 87. Bianchi hypothesizes that this rival may be Leonora Baroni, though the two had likely crossed paths before.

87 Costa, *La selva di Diana*, 93. Contrast with Gaspara Stampa, who states that she, like Icarus, "dared so much" ("osar molto"). Stampa, *The Complete Poems*, 166–7.

88 "Sono gl'honori entro gl'horror sommersi"; Costa, *La selva di Diana*, 88–9.

89 Costa, *La selva di Diana*, 90.

90 Costa, *La selva di Diana*, 92, 90.

91 See chapter 5, 16–17.

92 "traduzzione estemporale… scherzo dell'istesso autore"; Costa, *Lo stipo*, 141.

93 Costa, *Lo stipo*, 141; Gaudenzi, *La galleria dell'inclito Marino*, 153–60.

94 "col volto irato, vanne, o Costa, / vanne da me"; Costa, *Lo stipo*, 142.

95 "fredda nell'amore." Costa, *Lo stipo*, 142.

96 See Brunelli, "Gaudenzi, Paganino."

97 Ovid, *Tristia*, II.313.

98 "Non brama ch'altra donna ivi risieda / [...] / [E] sdegna comun con l'altre haver la preda"; Costa, *Lo stipo*, 145.

99 "Plettro frale [...] / Ella è di mille Apolli unica reggia"; Costa, *Lo stipo*, 145.

100 "per bere in Arno eternità verace / lo scostarsi dal Tebro a Costa piace"; Costa, *Lo stipo*, 146.

101 "schiere d'amanti"; Costa, *La selva di cipressi*, 230.

102 Costa, *La selva di cipressi*, 233.

103 "ludibrio del dolor, scherno del mondo"; Costa, *La selva di cipressi*, 235.

104 Costa, *La selva di cipressi*, 237. Emphasis is mine.

105 Costa, *La selva di cipressi*, 245.

106 "Cangiar di ciel nulla mi giova"; Costa, *La selva di cipressi*, 242.

107 "Muterò servitù, cangirò regno / [...] / Ti lascio Aminta, e vado a ciel straniero / più ch'a me questo fusse [...] / Forse lunge da l'Arno men severo / il ciel sarammi, e sorte havrò men ria"; Costa, *La selva di cipressi*, 247.

108 Costa, *La selva di cipressi*, 254.

109 "se 'l Fato è rio, / Ha le sventure sue pari ad un Dio"; Costa, *La selva di cipressi*, 256.

110 Cox, *Women's Writing in Italy*, 226; Cox, "Declino e caduta della scrittura femminile," 157–9.

111 "già credei, come donna, o mia follia, / ch'ogni alto core del mio plettro frale / gioir dovesse, e che de l'opra mia / godimento trahesse al merto eguale"; Costa, *La selva di cipressi*, 253.

112 "col soccorso / Vostro m'havete messa in un periglio / Che son quas' un'agnella in man d'un orso." Costa, "Le sette giornate," fol. 271r.

113 "Io v'ubidij perché… / simai il vostro amore." Costa, "Le sette giornate," 272v.

114 "fallace e dipinto." Costa, "Le sette giornate," 272v.

115 Costa, "Le sette giornate," 272v–73r.

116 Costa, "Le sette giornate," 273v–74r.

117 See chapter 2, 61–2.

118 "hormai conosco il cortegiano stile"; "Bella donna si duole della corte mentre il suo amante per servire in essa si parte da lei, e la lascia inferma"; Costa, *La chitarra*, 309–15. The lines are found on pp. 312–13, citation on 313.

119 "fingendo parlar di te per gioco, / procuran contro te le tue rovine"; "l'invida tien sicura sede"; "un fido cor divien deriso"; Costa, *La chitarra*, 314–15.

120 "in corte non sta ben, chi non sa fingere"; Costa, *La chitarra*, 315.

121 The poem echoes Aretino's *Lamento de uno cortigiano* (in which envy is similarly described as the lynchpin of courtly life); Aretino, *Operette politiche e satiriche*, 2:51–60. See also Faini, "Un'opera dimenticata di Pietro Aretino."

122 "E che peggio può dirsi, oh me dolente! / Che Cortegiano, ohime, che Corte, hai [*sic*] lasso?"; Costa, *Lo stipo*, 227.

123 "invidia alberga e nacque"; Costa, *Lo stipo*, 224.

124 Costa, *Lo stipo*, 237.

125 "intenta ad arricchire"; Costa, *Lo stipo*, 5.

126 "schiuma d'inferno"; Costa, *Lo stipo*, 242.

127 See also Coller, *Women, Rhetoric, and Drama*, 42–5.

128 Chapter 2, 65.

129 Costa, *The Buffoons*, 86–7, lines 46–51.

130 Costa, *The Buffoons* I.vii.62–7.

131 Costa, *The Buffoons* III.i.41–51.

132 "un'arte benedetta"; Costa, *The Buffoons* III.i.52.

133 Costa, *The Buffoons* III.i.88–92. Tordo specifies that the Armenians operate under the Uffizi.

134 See chapter 2, 74–5.

135 "Non si trova il signore senza il buffone, né il buffone senza il signore"; Garzoni, *La piazza universale*, 352.

136 "strade e mezzi"; Ricci, *Il Tedeschino*, 87.

137 Ricci, *Il Tedeschino*, 89.

138 "ad onor de' buoni e veri buffoni ed ad onta de' falsi ed infami"; Ricci, *Il Tedeschino*, 105.

139 Ricci, *Il Tedeschino*, 72.

140 "Voi mi pigliate in cambio, non son io / Un buffonaccio da tutti mistieri. / Son buon trattenitore, omo scaltrito / … / Bench'io faccia il buffone, / Ne la mia villa nacqui cavaliero"; Costa, *The Buffoons*, II.iii.45–7, 57–8, 210–11.

141 On the buffoonish gags and dialogue, see Strappini, *La tragedia del buffone*, 264–71.

142 Costa, *The Buffoons*, I.xi.85–9. On Ricci's movements, *Il Tedeschino*, 71–73.

143 "Sempre per util mio, / Ho cangiato mantello"; "quella che si faccia in corte"; Costa, *The Buffoons*, I.x.79–80, 93.

144 Costa, "Le sette giornate," 297r.

145 "solitaria ancella… in angusto claustro, angusta cella"; Costa, "Le sette giornate," 297v–98r.

146 "senza nessuno aiuto… e senza nessuno per me"; "vedova e povera virtuosa"; BAV, Chigi I.vii.273, fol. 125r. See Introduction, 20.

147 *Gran Prence, a te, che di Quirino al trono*, BAV, Chigi I.vii.273, fol. 126r.

148 "senzza [*sic*] nessuno per noi, e tra gente che ne vorrebeno anichilare affatto e levorne quel poco che abbiamo ricuperato"; 17 June 1657, ASF MdP 5466, c. 341r–v; also transcribed in Mamone, *Mattias de' Medici*, 557 (#1167).

149 ASF MdP 5465, c. 679r; also transcribed in Mamone, *Mattias de' Medici*, #1093.

150 "Signora di se stessa… Da gentil donna vivo, et oscurare / il mio nome non può l'invida istessa / che fermato il pensiero e il piè securo, / poco dell'altrui dire mi affanno e curo"; Costa, *La chitarra*, 394.

Conclusion

1 Virginia Cox labels these periods of "Affirmation (1580–1620)" and "Backlash (1590–1650)" in *Women's Writing in Italy*.

2 "donna non men savia che dotta, e molto versata nelle lettere amene [...] non solamente sormontò la condizione del donnesco ingegno; ma non pochi rimatori anche rinomati suoi coetanei, di manière che a gran ragione fu universalmente applaudita"; Crescimbeni, *L'istoria della volgar poesia*, 202.

3 "Doppo un lungo combattimento di variati accidenti della mia vita, la mia avversa fortuna sazia, o per dir meglio, stanca di più tiranneggiarmi, m'ha permesso su l'Arno quella quiete, che su 'l Tebro mi negò sempre"; Costa, *La chitarra* dedication.

4 "il voler cantar su l'Arno mentre io nacqui su 'l Tebro. Ma perché ho l'animo spogliato d'ogni prosunzione, e del tutto lontano di voler pareggiare il virtuoso e lodevol modo ch'ivi si tiene nel comporre; mi sono ardita di dare alla luce questo picciolo volume"; "se non gradite almeno compatite; e come parto di donna … protette"; Costa, *La chitarra*, letter to the reader.

5 Costa, *La chitarra*, †1r. Robarts ("Challenging Male Authored Poetry," 90–1) also discusses this sonnet, rightly connecting it to the volume's *caramogi* and *zerbini* poems, discussed in chapter 2, 70–1.

6 "Sempre per util mio, / Ho cangiato mantello"; "quella che si faccia in corte"; Costa, *The Buffoons*, I.x.79–80, 93.

7 Croce, *Nuovi saggi*, 11.

8 Metlica, *Le seduzioni della pace*, 13.

Bibliography

Primary Sources

Manuscript Sources

FLORENCE
Archivio dell'Opera del Duomo
Registro delle fedi di battesimo di San Giovanni, Reg. 262.
Registro delle fedi di battesimo di San Giovanni, Reg. 263.

Archivio di Stato di Firenze (ASF)
Mediceo del principato (MdP) 1503. Letters of Desiderio Montemagni, 1649–50.
Mediceo del principato 1505. Letters of Desiderio Montemagni, 1652.
Mediceo del principato 4653. Letters from Giovan Battista Barducci in France, 1647–8.
Mediceo del principato 5320. Letters to Giovan Carlo de' Medici, 1652.
Mediceo del principato 5458. Letters to Mattias de' Medici, 1656.
Mediceo del principato 5465. Letters to Mattias de' Medici, 1657.
Mediceo del principato 5466. Letters to Mattias de' Medic, 1657.
Mediceo del principato 5561. Letters to Leopoldo de' Medici, 1646–74.
Mediceo del principato 6379.
Mediceo del principato 6380.
Misc. medicea 504, Inserts 1–30.
Settimanni, Francesco. "Memorie Fiorentine," Manoscritti 134 (VIII.1626–30)

Biblioteca Nazionale Centrale di Firenze (BNCF)
"Al serenissimo Ferdinando Secondo gran duca di Toscana venuto a Roma incognito."
    II.II.277.
"Bisdosso overo Diario di Francesco Bonazini." Magl. XXV.42.
Cervoni, Isabella. "Canzone… sopra 'l felicissimo natale del serenissimo principe di
    Toscana." Magl. VII.138.

Costa, Margherita. "Festa reale per ballo de' cavalli." 1640. II.II.371.

Inventory of Vittoria della Rovere's Library. Magl. X.44.

Marmi, Anton Francesco. "Miscellanea di diverse notizie letterarie e storiche raccolte per lo più dagli eruditissimi discorsi del Signor Antonio Magliabechi." Magl. VIII.15 and Magl. VIII.16.

Notes of Antonio Magliabechi. Magl. IX.14.

"Relazione degli onori fatti da [...] imperat[atore] a Ferdinando II de' Medici, Gran Duca di Toscana, in Praga l'anno 1628," Magl. XXVII.40.

Rime varie. II.II.295

"Vita, carcere, et azioni e morte del Capitano Tiberio Squilletti da Catanzano, detto comunemente Fra Paolo." Arch. Capponi 139, fols. 99r–116r.

LUCCA

Biblioteca Statale

Coreglia, Isabetta. "Raccolta di varie composizioni della sig[no]Ra Elisabetta Coreglia di Lucca detta Nerina," MS 205.

PARIS

Archives du Ministère des Affaires Étrangères

Lettre du grand duc de Toscane du 23 julliet 1647 à Mazarin. Aff. Etr. Toscane, 128CP/5.

Bibliothèque Mazarine

Puget de La Serre, Jean. "Temple de la gloire." MS 2212.

Bibliothèque Nationale de France

Andreini, Giovan Battista. "La Ferinda." MS italien 1088.

Letter of 22 May 1647 from Cardinal Mazarin to the Marquis de Fontenay. Dupuy 775.

ROME

Archivio Doria Pamphili (ADP)

Costa, Margherita. "Le sette giornate, o Vero il viaggio di Loreto della Signora Margherita Costa al S[Ignor] C[Onte]." c. 1644. Fondo Archiviolo, XX, busta 122, fols. 268r–297v.

"Miscellanea: Idea critica degli autori greci e latini indice della libreria del principe D. Camillo Sen. Tom. III." Fondo Archiviolo 106.

Archivio di Stato di Roma (ASR)

Notai dell'A.C. Testamenti 82, fols. 343r–345r.

Trenta notari capitolini, Officio 9, settembre 1636.

Biblioteca Apostolica Vaticana (BAV)

Avvisi. Cappon. 63.

Avvisi, 1646–1651. Barb. lat. 6366.

Costa, Margherita. "Cecilia martire." Barb. lat. 4069.

– Letter and poem to Mario Chigi, 4 May 1657. Chigi I.VII.273.

– "Sonetto stampato... all'ecc. principe di Palestrina per la festa a cavallo fatta da S.E. alla maestà di Cristina Regina di Svezia." Archivio Barberini, Indice 1, 1088.

Eclissi, Antonio. "Forma della chiesa profanata di S.to Urbano papa primo posto nel loco detto La Caffarella [...]" Barb. lat. 4402, fols. 1r–19r. Painted illustrations.

"*L'Orfeo* / Personaggi dell'opera." Barb. lat. 4059.

Marazzoli, Marco. Musical scores. Chigi Q.VIII.177.9.

"Pitture della Chiesa di S. Urbano alla Caffarella." Barb. lat. 4408, fols. 51r–66r.

"Racconto istorico del trionfo in Vaticano di Christina Regina di Svetia alla santità di N[ostro] Si[gnore] Alessandro PP VII, Roma." Urb. lat. 1681.

"Ragguaglio della festa de' caroselli fata dal Sig[no]re Principe di Palestrina alla Regina di Svezia." Barb. lat. 4913.

BIBLIOTECA CASANATENSE

Ameyden, Teodoro. "Diario della città e corte di Roma notato da deone hora temi Dio." MS 1832.

TURIN

Archivio di Stato di Torino, Castello (AST-Castello)

Castiglione, Valeriano. "Historia della reggenza di Madama reale Christina di Francia, duchessa di Savoia, regina di Ciprio, tutrice delli serenissimi Duchi Francesco Giacino e Carlo Emanuele II." 1656. Storia della real casa, m. 17.

Lettere ministri, Roma, m. 35.

Lettere ministri, Roma, m. 37.

Lettere ministri, Roma, m. 38.

Lettere, principi diversi, m. 18.

Archivio di Stato di Torino, Piave (AST-Piave)

Patenti controllo finanza. 1645–6.

Patenti controllo finanza. 1646–7.

Biblioteca Nazionale Universitaria di Torino (BNUT)

"Dono del re del'Alpi a Madama reale, festa per il giorno natale, li diece febraro MDCXLV, ballato in Rivoli." Q.V.60.

"Il dono del re dell'Alpi." Musical scores. Qm.II.84 (A–D).

VENICE

Archivio di Stato di Venezia (ASV)

Faustini papers. Scuola Grande San Marco, b. 112.

Notarile, Atti, b. 3551, fols. 107v–108r.

PRINT SOURCES

Abriani, Paolo. *Poesie*. Venice: Francesco Valvasense, 1663.

Adimari, Alessandro. *La Melpomene*. Florence: Massi e Landi, 1640.

— *La Tersicore, o vero Scherzi, e paradossi poetici sopra la beltà delle donne fra' difetti ancora, ammirabili, e vaghe*. Florence: Massi e Landi, 1637.

Allacci, Leone. *Drammaturgia*. Rome: Il Mascardi, 1666.

— *Drammaturgia di Lione Allacci accresciuta e continuata fino all'anno MDCCLV*. Venice: Giambatista Pasquali, 1755.

Andreini, Isabella. *Mirtilla, A Pastoral*. Edited by Valeria Finucci. Translated by Julie Kisacky. Toronto: Iter; Tempe: Arizona Center for Medieval and Renaissance Studies, 2018.

— *Rime*. Paris: Claudio de Monstr'œil, 1603.

— *Selected Poems of Isabella Andreini*. Edited by Anne MacNeil. Translated by James Wyatt Cook. Oxford: Scarecrow Press, 2005.

Anguillara, Giovanni Andrea dell'. *Le metamorfosi d'Ovidio*. Edited by Alessio Cotugno. Manziana (Rome): Vecchiarelli Editore, 2019.

Aretino, Pietro. *Operette politiche e satiriche*. Edited by Marco Faini. Vol. 2. Rome: Salerno Editrice, 2012.

Ariosto, Ludovico. *Orlando furioso*. Edited by Lanfranco Caretti. Turin: Einaudi, 1992.

Armanni, Vincenzo. *Della nobile & antica famiglia de' Capizucchi, baroni romani*. Rome: Nicol'Angelo Tinassi, 1668.

Baldinucci, Filippo. *Notizie de' professori del disegno da Cimabue in qua*. Florence: Batellli e Compagni, 1846.

Bardi, Ferdinando. *Descrizione delle feste fatte in Firenze per le reali nozze de' serenissimi sposi Ferdinando II, gran duca di Toscana, e Vittoria, principessa d'Urbino*. Florence: Zanobi Pignoni, 1637.

Baronio, Cesare. *Annales ecclesiastici*. 12 vols. Rome: Ex Typographia Vaticana, 1588–1607.

Bergalli, Luisa. *Componimenti poetici delle più illustri rimatrici d'ogni secolo*. 2 vols. Venice: Antonio Mora, 1726.

Boccaccio, Giovanni. *Boccaccio's Exposition on Dante's Comedy*. Translated by Michael Papio. Toronto: University of Toronto Press, 2009.

— *Famous Women*. Edited and translated by Virginia Brown. Cambridge, MA: Harvard University Press, 2001.

— *Genealogy of the Pagan Gods*. Edited and translated by Jon Solomon. 2 vols. Cambridge, MA: Harvard University Press, 2011.

Boccalini, Traiano. *Ragguagli di Parnaso e scritti minori*. Edited by Luigi Firpo. 3 vols. Bari: Gius. Laterza, 1948.

Bosio, Antonio. *Historia Passionis b. Caeciliae virginis, Valeriani, Tiburtii et Maximi martyrum*. Rome: Apud Stephanum Paulinum, 1600.

Capponi, Giovanni. *Amore prigioniero in Delo, torneo fatto da' signori academici Torbidi in Bologna li XX di marzo MDCXXVIII*. Bologna: Per gli heredi di Vittorio Benacci, 1628.

Caracciolo, Pasquale. *La gloria del cavallo*. Venice: Giolito, 1566.

Carteggi italiani inediti o rari, antichi e moderni, edited by Filippo Orlando. Florence: Fratelli Bocca, 1892.

Castellamonte, Amedeo. *Venaria reale: Palazzo di piacere, e di caccia...* Turin: Bartolomeo Zapatta, 1674.

Castelletti, Bastiano. *La trionfatrice Cecilia vergine, e martire romana*. Florence: Filippo Giunti, 1594.

Castiglione, Baldassarre. *Il cortigiano*. Edited by Amedeo Quondam. Milan: Mondadori, 2002.

– *The Book of the Courtier*. Edited by Daniel Javitch. New York: W.W. Norton, 2002.

Castiglione, Valeriano. *Le pompe torinesi nel ritorno dell'Altezza Reale di Carlo Emanuele II, duca di Savoia, principe di Piemonte, re di Cipro, ecc.* Turin: Per Gio. Giacomo Rustis, 1645.

Catullus. *The Poems of Catullus*. Translated by Guy Lee. Oxford: Clarendon Press, 1990.

Cavalli, Francesco. *La Calisto*. Edited by Jennifer Williams Brown. Collegium Musicum, Yale University, Second Series. Middleton, WI: A-R Editions, 2007.

– *La Calisto*. Edited by Álvaro Torrente and Nicola Badolato. Kassel, Basel, London, New York and Prague: Bärenreiter-Verlag, 2011.

Chiabrera, Gabriello. *Canzonette, rime varie, dialoghi*. Edited by Luigi Negri. Turin: UTET, 1964.

Cinelli Calvoli, Giovanni. *Biblioteca volante*. Vol. 2. Venice: Giambattista Albrizzi, 1735.

Costa, Margherita. *Al serenissimo Ferdinando II, gran duca di Toscana, per la festa di San Gio. Batista*. Venice, 1638.

– *Al serenissimo Principe Gio. Carlo di Toscana per la carica di generalissimo del mare*. Florence: Stamperia nuova del Massi e Landi, [n.d.].

– *Alla serenissima Margherita de Medici, Duchessa di Parma, per l'arrivo in Fiorenza*. Venice, 1638.

– *Alla serenissima Vittoria della Rovere, gran duchessa di Toscana, per la festa di San Gio. Batista*. Venice, 1638.

– *All'altezza serenissima di Ferdinando Secondo gran duca di Toscana, nel giorno della sua nascita*. Florence: Stamperia de' Landi, 1655.

– *Cecilia martire*. Rome: Mascardi, 1644.

– *Festa reale per balleto a cavallo*. Paris: Sebastiano Cramoisy, 1647.

– *Flora feconda*. Florence: Massi e Landi, 1640.

– *Gl'amori della luna*. Venice: Per il Giuliani, 1654.

– *Il violino*. [Frankfurt]: [Daniel Wastch], 1638.

– *Istoria del viaggio d'Alemagna del serenissimo gran duca di Toscana Ferdinando Secondo*. [Venice], 1628.

– *La chitarra*. [Frankfurt]: [Daniel Wastch], 1638.

– *La Flora feconda*. Florence: Massi e Landi, 1640.

– *La selva di cipressi*. Florence: Massi e Landi, 1640.

– *La selva di Diana*. Paris: Sebastiano Cramoisy, 1647.

– *La tromba di Parnaso*. Paris: Sebastiano Cramoisy, 1647.

– *Lettere amorose*. [Venice], 1639.

– *Love Letters. A Bilingual Edition*. Edited and translated by Sara Díaz. Forthcoming.

– "Li buffoni." In *Commedia dell'arte*, edited by Siro Ferrone, 1:235–359. Milan: Mursia, 1986.

– *Li buffoni*. Florence: Massi e Landi, 1641.

– *Lo stipo*. [Venice], 1639.

– *Per l'incendio di Pitti*. Florence: Stamperia nuova, 1638.

– *The Buffoons, A Ridiculous Comedy: A Bilingual Edition*. Edited and translated by Sara Díaz and Jessica Goethals. Toronto: Iter; Tempe: Arizona Center for Medieval and Renaissance Studies, 2018.

– *Voice of a Virtuosa and Courtesan: Selected Poems of Margherita Costa*. Edited by Natalia Costa-Zalessow. Translated by Joan E. Borrelli. New York: Bordighera Press, 2015.

Crescimbeni, Giovanni Mario. *L'istoria della volgar poesia*. 6 vols. Venice: Lorenzo Basegio, 1730.

Dante Alighieri. *Inferno*. Translated by Robert and Jean Hollander. New York: Anchor Books, 2000.

– *Purgatory*. Translated by Robert and Jean Hollander. New York: Anchor Books, 2003.

D'Agliè, Filippo. *Le delitie, relatione della vigna di Madama reale Christiana di Francia…* Gio. Giacomo Rustis, 1667.

De Blasi, Jolanda, ed. *Antologia delle scrittrici italiane dalle origini al 1800*. Florence: Nemi, 1930.

Erythraeus, Janus Nicius [ps., Gian Vittorio Rossi]. *Eudemiae*. Amsterdam: Iodocum Kalcovium et socios, 1645.

– *Gian Vittorio Rossi's "Eudemiae libri decem."* Edited and translated by Jennifer K. Nelsen. Tübingen: Narr Francke Attempto, 2021.

– *Pinacotheca imaginum illustrium doctrinae vel ingenii laude virorum*. 3 vols. Amsterdam: Iodocum Kalcovium et socios, 1645-48.

Ferrero, Giuseppe Guido, ed. *Marino e i marinisti*. Milan, Naples: Riccardo Ricciardi Editore, 1954.

Fiaschi, Cesare. *Trattato dell'imbrigliare, maneggiare, et ferrare cavalli*. Bologna: Anselmo Giaccarelli, 1556.

Fontanella, Girolamo. *Nove cieli*. Naples: Roberto Mollo, 1640.

Franceschi, Lorenzo. *Ballo e giostra de' venti nelle nozze del serenissimo prinicipe e della serenissima principessa di Toscana, arciduchessa d'Austria*. Florence: Giunti, 1608.

Franco, Veronica. *Poems and Selected Letters*. Edited and translated by Ann Rosalind Jones and Margaret F. Rosenthal. Chicago: University of Chicago Press, 1998.

Galilei, Galileo. *Dialogo… sopra i due massimi sistemi del mondo tolemaico, e copernicano*. Florence: Per Gio. Batista Landini, 1632.

– *Le opere*. Edited by Antonio Favaro. 20 vols. Florence: Giunti Barbera, 1890.

– *Opere*. 2 vols. Bologna: Dozza, 1656.

– *Sidereus Nuncius, or the Sidereal Messenger*. Translated by Albert Van Helden. Chicago: University of Chicago Press, 1989.

Galilei, Galileo, and Christoph Scheiner. *On Sunspots*. Translated by Eileen Reeves and Albert Van Helden. Chicago: University of Chicago Press, 2010.

Gallonio, Antonio. *Historia delle sante vergini romane*. Rome: Ascanio e Girolamo Donangeli, 1591.

Garella, Nanni. *Li buffoni*. Bologna: Luca Sossella editore, 2018.

Garzoni, Tommaso. *La piazza universale di tutte le professioni del mondo*. Venice: Giovanni Battista Somasco, 1585.

Gaudenzi, Paganino. *La galleria dell'inclito Marino*. Pisa: Ferdinando Chelli e Francesco Stefanelli, 1648.

Getto, Giovanni, ed. *Opere scelte di Giovan Battista Marino e dei marinisti*. Turin: UTET, 1962.

Gianni, Angelo, ed. *Anch'esse "quasi simili a Dio": Le donne nella storia della letteratura italiana, in gran parte ignote o misconosciute, dalle origini alla fine dell'Ottocento*. Viareggio: M. Baroni, 1997.

Gigli, Giacinto. *Diario di Roma*. Edited by Manlio Barberito. 2 vols. Rome: Colombo, 1994.

Giuglaris, Luigi. *Funerale fatto nel duomo di Torino alla gloriosa memoria [di]… Vittorio Amedeo Duca di Savoia*. Turin: Eredi di G. D. Tarino, 1638.

Grazzini, Anton Francesco ("Il Lasca"). *Primo libro dell'opere burlesche*. Florence: Bernardo Giunta, 1548.

– *Tutti i trionfi, carri, mascherate o canti carnascialeschi andati per Firenze dal tempo del magnifico Lorenzo de' Medici, fino all'anno 1559*. 2 vols. Lucca: Benedini, 1750.

Grisone, Federico. *Gli ordini di cavalcare*. Naples: Suganappo, 1550.

Guarini, Battista. *Il pastor fido*. Edited by Elisabetta Selmi. Venice: Marsilio, 1999.

Guidiccioni, Lelio. *Rime*. Rome: Manelfo Manelfi, 1637.

Harrach, Ernst Adalbert von. *Die diarien und tagzettel des kardinals Ernst Adalbert von Harrach (1598–1667)*. Edited by Katrin Keller and Alessandro Catalano. 7 vols. Vienna: Böhlau, 2010.

Holstenius, Lucas. *Index Bibliothecae qua Franciscus Barberinus S. R. E. Cardinalis vicecancellarius magnificentissimas suae familiae ad Quirinalem aedes magnificentiores reddidit*. 3 vols. Rome: Typis Barberinis, 1681.

I caramogi palio e mascherata fatta in Firenze il dì 26 d'agosto 1629. Florence: Zanobi Pignoni, 1629.

Jonson, Ben. *Volpone and Other Plays*. New York: Penguin Books, 2004.

Knox, John. *The First Blast of the Trumpet against the Monstrous Regiment of Women*. Geneva, 1558.

Le Moyne, Pierre. *La gallerie des femmes fortes*. Paris: Antoine de Sommaville, 1647.

Livy. *Ab urbe condita*. Translated by B.O. Foster. 8th ed. Cambridge, MA: Harvard University Press, 1976.

Loredano, Gio. Francesco. *Delle bizzarrie academiche. Parte seconda*. Bologna: Carlo Venero, 1646.

Mamone, Sara, ed. *Mattias de' Medici serenissimo mecenate dei virtuosi: Notizie di spettacolo nei carteggi medicei. Carteggio di Mattias de' Medici (1629–1667)*. Florence: Le Lettere, 2013.

— *Serenissimi fratelli principi impresari. Notizie di spettacolo nel carteggi medicei. Carteggi di Giovan Carlo de' Medici e di Desiderio Montemagni suo segretario (1628–1664)*. Florence: Le Lettere, 2003.

Mandosio, Prospero. *Bibliotheca romana, seu romanorum scriptorum centuriae*. Vol. 2. Rome: Ignati de Lazzaris, 1682.

Maoro, Giovanni Domenico. *Descrittione della chiesa parocchiale del Santissimo Salvatore della corte di Roma, nel rione di Trastevere, divisa in due parti*. Velletri: Pietro Guglielmo Caffasso, 1677.

Marinella, Lucrezia. *Exhortations to Women and to Others If They Please*. Edited and translated by Laura Benedetti. Toronto: Iter and the Centre for Renaissance and Reformation Studies, 2012.

— *La Colomba sacra: Poema heroico*. Venice: Giovanni Battista Ciotti, 1595.

— *Vita del serafico et glorioso S. Francesco e Le vittorie di Francesco il Serafico. Li passi gloriosi della diva Chiara*. Edited by Armando Maggi. Ravenna: Longo editore, 2018.

Marino, Giovan Battista. *Dicerie sacre e La strage de gl'innocenti*, edited by Giovanni Pozzi. Turin: Einaudi, 1960.

— *La lira*. Edited by Maurizio Slawinski. 3 vols. Turin: Edizioni RES, 2007.

— *Lettere*. Edited by Marziano Guglielminetti. Turin: Einaudi, 1966.

— *Rime lugubri*. Edited by Vincenzo Guercio. Modena: F.C. Panini, 1999.

Mascardi, Agostino. *Dell'arte historica*. Rome: Giacomo Facciotti, 1636.

Melzo, Lodovico. *Regole militari del cavalier Melzo sopra il governo e servitio della cavalleria*. Antwerp: Gioachimo Trognæsio, 1611.

Ménestrier, Claude-François. *Des représentations en musique anciennes et modernes*. Paris: René Guignard, 1681.

Moniglia, Giovanni Andrea. *Il mondo festeggiante: Balletto a cavallo...* Florence: Nella stamperia di S.A.S., 1661.

Morandini, Giuliana, ed. *Sospiri e palpiti: Scrittrici italiane del Seicento*. Genoa: Marietti, 2001.

Morassini, Lorenzo. *Rime*. Florence: Filippo Papini & Francesco Sabatini, 1641.

Motteville, Françoise de. *Memoirs of Madame de Motteville on Anne of Austria and Her Court*. Translated by Katharine Prescott Wormeley. 3 vols. Boston: Hardy, Pratt, 1902.

Nolfi, Vincenzo. *Ginipedia, overo Avvertimenti civili per donna nobile*. Venice: Heredi di Gio. Guerigli, 1631.

Ovid. *Fasti*. Translated by James George Frazer. 2nd ed. Cambridge, MA: Harvard University Press, 1989.

— *Heroides. Amores*. Translated by Grant Showerman. Cambridge, MA: Harvard University Press, 1914.

— *Metamorphoses*. Translated by Frank J. Miller. 2 vols. Cambridge, MA: Harvard University Press, 1916.

— *The Art of Love and Other Poems*. Translated by J.H. Mozley. Cambridge, MA: Harvard University Press, 1929.

— *Tristia. Ex Ponto*. Translated by A.L. Wheeler. Cambridge, MA: Harvard University Press, 1924.

Pentolini, Francesco. *Le donne illustre*. Livorno: Gio. Vincenzo Falorni, 1776.

Pizan, Christine de. *The Book of the City of Ladies*. Translated by Earl Jeffrey Richards. New York: Persea Books, 1982.

Priorato, Galeazzo Gualdo. *Historia della sacra real Maestà di Christina Alessandra Regina di Svetia*. Venice: Per il Baba, 1656.

Puget de La Serre, Jean. *L'Isthoire* [sic] *et les portraits des imperatrices, des reynes, et des illustres princesses de l'auguste maison d'Austriche, qui ont porté le nom d'Anne*. Paris: P. de Bresche, 1648.

Quadrio, Francesco Saverio. *Ragione e storia d'ogni poesia*. 7 vols. Milan: Francesco Agnelli, 1739.

Ricci, Bernardino. *Il Tedeschino, overo Difesa dell'arte del cavalier del piacere. Con l'epistolario e altri documenti*. Edited by Teresa Megale. Florence: Le Lettere, 1995.

Rinuccini, Camillo. *Descrizione delle feste fatte nelle reali nozze de' serenissimi prinicipi di Toscana duca Cosimo de' Medici e Maria Maddalena arciduchessa d'Austria*. Florence: Giunti, 1608.

Rinuccini, Ottavio. *Arianna*. Florence: Giunti, 1608.

Risposta de begl'imbusti a' caramogi. Palio, e mascherata fatta in Firenze il dì 28 d'agosto 1629. Florence: Pietro Cecconcelli, 1629.

Rondinelli, Francesco. *Relazione del contagio stato in Firenze l'anno 1630 e 1633*. Florence: Gio. Batista Landini, 1634.

Ronna, Antoine, ed. *Parnaso italiano: Poeti italiani contemporanei maggiori e minori*. Paris: Baudry, 1843.

Sabbattini, Nicola. *Pratica di fabricar scene e machine ne' teatri*. Ravenna: Pietro de' Paoli e Gio. Battista Giovannelli, 1638.

Salvadori, Andrea. *Guerra d'amore, festa del serenissimo gran duca di Toscana Cosimo Secondo*. Florence: Zanobi Pignoni, 1615.

– *La Flora, overo Il natal de' fiori*. Florence: Pietro Cecconcelli, 1628.

– *Poesie*. 2 vols. Rome: Michele Ercole, 1668.

– *Sonetti... in lode del campo imperiale, e in morte del re di Svezia*. Florence: Cecconcelli, 1633.

Scala, Flaminio. *Il teatro delle favole rappresentative*. Edited by Ferruccio Marotti. 2 vols. Milan: Il Polifilo, 1976.

Scelta di lettere amorose di Ferrante Pallavicino, Luca Asserino, Margarita Costa, Girolamo Parabosco et d'altri eruditi scrittori Italiani. Venice: Giacomo Bortoli, 1656.

Sempronio, Giovanni Leone. *La selva poetica*. Bologna: Clemente Ferroni, 1633.

Spezzani, Antonio. *Rappresentatione di S. Cecilia*. Bologna: Gio. Rossi, 1581.

Stampa, Gaspara. *The Complete Poems: The 1554 Edition of the "Rime," A Bilingual Edition*. Edited by Jane Tylus and Troy Tower. Translated by Jane Tylus. Chicago: University of Chicago Press, 2010.

Strozzi, Giulio. *I cinque fratelli sonetti...* Venice: Il Deuchino, 1628.

Successi del mondo. Turin: Pietro Antonio Socini.

Talenti, Crisostomo. *Dialogo... per le felicissime nozze de' serenissimi di Toscana*. Florence: Cristofano Marescotti, 1608.

Tarabotti, Arcangela. *Antisatire: In Defense of Women, against Francesco Buoninsegni.* Edited and translated by Elissa Weaver. Toronto: Iter; Tempe: Arizona Medieval and Renaissance Studies, 2020.

Tarde, Jean. *Borbonia Sidera.* Paris: Apud Ioannem Gesselin, 1620.

Tasso, Torquato. *Aminta, A Pastoral Play.* Edited and translated by Charles Jernigan and Irene Marchegiani Jones. New York: Italica Press, 2000.

– *Discorso della virtù feminile e donnesca.* Edited by Maria Luisa Doglio. Palermo: Sellerio editore, 1997.

– *Gerusalemme liberata.* Edited by Lanfranco Caretti. 2nd ed. Turin: Einaudi, 1993.

– *Rime.* Edited by Franco Gavazzeni and Vercingetorige Martignone. Alessandria: Edizioni dell'Orso, 2004.

Tesauro, Emanuele. *Panegirici.* Turin: Bartolomeo Zavatta, 1659.

Theatrum Statuum Regiae Celsitudinis Sabaudiae Ducis, Pedemontii Principis, Cypri Regis. Amsterdam: Joan Blaeu, 1682.

Tigliamochi degli Albizi, Barbera. *Ascanio errante.* Florence: Stamperia de' Landini, 1640.

Tondini, Giovanni Battista. *Delle lettere di uomini illustri pubblicate ora per la prima volta.* 2 vols. Macerata: Bartolomeo Capitani, 1782.

Valentino, Giambattista. *La Cecala napoletana.* Naples: Luc'Antonio di Fusco, 1974.

Vida, Marco Girolamo. *Christiad.* Translated by James Gardner. Cambridge, MA: Harvard University Press, 2009.

Villifranchi, Giovanni. *Descrizzione della barriera e della mascherata fatte in Firenze a' XVII e a' XIX di febbraio 1613.* Florence: Bartolommeo Sermartelli e fratelli, 1613.

Virgil. *Aeneid Book XII.* Edited by Richard Tarrant. Cambridge: Cambridge University Press, 2012.

– *The Aeneid.* Translated by Robert Fitzgerald. 3rd ed. New York: Random House, 1983.

Vittori, Loreto. *La Galatea.* Edited by Thomas D. Dunn. Middleton, WI: A-R Editions, 2002.

Voragine, Jacobus de. *Golden Legend: Readings on the Saints.* Translated by William Granger Ryan. Princeton, NJ: Princeton University Press, 2012.

Xenophon. "On the Art of Horsemanship." In *Scripta Minora*, translated by E.C. Marchant, 2nd ed., 295–363. Cambridge, MA: Harvard University Press, 1946.

Secondary Sources

Acton, Harold. *The Last Medici.* London: Faber & Faber, 1930.

Adami, Giuseppe. "Sham Fights and Mock Sieges: An Enduring Antiquity in the Medieval and Pre-Modern Representation of War." *Drammaturgia* XVI, no. 6 (2019): 7–47.

Ademollo, Alessandro. *I primi fasti della musica italiana a Parigi (1645–1662).* Milan: Ricordi, 1884.

Aercke, Kristiaan. *Gods of Play: Baroque Festive Performances as Rhetorical Discourse.* Albany: State University of New York Press, 1994.

Aguilar, Mónica García. "Margherita Costa y la comedia bufonesca del siglo XVII." In *Escritoras italianas fuera del canon*, edited by Daniele Cerrato, 181–96. Seville: Benilde Ediciones, 2017.

Alberti, Maria. "Le 'barriere' di Cosimo II granduca di Toscana." In *Musica in torneo nell'Italia del Seicento*, edited by Paolo Fabbri, 81–102. Lucca: LIM Editrice, 1999.

Amati, Girolamo, ed. *Bibliografia romana: Notizie della vita e delle opere degli scrittori romani dal secolo XI fino ai nostri giorni*. Vol. 1. Rome: Tipografia eredi Botta, 1880.

Andrews, Richard. *Scripts and Scenarios: The Performance of Comedy in Renaissance Italy*. Cambridge, MA: Cambridge University Press, 1993.

Angiolini, Franco. "Il lungo seicento (1609–1737): Declino o stabilità?" In *Storia della civiltà toscana*, Vol. 3: *Il principato mediceo*, edited by Elena Fasano Guarini, 41–76. Florence: Casa di Risparmio, 2003.

Arecchi, Kathleen Hickey. "Six Political Lament-Cantatas by Luigi de' Rossi (ca. 1597–1653)." DMA dissertation, University of Maryland College Park, 1993.

Ariew, Roger. "Theory of Comets at Paris during the Seventeenth Century." *Journal of the History of Ideas* 53, no. 3 (1992): 355–72.

Arlia, Costantino. "Un bandito e una cortigiana letterati." *Il bibliofilo* II, nos. 8–9 (1881): 164–6.

Arnaldi di Balme, Clelia, and Franca Varallo, eds. *Feste barocche: Cerimonie e spettacoli alla corte del Savoia tra Cinque e Settecento*. Milan: Silvana Editoriale, 2009.

Asor Rosa, Alberto. *La lirica del Seicento*. Bari: Laterza, 1975.

Bacherini, Maria Adelaide Bartoli. *"Per un regale evento": Spettacoli nuziali e opera in musica alla corte dei Medici*. Florence: Centro Di, 2000.

Badolato, Nicola. "Cantanti, librettisti e impresari nelle *Poesie* di Paolo Abriani (1663)." *Studi secenteschi* LXI (2020): 131–49.

Bardazzi, Simone. "'Istoria del viaggio di Alemagna del serenissimo granduca di Toscana Ferdinando Secondo.'" In *I Gonzaga e l'impero: Itinerari dello spettacolo; con una selezione di materiali dall'Archivio Informatico Herla (1560–1630)*, edited by Umberto Artioli and Cristina Grazioli, 175–95. Florence: Casa Editrice Le Lettere, 2005.

Barkan, Leonard. *The Gods Made Flesh: Metamorphosis and the Pursuit of Paganism*. New Haven: Yale University Press, 1986.

Barker, Sheila. "Pasquinades and Propaganda: The Reception of Urban VIII." In *The Papacy since 1500: From Italian Prince to Universal Pastor*, edited by James Corkery and Thomas Worcester, 69–89. Cambridge: Cambridge University Press, 2010.

Barocchi, Paola. "Ferdinando II da Firenze a Praga nel 1628." *Annali della Scuola Normale Superiore di Pisa*, Quaderni 1/2 (1996): 305–24.

Barocchi, Paola, and Giovanna Gaeta Bertelà, eds. *Collezionismo mediceo e storia artistica*. Vol. 3, *Il cardinal Giovan Carlo, Mattias e Leopoldo 1628–1667*. 4 vols. Florence: Studio per Edizioni Scelte, 2005.

Barry, Jean-Claude. "Les airs relevés et leur histoire." In *Les arts de l'équitation dans l'Europe de la Renaissance: VIe colloque de l'Ecole nationale d'équitation au Château d'Oiron (4 et 5 octobre 2002)*, edited by Patrice Franchet d'Espèrey and Monique Chatenet, 183–96. Arles: Actes Sud, 2009.

Battistini, Andrea. *Il barocco: Cultura, miti, immagini*. Rome: Salerno, 2000.

Baudi di Vesme, Alessandro, and Phyllis D. Massar. *Stefano della Bella: Catalogue Raisonné*. 2 vols. New York: Collectors Editions, 1971.

Baumgartner, Frederic J. "Sunspots or Sun's Planets: Jean Tarde and the Sunspot Controversy of the Early Seventeenth Century." *Journal for the History of Astronomy* 18, no. 1 (1987): 44–54.

Béhar, Pierre, and Helen Watanabe-O'Kelly. *Spectacvlvm Evropævm: Theatre and Spectacle in Europe (Histoire du spectacle en Europe, 1580–1750)*. Wiesbaden: Harrassowitz Verlag, 1999.

Bellesi, Sandro. "I ritratti delle sorelle Costa di Cesare Dandini e Stefano della Bella." In *Con dolce forza: Donne nell'universo musicale del Cinque e Seicento*, edited by Laura Donati, 65–74. Florence: Polistampa, 2018.

Benadusi, Giovanna. "Carteggi e negozi della granduchessa Vittoria della Rovere (1634–1694)." In *Le donne Medici nel sistema europeo delle Corti, XVI–XVIII secoli*, edited by Giulia Calvi and Riccardo Spinelli, 415–31. Florence: Polistampa, 2008.

– "The Gender Politics of Vittoria della Rovere." In *Medici Women: The Making of a Dynasty in Grand Ducal Tuscany*, edited by Giovanna Benadusi and Judith C. Brown, 264–301. Toronto: Centre for Reformation and Renaissance Studies, 2015.

Bendinelli, Goffredo, and Luigia Maria Tosi. "Stipo." In *Enciclopedia italiana*, 1936.

Benedetti, Laura. "Saintes et guerrières: l'héroïsme féminin dans l'oeuvre de Lucrezia Marinella." In *Les femmes et l'écriture; l'amour profane et l'amour sacré*, edited by Claude Cazalé Bérard, 93–109. Paris: Presses Universitaires de Paris, 2005.

Benocci, Carla. *Le belle: Ritratti di dame del Seicento e del Settecento nelle residenze feudali del Lazio*. Rome: Pieraldo Editore, 2004.

Bernardi, Marziano, ed. *Il Castello del Valentino*. Turin: Società editrice torinese, 1949.

Bertelli, Sergio. "Palazzo Pitti dai Medici ai Savoia." In *La corte di Toscana dai Medici ai Lorena*, edited by Anna Bellinazzi and Alessandra Contini, 11–109. Rome: Ministero per i beni e le attività culturali, 2002.

Besutti, Paola. "Costa, Anna Francesca." In *Grove Music Online, Oxford Music Online*. Oxford University Press, 2002. https://doi-org.libdata.lib.ua.edu/10.1093/gmo/9781561592630.article.O006274.

– "Sardelli, Anna Maria ('La Campaspe')." In *Grove Music Online, Oxford Music Online*. Oxford University Press, 2001. https://doi-org.libdata.lib.ua.edu/10.1093/gmo/9781561592630.article.41031.

Bettella, Patrizia. *The Ugly Woman: Transgressive Aesthetic Models in Italian Poetry from the Middle Ages to the Baroque*. Toronto: University of Toronto Press, 2005.

Biagioli, Mario. *Galileo, Courtier: The Practice of Science in the Culture of Absolutism*. Chicago: University of Chicago Press, 1993.

Bianchi, Dante. "Una cortigiana rimatrice del Seicento: Margherita Costa." *Rassegna critica della letteratura italiana* 29 (1924): 1–31 and 187–203.

– "Una cortigiana rimatrice del Seicento: Margherita Costa." *Rassegna critica della letteratura italiana* 30 (1925): 158–211.

Bianconi, Lorenzo. *Music in the Seventeenth Century*. Translated by David Bryant. 2nd ed. Cambridge: Cambridge University Press, 1989.

Bianconi, Lorenzo, and Thomas Walker. "Dalla *Finta pazza* alla *Veremonda*: Storie di Febiarmonici." *Rivista italiana di musicologia* 10 (1975): 379–454.

– "Production, Consumption, and Political Function of Seventeenth-Century Opera." *Early Music History* 4 (1984): 209–96.

Bisceglia, Anna, Matteo Ceriana, and Simona Mammana, eds. *Buffoni, villani e giocatori alla corte dei Medici*. Livorno: Sillabe, 2016.

"Bizzarria." In *Vocabolario degli Accademici della Crusca*, http://www.lessicografia.it/.

Bizze. "Un avventuriere e Margherita Costa." *Giornale di erudizione: Corrispondenza letteraria, artistica e scientifica* 5, nos. 17 and 18 (September 1894): 261–3.

Bjurström, Per. *Feast and Theatre in Queen Christina's Rome*. Stockholm: Nationalmusei, 1966.

Blumenthal, Arthur R. *Theater Art of the Medici*. Hanover, NH: University Press of New England, 1980.

Bouquet, Marie-Thérèse. *Il teatro di corte dalle origini al 1788*, vol. 1, *Storia del teatro regio di Torino*, 5 vols. Turin: Cassa di Risparmio di Torino, 1976.

Bouquet-Boyer, Marie-Thérèse. "Les états de Savoie et Christine de France: Les fragiles equilibres d'une politique culturelle et artistique (1619-1663)." In *La France et l'Italie au temps de Mazarin*, edited by Jean Serroy, 135–9. Grenoble: Presses Universitaires de Grenoble, 1986.

– "Musical Enigmas in Ballet at the Court of Savoy." Translated by Margaret M. McGowan. *Dance Research: The Journal of the Society for Dance Research* 4, no. 1 (1986): 29–44.

Brazeau, Bryan. "'Defying Gravity': Prose Epic and Heroic Style in Lucrezia Marinella's 1602 *Vita di Maria Vergine*." *Classical Receptions Journal*, 13.1 (2021): 107–25.

– "The Better Fortitude Unsung?: Christian Epic, Heroism, and Interiority in Sixteenth-Century Italy." PhD dissertation, New York University, 2015.

Brege, Brian. *Tuscany in the Age of Empire*. Cambridge, MA: Harvard University Press, 2021.

Brosius, Amy. "Courtesan Singers as Courtiers: Power, Political Pawns, and the Arrest of Virtuosa Nina Barcarola." *Journal of the American Musicological Society* 73, no. 2 (2020): 207–66.

– "'Il suon, lo sguardo, il canto': The Function of Portraits of Mid-Seventeenth-Century Virtuose in Rome." *Italian Studies* 63, no. 1 (2008): 17–39.

– "Singers Behaving Badly: Rivalry, Vengeance, and the Singers of Cardinal Antonio Barberini." *Women and Music: A Journal of Gender and Culture* 19 (2015): 45–53.

Brown, Pamela Allen. *The Diva's Gift to the Shakespearean Stage*. Oxford: Oxford University Press, 2021.

– "The Mirror and the Cage." In *Historical Affects and the Early Modern Theater*, edited by Ronda Arab, Michelle Dowd, and Adam Zucher, 137–51. New York: Routledge, 2015.

Brunelli, Giampiero. "Gaudenzi, Paganino." In *Dizionario Biografico degli Italiani*. Vol. 52, 1999. http://www.treccani.it/enciclopedia/paganino-gaudenzi_(Dizionario -Biografico)/.

Bruni, Roberto. "Editori e tipografi a Firenze nel Seicento." *Studi secenteschi* 45 (2004): 325–419.

Bucchi, Gabriele. *"Meraviglioso diletto": La traduzione poetica del Cinquecento e le 'Metamorfosi d'Ovidio' di Giovanni Andrea dell'Anguillara*. Pisa: ETS, 2011.

Butler, Alban. *Butler's Lives of the Saints: August*. Collegeville, MN: Liturgical Press, 1998.

Callard, Caroline. *Le prince et la république: Histoire, pouvoir et société dans la Florence des Médicis au XVIIe siècle*. Paris: PUPS, 2007.

Caluori, Eleanor. "The Cantatas of Luigi Rossi (Volume One and Two)." PhD dissertation, Brandeis University, 1972.

Calvi, Giulia. *Histories of a Plague Year: The Social and the Imaginary in Baroque Florence*. Translated by Dario Biocca and Bryant T. Ragan, Jr. Berkeley: University of California Press, 1989.

Camerano, Alessandra. "Donne oneste o meretrici? Incertezza dell'identità fra testamenti e diritto di proprietà a Roma." *Quaderni storici* 33, no. 99 (3) (1998): 637–75.

Cammarata, Silvia Maria Sara, and Marco Testa. "Castello del Valentino." In *Scambi artistici tra Torino e Milano, 1580–1714: Cantiere di studio*, edited by Alessandro Morandotti and Gelsomina Spione. Milan: Scalpendi editore, 2018.

Campbell, David A. *Greek Lyric*. Cambridge, MA: Harvard University Press, 1982.

Campbell, Julie D. *Literary Circles and Gender in Early Modern Europe: A Cross-Cultural Approach*. Burlington, VT: Ashgate, 2006.

– "Marie de Beaulieu and Isabella Andreini: Cross-Cultural Patronage at the French Court." *Sixteenth Century Journal* 45, no. 4 (2015): 851–74.

Campbell, Malcolm. "Medici Patronage and the Baroque: A Reappraisal." *Art Bulletin* 48, no. 2 (1966): 133–46.

Campbell, Stephen J. *The Cabinet of Eros: Renaissance Mythological Painting and the Studiolo of Isabella d'Este*. New Haven: Yale University Press, 2004.

Canonici Fachini, Ginevra. *Prospetto biografico delle donne italiane rinomate in letteratura dal secolo decimoquarto fino a' giorni nostri*. Venice: Alvisopoli, 1824.

Capponi, Niccolò. "Le Palle di Marte: Military Strategy and Diplomacy in the Grand Duchy of Tuscany under Ferdinand II de' Medici (1621–1670)." *Journal of Military History* 68, no. 4 (2004): 1105–41.

Capucci, Martino. "Costa, Margherita." In *Dizionario Biografico degli Italiani*. Vol. 30, 1984. https://www.treccani.it/enciclopedia/margherita-costa_%28Dizionario-Biografico%29/.

Caratti, Silvia, and Mayla Ordano. "'Successi del mondo' (1645–1669): Spoglio delle notizie di interesse musicale." *Fonti musicali italiane* 16 (2011): 41–91.

Caresio, Franco, ed. *Residenze sabaude*. Turin: EDA, 2000.

Carter, Tim. "A Florentine Wedding of 1608." *Acta musicologica* 55, no. 1 (1983): 89–107.

– "Costa, (Maria) Margherita [Margarita]." In *Grove Music Online, Oxford Music Online*. https://doi.org/10.1093/gmo/9781561592630.article.O010035.

– "Epyllia and Epithalamia: Some Narrative Frames for Early Opera." *The Italianist,* 40, no. 3 (2021): 382–99.

– "Lamenting Ariadne?" *Early Music* 27, no. 3 (1999): 395–405.

– "Rediscovering *Il rapimento di Cefalo.*" *Journal of Seventeenth-Century Music* 9, no. 1 (2003). https://sscm-jscm.org/v9/no1/carter.html.

Casini, Matteo. "La corte, i cerimoniali, le feste." In *Storia della civiltà toscana,* vol. 3, *Il principato mediceo,* edited by Elena Fasano Guarini. Florence: Le Monnier, 2003.

Castiglione, Caroline. *Patrons and Adversaries: Nobles and Villagers in Italian Politics, 1640–1760.* Oxford: Oxford University Press, 2005.

Cerbo, Anna. *Metamorfosi del mito classico da Boccaccio a Marino.* Pisa: Edizioni ETS, 2001.

Cheng, Sandra. "Parodies of Life: Baccio del Bianco's Comic Drawings of Dwarfs." In *Parody and Festivity in Early Modern Art,* edited by David R. Smith, 127–42. Burlington, VT: Ashgate, 2012.

Cherchi, Paolo. "A Dossier for the Study of Jealousy." In *Eros and Anteros: The Medical Traditions of Love in the Renaissance,* edited by Donald Beecher and Massimo Ciavolella, 123–34. Ottawa: Doverhouse, 1992.

Chiarini, Marco. *Pitti Palace: Guide to the Collections and Complete Catalogue of the Palatine Gallery.* Boston: Sandak, 1992.

Chiesa, Mario. "Il poema sacro secentesco: Uno sguardo ai frontespizi." In *Dopo Tasso: Percorsi del poema eroico,* edited by Guido Arbizzoni, Marco Faini, and Tiziana Mattioli, 285–309. Rome: Antenore, 2005.

Ciancarelli, Roberto. "Frammenti e scritture comiche: Con un 'campionario' di documenti inediti." *Teatro e Storia* 33 (2012): 85–123.

Ciavolella, Massimo. "Text as (Pre)Text: Erudite Renaissance Comedy and the *Commedia Ridicolosa*: The Example of Gian Lorenzo Bernini's *L'impresario*" *Rivista di Studi Italiani* 10 (1992): 22–34.

Claretta, Gaudenzio. *Storia della reggenza di Cristina di Francia, Duchessa di Savoia.* 3 vols. Turin: Stabilmente Civelli, 1868.

Clubb, Louise George. "The Pastoral Play: Conflations of Country, Court, and City." In *Il teatro italiano del Rinascimento,* edited by Maristella de Panizza Lorch, 65–73. Milan: Edizione di Comunità, 1980.

Cochrane, Eric. *Florence in the Forgotten Centuries, 1527–1800: A History of Florence and the Florentines in the Age of the Grand Dukes.* Chicago: University of Chicago Press, 2013.

Coelho, Victor. "The Baroque Guitar: Players, Paintings, Patrons, and the Public." In *The World of Baroque Music: New Perspectives,* 169–84. Bloomington: Indiana University Press, 2006.

Cole, Janie. *Music, Spectacle and Cultural Brokerage in Early Modern Italy: Michelangelo Buonarroti il Giovane.* 2 vols. Florence: Olschki, 2011.

Coller, Alexandra. *Women, Rhetoric, and Drama in Early Modern Italy.* New York: Routledge, 2017.

Conrieri, Davide. "La cultura letteraria e teatrale." In *Storia della civiltà toscana*, vol. 3, *Il principato mediceo*, edited by Elena Fasano Guarini, 355–90. Florence: Le Monnier, 2003.

Cope, Jackson. "Bernini and Roman *Commedie Ridicolose*." *PMLA* 102, no. 2 (1987): 177–86.

Corsaro, Antonio. *La regola e la licenza: Studi sulla poesia satirica e burlesca fra Cinque e Seicento*. Rome: Vecchiarelli Editore, 1999.

Cosentino, Paola. "Allegorie del potere femminile: La politica spettacolare delle reggenti nelle corti italiane del Seicento." Edited by Elisabetta Selmi and Enrico Zucchi. Bologna: Emil di Odoya, 2016.

Costa-Zalessow, Natalia. "Alla scoperta di Margherita Costa." *altrelettere* (2021): 13–26.

— "Margherita Costa." In *Dictionary of Literary Biography*, vol. 339, *Seventeenth-Century Italian Poets and Dramatists*, edited by Albert N. Mancini and Glenn Palen Pierce, 113–18. Gale Cengage Learning. Detroit, 2008.

— *Scrittrici italiane dal XIII al XX secolo: Testi e critica*. Ravenna: Longo editore, 1982.

— "Una poesia femminista del 1672 anonima e dimenticata, da attribuire a Margherita Costa." *Esperienze letterarie*, 2010.

Cox, Virginia. "Declino e caduta della scrittura femminile nell'Italia del Seicento." In *Verso una storia di genere della letteratura italiana: Percorsi critici e gender studies*, edited by Virginia Cox and Chiara Ferrari, 157–84. Bologna: Il Mulino, 2001.

— "Members, Muses, Mascots: Women and Italian Academies." In *The Italian Academies 1525–1700*, 132–69.

— "Re-Thinking Counter-Reformation Literature." In *Innovation in the Italian Counter-Reformation*, edited by Shannon McHugh and Anna Wainwright, 13–55. Newark: University of Delaware Press, 2020.

— *The Prodigious Muse: Women's Writing in Counter-Reformation Italy*. Baltimore: Johns Hopkins University Press, 2011.

— *Women's Writing in Italy, 1400–1650*. Baltimore: Johns Hopkins University Press, 2008.

Crawford, Katherine. *Perilous Performances: Gender and Regency in Early Modern France*. Cambridge, MA: Harvard University Press, 2004.

Croce, Benedetto. *Nuovi saggi sulla letteratura italiana del Seicento*. Bari: Laterza, 1931.

— *Storia della età barocca in Italia: Pensiero-poesia e letteratura vita morale*. Bari: Laterza, 1929.

Croce, Franco. "Introduzione al barocco." In *I capricci di Proteo*, 25–40.

Cruz, Anne J., and Mihoko Suzuki, eds. *The Rule of Women in Early Modern Europe*. Urbana: University of Illinois Press, 2009.

Curnis, Michele. "Novelli Endimioni e falsi Atteoni nella *Diana Schernita* (Roma 1629)." In *Il mito di Diana nella cultura delle corti: Arte letteratura musica*, edited by Giovanni Barberi Squarotti, Annarita Colturato, and Clara Goria. Florence: Olschki, 2018.

Cusick, Suzanne G. *Francesca Caccini at the Medici Court: Music and the Circulation of Power*. Chicago: University of Chicago Press, 2009.

– "'There Was Not One Lady Who Failed to Shed a Tear': Arianna's Lament and the Construction of Modern Womanhood." *Early Music* 22, no. 1 (1994): 21–41.

D'Addario, Arnaldo. "Adimari, Alessandro." In *Dizionario Biografico degli Italiani*. Vol. 1, 1960. https://www.treccani.it/enciclopedia/alessandro-adimari_%28Dizionario -Biografico%29/.

Dameri, Annalisa, and Costanza Roggero. "Il Castello del Valentino." In *Le residenze sabaude*, edited by Costanza Roggero and Alberto Vanelli, 107–22. Turin: Allemandi, 2009.

De Dominicis, Claudio. *Membri del Senato della Roma pontifica: Senatori, conservatori, caporioni e loro priori e lista d'oro delle famigli dirigenti (Secc. X–XIX)*. Rome: Fondazione Marco Besso, 2009.

De Felice, Renzo. "Agliè, Filippo San Martino conte di." In *Dizionario Biografico degli Italiani*, Vol. 1, 1960. https://www.treccani.it/enciclopedia/filippo-san-martino -conte-di-aglie_(Dizionario-Biografico)/.

De Liso, Daniela. "Le *Lettere amorose* di Margherita Costa." In *(Auto)Narrativas: Hacia la construcción de un canon alternativo en italiano*, edited by Sara Velázquez García and Laureano Núñez García, 47–64. Salamanca: Ediciones Universidad de Salamanca, 2020.

– "Margherita Costa a Parigi: *La selva di Diana*." *altrelettere* (2021): 27–42.

DeCoste, Mary-Michelle. *Hopeless Love: Boiardo, Ariosto, and Narratives of Queer Female Desire*. Toronto: University of Toronto Press, 2009.

Decroisette, Françoise. "*L'Armida trionfante* di Ferdinando Saracinelli (1637): La vittoria dello spettacolo totale." In *L'arme e gli amori; Ariosto, Tasso, and Guarini in Late Renaissance Florence*, edited by Massimiliano Rossi and Fiorella Gioffreddi Superbi, 285–96. Florence: Olschki, 2001.

– "Les fêtes du mariage de Cosme III avec Marguerite Louise d'Orléans à Florence, 1661." Edited by Jean Jacquot and Elie Konigson, 3:421–36. Paris: CNRS, 1975.

Defabiani, Vittorio. "Una 'metafora attuosa': Il balletto alla corte sabauda." In *Le capitali della festa: Italia settentrionale*, edited by Marcello Fagiolo, 61–7. Rome: De Luca Editori d'Arte, 2007.

Defabiani, Vittorio, and Chiara Devoti. "La corte, la festa, la città." In *Le capitali della festa: Italia settentrionale*, edited by Marcello Fagiolo, 50–7. Rome: De Luca Editori d'Arte, 2007.

DeJean, Joan. *Fictions of Sappho, 1546–1937*. Chicago: University of Chicago Press, 1989.

Delbrück, Hans. *The Dawn of Modern Warfare*. Translated by Walter J. Renfroe Jr. Lincoln: University of Nebraska Press, 1985.

Delehaye, Hippolyte. *Étude sur le légendier romain: Les saints de novembre et de décembre*. Brussels: Société des Bollandistes, 1936.

– *Les passions des martyrs et les genres littéraires*. Brussels: Société des Bollandistes, 1966.

Di Macco, Michela, and Giovanni Romano, eds. *Diana trionfatrice: Arte di corte del Piemonte del Seicento*. Turin: U. Allemandi, 1989.

Di Maro, Maria. "'Il cor si finge un ghiaccio e in guoco giace': Amore e gelosia nella produzione lirica di Margherita Costa." *altrelettere* (2021): 43–74.

– "«Ogni bizzarro humore e bizzarria / son tenuti istrumenti di pazzia»: burla e satira ne *La chitarra* di Margherita Costa." In *Letteratura e Potere/Poteri,* edited by Andrea Manganaro, Giuseppe Traina, and Carmelo Tramontana. Rome, AdI Editori, 2023. https://www.italianisti.it/pubblicazioni/atti-di-congresso/letteratura-e-potere/Di%20Maro.pdf.

– "Una poetessa del XVII secolo: Margherita Costa." In *(Auto)Narrativas: Hacia la construcción de un canon alternativo en italiano,* edited by Sara Velázquez García and Laureano Núñez García, 81–98. Salamanca: Ediciones Universidad de Salamanca, 2020.

Diaz, Furio. *Il granducato di Toscana: I medici.* Turin: UTET, 1987.

Díaz, Sara. "Exceptional Bodies and Ludic Lovers: Humor, Disability, and the Grotesque in Margherita Costa's 1639 *Lettere Amorose.*" *Early Modern Women: An Interdisciplinary Journal* 16, no. 2 (2022): 265–88.

_ "L'opre del Zerbinar: l'effeminatezza nelle opere fiorentine di Margherita Costa." *altrelettere* (2023): 25–41.

Doglio, Maria Luisa, and Guglielminetti, Marziano. "La letteratura a corte." In *Storia di Torino,* vol. 3, *Dalla dominazione francese alla ricomposizione dello stato (1536–1630),* edited by Giuseppe Ricuperati, 599–672. Turin: Einaudi, 1998.

Driscoll, Kate. "'La donna di poche parole' from Page to Stage: Envoicing Enchantment in Epic Poetry and Early Opera." *The Italianist* 41, no. 1 (2021): 1–22.

Eisenhardt, Lex. *Italian Guitar Music of the Seventeenth Century: Battuto and Pizzicato.* Rochester: University of Rochester Press, 2015.

Erdmann, Axel. *My Gracious Silence: Women in the Mirror of 16th Century Printing in Western Europe.* Lucerne: Gilhofer & Ranschburg, 1999.

Evangelisti, Silvia. "Vincenzo Nolfi's *Ginipedia* (1631): Household Management and Civic Femininity in Seventeenth-Century Italy." In *Conduct Literature for and about Women in Italy, 1470–1900,* edited by Helena Sanson and Francesco Lucioli, 63–80. Paris: Classiques Garnier, 2016.

Everson, Jane E., Denis Reidy, and Lisa Sampson, eds. *The Italian Academies 1525–1700: Networks of Culture, Innovation and Dissent.* Oxford: Legenda, 2016.

Faini, Marco. "La poetica dell'epica sacra tra Cinque e Seicento in Italia." *The Italianist* 35, no. 1 (2015): 27–60.

– "Un'opera dimenticata di Pietro Aretino: *Il lamento de uno cortigiano.*" *Filologia e critica* 32 (2007): 75–91.

Fantappié, Francesca. "'Angela Senese' alias Angela Signorini Nelli. Vita artistica di un'attrice nel Seicento italiano: Dal Don Giovanni ai libertini." *Bullettino senese di storia patria* 116 (2009): 212–67.

Fantoni, Marcello. *La corte del granduca: Forme e simboli del potere mediceo fra Cinque e Seicento.* Rome: Bulzoni, 1994.

Favaro, Antonio. *La libreria di Galileo Galilei descritta ed illustrata.* Rome: Tipografia delle matematiche e fisiche, 1887.

Festa, Lisa Ann. "Representations of Saint Cecilia in Italian Renaissance and Baroque Painting and Sculpture." PhD dissertation, Rutgers University, 2004.

Fichter, Andrew. *Poets Historical: Dynastic Epic in the Renaissance.* New Haven: Yale University Press, 1982.

Finocchiaro, Maurice A. *Retrying Galileo, 1633–1992.* Berkeley: University of California Press, 2005.

Fosi, Irene. *All'ombra dei Barberini: Fedeltà e servizio nella Roma barocca.* Rome: Bulzoni, 1997.

Franchet d'Espèrey, Patrice. "L'équitation italienne, sa transmission et son évolution en France au temps de la Renaissance." In *Les arts de l'équitation dans l'Europe de la Renaissance. VIe colloque de l'Ercole nationale d'equitation au Château d'Oiron (4 et 5 octobre 2002),* edited by Patrice Franchet d'Espèrey and Monique Chatenet, 158–82. Arles: Actes Sud, 2009.

– "The Ballet d'Antoine de Pluvinel and the Maneige Royal." In *Dynastic Marriages 1612/1615: A Celebration of the Habsburg and Bourbon Unions,* edited by Margaret M. McGowan, 115–36. Farnham: Ashgate, 2013.

Franchi, Saverio. "L'Aretusa." In *Annali della stampa musicale romana dei secoli XVI–XVIII,* 1:353–6. Rome: IBIMUS, 2006.

– "Mascardi, Giacomo." In *Dizionario Biografico degli Italiani.* Vol. 71, 2008. http://www.treccani.it/enciclopedia/giacomo-mascardi_(Dizionario-Biografico)/.

Freitas, Roger. *Portrait of a Castrato: Politics, Patronage, and Music in the Life of Atto Melani.* Cambridge: Cambridge University Press, 2009.

Galassi, Cristina. *Ritratto di una virtuosa canterina: Eleonora Baroni e il pittore Fabio della Corgna al tempo dei Barberini.* Perugia: Aquaplano, 2017.

Garrard, Mary D. *Artemisia Gentileschi: The Image of the Female Hero in Italian Baroque Art.* Princeton: Princeton University Press, 1989.

Gerbino, Giuseppe. *Music and the Myth of Arcadia in Renaissance Italy.* Cambridge: Cambridge University Press, 2009.

Getto, Giovanni. *Il barocco letterario in Italia.* Milan: Mondadori, 2000.

Ghadessi, Touba. *Portraits of Human Monsters in the Renaissance: Dwarves, Hirsutes, and Castrati as Idealized Anatomical Anomalies.* Kalamazoo: Medieval Institute Publications, 2018.

Ghisi, Federico. "Ballet Entertainments in Pitti Palace, Florence, 1608–1625." *Musical Quarterly* 35 (1949): 421–36.

– "'Il mondo festeggiante': Balletto a Cavallo in Boboli." Edited by Riccardo Bacchelli, 233–42. Milan: Ricciardi, 1973.

Ghislanzoni, Alberto. *Luigi Rossi: Biografia e analisi delle opere.* Rome: Bocca, 1954.

Giachino, Luisella. "*Cicero libertinus*: La satira della Roma barberiniana nell'*Eudemia* dell'Eritreo." *Studi secenteschi* 43 (2002): 185–215.

Gianturco, Carolyn. "Nuove considerazioni su 'Il Tedio del Recitativo' delle prime opere romane." *Rivista italiana di musicologia* 17, no. 2 (1982): 212–39.

Giles, Roseen. "Giambattista Marino's *L'Adone*: A Drama of Madrigals." *Genre Bending in Early Modern Performative Culture* 40, No. 3 (2020): 419–40.

– "The (Un)Natural Baroque: Giambattista Marino and Monteverdi's Late Madrigals." PhD dissertation, University of Toronto, 2016.

Glixon, Beth. "Private Lives of Public Women: Prima Donnas in Mid-Seventeenth-Century Venice." *Music & Letters* 76 (1995): 509–31.

Glixon, Beth, and Jonathan Glixon. *Inventing the Business of Opera: The Impresario and His World in Seventeenth-Century Venice.* Oxford: Oxford University Press, 2005.

Goethals, Jessica. "*Cadde a tai note*: Il lamento tra *La Flora feconda* e *La selva di cipressi* di Margherita Costa." *altrelettere* (2023): 42–64.

– "*Li buffoni*, Fessa e la nuova malmaritata di Margherita Costa." *Versants* 69, no. 2 (2022): 145–61.

– "The Bizarre Muse: The Poetics and Persona of Margherita Costa." *Early Modern Women: An Interdisciplinary Journal* 12, no. 1 (2017): 48–72.

– "The Patronage Politics of Equestrian Ballet: Allegory, Allusion, and Satire in the Courts of Seventeenth Century Italy and France." *Renaissance Quarterly* 70, no. 4 (2017): 1397–1448.

– "The Singing Saint: The Martyrdom of St. Cecilia in Seventeenth-Century Literature and Theater." *Women Language Literature in Italy / Donne Lingua Letteratura in Italia* 2 (2020): 43–61.

– "Worth Its Salt: A Ridiculous Defence of Buffoonery." *The Italianist* 40, no. 3 (2020): 362–81.

Goodson, Caroline J. "Material Memory: Rebuilding the Basilica of S. Cecilia in Trastevere, Rome." *Early Medieval Europe* 15, no. 1 (2007): 2–34.

Gordon, Bonnie. *Monteverdi's Unruly Women: The Power of Song in Early Modern Italy.* Cambridge: Cambridge University Press, 2004.

Gough, Melinda J. "Tasso's Enchantress, Tasso's Captive Woman." *Renaissance Quarterly* 54, no. 2 (2001): 523–52.

Green, C.M.C. *Roman Religion and the Cult of Diana at Aricia.* Cambridge: Cambridge University Press, 2012.

Gregori, Mina. "Nuovi accertamenti in Toscana sulla pittura 'caricata' e giocosa." *Arte antica e moderna* 4, vol. 13–16 (1961): 400–12.

Grifi, Elvira. *Saunterings in Florence: A New Artistic and Practical Hand-Book for English and American Tourists.* Florence: R. Bemporad & Figlio, 1899.

Griseri, Andreina. *Il diamante: La villa di Madama Reale Cristina di Francia.* Turin: Istituto bancario San Paolo di Torino, 1998.

Hall, Crystal. "Margherita Costa." *Galileo's Library* (blog). https://research.bowdoin.edu/galileos-library/book-isotopes/margherita-costa/.

Hammond, Frederick. *The Ruined Bridge: Studies in Barberini Patronage of Music and Spectacle, 1631–1679.* Sterling Heights, MI: Harmonie Park Press, 2010.

Hanley, Sarah. "Configuring the Authority of Queens in the French Monarchy, 1600s–1840s." *Historical Reflections / Réflexions Historiques* 32 (2006): 453–64.

– "The Salic Law." In *Political and Historical Encyclopedia of Women*, edited by Christine Fauré, 2–17. New York: Routledge, 2003.

Harness, Kelley. *Echoes of Women's Voices: Music, Art, and Female Patronage in Early Modern Florence.* Chicago: University of Chicago Press, 2006.

– "Habsburgs, Heretics, and Horses: Equestrian Ballets and Other Staged Battles in Florence during the First Decade of the Thirty Years War." In *L'arme e gli amori:*

Ariosto, Tasso, and Guarini in Late Renaissance Florence, edited by Massimiliano Rossi and Fiorella Giofreddi Superbi, 255–83. Florence: Olschki, 2001.

– "'Nata à maneggi & essercizii grandi': Archduchess Maria Magdalena and Equestrian Entertainments in Florence, 1608–1625." In *"La Liberazione di Ruggiero dall'isola d'Alcina": Räume und inszenierungen in Francesca Caccinis ballettoper (Florenz, 1625)*, edited by Christine Fischer, 89–108. Zurich: Chronos, 2015.

Harper, James C. "Tapestry Production in Seventeenth-Century Rome: The Barberini Manufactory." In *Tapestry in the Baroque: Threads of Splendor*, 293–324. New Haven: Yale University Press, 2007.

Heilbron, J.L. *Galileo*. Oxford: Oxford University Press, 2010.

Heller, Wendy. *Emblems of Eloquence: Opera and Women's Voices in Seventeenth-Century Venice*. Berkeley: University of California Press, 2003.

– "Ovid's Ironic Gaze: Voyeurism, Rape, and Male Desire in Cavalli's *La Calisto*." In *Eroticism in Early Modern Music*, edited by Bonnie Blackburn and Laurie Stras, 204–25. London: Routledge, 2016.

Henderson, John. *Florence under Siege: Surviving Plague in an Early Modern City*. New Haven: Yale University Press, 2019.

Henke, Robert. *Performance and Literature in the Commedia dell'Arte*. Cambridge: Cambridge University Press, 2002.

Herissone, Rebecca. "Daniel Henstridge and the Aural Transmission of Music in Restoration England." In *Beyond Boundaries: Rethinking Music Circulation in Early Modern England*, edited by Linda Phyllis Austern, Amanda Eubanks Winkler, and Candace Bailey, 165–86. Bloomington: Indiana University Press, 2017.

Hester, Nathalie. "Baroque Italian Epic from Granada to the New World: Columbus Conquers the Moors." In *The New World in Early Modern Italy, 1492–1750*, edited by Elizabeth Horodowich and Lia Markey, 270–87. New York: Cambridge University Press, 2017.

Hills, Helen. "The Baroque: The Grit in the Oyster of Art History." In *Rethinking the Baroque*, edited by Helen Hills, 11–36. Burlington, VT: Ashgate, 2011.

Holford-Strevens, Leofranc. "'Her Eyes Became Two Spouts': Classical Antecedents of Renaissance Laments." *Early Music* 27, no. 3 (1999): 379–93.

Holzer, Robert. "Music and Poetry in Seventeenth-Century Rome: Settings of the Canzonetta and Cantata Texts of Francesco Balducci, Domenico Benigni, Francesco Melosio, and Antonio Abati." PhD dissertation, University of Pennsylvania, 1990.

– "'Sono d'altro garbo … le canzonette che si cantano oggi': Pietro della Valle on Music and Modernity in the Seventeenth Century." *Studi musicali* (1992): 253–306.

Hunt, John M. *The Vacant See in Early Modern Rome: A Social History of the Papal Interregnum*. Leiden: Brill, 2016.

I capricci di Proteo: Percorsi e linguaggi del barocco: Atti del convegno internazionale di Lecce, 23–26 ottobre 2000. Rome: Salerno Editrice, 2000.

Jaffe-Berg, Erith. *Commedia dell'Arte and the Mediterranean: Charting Journeys and Mapping "Others."* Farnham: Ashgate, 2015.

Jansen, Sharon L. *The Monstrous Regiment of Women: Female Rulers in Early Modern Europe*. New York: Palgrave Macmillan, 2002.

Jeanneret, Christine. "Gender Ambivalence and the Expression of Passions in the Performances of Early Roman Cantatas by Castrati and Female Singers." In *The Emotional Power of Music: Multidisciplinary Perspectives on Musical Arousal, Expression, and Social Control*, edited by Tom Cochrane, Bernardino Fantini, and Klaus R. Scherer. Oxford: Oxford University Press, 2013.

Johnson, Charles. *Stefano della Bella, Baroque Printmaker: The I. Webb Surratt, Jr. Print Collection*. Richmond: Marsh Art Gallery, University of Richmond Museums, 2001.

Kaborycha, Lisa, ed. and trans. *A Corresponding Renaissance: Letters Written by Italian Women, 1375–1650*. Oxford: Oxford University Press, 2015.

Keller, Katrin, and Marion Romberg. "The *Tagzettel* and Diaries of Cardinal Ernst Adalbert von Harrach: A Source for Central European History of the 17th Century." *Medieval History Journal* 13 (2010): 287–314.

Kendrick, Robert L. "What's So Sacred about 'Sacred' Opera? Reflections on the Fate of a (Sub)Genre." *Journal of Seventeenth-Century Music* 9, no. 1 (2003). https://sscm-jscm.org/v9/no1/kendrick.html#n7.

Kerr, Rosalind. *The Rise of the Diva on the Sixteenth-Century Commedia dell'Arte Stage*. Toronto: University of Toronto Press, 2015.

Kettering, Sharon. "Favour and Patronage: Dancers in the Court Ballets of Early Seventeenth-Century France." *Canadian Journal of History / Annales Canadiennes d'histoire* 43 (2008): 391–415.

– "Patronage in Early Modern France." *French Historical Studies* 17, no. 4 (1992): 839–62.

– "The Patronage Power of Early Modern French Noblewomen." *Historical Journal* 32, no. 4 (1989): 817–41.

Kleinman, Ruth. *Anne of Austria, Queen of France*. Columbus: Ohio State University Press, 1985.

Kolrud, Kristine. "The Gem and the Mirror of Heroic Virtue: Emanuele Tesauro and the Heroic at the Court of Savoy." In *Shaping Heroic Virtue: Studies in the Art and Politics of Supereminence in Europe and Scandinavia*, edited by Stefano Fogelberg Rota and Andreas Hellerstedt. Leiden: Brill, 2015.

Kutsch, K. J., and Leo Riemens, eds. *Großes Sängerlexikon*. Munich: K.G. Saur, 2003.

Lamothe, Virginia Christy. "The Theater of Piety: Sacred Operas for the Barberini Family (Rome, 1632–1643)." PhD dissertation, University of North Carolina at Chapel Hill, 2009.

Langdon, Gabrielle. *Medici Women: Portraits of Power, Love and Betrayal from the Court of Duke Cosimo I*. Toronto: University of Toronto Press, 2007.

Langdon, Helen. *Salvator Rosa: Paint and Performance*. London: Reaktion Books, 2022.

Langedijk, Karla. *The Portraits of the Medici, 15th–18th Centuries*. 3 vols. Florence: Studio per Edizioni Scelte, 1981.

Lapidge, Michael. *The Roman Martyrs: Introduction, Translations, and Commentary*. Oxford: Oxford University Press, 2018.

Lattarico, Jean-François. "*Lo scherno degli dei*: Myth and Derision in the *Dramma per Musica* of the Seventeenth Century." In *(Dis)Embodying Myths in Ancien Régime Opera: Multidisciplinary Perspective*, edited by Bruno Forment, 17–32. Leuven: Leuven University Press, 2012.

Lazzeri, Alessandro. *Il principe e il diplomatico: Ferdinando II tra il destino e la storia*. Florence: Edizioni Medicea, 1996.

LeGuin, Elisabeth. "Man and Horse in Harmony." In *The Culture of the Horse: Status, Discipline, and Identity in the Early Modern World*, edited by Karen Raber and Treva J. Tucker, 175–95. New York: Palgrave Macmillan, 2005.

Leone, Stephanie C. *The Palazzo Pamphilj in Piazza Navona: Constructing Identity in Early Modern Rome*. London: Harvey Miller Publishers, 2008.

Lewis, John Michael. *Galileo in France: French Reactions to the Theories and Trial of Galileo*. New York: Peter Lang, 2006.

Liborio, Francesca Maria. *La scena della città: Rappresentazioni sceniche nel Teatro di Cremona 1748–1900*. Cremona: Editrice Turris, 1994.

Lincoln, Evelyn. "Printers and Publishers in Early Modern Rome." In *A Companion to Early Modern Rome, 1492–1692*, 546–63. Leiden: Brill, 2019.

Lipking, Lawrence. *Abandoned Women and the Poetic Tradition*. Chicago: University of Chicago Press, 1988.

Lirosi, Alessia. "Il corpo di Santa Cecilia (Roma, III–XVII secolo)." *Mélanges de l'École Française de Rome* 122, no. 1 (2010): 5–51.

Longhi, Silvia. *Lusus: Il capitolo burlesco nel Cinquecento*. Padua: Antenore, 1983.

Lyden, Émile Mignot de. *Le théâtre d'autrefois et d'aujourd'hui: Cantatrices et comédiens 1532–1882*. Paris: E. Dentu, 1882.

MacLean, Ian. *Woman Triumphant: Feminism in French Literature, 1610–1652*. Oxford: Clarendon Press, 1977.

MacNeil, Anne. *Music and Women of the Commedia dell'Arte in the Late Sixteenth Century*. Oxford: Oxford University Press, 2003.

– "Weeping at the Water's Edge." *Early Music* 27, no. 3 (1999): 406–17.

Magnuson, Torgil. *Rome in the Age of Bernini*. 2 vols. Stockholm: Almquist and Wiksell International, 1982–6.

Mallick, Oliver. "Clients and Friends: The Ladies-in-Waiting at the Court of Anne of Austria (1615–66)." In *The Politics of Female Households: Ladies-in-Waiting across Early Modern Europe*, 231–64. Leiden: Brill, 2014.

Mamone, Sara. "Most Serene Brothers-Princes-Impresarios: Theater in Florence under the Management and Protection of Mattias, Giovan Carlo, and Leopoldo de' Medici." *Journal of Seventeenth-Century Music* 9, no. 1 (2003). http:// sscm-jscm.org/v9/no1/ mamone.html.

Marcigliano, Alessandro. "Cavallerie a Ferrara: 1561–1570." In *Italian Renaissance Festivals and Their European Influence*, edited by J. R. Mulryne and Margaret Shewring, 197–222. Lewiston, NY: Edwin Mellen Press, 1992.

Marcotti, G. "Fra Paolo." *Gazzetta letteraria, artistica e scientifica*, 10 July 1886.

Mariti, Luciano. *Commedia ridicolosa: Comici di professione, dilettanti, editoria teatrale nel Seicento; Storia e testi.* Rome: Bulzoni, 1979.

Markey, Lia. *Imagining the Americas in Medici Florence.* University Park, PA: Penn State University Press, 2016.

Marongiu, Paola. "*L'Ascanio errante* di Barbera Tigliamochi degli Albizi: Un'*Eneide* rivisitata in versione toscana e femminista." *Critica etteraria* 2 (2016): 225–51.

– "Margherita Costa: Una scrittrice femminista del XVII secolo." *Critica letteraria* 190 (2021): 115–33.

Marotti, Ferruccio, and Giovanna Romei, eds. *La professione del teatro.* Rome: Bulzoni, 1991.

Martelli, Francesco, ed. *Il viaggio in Europa di Pietro Guerrini (1682–1686): Edizione della corrispondenza e dei disegni di un inviato di Cosimo III de' Medici.* 2 vols. Florence: Olschki, 2005.

Martin, Henri-Jean. "Un grand editeur parisien au XVIIe siècle: Sébastien Cramoisy." *Gutenberg-Jahrbuch* (1957): 179–88.

Martini, Alessandro. "Le nuove forme del canzoniere." In *I capricci di Proteo,* 199–226.

Massar, Phyllis D. "Presenting Stefano della Bella." *Metropolitan Museum of Art Bulletin* 27, no. 3 (1968): 159–76.

– *Presenting Stefano della Bella, Seventeenth-Century Printmaker.* New York: Metropolitan Museum of Art, 1971.

– "Valerio Spada, Seventeenth-Century Florentine Calligrapher and Draughtsman." *Master Drawings* 19, no. 3 (1981): 251–75, 319–44.

Masson, Georgina. "Papal Gifts and Roman Entertainments in Honour of Queen Christina's Arrival." In *Queen Christina of Sweden: Documents and Studies,* 244–61. Stockholm: Norstedt and Söner, 1966.

Mazzoleni, Achille. "Aci e Galatea nella letteratura e nell'arte." *Rendiconti e memorie della R. Accademia di scienze, lettere e arti degli delanti* 3, no. 2 (1903): 89–158.

McClary, Susan. *Desire and Pleasure in Seventeenth-Century Music.* Berkeley: University of California Press, 2012.

McClure, George. *Parlour Games and the Public Life of Women in Renaissance Italy.* Toronto: University of Toronto Press, 2013.

McGowan, Margaret M. *Dance in the Renaissance: European Fashion, French Obsession.* New Haven: Yale University Press, 2008.

– "Deux fêtes en Savoie en 1644 et 1645." *Baroque* 5 (1972). http://baroque.revues.org/373.

– *L'art du ballet de cour en France, 1581–1643.* Paris: Centre National de la Recherche Scientifique, 1963.

McIver, Katherine A., and Cynthia Stollhans, eds. *Patronage, Gender, and the Arts in Early Modern Italy: Essays in Honor of Carolyn Valone.* New York: Italica Press, 2015.

Megale, Teresa. "Altre novità su Anna Francesca Costa e sull'allestimento dell'*Ergirodo.*" *Medioevo e rinascimento* 4 (1993): 137–42.

– "Il principe e la cantante: Riflessi impresariali di una protezione." *Medioevo e rinascimento* 6 (1992): 211–33.

– "La commedia decifrata: Metamorfosi e rispecchiamenti in *Li buffoni* di Margherita Costa." *Il castello di Elsinore* 1, no. 2 (1988): 64–76.

– "Sorelle, cantanti, rivali: I teatri di Margherita e Anna Francesca Costa nel primo Seicento." *altrelettere* (2023): 65–89.

– "Sproporzioni: Il teatro dell'assurdo buffonesco all'ombra dei Medici." In Bisceglia, Ceriana, and Mammana, *Buffoni, villani e giocatori alla corte dei Medici*, 68–71.

– "Su un dipinto buffonesco del Sustermans." *Ariel* 9, no. 1 (1994): 123–5.

Meine, Sabine. "Cecilia without a Halo: The Changing Musical Virtus." *Music in Art* 29, no. 1/2 (2004): 104–12.

Menchini, Carmen. "Funeral Oratory at the Medici Court: The Representation of the First Grand Dukes." *EUI Working Papers* 20 (2008).

Merola, Valeria. "Il mito in scena: Endimione e Diana ne *Gli amori della luna* di Margherita Costa." *altrelettere* (2021): 75–93.

Merrick, Jeffrey. "The Cardinal and the Queen: Sexual and Political Disorders in the Mazarinades." *French Historical Studies* 18, no. 3 (Spring 1994): 667–99.

Mertz, Jörg Martin. *Pietro da Cortona and Roman Baroque Architecture*. New Haven: Yale University Press, 2008.

Metlica, Alessandro. *Le seduzioni della pace: Giovan Battista Marino, le feste di corte e la Francia barocca*. Bologna: Il Mulino, 2020.

Michelassi, Nicola. "Balbi's Febiarmonici and the First 'Road Shows' of *Giasone* (1649–1653)." In *Readying Cavalli's Operas for the Stage*, edited by Ellen Rosand, 307–20. Burlington, VT: Ashgate, 2017.

– "Il teatro del Cocomero di Firenze: Uno stanzone per tre accademie (1651–1665)." *Studi secenteschi* 40 (1999): 149–86.

– "'Regi protettori' e 'virtuosi trattenimenti': Principi medicei e intellettuali fiorentini del Seicento tra corte, teatro e accademia." In *Naples, Rome, Florence: Une histoire comparée des milieux intellectuels italiens (XVII–XVIIIᵉ siècles)*, edited by Jean Boutier, Brigitte Marin, and Antonella Romano, 445–72. Rome: Publications de l'École française de Rome, 2005. https://books.openedition.org/efr/2352.

Migiel, Marilyn. "Tasso's Erminia: Telling an Alternate Story." *Italica* 64, no. 1 (1987): 62–75.

– *Veronica Franco in Dialogue*. Toronto: University of Toronto Press, 2022.

Milburn, Erika. "'D'invidia e d'amor figlia sì ria': Jealousy and the Italian Renaissance Lyric." *Modern Language Review* 97, no. 3 (2002): 577–91.

Minor, Vernon Hyde. *The Death of the Baroque and the Rhetoric of Good Taste*. Cambridge: Cambridge University Press, 2006.

Mirollo, James V. *The Poet of the Marvelous: Giambattista Marino*. New York: Columbia University Press, 1963.

Modesti, Adelina. *Women's Patronage and Gendered Cultural Networks in Early Modern Europe: Vittoria della Rovere, Grand Duchess of Tuscany*. New York: Routledge, 2019.

Modolo, Elisa. "Metamorphosis of the Metamorphoses: Italian Rewritings of Ovid between Renaissance and Baroque." PhD dissertation, University of Pennsylvania, 2015.

Monaldini, Sergio. *L'orto dell'Esperidi: Musici, attori e artisti nel patrocinio della famiglia Bentivoglio, 1646–1685*. Lucca: Libreria Musicale Italiana, 2000.

Muir, Edward. *The Culture Wars of the Late Renaissance: Skeptics, Libertines, and Opera*. Cambridge, MA: Harvard University Press, 2007.

Murata, Margaret. *Operas for the Papal Court, 1631–1668*. Ann Arbor: UMI Research Press, 1981.

– "Why the First Opera Given in Paris Wasn't Roman." *Cambridge Opera Journal* 7, no. 2 (July 1995): 87–105.

Nagler, A.M. *Theatre Festivals of the Medici, 1539–1637*. New Haven: Yale University Press, 1964.

Nettl, Paul. "Equestrian Ballets of the Baroque Period." *Musical Quarterly* 19, no. 1 (1933): 74–83.

Newcomb, Anthony. "Courtesans, Muses, or Musicians? Professional Women Musicians in Sixteenth-Century Italy." In *Secular Renaissance Music*, edited by Jane Bowers and Judith Tick, 90–115. Urbana: University of Illinois Press, 1987.

Nordera, Marina. "Ballet de Cour." In *The Cambridge Companion to Ballet*, edited by Marion Kant, 20–31. Cambridge: Cambridge University Press, 2000.

Noreen, Kirstin. "Lay Patronage and the Creation of Papal Sanctity during the Gregorian Reform: The Case of Sant'Urbano alla Caffarella, Rome." *Gesta* 40, no. 1 (2001): 39–59.

– "Recording the Past: Seventeenth-Century Watercolor Drawings of Medieval Monuments." *Visual Resources* 91 (2000): 1–26.

Norman, Joanna. "In Public and in Private: A Study of Festival in Seventeenth-Century Rome." In *Occasions of State: Early Modern European Festivals and the Negotiation of Powe*, edited by J.R. Mulryne, Krista De Jonge, R.L.M. Morris, and Pieter Martens, 229–46. New York: Routledge, 2018.

Nussdorfer, Laurie. *Civic Politics in the Rome of Urban VIII*. Princeton, NJ: Princeton University Press, 1992.

– "Print and Pageantry in Baroque Rome." *Sixteenth Century Journal* 29, no. 2 (1998): 439–64.

O'Bryan, Robin. "Grotesque Bodies, Princely Delight: Dwarfs in Italian Renaissance Court Imagery." *Preternature: Critical and Historical Studies on the Preternatural* 1, no. 2 (2012): 252–88.

Oresko, Robert. "The House of Savoy in Search for a Royal Crown in the Seventeenth Century." In *Royal and Republican Sovereignty in Early Modern Europe*, edited by Robert Oresko, G.C. Gibbs, and H.M. Scott, 272–350. Cambridge: Cambridge University Press, 1997.

Osborne, Toby. *Dynasty and Diplomacy in the Court of Savoy: Political Culture and the Thirty Years' War*. Cambridge: Cambridge University Press, 2002.

– "Language and Sovereignty: The Use of Titles and Savoy's Royal Declaration of 1632." In *Political, Religious, and Social Conflict in the States of Savoy, 1400–1700*, edited by Sarah Alyn Stacey, 15–34. Bern: Peter Lang, 2014.

– "The House of Savoy and the Theatre of the World: Performances of Sovereignty in Early Modern Family." In *Sabaudian Studies: Political Culutre, Dynasty, and Territory, 1400–1700*, edited by Matthew Vester, 167–90. Kirksville, MO: Truman State University Press, 2013.

Panofsky, Erwin. "More on Galileo and the Arts." *Isis* 47, no. 2 (1956): 182–5.

Parker, Deborah. *Bronzino: Renaissance Painter as Poet.* Cambridge: Cambridge University Press, 2000.

Pepper, D. Stephen. *Guido Reni: A Complete Catalogue of His Works with an Introductory Text.* Oxford: Phaidon, 1984.

Persson, Fabian. *Women at the Early Modern Swedish Court.* Amsterdam: Amsterdam University Press, 2021.

Petrucci, Francesco. *Ferdinand Voet (1639–1698), detto Ferdinando de' ritratti.* Rome: Ugo Bozzi, 2005.

Piantoni, Luca. "Le *Lettere amorose* di Margherita Costa (1639) tra sperimentalismo e 'divertissement.'" *Studi secenteschi* 59 (2018): 33–51.

Piccinini, Francesca. "Carnevale di Roma del 1656: Un carosello a Palazzo Barberini." In Strappino, *I luoghi dell'immaginario barocco,* 123–33.

Picozzi, Maria Grazia. "Orfeo Boselli and the Interpretation of the Antique." In *The Rediscovery of Antiquity: The Role of the Artist,* edited by Jane Fejfer, Tobias Fischer-Hansen, and Annette Rathje, 89–122. Copenhagen: Museum Tusculanum Press, University of Copenhagen, 2003.

Piechocki, Katharina N. "Clouds, Nuptials, Nubifications: At the Origins of Operatic Poetics." *Romance Quarterly* 68, no. 3 (2021): 160–76.

Pirrotta, Nino. "Costa, Margherita." In *Enciclopedia dello spettacolo,* 3: col. 1555. Rome: Le Maschere, 1956.

Pollak, Martha D. *Turin, 1564–1680: Urban Design, Military Culture, and the Creation of the Absolutist Capital.* Chicago: University of Chicago Press, 1991.

Porter, William V. "Lamenti recitativi da camera." In *Con che soavità: Studies in Italian Opera, Song, and Dance, 1580–1740,* edited by Iain Fenlon and Tim Carter, 73–110. Oxford: Clarendon Press, 1995.

– "Northwestern University's Seventeenth-Century Manuscript of Roman Cantatas." In *A Compendium of American Musicology: Essays in Honor of John F. Ohl,* edited by Enrique Alberto Arias, Susan M. Filler, William V. Porter, and Jeffrey Wasson, 92–121. Evanston, IL: Northwestern University Press, 2001.

Primarosa, Yumi. "I volti della musica: Cantatrici, musici e buffoni alla corte di Roma nei ritratti di Ottavio Leoni." *Storia dell'arte* 41 (2015): 63–85.

Prunières, Henry. *L'opéra italien en France avant Lulli.* Paris: Champion, 1913.

Quaintance, Courtney. "Singing Women, Saint Cecilia, and Self-Fashioning in Seventeenth-Century Rome." In *Gendering the Renaissance: Text and Context in Early Modern Italy,* edited by Meredith K. Ray and Lynn Lara Westwater, 197–229. Newark: University of Delaware Press, 2023.

Quatremère de Quincy, Antoine-Chrysostome. *The True, the Fictive, and the Real: The Historical Dictionary of Architecture.* Translated by Samir Younés. London: Papadakis, 1999.

Quint, David. *Epic and Empire: Politics and Generic Form from Virgil to Milton.* Princeton, NJ: Princeton University Press, 1993.

Quondam, Amedeo. *Le "carte messaggiere": Retorica e modelli di comunicazione epistolare: Per un indice dei libri di lettere del Cinquecento*. Rome: Bulzoni, 1981.

– *Paradigmi e tradizioni*. Rome: Bulzoni, 2005.

Raizen, Karen T. "Monsters of the Pastoral Stage and the Nature of the Unnatural." *I Tatti Studies in the Italian Renaissance* 21, no. 2 (2018): 423–46.

Ranum, Patricia. *Portraits around Marc-Antoine Charpentier*. Baltimore: Dux Femina Facti, 2004.

Rasi, Luigi. *La caricatura e i comici italiani*. Florence: R. Bemporad e Figlio, 1907.

Ray, Meredith K. "Renaissance of Women: New Directions in North American Scholarship on Early Modern Italian Literature." *Bruniana & Campanelliana* 26, no. 1 (2020): 283–95.

– *Writing Gender in Women's Letter Collections of the Italian Renaissance*. Toronto: University of Toronto Press, 2009.

Reeves, Eileen. *Evening News: Optics, Astronomy, and Journalism in Early Modern Europe*. Philadelphia: University of Pennsylvania Press, 2014.

Refini, Eugenio. "Echoes of Ariadne in the Musical Reception of Ariosto and Tasso." *Renaissance Quarterly* 73, no. 2 (2020): 527–66.

– "'*Parole tronche et imperfette*': The Lament as a 'Mode' across Poetical and Musical Genres." *The Italianist* 40, no. 3 (2020): 441–62.

– "Prologhi figurati: Appunti sull'uso della prosopopea nel prologo teatrale del Cinquecento." *Italianistica* 35, no. 3 (2006): 61–86.

Richardson, Brian. *Women and the Circulation of Texts in Renaissance Italy*. Cambridge: Cambridge University Press, 2020.

Rietbergen, Peter. *Power and Religion in Baroque Rome: Barberini Cultural Policies*. Leiden: Brill, 2006.

Robarts, Julie. "Challenging Male Authored Poetry: Margherita Costa's Marinist Lyrics (1638–1639)." PhD dissertation, University of Melbourne, 2019.

– "Marinism and Macrotextuality in Margherita Costa's Early Printed Books." *altrelettere* (2023): 3–24.

Robin, Diana. *Publishing Women: Salons, the Presses, and the Counter-Reformation in Sixteenth-Century Italy*. Chicago: University of Chicago Press, 2007.

Rodini, Robert J. *Antonfrancesco Grazzini: Poet, Dramatist, and Novelliere, 1503–1584*. Madison: University of Wisconsin Press, 1970.

Rosa, Alberto Asor, and Salvatore S. Nigro. *I poeti giocosi dell'età barocca*. Rome: Laterza, 1999.

Rosand, Ellen. "Barbara Strozzi, 'Virtuosissima cantatrice': The Composer's Voice." *Journal of the American Musicological Society* 31, no. 2 (1978): 241–81.

– *Monteverdi's Last Operas: A Venetian Trilogy*. Berkeley: University of California Press, 2007.

– *Opera in Seventeenth-Century Venice: The Creation of a Genre*. Berkeley: University of California Press, 1991.

– "The Descending Tetrachord: An Emblem of Lament." *The Musical Quarterly* 65, no. 3 (1979): 346–59.

Rosenthal, Margaret F. *The Honest Courtesan: Veronica Franco, Citizen and Writer in Sixteenth-Century Venice*. Chicago: University of Chicago Press, 1992.

Ross, Sarah C.E., and Rosalind Smith, eds. *Early Modern Women's Complaint: Gender, Form and Politics*. Cham: Palgrave Macmillan, 2020.

Ross, Sarah Gwyneth. "Weird Humanists." *I Tatti Studies in the Italian Renaissance* 22, no. 2 (2019): 345–54.

Rosselli, John. "From Princely Service to the Open Market: Singers of Italian Opera and Their Patrons, 1600–1850." *Cambridge Opera Journal* 1, no. 1 (1989): 1–32.

– *Singers of Italian Opera: The History of a Profession*. Cambridge: Cambridge University Press, 1995.

Rua, Giuseppe. *Poeti della corte di carlo Emanuele I di Savoia*. Turin: Ermanno Loescher, 1899.

Russo, Emilio. *Marino*. Rome: Salerno Editrice, 2008.

Rutgers, Jaco. "A Frontispiece for Galileo's *Opere*: Pietro Anichini and Stefano della Bella." *Print Quarterly* 29, no. 1 (2012): 3–12.

Salvi, Marcella. "'Il solito è sempre quello; l'insolito è più nuovo': *Li buffoni* e le prostitute di Margherita Costa tra tradizione e innovazione." *Forum italicum* 38, no. 2 (2004): 376–99.

Sampson, Lisa. *Pastoral Drama in Early Modern Italy: The Making of a New Genre*. London: Legenda, 2006.

Sanger, Alice E. *Art, Gender, and Religious Devotion in Grand Ducal Tuscany*. Farnham: Ashgate, 2014.

Sani, Bernardina. *La fatica virtuosa di Ottavio Leoni*. Turin: Umberto Allemandi, 2005.

Santacroce, Simona. "'La ragion perde dove il senso abonda': *La catena d'Adone* di Ottavio Tronsarelli." *Studi secenteschi* 55 (2014): 136–53.

Sartori, Claudio. *Libretti italiani a stampa dalle origini al 1800*. 5 vols. Cuneo: Bertola & Locatelli, 1990.

Saslow, James M. *The Medici Wedding of 1589: Florentine Festival as Theatrum Mundi*. New Haven: Yale University Press, 1996.

Scalabrini, Massimo. *Commedia e civiltà: Dinamiche anticonflittuali nella letteratura italiana del Cinquecento*. Ravenna: Angelo Longo Editore, 2022.

Scanzani, Barbara. "Camilla e Costanza Barberini: Lettere a Urbano VIII." In *Scritture di Donne: La memoria restituita: Atti del vonvegno, Roma, 23–24 marzo 2004*, edited by Marina Caffiero and Manola Ida Venzo, 167–83. Rome: Viella, 2007.

Schiesari, Juliana. "Pedagogy and the Art of Dressage in the Italian Renaissance." In *Animals and Early Modern Identity*, edited by Pia F. Cuneo, 375–89. Farnham: Ashgate, 2014.

Schleuse, Paul. *Singing Games in Early Modern Italy: The Music Books of Orazio Vecchi*. Bloomington: Indiana University Press, 2015.

Scott, John Beldon. "Fashioning a Capital: The Politics of Urban Space in Early Modern Turin." In *The Politics of Space: European Courts ca. 1500–1750*, edited by Marcello Fantoni, George Gorse, and Malcolm Smuts, 141–70. Rome: Bulzoni, 2009.

Selmi, Elisabetta. "'Inchiostri purgati' e il 'Parnaso in pulpito' (memoria e riscrittura tassiana nell'epica sacra del Seicento)." In *Dopo Tasso: Percorsi del poema eroico*, edited by Guido Arbizzoni, Marco Faini, and Tiziana Mattioli, 423–75. Rome: Antenore, 2006.

Snyder, Jon R. *Dissimulation and the Culture of Secrecy in Early Modern Europe.* Berkeley: University of California Press, 2009.

– *L'estetica del barocco.* Bologna: Il Mulino, 2005.

Solerti, Angelo. *Musica, ballo, e drammatica alla corte medicea dal 1600 al 1637.* Florence: R. Bemporad & Figlio, 1905.

Solinas, Francesco. "Simon Vouet, Suonatrice di Chitarra." In *Maria de' Medici (1573–1642): Una principessa fiorentina sul trono di Francia*, edited by Caterina Caneva and Francesco Solinas, 305–7. Florence: Sillabe, 2005.

Solomon, Jon. "The Influence of Ovid in Opera." In *A Handbook to the Reception of Ovid*, edited by John F. Miller and Carole E. Newlands, 371–85. Oxford: John Wiley & Sons, 2014.

Spangler, Jonathan. "Mother Knows Best: The Dowager Duchess of Guise, a Son's Ambitions, and the Regencies of Marie de Medici and Anne of Austria." In *Aspiration, Representation and Memory: The Guise in Europe, 1506–1688*, edited by Jessica Munns, Penny Richards, and Jonathan Spangler, 125–46. New York: Routledge, 2015.

Spinelli, Riccardo. "Temi edificanti e scelte licenziose nelle decorazioni affrescate della Villa Medici Corsini a Mezzomonte." In *L'arme e gli amori: La poesia di Ariosto, Tasso e Guarini nell'arte fiorentina del Seicento*, edited by Massimiliano Rossi and Fiorella Giofreddi Superbi, 2:341–71. Florence: Olschki, 2004.

Spini, Giorgio. *Ricerca dei libertini: La teoria dell'impostura delle religioni nel Seicento italiano.* Florence: La Nuova Italia, 1983.

"Squilletti, the Celebrated Bandit." In *The Monthly Traveller*, 4:107–9. Boston: Badger & Porter, 1833.

"Squilletti, the Celebrated Bandit." *The Lady's Book*, 1833, 87–9.

Staiti, Nico. *Le metamorfosi di Santa Cecilia: L'immagine e la musica.* Innsbruck: StudienVerlag; Lucca: LIM, 2002.

Stampino, Maria Galli. "A Regent and Her Court: Towards a Study of Maria Maddalena d'Austria's Patronage (Florence 1621–28)." *Forum Italicum* 40, no. 1 (2006): 22–35.

Stein, Louise K. "How Opera Traveled." In *The Oxford Handbook of Opera*, edited by Helen M. Greenwald, 243–61. Oxford: Oxford University Press, 2014.

Stella, Clara. "Il *Cecilia martire* di Margherita Costa (1644): Pentimento e *renovatio* alla corte dei Barberini." *Studi secenteschi* 62 (2022): 75–102.

– "Tra 'infiammate stille' e 'lacci cari': La Cecilia di Margherita Costa (1644)." *altrelettere* (2021): 94–116.

Stoppino, Eleonora. *Genealogies of Fiction: Women Warriors and the Dynastic Imagination in the Orlando Furioso.* New York: Fordham University Press, 2011.

Storey, Tessa. *Carnal Commerce in Counter-Reformation Rome.* Cambridge: Cambridge University Press, 2008.

Strappini, Lucia. *I luoghi dell'immaginario barocco: Atti del convegno di Siena, 21–23 ottobre 1999.* Naples: Liguori Editore, 2006.

– *La tragedia del buffone: Percorsi del comico e del tragico nel teatro del XVII secolo*. Rome: Bulzoni, 2003.

Straussman-Pflanzer, Eve. "Court Culture in 17th-Century Florence: The Art Patronage of Medici Grand Duchess Vittoria Della Rovere (1622–1694)." PhD dissertation, New York University, 2010.

Strong, Roy. *Art and Power: Renaissance Festivals, 1450–1650*. Berkeley: University of California Press.

Sustermans: Sessant'anni alla corte dei Medici: Firenze, Palazzo Pitti, luglio-ottobre 1983 (Exh. Cat.). Florence: Centro Di, 1983.

Talbot, Michael. "Vendramin." In *Grove Music Online, Oxford Music Online*. Oxford University Press, 2002. https://doi-org.libdata.lib.ua.edu/10.1093/gmo/9781561592630.article.O905438.

Tempesti, Anna Forlani. *Mostra di incisioni di Stefano della Bella*. Florence: Olschki, 1973.

Th. Van Veen, Henk. *Cosimo I de' Medici and His Self-Representation in Florentine Art and Culture*. Translated by Andrew McCormick. Cambridge: Cambridge University Press, 2006.

– "Keeping Sight of the Piazza: Gabriello Chiabrera and the Art of Praising the Medici." In *L'arme e gli amori: Ariosto, Tasso and Guarini in Late Renaissance Florence*, edited by Massimiliano Rossi and Fiorella Gioffreddi Superbi, vol. 1, 99–118. Florence: Olschki, 2004.

Tiraboschi, Girolamo. *Storia della letteratura italiana*. Vols. 10–13. Rome: Luigi Perego Salviani, 1785.

Tobey, Elizabeth M. "The Legacy of Federico Grisone." In *The Horse as Cultural Icon: The Real and the Symbolic Horse in the Early Modern World*, edited by Peter Edwards, Karl A.E. Enenkel, and Elspeth Graham, 143–73. Leiden: Brill, 2012.

Treadwell, Nina. *Music and Wonder at the Medici Court: The 1589 Interludes for "La Pellegrina."* Bloomington: Indiana University Press, 2008.

Treasure, Geoffrey. *Mazarin*. London: Routledge, 1995.

Treherne, Matthew. "Pictorial Space and Sacred Time: Tasso's *Le lagrime della Beata Vergine* and the Experience of Religious Art in the Counter-Reformation." *Italian Studies* 62, no. 1 (2007): 5–25.

Trinchieri Camiz, Franca. "Santa Cecilia: 'Cantatrice in terra… suonatrice al mondo' nel primo Seicento romano." In *Le immagini della musica: Atti del seminario di iconografia musicale*, edited by Francesca Zannoni, 59–68. Rome: Fratelli Palombi Editori, 1996.

Tucker, Treva J. "Early Modern French Noble Identity and the Equestrian 'Airs above the Ground'." In *The Culture of the Horse: Status, Discipline, and Identity in the Early Modern World*, edited by Karen Raber and Treva J. Tucker, 273–309. New York: Palgrave Macmillan, 2005.

Turner, James Grantham. *Schooling Sex: Libertine Literature and Erotic Education in Italy, France, and England, 1534–1685*. Oxford: Oxford University Press, 2003.

Turner, Nicholas. *Roman Baroque Drawings c. 1620 to c. 1700*. London: BMP, 1999.

Tyler, James, and Paul Sparks. *The Guitar and Its Music: From the Renaissance to the Classical Era*. New York: Oxford University Press, 2002.

Tylus, Jane. "Colonizing Peasants: The Rape of the Sabines and Renaissance Pastoral." *Renaissance Drama* 23 (1992): 113–38.

– "Imagining Narrative in Tasso: Revisiting Erminia." *MLN* 127, no. 1 (2012): 45–64.

– "Naming Sappho: Gaspara Stampa and the Recovery of the Sublime in Early Modern Europe." In *Rethinking Gaspara Stampa in the Canon of Renaissance Poetry*, edited by Unn Falkeid and Aileen Feng, 15–38. Farnham: Ashgate, 2015.

Ugolini, Paola. *The Court and Its Critics: Anti-Courtly Sentiments in Early Modern Italy*. Toronto: University of Toronto Press, 2020.

Van Orden, Kate. "From *Gens d'armes to Gentilshommes*: Dressage, Civility, and the Ballet à Cheval." In *The Culture of the Horse: Status, Discipline, and Identity in the Early Modern World*, edited by Karen Raber and Treva J. Tucker, 197–222. New York: Palgrave Macmillan, 2005.

– *Music, Discipline, and Arms in Early Modern France*. Chicago: University of Chicago Press, 2005.

Varallo, Franca. "Le feste da Maria Cristina a Giovanna Battista." In *Storia di Torino*, vol. 4, *La città fra crisi e ripresa (1630–1730)*, edited by Giuseppe Ricuperati, 483–502. Turin: Einaudi, 2002.

– "Le feste sabaude nella storia e nella storiografia." In *Feste barocche: Cerimonie e spettacoli alla corte del Savoia tra Cinque e Seicento*, edited by Clelia Arnaldi di Balme and Franca Varallo, 13–25. Milan: Silvana Editoriale, 2009.

Vavoulis, Vassilis. "A Venetian World in Letters: The Massi Correspondence at the Hauptstaatsarchiv in Hannover." *Notes* 59, no. 3 (2003): 556–609.

Vesme, Alexandre Baudi de, and Phyllis D. Massar. *Stefano della Bella: Catalogue Raisonné*. 2 vols. New York: Coll. Edition, 1901.

Viale Ferrero, Mercedes. *Feste delle Madame Reali di Savoia*. Turin: Istituto Bancario San Paolo di Torino, 1965.

Vianello, Daniele. *L'arte del buffone: Maschere e spettacolo tra Italia e Baviera nel XVI secolo*. Rome: Bulzoni, 2005.

Viatte, Françoise. "Allegorical and Burlesque Subjects by Stefano della Bella." *Master Drawings* 15, no. 4 (1977): 347–65, 425–44.

Vincenti, Maria Cristina. *Diana: Storia, mito e culto della grande dea di Aricia*. Rome: Palombi, 2010.

Vodret, Rossella, and Claudio Strinati. "Painted Music: 'A New and Affecting Manner.'" In *The Genius of Rome, 1592–1623*, edited by Beverly Louise Brown, 92–115. London: Royal Academy of Arts, 2001.

Waddy, Patricia. *Seventeenth-Century Roman Palaces: Use and the Art of the Plan*. Cambridge, MA: MIT Press, 1990.

Wainwright, Anna. "The Fair Warrior in the City of Florence: Maddalena Salvetti's Poems to Christine of Lorraine." In *Innovation in the Italian Counter-Reformation*, edited by

Shannon McHugh and Anna Wainwright, 127–44. Newark: University of Delaware Press, 2020.

Warrack, John. *German Opera: From the Beginnings to Wagner*. Cambridge: Cambridge University Press, 2001.

Watanabe-O'Kelly, Helen. "The Equestrian Ballet in Seventeenth-Century Europe – Origin, Description, Development." *German Life and Letters* 36, no. 3 (1983): 198–212.

– *Triumphall Shews: Tournaments at German-Speaking Courts in Their European Context, 1560–1730*. Berlin: Mann, 1992.

Weaver, Robert Lamar. *A Chronology of Music in the Florentine Theater, 1590–1750: Operas, Prologues, Finales, Intermezzos and Plays with Incidental Music*. Detroit: Detroit Studies in Music Bibliography, 1978.

Wilbourne, Emily. "Little Black Giovanni's Dream: Black Authorship and the 'Turks, and Dwarves, the Bad Christians' of the Medici Court." In *Acoustemologies in Contact: Sounding Subjects and Modes of Listening in Early Modernity*, edited by Emily Wilbourne and Suzanne G. Cusick, 135–66. Cambridge, UK: Open Book Publishers, 2021.

– *Seventeenth-Century Opera and the Sound of the Commedia dell'Arte*. Chicago: University of Chicago Press, 2016.

Williamson, Paul. "Notes on the Wall-Paintings in Sant'Urbano alla Caffarella, Rome." *Papers of the British School at Rome* 55 (1987): 224–8.

Wind, Barry. *"A Foul and Pestilent Congregation": Images of "Freaks" in Baroque Art*. Burlington, VT: Ashgate, 1998.

Witzenmann, Wolfgang. *The Italian Cantata in the Seventeenth Century*, vol. 4, *Cantatas by Marco Marazzoli*. New York: Garland, 1986.

Woodward, David. *Catalogue of Watermarks in Italian Printed Maps, ca 1540–1600*. Chicago: Chicago University Press, 1996.

Wootton, David. *Galileo: Watcher of the Skies*. New Haven: Yale University Press, 2010.

Yavneh, Naomi. "'Dal rogo alle nozze': Tasso's Sofronia as Martyr Manque." In *Renaissance Transactions: Ariosto and Tasso*, edited by Valeria Finucci. Durham, NC: Duke University Press, 1999.

Zanrè, Domenico. *Cultural Non-Conformity in Early Modern Florence*. Farnham: Ashgate, 2004.

Zaslaw, Neal. "The First Opera in Paris: A Study in the Politics of Art." In *Jean-Baptiste Lully and the Music of the French Baroque: Essays in Honor of James R. Anthony*, edited by John Hadju Heyer, 7–23. Cambridge: Cambridge University Press, 1989.

Index

Milton Keynes UK
Ingram Content Group UK Ltd.
UKHW022301040324
438897UK00016B/102/J